Lecture Notes in Computer Science 11981

More information about this series at http://www.springer.com/series/7410

Apostolos P. Fournaris · Manos Athanatos ·
Konstantinos Lampropoulos · Sotiris Ioannidis ·
George Hatzivasilis · Ernesto Damiani ·
Habtamu Abie · Silvio Ranise ·
Luca Verderame · Alberto Siena ·
Joaquin Garcia-Alfaro (Eds.)

Computer Security

ESORICS 2019 International Workshops,
IOSec, MSTEC, and FINSEC
Luxembourg City, Luxembourg, September 26–27, 2019
Revised Selected Papers

 Springer

Editors
Apostolos P. Fournaris (iD)
Industrial Systems Institute/Research
Center ATHENA
Patras, Greece

Konstantinos Lampropoulos
University of Patras
Patras, Greece

George Hatzivasilis (iD)
Foundation for Research
and Technology - Hellas (FORTH)
Heraklion, Greece

Habtamu Abie (iD)
Norwegian Computing Center
Oslo, Norway

Luca Verderame (iD)
University of Genoa
Genoa, Italy

Joaquin Garcia-Alfaro (iD)
Télécom SudParis
Evry, France

Manos Athanatos
Foundation for Research
and Technology - Hellas (FORTH)
Heraklion, Greece

Sotiris Ioannidis
Foundation for Research
and Technology - Hellas (FORTH)
Heraklion, Greece

Ernesto Damiani (iD)
University of Milan
Milan, Italy

Silvio Ranise (iD)
Fondazione Bruno Kessler
Trento, Italy

Alberto Siena (iD)
Fondazione Bruno Kessler
Trento, Italy

ISSN 0302-9743   ISSN 1611-3349 (electronic)
Lecture Notes in Computer Science
ISBN 978-3-030-42050-5   ISBN 978-3-030-42051-2 (eBook)
https://doi.org/10.1007/978-3-030-42051-2

LNCS Sublibrary: SL4 – Security and Cryptology

This Springer imprint is published by the registered company Springer Nature Switzerland AG
The registered company address is: Gewerbestrasse 11, 6330 Cham, Switzerland

IOSec 2019 Preface

The recent advancements of ICT have provided the opportunity for companies, public administrations, and various critical infrastructures to offer new and innovative services and at the same time lower their operational costs. These advancements, however, were quickly adopted without proper evaluation of their impact on security, leaving current IT (Information Technology) and OT (Operation Technology) systems vulnerable to various kinds of cyber attacks. Furthermore, cyber-security protection of IT and/or OT networks, data, and storage areas in small and medium enterprises (SMEs) is also problematic since such companies do not have the resources, expertise, as well as funds to support and maintain cyber-security operations in their premises. The International Workshop on Information & Operational Technology (IT & OT) security systems aims to bring together viewpoints from diverse areas to explore the commonalities of security problems and solutions for advancing the collective science and practice of IT and OT security protection, as well as promote security awareness and cyber-security solutions for the SME community. More specifically, topics that were addressed during the workshop include security architectures and frameworks for enterprises, SMEs, public administration or critical infrastructures, threat models for IT and OT systems and communication networks, cyber-threat detection, classification and profiling, incident management, security training and awareness, risk assessment, safety and security, hardware security, cryptographic engineering, secure software development, malicious code analysis, as well as security testing platforms.

In 2019, the workshop took place in September in collocation with the ESORICS 2019 conference and had collected inputs from various security research fields that can be applicable in the IT/OT security strengthening. The workshop lasted half a day and received 18 submitted papers, of which 7 were accepted to appear as revised selected papers in these post-proceedings, thus achieving an acceptance rate of 38%.

This volume contains the research outcomes of the IOSec 2019 workshop by including extended versions of all the scientific works that were presented during the workshop. IOSec 2019 was sponsored by the SMESEC European Union Innovation action project "Cybersecurity for small and medium-sized enterprises" that develops a lightweight cyber-security framework for thorough protection of SMEs against cyber-security threats.

Finally, the organizers of IOSec 2019 would like to thank those who contributed to the realization of the IOSec 2019 workshop, the ESORICS 2019 Organizing Committee, the IOSec Program Committee and the reviewers who helped with the review process, and finally Springer for aiding us with the post-conference proceedings volume publication.

December 2019

Apostolos P. Fournaris
Sotiris Ioannidis

IOSec 2019 Organization

General Chairs

Apostolos P. Fournaris   ISI - Athena Research Center, Greece
Sotiris Ioannidis   Foundation for Research and Technology - Hellas, Greece

Publication and Publicity Chairs

Manos Athanatos   Foundation for Research and Technology - Hellas, Greece
Konstantinos Lampropoulos   University of Patras, Greece

Program Committee

Apostolis Zarras   Maastricht University, The Netherlands
Apostolos P. Fournaris   ISI - Athena Research Center, Greece
Christos Tselios   Citrix Systems Inc., USA
Ciprian Oprisa   Bitdefender, Romania
Dimitrios Serpanos   ISI - Athena Research Center and University of Patras, Greece
Dusan Jakovetic   University of Novi Sad, Serbia
Elias Athanasopoulos   University of Cyprus, Cyprus
Francesco Regazzoni   University of Lugano, Switzerland
Giorgos Vasiliadis   Foundation for Research and Technology - Hellas, Greece
Jose F. Ruiz   ATOS, Spain
Manos Athanatos   Foundation for Research and Technology - Hellas, Greece
Marco Spruit   Utrecht University, The Netherlands
Michael Sirivianos   Cyprus University of Technology, Cyprus
Neeraj Suri   University of Lancaster, UK
Nicolas Sklavos   University of Patras, Greece
Odysseas Koufopavlou   University of Patras, Greece
Paris Kitsos   University of Peloponnese, Greece
Rodrigo Díaz   ATOS, Spain
Samuel Fricker   FHNW Fachhochschule Nordwestschweiz, Switzerland
Sotiris Ioannidis   Foundation for Research and Technology - Hellas, Greece
Spyros Denazis   University of Patras, Greece

Stefan Katzenbeisser   Technical University of Darmstadt, Germany
Vassilis Prevelakis   TU Braunschweig, Germany
Xavi Masip   Universitat Politècnica de Catalunya, Spain
Fady Copty   IBM Research, Israel

MSTEC 2019 Preface

This volume contains the papers presented at the First Model-driven Simulation and Training Environments for Cybersecurity (MSTEC 2019) workshop, held on September 27, 2019, in Luxembourg.

The MSTEC 2019 workshop addressed recent advances in the field of cyber modeling and simulation. It aimed to provide a forum of practitioners and researchers to discuss cyber modeling and simulation (M&S) as well as its application to the development of cyber-security training scenarios and courses of action (COAs). Specifically, it focused on the verification and validation (V&V) process, which provides the operational community with confidence in knowing that cyber models represent the real world, and discusses how defense training may benefit from cyber models. It also investigated advances in emulators, simulators, and their potential combination. The papers presented at MSTEC 2019 took a holistic approach to the overall system assurance process, presenting advances in the simulation of people, policies, processes, and technologies currently available in the field. The workshop aimed to connect the multiple threads that currently compose M&S into a coherent view of what is usable in order to train experts and non-computer-savvy users toward assured operation of critical systems.

There were 15 submissions. Each submission was reviewed by at least 2, and on the average 2.0, Program Committee members. The committee decided to accept 7 papers. The program also included an invited talk by Prof. Vasilis Prevelakis on the topic of Cybersecurity for the Protection of Critical Infrastructures.

The main sponsorship was provided by the European Union Horizon's 2020 research and innovation program THREAT-ARREST under grant agreement No. 786890 (https://www.threat-arrest.eu/).

We would like to thank the committee members and the reviewers for their voluntary effort as well as all the authors of the submitted papers for their contributions.

December 2019

Sotiris Ioannidis

MSTEC 2019 Organization

General Chairs

Ernesto Damiani	University of Milan, Italy
Vassilis Prevelakis	Technical University of Braunschweig, Germany
George Spanoudakis	Sphynx Technology Solutions AG, Switzerland
Michael Vinov	IBM Research, Israel

Program Chair

Sotiris Ioannidis	FORTH, Greece

Program Committee

George Hatzivasilis	FORTH, Greece
Fulvio Frati	University of Milan, Italy
Marinos Tsantekidis	Technical University of Braunschweig, Germany
Kostantinos Fysarakis	Sphynx Technology Solutions AG, Switzerland
Ludger Goeke	Social-Engineering Academy, Germany
Hristo Koshutanski	ATOS, Spain
George Leftheriotis	TUV Hellas, Greece
George Tsakirakis	ITML, Greece
Othonas Soultatos	City University of London, UK

Additional Reviewers

Elvina Riccobene	University of Milan, Italy
Iason Somarakis	Sphynx Technology Solutions AG, Switzerland
Eftychia Lakka	FORTH, Greece
Manolis Michalodimitrakis	FORTH, Greece

FINSEC 2019 Preface

In the (cyber-physical) security research context, it is even more important to deeply investigate the topic in order to anticipate cyber-criminal activities as much as possible, hence providing adequate security to the considered system. Considering critical infrastructures, this is a crucial topic, due to the possible effects of malicious activities. To address this, FINSEC is a forum for researchers and practitioners working on cyber-physical security in the critical financial infrastructures. Financial infrastructures run the core of the modern economies, and manage every day a vast amount of virtual and physical money and assets. Security incidents in the financial critical infrastructure lead directly to significant economic damages for individuals and companies as well, while decreasing trust in financial institutions and questioning their social value. On the other hand, financial infrastructures and services are more critical, sophisticated, and interconnected than ever before, which makes them increasingly vulnerable to security attacks, as confirmed by the steady rise of cyber-security incidents, such as phishing or ransomware attacks, but also cyber-physical incidents, such as physical violation of devices or facilities.

In order to address these challenges, the FINSEC 2019 workshop had the objective of bringing together researchers and practitioners from the cyber-(physical) security and financial domain, to rethink cyber-security in light of latest technological developments (e.g., FinTech, Cloud Computing, Blockchain, Big Data, AI, Internet of Things (IoT), Mobile-first services, Mobile payments, etc.). Specifically, value was given to contributions capable of fostering new, intelligent, collaborative, and more dynamic approaches to detect, prevent, and mitigate security incidents, such as (i) intelligent monitoring and data collection of security related information; (ii) predictive analytics over the collected data based on AI (i.e. deep learning mechanisms) that enable the identification of complex attack patterns; (iii) triggering preventive and mitigation measures in advance (before the occurrence of the attack); and (iv) allowing all stakeholders to collaborate invulnerability assessment, risk analysis, threat identification, threat mitigation, and compliance.

The workshop called the attention of the critical financial infrastructures research communities in order to stimulate integrated (cyber-physical) security of critical financial infrastructure. The First International Workshop on Security for Critical Financial Infrastructures and Services (FINSEC 2019) was held in Luxembourg. The workshop was organized in conjunction with the 24th European Symposium on Research in Computer Security (ESORICS 2019). The format of the workshop included technical presentations followed by presentations of preliminary project results from two H2020 projects, FINSEC and DEFENDER. The workshop was attended by around 20 people on average.

The workshop received eight submissions for review, from authors of five distinct countries. After a thorough peer-review process, four papers were selected for presentation at the workshop. The review process focused on the quality of the papers, their scientific novelty, and applicability to the protection of critical financial infrastructure and services, with an acceptance rate of 50%. The accepted articles represent an interesting mix of techniques for the Identification, Mitigation, Security Information Sharing, and Threats Mapping in critical financial infrastructure and services.

Finally, the organizers of the FINSEC 2019 workshop would like to thank the FINSEC 2019 Program Committee, whose members made the workshop possible with their rigorous and timely review process. We would also like to thank the University of Luxembourg for hosting the workshop, and the ESORICS 2019 workshop chair for the valuable help and support.

December 2019   Habtamu Abie
                                                                Silvio Ranise
                                                              Luca Verderame
                                                               Alberto Siena

FINSEC 2019 Organization

General Chairs

Habtamu Abie	Norwegian Computing Center, Norway
Silvio Ranise	Fondazione Bruno Kessler (FBK), Italy

Program Chairs

Luca Verderame	University of Genova, Italy
Alberto Siena	Fondazione Bruno Kessler (FBK), Italy
Enrico Cambiaso	National Research Council (CNR), Italy

Program Committee

Dieter Gollmann	Hamburg University of Technology, Germany
Sokratis Katsikas	Norwegian University of Science and Technology, Norway
Javier Lopez	University of Malaga, Spain
Fabio Martinelli	IIT-CNR, Italy
Einar Arthur Snekkenes	Norwegian University of Science and Technology, Norway
Omri Soceanu	IBM Research, Israel
Stamatis Karnouskos	SAP Research, Germany
Reijo Savola	VTT Technical Research Centre of Finland, Finland
Alessandro Armando	University of Genoa, Italy
Alessio Merlo	University of Genoa, Italy
Cristina Alcaraz	University of Malaga, Spain
Giovanni Livraga	University of Milan, Italy
Gustavo Gonzalez-Granadillo	ATOS, Spain
Stefan Poslad	Queen Mary University of London, UK
Shouhuai Xu	University of Texas at San Antonio, USA
Christos Xenakis	University of Piraeus, Greece
Mauro Conti	University of Padua, Italy
Audun Josang	University of Oslo, Norway

Contents

IOSec Workshop

A Comprehensive Technical Survey
of Contemporary Cybersecurity Products
and Solutions

Christos Tselios[1]([✉]), George Tsolis[1], and Manos Athanatos[2]

[1] Citrix Systems Inc., Patras, Greece
[2] Foundation for Research and Technology - Hellas (FORTH), Heraklion, Greece
{christos.tselios,george.tsolis}@citrix.com

Abstract. As the complexity of applications and software frameworks increases, cybersecurity becomes more challenging.The potential attack surface keeps expanding while each product has its own peculiarities and requirements leading to tailor-made solutions per case.These are the primary reasons which render security solutions expensive, highly complex and with significant deployment delay. This technical survey intends to reveal the pillars of today's cybersecurity market, as well as identify emerging trends,key players and functional aspects. Such an insight will allow all interested parties to optimize the design process of a contemporary and future-proof cybersecurity framework for end-to-end protection.

Keywords: Cybersecurity · Optimization · Market analysis

1 Introduction

As the complexity of applications and software frameworks increases, cybersecurity becomes more challenging [5]. The attack surface keeps expanding while each product has its own peculiarities and requirements leading to tailor-made solutions per case. This is the primary reason which renders security solutions expensive, highly complex and with significant deployment delay. Larger companies are willing to pay the protection premium since a potential breach could have severe economical and reputational impact. Alas, small-medium enterprises (SMEs) and public administrations with limited budget are generally reluctant to invest in cybersecurity. They plan and operate without thinking about security, designing new services and products with two main objectives in mind: time to market and cost minimization.

The most important factor to boost cybersecurity in SMEs, public administrations and organizations with restricted budget in general, is to link it with its economic impact and the market that is forming around it. One must admit that, in most cases, cybersecurity is promoted with no economic impact. And even though all companies agree that boosting their security will eliminate service disruption and data recovery costs, the truth is that the majority would

© Springer Nature Switzerland AG 2020
A. P. Fournaris et al. (Eds.): ESORICS 2019 Workshops, LNCS 11981, pp. 3–18, 2020.
https://doi.org/10.1007/978-3-030-42051-2_1

be more interested in advancing their security methods if they could identify opportunities for additional economic profit (e.g. new services, clients, markets etc.). This technical survey intends to reveal the most important cybersecurity market pillars, identify emerging trends in cybersecurity and identify key players and performance capabilities. Such an insight will allow all interested parties to optimize the design process of a contemporary and future-proof cybersecurity solution and will also shed some light on how the integrated framework of the SMESEC Project [4] intends to deliver end-to-end cybersecurity protection.

Cyber-attacks become more and more sophisticated, rendering legacy solutions no longer adequate for today's systems and services. Cybersecurity solutions evolve and become more "intelligent" with technologies like machine learning, statistical analysis, user behavioral analysis etc. but these solutions are offered to closed standalone products. This consortium argues that the complexity of managing cybersecurity world cannot be one man's job. Not all products can address or have the optimal solutions for all the different cases of cyber-attacks (viruses, malware, ransomware, intrusion detection, DDoS etc.). A proper framework must be able to adopt the latest innovations by integrating products (not only from security) with focused solutions from different providers very fast and considerably easy.

2   Identifying Imperative Cybersecurity Market Segments

Cyber-protection is a constant circular process which can be described in the following high level steps: (i) perform a risk assessment, (ii) develop a security plan, (iii) deploy the right defenses, (iv) monitor and (v) re-perform risk assessment. It is clear that this process is expensive and time consuming. Current solutions offered by security companies are off-the-shelf products charged by the number of protected end-devices and cannot be easily modified to accommodate the specific needs of small businesses. In addition, steps like risk assessment and security plan deployment are not always included and SMEs need to (a) evaluate and integrate extra modules thus increasing the overall cost or (b) settle with a product which might not be the optimal solution for their use cases. It is therefore important to take a step back and identify, categorize and analyze some important existing and upcoming security market segments, along with the key players and dominant products in each case.

2.1   Contemporary Security Market Segments and Related Products

Encryption refers to the process of protecting sensitive data by converting to an encoded form that can be decrypted by means of a protected key. This method ensures that even if security is breached in other levels, data will still be highly protected and will be useless to any malicious user. In fact, encryption is one of the first requirements when it comes to protecting sensitive data. Apart from the key players and proprietary solutions presented in Table 1, there is a wide range of open source solutions which cover different aspects like file, filesystem, and network encryption such as VeraCrypt[1] and CryptTool[2]. None of the SMESEC contributed products is now directly related to the encryption market, thus it makes this particular market attractive for adding the specific capabilities to the SMESEC.

Symantec[3] is a key player in the specific domain with an encryption portfolio that includes endpoint, file and folder and email encryption. Integration with Symantec Data Loss Prevention automatically encrypts sensitive data being moved onto removable media devices or residing in emails and files. Robust management features include individual and group key management, automated policy controls, and out-of-the-box, compliance-based reporting. Heterogeneous management capabilities include support for native OS encryption (FileVault2) and Opal compliant self-encrypting drives. Sophos[4] introduces the most complete data protection solution on the market today, protecting data on multiple devices and operating systems. Whether data resides on a laptop, a mobile device, or being collaborated upon via the cloud or other file sharing method, SafeGuard Encryption is built to match organizational workflow and processes without slowing down productivity.

Table 1. Encryption-related solutions

Kaspersky Lab	Kaspersky Endpoint Security offers data encryption with highly integrated security policies that can be aligned with application and device controls for data protection in case devices or files are lost or stolen
Symantec	Symantec's encryption portfolio includes endpoint, file/folder and email encryption. Integration with Symantec Data Loss Prevention automatically encrypts sensitive data being moved onto removable media devices or residing in emails and files
McAfee, Inc.	McAfee Complete Data Protection secures critical data on endpoint devices with powerful enterprise-grade drive encryption. This endpoint encryption suite also enables management of native encryption on Macs and Windows systems

Governance, Risk Management and Compliance (GRC) create an acronym often used to describe the organization efficiency to achieve its objectives, address uncertainty and act with integrity. In these three terms, (i) Governance refers to the processes involved to assure that the organization handles information properly across all workflows, (ii) Risk Management stands for predicting and handling possible risks that may slow the organization achieving the goals and (iii) Compliance includes all the processes to adhere with laws and regulations, as well as company policies.

---

[1] https://www.veracrypt.fr/en/Home.html.
[2] https://www.cryptool.org/en/.
[3] https://www.symantec.com/products/endpoint-encryption.
[4] https://www.sophos.com/en-us/products/safeguard-encryption.aspx.

This market segment covers some security aspects that usually SMEs neglect to address, for instance who has the rights to the obtained datasets, whether datasets adhere to company or other legal compliances, and how to deal with issues identified through the initial risk management process. This kind of services often comes on top of other first level security solutions, and SMESEC aims to address this space as well.By collecting traffic, usage, and other data from the underlying infrastructure (firewall, antivirus, etc.) the integrated framework can re-assess the risk periodically, whereas the overall architecture should take into account general governance and compliance constraints (Table 2).

Table 2. Key players in the GRC domain

RSA Security LLC (part of EMC)	RSA Archer eGRC Solutions allows developing an efficient, collaborative enterprise governance, risk and compliance (eGRC) program across IT, finance, operations and legal domains. These solutions include policy, risk, compliance, enterprise, incident, vendor, threat, business continuity and audit management
IBM Corporation	The IBM OpenPages GRC Platform delivers a modular platform for intrinsic GRC, enabling businesses to deploy scalable solutions for managing enterprise-wide risk and compliance. Designed for increasing overall productivity and efficiency, the platform supports agile implementation for rapid time to value
MetricStream	MetricStream offers an advanced and comprehensive IT GRC software solution for streamlining IT GRC processes, effectively managing IT risk, and meeting IT regulatory requirements. The MetricStream solution enables companies to implement a formal framework to rigorously measure, mitigate, and monitor IT risks
Galvanize	Galvanize's software helps organizations successfully manage risk, compliance, audit, and security needs effectively. The available platform provides the most intuitive and flexible solutions for GRC, security risk intelligence, vendor/third-party risk management, KPI/KRI metrics, and on-demand applications

Security Information and Event Management (SIEM) is a technology that enables the aggregation of data produced by multiple devices, network infrastructure, systems, and applications. Data logs may be the primary source of information but SIEM systems are able to absorb and identify other complex data structures as well. These characteristics, allow SIEM systems not only to monitor systems and users but also comply with policies and standards as well.

Undoubtedly, SIEM is a key component in a security solution, especially when multiple products are involved. The ability of SIEM products to ingest large amounts of heterogeneous data from several sources, correlate, create and visualize insights, makes it indispensable component in a security architecture (Table 3).

Table 3. Key players in the Security Information and Event Management domain

Microfocus	The ArcSight SIEM by Microfocus is s comprehensive solution that enables cost-effective compliance and provides advanced security analytics for identifying threats and/or risk management
McAfee, Inc.	McAfee Enterprise Security Manager brings event, threat, and risk data together to provide strong security intelligence, rapid incident response, seamless log management, and compliance reporting–delivering the context required for adaptive security risk management
LogRythm Inc.	LogRhythm's security intelligence and analytics platform enables organizations to detect, prioritize and neutralize cyber threats that penetrate the perimeter or originate from within
Splunk Inc.	Splunk's Security Intelligence Platform, combines Splunk Enterprise and Splunk App for Enterprise Security, to offer an overview of all existing data threats
RSA Security LLC (part of EMC)	RSA NetWitness Logs and Packets goes beyond baseline SIEM capabilities. Designed for scale and heavy analytic loads, the product will spot sophisticated attacks and will prioritize alerts

Intrusion Detection and Prevention Systems (IDS/IPS) implement threat deterrent technologies which monitor live network traffic [2] to detect and prevent vulnerabilities [3], based on a given set of rules. Besides the proprietary solutions presented in Table 4 there are some popular open-source solutions such as Suricata[5] and Snort[6].

Table 4. Dominant IDS/IPS solutions and key players

Cisco Systems, Inc.	The Cisco FirePOWER Next-Generation IPS (NGIPS) solution offers advanced threat protection by integrating real-time contextual awareness, intelligent security automation and superior performance
IBM Corporation	IBM Security Network Intrusion Prevention System appliances are designed to stop constantly evolving threats before they impact your business. This means providing both high levels of protection and performance, while lowering the overall cost and complexity associated with deploying and managing a large number of point solutions
Trend Micro, Inc.	The TippingPoint Next-Generation Intrusion Prevention System (IPS) offers comprehensive threat protection against advanced and evasive targeted attacks with high accuracy. Using a combination of technologies such as deep packet inspection, threat reputation, and advanced malware analysis. It provides enterprises with a proactive approach to security

---

[5] https://suricata-ids.org/.
[6] https://www.snort.org.

Distributed Denial-of-Service (DDoS) refers to attacks from multiple sources to a single target in order to make it unable to provide a service by causing denial of service due to flooding by immense traffic. Such attacks directly affect the organization operations by denying access to legitimate users, therefore mitigation solutions have been developed, as shown in Table 5.

Table 5. Distributed DoS protection key players and products

Cloudflare Inc.	CloudFlare's advanced DDoS protection, provisioned as a service at the network edge, matches the sophistication and scale of DDoS threats and can be used to mitigate DDoS attacks of all forms and sizes including those that target the UDP and ICMP protocols, as well as SYN/ACK, DNS amplification and Layer 7 attacks
Arbor (now part of NetScout)	Arbor Cloud is a DDoS service powered by the world's leading experts in DDoS mitigation, together with the most widely deployed DDoS protection technology
Verisign Inc. (now part of Symantec)	Verisign DDoS Protection Services help organizations reduce the risk of catastrophic DDoS attacks by detecting and filtering malicious traffic aimed at disrupting or disabling their internet-based services. Unlike traditional solutions, Verisign DDoS Protection Services filter harmful traffic upstream of the organizational network or in the cloud
Akamai	Kona Site Defender combines automated DDoS mitigation with a highly scalable and accurate WAF to protect websites from a wide range of online threats, including network- and application-layer DDoS, SQL injection and XSS attacks – without compromising the user experience. Kona Site Defender can stop the largest attacks and leverages Akamai's visibility into global web traffic to help organizations respond to the latest threats
Imperva	The Imperva Incapsula service delivers a multi-faceted approach to DDoS defense, providing blanket protection from all DDoS attacks to shield your critical online assets from these threats. Incapsula DDoS protection services are backed by a 24 × 7 security team, 99.999% uptime SLA, and a powerful, global network of data centers
F5 Networks Inc.	F5's DDoS Protection solution protects the fundamental elements of an application (network, DNS, SSL, and HTTP) against distributed denial-of-service attacks. Leveraging the intrinsic security capabilities of intelligent traffic management and application delivery, F5 protects and ensures availability of an organization's network and application infrastructure under the most demanding conditions

Web Application Firewall (WAF) differ from the typical firewall as they focus mainly on protecting the web traffic (HTTP protocol) from a variety of attacks, such as Cross-Site Scripting (XSS) or SQL injection. WAFs are able to inspect the payload of the HTTP traffic, decide if this is legit, and provide input to other tools like SIEMs.

Several businesses today depend on web applications due to platform independency, easy-of-deployment which together with the evolution of cloud computing [6] generated a whole new market. It is WAFs which protect these valuable applications and nullify attacks targeting other dependant assets (Table 6).

Table 6. Web Application Firewall solutions

Citrix Systems Inc.	Citrix ADC prevents inadvertent or intentional disclosure of confidential information and aids in compliance with information security regulations such as PCI-DSS[a]
F5 Networks Inc.	BIG-IP Application Security Manager is an on-premises web application firewall (WAF) with relatively advanced firewall. It secures applications against layer 7 distributed denial-of-service (DDoS) attacks and application vulnerabilities
Barracuda Networks Inc.	Barracuda Web Application Firewall is a solution for organizations looking to protect web applications from data breaches and defacement. With the Barracuda Web Application Firewall, administrators do not need to wait for clean code or even know how an application works to secure their applications. Organizations can ensure robust security with a Barracuda Web Application Firewall hardware or virtual appliance, deployed either on-premises or in the cloud

[a]https://www.pcisecuritystandards.org/

Secure Web Gateways (SWG) protect company assets while surfing and enforce the policy companies to the network traffic. They may offer a range of capabilities, including URL filtering, antivirus/antimalware protection, SSL traffic inspection, etc.

Secure Web Gateways can offer a wide range of protections for web traffic, covering not only incoming but outgoing traffic as well. Characteristics such as URL filtering or anti-malware protection can help into preventing malicious content and code entering the organization. The ability to inspect secure traffic makes it also attractive as much of the malware can be transported over secure web connections that otherwise pass uninspected (Table 7).

Table 7. Key players delivering Secure Web Gateway solutions

Symantec	Symantec Secure Web Gateway (previously Blue Coat SWG) consolidates a broad set of features to authenticate users, filter web traffic, identify cloud application usage, provide data loss prevention, deliver threat prevention, and ensure visibility into encrypted traffic
Zscaler	Zscaler Web Security provides security, visibility and control, going beyond the basics of web content filtering. Delivered in the cloud, Zscaler includes web security integrated with a robust network security platform that features advanced threat protection, real-time analytics and forensics
Cisco Systems Inc.	Get advanced threat defense, advanced malware protection, application visibility and control, insightful reporting, and secure mobility. The Cisco Web Security Appliance (WSA) combines all of these forms of protection and more in a single solution

Endpoint Security and Protection Platforms (EPP) intend to protect endpoints such as workstations, servers or mobile devices from viruses, trojans, spyware, malware, or phishing attacks.

EPP is one of the traditional markets in terms of awareness, as antivirus solutions used to be present in SME environments several years ago. The increasing complexity of viruses and malware today, rendered these solutions even more necessary, and the integration with other security products is definitely an advantage when it comes to the prevention of this kind of threats (Table 8).

Table 8. Leading Endpoint Security and Protection Platforms

Sophos	Sophos Endpoint Protection makes it simple to secure Windows, Mac, and Linux systems against malware and advanced threats, such as targeted attacks
Trend Micro	Trend Micro endpoint security provides the necessary threat protection and data security to users and corporate information across every device and application
Webroot Inc.	Webroot SecureAnywhere Endpoint Protection leverages cloud-based real-time intelligence to protect organizations against ever-evolving threats
BitDefender	Bitdefender's GravityZone Endpoint Security provides the highly scalable endpoint security solution that businesses require to protect against malware and web threats
Symantec	Symantec Endpoint Protection: Proactively detect and block today's most advanced threats with an endpoint protection solution that goes beyond antivirus
Kaspersky Lab	World-class security for all your endpoints – including laptops, desktops, file servers and mobile devices. Advanced security for workstations & File servers. Multi-layer mobile security and management. Application Control, Device Control & Web Control. Centralized management console for all functions

Application Security Testing (AST) helps developers, administrators, and enterprises to identify security vulnerabilities by performing exhausting testing on various aspects of the software. AST is usually an operation that does not run in the front-line, but a careful testing of a hardware or software applications before deployment can prevent future attacks. Testing can take place even before deployment, but also while a product has been deployed, providing continuously feedback. Another possible benefit will be enriching tests with even more attack scenarios and consuming this information in an automated manner (Table 9).

Table 9. Application Security Testing

IBM Corporation	IBM Security AppScan Standard helps organizations decrease the likelihood of web application attacks and costly data breaches by automating application security vulnerability testing. IBM Security AppScan Standard can be used to reduce risk by permitting you to test applications prior to deployment and for ongoing risk assessment in production environments
WhiteHat Security	WhiteHat Sentinel is a Software-as-a-Service (SaaS) platform that enables your business to quickly deploy a scalable application security program across the entire software development lifecycle (SDLC). Combining advanced scanning technology with a large application threat research team, WhiteHat Security accurately identifies the enterprise vulnerabilities and scale to meet any demand
Microfocus	Fortify on Demand is an application security testing and program management solution that enables customers to easily create, supplement and expand a software security assurance program through a managed service dedicated to delivery and customer support

2.2 Emerging Security Market Sectors and Key Players

A number of emerging markets that will expand significantly in next few years is those including certain characteristics such as: (i) intelligent methods of detecting/mitigating attacks, rather than a rule or signature-based approach (ii) advanced behaviour analysis and user profiling (iii) a centralized way of collecting, correlating and extracting intelligence from multiple endpoints, providing higher level of confidence for the risks than individual indications. Some of the key players in these markets and a short description of their products follow in the following sections.

Deception Technology is an emerging market segment in cybersecurity. The main goal of deception technology solutions is the deployment of several decoys in parts of the infrastructure that are indistinguishable with the real servers. If an attacker gains access, these decoys act as an easy target and quickly notify as well as trigger appropriate actions against the intruder (Table 10).

Table 10. Deception Technology key players

TrapX	TrapX is a cyber security company founded in 2010 and headquartered in California, US. TrapX "Deception grid" platform provides deception based advance threat defense solution. TrapX has a number of out-of-box use cases for detecting zero-day malware, ransomware and attacks through compromised accounts
Cymmetria	Cymmetria, founded in 2014 and headquartered in California, US, has a deception platform called "Mazerunner", which intercepts the attacker during the reconnaissance phase and carefully lead them to a monitored deception network where they are analyzed for their tactics, techniques and procedures employed for attacking the enterprise
Acalvio	Acalvio provides Advanced Threat Defense (ATD) solutions to detect, engage and respond to malicious activity inside the enterprise networks. Acalvio holds patents in deception and data science and have developed their product "Deception2.0" around that. Acalvio is founded in 2015 and headquartered in California, USA

Endpoint Detection and Response. Endpoint Detection and Response (EDR) is the evolution of EPP. Typically, EDR involves the detection and mitigation to a more sophisticated process including detection, analytics and prioritization of incident response.Currently there is some confusion over the exact borders of each market. However, the characteristics of the EDR products can be a driver for extending the capabilities of the EPP ones, either directly, or through the development of synergies between modules that will render existing frameworks capable of eventually providing EDR services (Table 11).

Table 11. Endpoint Detection and Response key players and products

Carbon Black	Carbon Black Enterprise Response is the most complete endpoint detection and response solution available to security teams who want a single platform for hunting threats, disrupting adversary behaviour and changing the economics of security operations. Only Carbon Black Enterprise Response continuously records all endpoint activity, centralizes and correlates that data with unified intelligence sources, and reveals a complete kill chain that pinpoints attack root cause to power live threat containment, banning and remediation activities. Built entirely on open APIs, Carbon Black Enterprise Response pushes and pulls data through the security infrastructure to automate and enhance adaptive threat response processes, helping to make it the dominant EDR solution among global enterprises
Cisco Systems Inc.	Cisco Advanced Malware Protection (AMP) is a security solution that addresses the full lifecycle of the advanced malware problem. It can not only prevent breaches, but gives you the visibility and control to rapidly detect, contain, and remediate threats if they evade front-line defences - all cost-effectively and without impacting operational efficiency
CrowdStrike	CrowdStrike is a leading provider of next-generation endpoint protection, threat intelligence, and pre- and post incident response services. CrowdStrike Falcon is the first true Software as a Service (SaaS) based platform for next-generation endpoint protection that detects, prevents, and responds to attacks, at any stage - even malware-free intrusions. Falcon's patented lightweight endpoint sensor can be deployed to over 100,000 endpoints in hours providing visibility into billions of events in real-time. CrowdStrike operates on a highly scalable subscription- based business model that allows customers the flexibility to use CrowdStrike-as-a-Service to multiply their security team's effectiveness and expertise with 24/7 endpoint visibility, monitoring, and response
FireEye	The FireEye Endpoint Threat Prevention for the FireEye Security Platform - HX Series was developed by Mandiant consultants for use during an incident response or compromise assessment. The management system consists of a hardware appliance that is installed in the primary network and an optional appliance that can be installed into the DMZ for managing off network endpoints

(*continued*)

Table 11. (*continued*)

Guidance Software (now part of OpenText)	EnCase Endpoint Security: Mitigate Threats, Maximize Productivity Enterprises demand EDR products to offer scalability, strong detection and incident response workflows, and open integrations to operate more efficiently. EnCase Endpoint Security v6 was designed to not only meet these needs, but then exceed them with a beautifully redesigned front-end user interface. The completely redesigned EnCase Endpoint Security v6 delivers improved performance, better usability, and enhanced capabilities. Moving to the newest version of EnCase Endpoint Security has never been easier or more exciting
RSA	RSA ECAT is a continuous endpoint solution providing contextual visibility beyond a single alert to provide incident responders and security analysts a full attack investigation platform to detect and respond in real-time against advanced attacks, known and unknown as well as malware and non-malware threats
Symantec	Symantec Advanced Threat Protection: Endpoint is a new solution to uncover, prioritize, and remediate advanced attacks across all of your endpoints, leveraging existing investments in Symantec Endpoint Protection. With one click of a button, you can search for, discover, and remediate any attack artifacts across all of your endpoint systems. And, if you have Symantec Advanced Threat Protection: Network or Symantec Email Security.cloud, Symantec's Synapse correlation technology will automatically aggregate events across all Symantec-protected control points to prioritize the most critical threats in your organization

Cloud Access Security Brokers (CASB) have appeared in an era where cloud applications become more and more an integral part of the organization workflow, manage corporate data but do not operate on private infrastructure. CASB is entity which provides common access policies from any corporate device to any cloud application (Table 12).

Identity and Access Management (IAM) is the process of managing digital identities, and access rights to enterprise resource and auditing in an automated manner. From a technical standpoint, IAMs are centralized management systems that consolidate the processes of authentication and auditing providing a single framework for access. Main goals in IAM are (i) Multi-factor authentication schemes, (ii) Integration with directory services (LDAP, Active Directory, etc.), (iii) Single Sign-On (SSO), (iv) Credentials management, (v) Auditing, (vi) Analytics.

Table 12. Cloud Access Security Broker key players and products

CipherCloud	Available as a service or virtual appliance, CipherCloud delivers a comprehensive set of protection controls across all cloud applications, including encryption, tokenization, activity monitoring, data loss prevention (DLP) and malware detection that can overcome cloud security concerns
Cisco Systems, Inc.	Cisco CloudLock focuses on the shadow IT challenge which matter: those cloud and third-party apps that directly connect into a corporate environment. CloudLock provides adequate control to decide which apps lead to productivity gains and which ones are a security risk in any organization
Adallom (now part of Microsoft)	Cloud access security broker Adallom announced that its cloud application security platform is now available as part of the HP Enterprise Security Products and HP Enterprise Services portfolios
Palerra LORIC (now part of Oracle)	Palerra enables organizations to protect business-critical cloud infrastructure and data with LORICTM, the cloud security automation platform. LORIC is delivered as a service and can be deployed in minutes
Palo Alto Networks	Aperture extends the visibility and granular control of our security platform into SaaS applications themselves – an area traditionally invisible to IT. Aperture solves this problem by looking into SaaS applications directly, providing full visibility into the day-to-day activities of users and data. Granular controls ensure policy is maintained to eliminate data exposure and threat risks
Skyhigh Networks	Skyhigh Cloud Security Manager enables IT to embrace and accelerate the adoption of cloud services while ensuring privacy, security, and compliance
Blue Coat (now part of Symantec)	The Blue Coat Cloud Data Protection Gateway is a software solution that delivers critical data privacy and security capabilities to users of public cloud applications

The core idea of IAM is the existence of some common user authentication service that not only allows access, but also audits the use of assets and reports possible malicious events. It also allows the correlation of events from multiple sources to single users through the common directory service. SMESEC does not have an offering in this field, however the study of the capabilities of IAM offerings can help SMESEC understand what should be needed to effectively handle the identifications of users and the correlation to specific access events (Table 13) .

Table 13. Identity and Access Management key players and products

IBM Corporation	IBM Security Identity and Access Manager provides automated and policy-based user lifecycle management and access controls throughout the enterprise. Available as an easy-to-manage virtual appliance, it pairs IBM Security Identity Manager with IBM Security Access Manager Platform for more secure user authentication and authorization to applications and data
Oracle Corporation	Oracle's complete, integrated next-generation identity management platform provides breakthrough scalability with an robust suite of identity management solutions
Sailpoint	IdentityIQ is SailPoint's governance-based identity and access management (IAM) software solution that delivers a unified approach to compliance, password management and provisioning activities for applications running on-premises or from the cloud. IdentityIQ meets the needs of large organizations with complex identity management processes who prefer to tailor their solution to align with unique business needs
Okta	The Okta identity management service provides directory services, SSO, strong authentication, provisioning, workflow, and reporting, all delivered as a multitenant IDaaS though some components reside on-premise
RSA Security LLC	RSA offers both RSA Identity Management and Governance (RSA IGA), a full-fledged identity management suite built from separately licensed components, and RSA VIA, an IDaaS suite composed of separately licensed SAAS point solutions

3   Towards a Holistic Cybersecurity Framework for SMEs

The previously mentioned security market analysis identified some key market segments along with the technical requirements of each one. Apart from the traditional segments, emerging ones are also presented since they are going to play a key role in the cybersecurity ecosystem over the next few years. It is imperative that any properly-designed framework must embrace some of the new features or provide the hooks to connect with third-party products there.

When the project started, the SMESEC consortium members [4] conducted a thorough technical analysis of the independent products contributed to be integrated in the overall platform. This analysis, as shown in Table 14, revealed that these products indeed provide a wide range of capabilities to cover the high-level requirements derived from the security market analysis. Some products can produce reports that go beyond the raw data and reveal more insights. The existence of processed data means less burden and traffic to other architecture components that will perform the data analysis. In addition, the integration effort should ensure that these requirements also stay on top during the design

Table 14. SMESEC products by market segment

Product name	Security areas	Market
ATOS XL-SIEM	Security information and event management	SIEM
BD GravityZone	Anti-virus/anti-malware	EPP, EDR
CITRIX ADC	SSL interception, URL filtering	WAF, DDoS
EGM test-as-a-service	Testing	AST
FHNW	Security readiness evaluation	GRC
FORTH EWIS & cloud	Intrusion detection/prevention systems	IDS/IPS
IBM angel-eye	Virtual patching	AST
IBM ExpliSAT	Software formal verification tool	AST
IBM anti-ROP	Anti-ROP solution	Moving target defence

and implementation of the unified framework. This analysis also investigated possible integration strategies in regards to architecture, platform deployment and cloud readiness, all of paramount importance for delivering a robust and noteworthy cybersecurity framework.

Not all products can address or have the optimal solutions for all the different cases of cyber-attacks. Efficient combination of existing feature is the key to successful cyber-attack mitigation, regardless of how sophisticated this may be. In addition, a proper framework must be able to adopt the latest innovations by integrating products (not only from security) with focused solutions from different providers very fast and considerably easy. These two elements are considered of paramount importance for the SMESEC consortium members and will be an integral part of the overall design, implementation and integration phase of the project. There is currently no contributed product focused on behaviour analysis, other than BD GravityZone which rather examines software behaviour. On the contrary, few products support risk assessment from raw events. This is an interesting point architecturally, as the collection of more events from all other products to them, can potentially reinforce their risk assessment capabilities.

4   Conclusions

There is no cybersecurity product capable of addressing every different case of cyber-attacks (viruses, malware, ransomware, intrusion detection, DDoS etc.), nor worthy of being considered as a holistic cybersecurity solution. Any framework must be able to adopt the latest innovations by integrating a variety of products and focused solutions from different providers, very fast and considerably easy.

Cybersecurity solutions are becoming more "intelligent" with technologies like machine learning [1], statistical and user behavioral analysis, in a struggle to mitigate the constantly more sophisticated and perplexed cyber-attacks. However, Not all products can address or have the optimal solutions for all the different cases of cyber-attacks, therefore it should be flexible and modular enough to adopt the latest innovations by integrating products (not only from security) with focused solutions from different providers very fast and considerably easy .

Based on the technical analysis of the contributed products and the market segment analysis, focus is given on placing the SMESEC framework in the security landscape. In the first phase, only as a sum of the products, but it is anticipated that the integration will produce some extra value to the overall solution. Some product extensions, as identified by partners, point to new features that would help SMESEC strengthen its position as a unified security framework, provide added-value to all individual products, and greatly improve the benefits for SMEs.

Acknowledgment. This work has received funding from the European Union's Horizon 2020 research and innovation programme under grant agreement No. 830927 (CONCORDIA). This work is also partly supported by the European Commission under the auspices of SMESEC Project, Horizon 2020 Research and Innovation action (Grant Agreement No. 740787). The views and opinions expressed are those of the authors and do not necessary reflect the official position of Citrix Systems Inc.

References

1. Buczak, A.L., Guven, E.: A survey of data mining and machine learning methods for cyber security intrusion detection. IEEE Commun. Surv. Tutor. **18**(2), 1153–1176 (2016). https://doi.org/10.1109/COMST.2015.2494502. Secondquarter
2. Butun, I., Morgera, S.D., Sankar, R.: A survey of intrusion detection systems in wireless sensor networks. IEEE Commun. Surv. Tutor. **16**(1), 266–282 (2014). https://doi.org/10.1109/SURV.2013.050113.00191. First
3. Gendreau, A.A., Moorman, M.: Survey of intrusion detection systems towards an end to end secure internet of things. In: 2016 IEEE 4th International Conference on Future Internet of Things and Cloud (FiCloud), pp. 84–90, August 2016. https://doi.org/10.1109/FiCloud.2016.20
4. SMESEC Project Consortium. https://smesec.eu/
5. Thakur, K., Qiu, M., Gai, K., Ali, M.L.: An investigation on cyber security threats and security models. In: 2015 IEEE 2nd International Conference on Cyber Security and Cloud Computing, pp. 307–311, November 2015. https://doi.org/10.1109/CSCloud.2015.71
6. Tselios, C., Politis, I., Tselios, V., Kotsopoulos, S., Dagiuklas, T.: Cloud computing: a great revenue opportunity for telecommunication industry. In: 51st FITCE Congress (FITCE), Poznan, Poland, vol. 6 (2012)

CyberSure: A Framework for Liability Based Trust

George Christou[1(✉)], Eva Papadogiannaki[1], Michalis Diamantaris[1],
Livia Torterolo[2], and Panos Chatziadam[1]

[1] Foundation of Research and Technology Hellas, Heraklion, Greece
{gchri,epapado,diamant,panosc}@ics.forth.gr
[2] Network Integration and Solutions, Genoa, Italy
livia.torterolo@nispro.it

Abstract. CyberSure is a programme of collaborations and exchanges between researchers aimed at developing a framework for creating and managing cyber insurance policy for cyber systems. Creating such policies will enhance the trustworthiness of cyber systems and provide a sound basis for liability in cases of security and privacy breaches in them. The framework is supported by a platform of tools enabling an integrated risk cyber system security risk analysis, certification and cyber insurance, based on the analysis of objective evidence during the operation of such systems. CyberSure develops its cyber insurance platform by building upon and integrating state of the art tools, methods and techniques. The development of the CyberSure platform is driven by certification, risk analysis and cyber insurance scenarios for cyber system pilots providing cloud and e-health services. Through these, CyberSure addresses the conditions required for offering effective cyber insurance for interoperable service chains cutting across application domains and jurisdictions. CyberSure platform aims to tackle the challenges of offering cyber insurance for interoperable service chains cutting across application domains and jurisdictions.

1 Introduction

The establishment of trust across interconnected cyber systems is very important. Widely approved, effective means of managing risks and uncertainty are cyber insurance and security certification. Certification is one way to offer and establish trust relations, since it provides the necessary evidence of the required regular assessment for the provision of a service against security control measures that are explicitly designed to defend against security risks. By definition, insurance enables trust, as it (i) establishes the responsibility of covering reinstating service provision costs following after interruptions or deviations from contractual obligations and/or regulatory standards and (ii) provides compensation for losses, suffered by service consumers due to improper service provision (e.g., loss of personal or commercially sensitive data) [9]. Certification and insurance have been used as instruments for risk mitigation and trust establishment in the provision of a wide spectrum of services and industries, such as construction services,

A. P. Fournaris et al. (Eds.): ESORICS 2019 Workshops, LNCS 11981, pp. 19–34, 2020.
https://doi.org/10.1007/978-3-030-42051-2_2

health services, hospitality services, and services in the banking sector. Moreover, for several types of such systems and services, providing certification and insurance is being mandated through legislation and regulations, as for instance in the case of health services, energy systems, vehicle maintenance systems and services, and shipping and logistics services. From the insurance perspective, offering cyber security certifications is a valid way to demonstrate that certain security controls have been implemented using the necessary standards. More specifically, in domains like online shopping, tourism services and pharmacies, we can observe a significant effect derived by the establishment of certification and cyber insurance. There have been several studies that indicate the ever increasing importance of cyber insurance, globally, as well as the challenges that occur. For instance, recent surveys present trends in the European Union cyber insurance market, including (i) fast expansion, (ii) significant investment and (iii) dramatic increase in cyber insurance costs and premiums.

Revenue opportunities resulted by cyber insurance can be achieved through meaningful cost savings. One solution is to take advantage of techniques that are able to produce accurate risk assessments, behaviour-based insurance contracts and dynamic pricing. In addition, having the ability to handle diverse consumer technology and fluctuations in legislations is necessary. Apparently, these trends require dynamic and automated establishment, management and adaptation of cyber insurance policies, including dynamic risk assessment and dynamic pricing. In addition, costs required to acquire customers can be reduced using analytics and increased insurance customisation to the characteristics of the subject of insurance. Still, all these requirements are not effectively addressed. More specifically, certification is yet based on labourintensive inspection and periodic offline testing of cyber systems and it does not strictly guarantee the preservation of every certified property between the certification audits. Furthermore, since the risk estimation and creation of cyber insurance policies happen during asynchronous periodic time periods, they are not able to effectively account for intermediate changes between these systems. Currently, risk estimation and creation of cyber insurance contracts are not able to consider fine-grained operational evidence obtained through monitoring and testing of cyber systems. Consequently, risk estimations are not accurate and, thus, insurance policies might not be effective for any of the entities associated.

CyberSure is an European Unions Horizon 2020 research and innovation programme (H2020-MSCA-RISE-2016). The project consortium comprises the following institutions and organizations: Foundation for Research and Technology - Hellas (FORTH), City University (CITY), Italian National Research Council (CNR), Cablenet, Hellas Direct, and Network Integrated Solutions S.r.l. (NIS). In paper, we present CyberSure, a framework that supports the creation and management of cyber insurance policies in order to establish trust in cyber systems and services. This framework is supported by a platform of integrated tools that enable: (i) the dynamic certification of security and privacy properties of cyber systems and services that need to be insured, (ii) the dynamic estimation of security and privacy risks for such systems and services, and finally, (iii) the development, monitoring and management of cyber insurance policies for these systems and services.

The main objectives of CyberSure are:

- To establish a process centric framework for automating the creation and management of cyber insurance policies for cyber systems, based on integrating proven techniques for the certification, audit and risk assessment of security and privacy (S&P) for such systems
- To develop a platform supporting the creation, monitoring and adaptation of cyber insurance policies for cyber systems and the services available through them
- To demonstrate the use of the CyberSure framework in real world trials in the areas of e-health and cloud services and, through them, carry a comprehensive evaluation covering technical, business and legal aspects, and demonstrating technology readiness
- To create conditions for improving cyber insurance practice and the trustworthiness of cyber systems and commercialising the use of the CyberSure platform and framework.

2   Related Work

In this section we present the various processes and components associated with Cyber Insurance. We discuss the current state of the art regarding each process and what are the main innovations of CyberSure framework.

2.1   Security Certification

Security certification is a way to evaluate and certify than a cyber infrastructure is in line with security standards [14]. The certification process results in a certificate, stating that an ICT system is compliant with a certification scheme, which defines the security properties and standards that should be complied with. The evaluation of the infrastructure can be either self assessed, i.e. the process is carried out by the owner of the infrastructure, or be conducted by a third-party organisation, i.e. a certification lab.

A notable certification scheme which spans certification process from the early stages of development up to the evaluation of the final infrastructure is the Common Criteria for Information Technology Security Evaluation [13]. Common Criteria evaluation results in a rating against an Evaluation Assurance Level (EAL). EALs are characterised by:

- The types of evidence that have been taken into account for evaluation (e.g., inspection, testing, formal verification).
- The agent who carried out the evaluation.
- The documentation/evidence that has to be produced and assessed for a successful evaluation.

There are numerous ISOs for information security standards. For example ISO/IEC 27001:2013 [6] dictates that the infrastructures information security risks will be examined systematically taking into account possible vulnerabilities, threats as well as possible impact of incidents. Moreover, an adequate set of information security controls will be designed and implemented in order to avoid and treat unacceptable risks. Finally, due to emerging threats, a management process must ensure that the information security controls are frequently updated in order to meet the infrastructures information security goals.

Despite the vast number of different approaches and certification that are available for the vast majority of IT ecosystems, the process is not automated and the evaluation relies on manual inspection with limited support from inspection tools. The EU project CUMULUS was designed to address these issues when it comes to certification. It is mainly used to automatically apply different types of certification schemes. Possible schemes can be based on data acquired by testing and monitoring.

CyberSure will explore possible ways in order to combine certification and risk management with cyber insurance. For this purpose, CUMULUS certification models will be developed and by automatically applying them to cyber infrastructures risk estimates, insurance policies and premiums will be dynamically adjusted. Thus, through the continuous monitoring and testing it will be possible to access the certification compliance of an infrastructure dynamically. Continuous monitoring is accomplished by deploying event captors at the client infrastructure which are responsible for transmitting certification evidence to CUMULUS monitors in a confidential manner (i.e. secure communication).

2.2   Risk Assessment and Management

Due to the continuously increasing criticality and complexity of cyber infrastructures, several methods and tools have been proposed with regards to risk assessment. The main challenge that is tackled by risk assessment is to identify and narrow down the possible cyber-attack events that could severely impact the operation of a cyber infrastructure. Part of effective risk assessment is the discovery of possible attack vectors. There are risk assessment strategies, which rely on high-level descriptions of the process that should be followed to identify risks and are not algorithmic. On the other hand, there exist more technical strategies, which provide tools in order to automate parts of the process.

A notable example of generic risk assessment methods is OCTAVE [7]. OCTAVE is mostly driven by operational risks and critical assets of an organization. At first, possible impact areas are identified (e.g. safety, health, etc.). The next step is to identify the critical information assets of the organization. The assets are categorized depending on the value and how depended is the operation of the infrastructure to that asset. At this step, the security requirements of each asset are also identified. Each asset that processes data is considered an information asset container. Beyond the outcome of a possible attack, an estimation of the consequences in case the threat scenario happens is calculated. The potential threats are then represented in threat trees. In order to assist with the traversal of the threat trees, OCTAVE provides worksheets and questionnaires.

Impact areas are then ordered in terms of severity depending on how many of the realized threats can affect them. Finally, a mitigation approach is decided for each risk. A risk can be mitigated, avoided, deferred or even accepted.

MAGERIT [2] is another method which follows a similar approach. Initially, informations regarding the assets of the infrastructure, the inter-connections between them and their value are collected. For each one of the assets et of possible threats is determined and already available safeguards are analysed in terms of effectiveness mitigating the risks. Next, the damage to an asset and the expected rate of occurrence of each threat is estimated. At the final step, for each risk, a treatment is decided. A risk can either be accepted and a monitoring scheme will be deployed in order to capture the occurrence of such risk, or treated. Treatment options include avoiding the risk by eliminating the source of the risk from the infrastructure, mitigating the risk by deploying mechanisms which can effectively reduce the impact and the likelihood of the threat, sharing the risk by outsourcing system components or using cyber-insurance, and finally fund the risk i.e. reserving funds in order to cover the impacts of the risk.

Other frameworks, such as MEHARI [1], combine a knowledge base created using MEHARI and adhere to the organization the risk management proposed by ISO 27002:27005. By creating the knowledge base of the infrastructure, the risk assessment can be tailored to the specific use case. The representation of the knowledge base offers the ability to develop a set of tools that will enhance the risk assessment. Moreover, risks can be analyzed in terms of events that can lead to each situation. When the risk assessment process is complete, decisions can be made with regards to what security measures should be implemented in order to assure that possible risk impacts are within acceptable margins. Finally, provided tools can be also used in order to assist security management over time by monitoring accepted risks.

More quantitative and tool based approaches like CORAS [10], provide customized language for modeling the risks and threats. CORAS is a framework for model-based security risk analysis consisting of a language, a method, and a tool. The language provides a graphical representation of main concepts and the relations between them. The method realizes an asset-driven defensive risk analysis and is supported by the tool implementing the language. The main concepts of risk assessment (such as threat agents, threats, vulnerabilities, impact, assets, etc.) are represented as nodes of specific types and are connected with the relations between them. Quantitative or qualitative values may be assigned to the nodes and relations for risk evaluation. The Unified Modeling Language (UML) is typically used to model the target of the analysis. The CORAS method provides a computerized tool designed to support documenting, maintaining and reporting analysis results through risk modeling.

In CyberSure risk assessment is part of the validation framework. Part of of the process ensures that the components of the system cooperate without side effects and that the business goals are achieved. The main innovation of the CyberSure framework is the semiautomatic way of collecting the information about the security risk level of the infrastructure. As described in this section, risk assessment relies mostly on questionnaires and highly generic methods, while there is only a small number of solutions that offer automation through tools (e.g. modeling languages). This is particularly cumbersome for insurance companies since, the data collected from such methods are coarse-grained The CyberSure framework integrates a certification checking module (CUMULUS [19]), which is able to validate part of this information. Finally, our proposed risk assessment process helps to quickly process the data and estimate the possible losses for an insurance company.

2.3 Insurance

Cyber Insurance is a quite new product offered by insurance companies, thus it still faces critical challenges [17]. The main challenge is that there are i not enough data regarding the assesment of cyber security incidents in order to produce accurate statistic conclusions. Since, data related to cyber security insidents are usually very sensitive and thus, companies avoid to disclose and share them with third parties. However this issue is mitigated in Europe through the Directive on security of networks and information systems [16].

Another major challenge originates from the fundamental properties of technology. The rapid evolution of both the systems and attacks and the complex interdependencies between cyber infrastructures assets impede the accurate identification and impact assessment of cyber risks [4]. Moreover, the cyber insurance coverage is inherently hard to define and the exceptions and correctness of the policy is more legal oriented than technological. Despite the challenges and the immaturity of cyber insurance services has a positive influence on cyber security [5].

In CyberSure, the automated security and risk assessment and dynamic certification will be used in order to develop a novel tool which will be able to tackle the challenges of cyber insurance. Insurance policies will be able to apply certification processes and depending on the results, specific risks will be highlighted in order to be covered. The automated processes will reduce the information asymmetries and will simplify the identification of interdependencies. Moreover, the quantitative risk assessment will process the evidence data and estimate the possible losses for the insurance company. Finally, the insurance component will select best pricing strategy.

3   Design

One of the main key challenges of CyberSure is to integrate proven state-of-the-art techniques in certification, risk assessment and insurance management into a unified framework for the management (i.e., creation, pricing, monitoring and adaptation) of cyber insurance policies for cyber systems. As can be seen in the architecture overview in Fig. 1, CyberSure develops a platform incorporating three basic components; (i) a certification infrastructure (supporting phase `Certification`), (ii) a risk management tool (supporting phases `Baseline risk analysis` and `Comprehensive risk assessment`) and (iii) the insurance management tools (supporting `Cyber insurance policy management` phase).

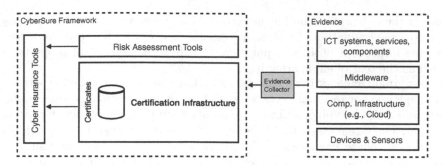

Fig. 1. The CyberSure framework.

This integration will be based on a generic process for cyber insurance management, which will orchestrate activities focusing on cyber systems risk modeling, certification, and cyber insurance policy management. This process supports integration by defining the expected data flows and interfaces between the activities of risk modeling, certification and cyber insurance management. Moreover, it supports both qualitative and quantitative types of analysis of cyber systems assurance at different levels and can be tailorable to the needs of individual service providers and insurers. As can be seen in Fig. 2, CyberSure's generic process for cyber insurance management involves the following four phases:

- `Baseline risk analysis`. Risk assessment methodologies and tools support the early analysis and specification of risk models, i.e., high level models of threat agents and attacks that may pose different types of risks to cyber system assets as well as the possible countermeasures that may be used to mitigate these risks.
- `Certification`. Based on the risk models developed in the previous phase, the CyberSure framework will generate executable cyber system certification models and use them to carry out assessments of the soundness and the effectiveness of the security controls that are used in such systems for mitigating risks. These assessments may be fully or semi-automated and will be based on static or dynamic testing, such as penetration testing, and/or continuous monitoring of the mechanisms of cyber systems, depending on the underpinning certification models. Depending on the outcomes of such assessments, certification may generate digital certificates providing basic risk level guarantees required for cyber insurance. This phase also generates the detailed operational evidence that underpins certificates as an additional means for assessing risks in cases where certificates won't be sufficient for risk assessment in the context of managing cyber insurance policies.
- `Comprehensive risk assessment`. The certificates and the operational evidence generated by `Certification` provide inputs to a subsequent comprehensive assessment of risk that may be required for formulating and pricing cyber insurance policies. The calculation of cyber system exposure to risk is probabilistic and is based on the analysis of the historic detailed evidence provided by certification. Calculating risk exposure is dynamic and makes

use of the outcome of continuous certification. Moreover, this phase will also involve the evaluation of the impact of risk on cyber system providers, such as the impact on business reputation, the theft of intellectual property, as well as the cost of eliminating it.

– `Cyber insurance policy management`. This phase covers the activities of managing cyber insurance contracts, such as policy creation, pricing, updating and claim handling, and will use inputs from previous phases. For example, Cyber system assets that have been identified as vulnerable to particular threats in phase `Baseline risk analysis`, will be the candidate subjects of insurance and may be used for customized policy creation and updates. The certificates and continuous operational evidence generated in phase `Certification` may be used as prerequisites for continuous policy validity checks. Furthermore, the cyber system assets risk exposure and impact estimates generated in phase `Comprehensive risk assessment`, may be used for policy pricing. The `Cyber insurance policy management` phase will also provide feedback to earlier phases. This feedback will arise from an analysis of claims referring to compromised assets across different policies, which may indicate the need to revise threat and certification models (used in phase `Baseline risk analysis` and `Certification`, respectively) and/or the risk exposure and the impact estimation methods used in `Comprehensive risk assessment`.

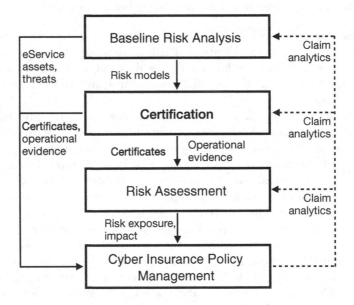

Fig. 2. CyberSure's generic process for cyber insurance management.

3.1   CyberSure's Internal Mechanisms and Tools

In this section we describe the tools incorporated and used for each one of the three basic components as well as relationship between them, as can be seen in Fig. 1.

Certification Infrastructure. The certification infrastructure integrated in the CyberSure platform has been developed by the EU F7 R&D project CUMULUS (Certification infrastrUcture for MUlti-Layer cloUd Services) [3,12,19]. This infrastructure can be used to define and execute automatically certification models. These certification models specify the security and privacy properties required of cloud services; how to acquire and analyse evidence in order to assess whether the provision of services satisfies these properties, and how to generate certificates that confirm the compliance of services with the required properties. Moreover, the CUMULUS infrastructure supports the collection and analysis of different types of evidence, including both static and dynamic test data. The data collection includes continuous monitoring data for cloud service provision, as well as data gathered from trusted platform modules that can guarantee the integrity of the software components, which are used to realize the services and the countermeasures against threats. The test and monitoring data that are required by a certification model in order to assess security properties are acquired by evidence collectors built into the software components that realize the services and/or the computational platforms where these services are deployed on (e.g., the cloud). To address the objectives of CyberSure, the CUMULUS certification models and infrastructure will be extended to support the specification of certification models that are based on unified concepts with the risk models used in phases `Certification` and `Cyber insurance policy management` of the general CyberSure process regarding the service assets, threats, and security countermeasures.

Risk Assessment Tools. The risk assessment tool RiS (Risk Integrated Service) integrated in the CyberSure platform has been developed by CNR (The Italian National Research Council) in order to support Information Security and IT Risk Management consulting services. CNR provides a a web-based solution that implements a risk process, based on ISO 31000 standard, that is able to assess, evaluate and manage IT risks of assets in scope. The main parameters analyzed are the asset severity, the threats and their probability of occurrence and the vulnerabilities. The `Risk assessment tools` is already able to provide a high-level risk scenario starting from a template of a predefined threats and vulnerabilities. We will also extend the functionalities provided in order to also support the `Comprehensive risk assessment` phase which requires the development of a new model able to calculate the cyber system exposure to risk on a probabilistic base and making use of historic/operational evidences provided by certification. In order to be consistent with the evolving threat and vulnerability landscape and to dynamically report on the increased levels of risk, this tool will integrate and correlate the outcome of the continuous certification process. Finally, it will be also extended to provide a cost-benefit analysis by exploiting the NeSSoS (Network of Excellence on Engineering Secure Future Internet Software Services and Systems) risk, cost management and assurance framework. NeSSoS also benefits from cooperation with the CUMULUS tool on acquiring the real evidence of the security configuration of the system and helping the insured customers to fill in the required input data, as well as verifying the correctness of the data provided.

Insurance Management Tools. The insurance management tools that will be integrated in the CyberSure platform derive from the main tools already adopted by HELLAS-DIRECT in managing insurance products in non-life insurance. These tools have the purpose of defining a price for the policy in order to fulfill the needs of the insured together with the target of the company, taking into account the updated risk profile of the insured. To achieve this goal, historical data conveniently classified will be given as the input of the models will allow the company to reach their targets, while also applying discounts or penalizations. The existing tools will be extended and modified in order to receive and integrate, as inputs, the outputs of the `Comprehensive risk assessment` and `Certification infrastructure`. The complete process and the tools used will be tailored according to the needs of the individual service providers and the insurers, since the goal of CyberSure is to support both complex cyber insurance scenarios that require automated certification as part of cyber insurance policy issuing and management but also simpler scenarios where certification might be performed in a non automated manner or not required at all.

3.2 Monitoring and Pricing Components

The CUMULUS framework facilitates the collection and analysis of different types of evidence and continuous monitoring of data, as well as data gathered from trusted platform modules that can guarantee the integrity of the software components. The monitoring data that are processed by a certification model, in order to evaluate the system properties, are acquired by evidence collectors deployed on the software components of the pilot systems, the health-care organization and the cloud provider, respectively.

The pricing component takes multiple inputs and estimates the pricing of each cyber insurance policy. The main input is the CyberSure comprehensive risk score, calculated using the previous components of the CyberSure platform, RiS and NeSSoS and the monitoring component by CUMULUS. The revenue of the company purchasing the policy affects the premiums in a positive way, since the higher the value of generated revenue, the higher the economic damage a possible cyber incident can have on the bottom line of the company. The critical dependency of business processes on IT, i.e. how a potential IT interruption would lead to a business interruption as well, is another factor affecting pricing. Past claims have been shown to be positively associated with future claims, and hence they are taken into account in pricing for cyber insurance. The specific industry and non-profit status of the company also affect the perceived risk of cyber incidents requiring pricing adjustments. Moreover, the type of data collected about customers, and whether this includes any sensitive personal data, has a quantifiable effect on pricing. Limits of insurance coverage, i.e. the maximum amount the insurance company will cover, and deductible amounts, i.e. the amount the insured party needs to cover before the insurance company starts paying their share, are two extra components of pricing [11,15,18].

4   Validation

In this section we discuss the validation procedure for the CyberSure framework [8]. CyberSure's validation process consists of a combination of three steps: (i) the technical, (ii) the business and (iii) the legal validation. Regarding the technical validation step, we will focus on assessing the integration of the standalone tools (i.e. CUMULUS, NESSOS, RIS and the pricing module), showing that the CyberSure platform as a whole works effectively from a technical point of view. Regarding the business validation step, the procedure aims to evaluate the business idea of the project, assessing the profitability and sustainability of the business model in respect to market and customer attractiveness. Finally, considering the legal validation step, the validation procedure aims to verify the platforms compliance with every European and national regulations, including GDPR. So far, CyberSure is under an initial validation state.

4.1   Criteria

In this section we define a set of different criteria that we aim to verify in order to ensure the quality of projects' outcomes. We divide these criteria into three categories: (i) technical, (ii) business and (iii) legal criteria. In the following paragraphs we discuss the aforementioned criteria.

Technical Criteria. From a technical point of view, CyberSure has to be validated in terms of methodology, software components, infrastructure, integration and communication. Since the CyberSure framework consists of a number of standalone tools, the validation of the platform has to be considered as an integration of the validation process of the tools. As already discussed, the main modules involved are: (i) CUMULUS, (ii) RIS, (iii) NESSOS and (iv) the pricing module. CUMULUS is a tool that is used to monitor security controls of IT infrastructures. The RIS service is a web application which relies on a database, hosted on the same server. The NESSOS tool is a web-based application that aims to evaluate risks of an organization. Finally, the pricing module is developed to estimate the price for various cyber insurance products, based on the input provided by other components of the CyberSure platform, the prices on similar products in the market and any additional factors that may be taken into account. Consequently, we need to verify that the evaluated pilot systems can interact with the proposed CyberSure platform and enable the real-time monitoring of the underlying assets.

As a result, for each one of the tools, the technical key factors to be evaluated include the following:

- *CUMULUS*: Ability to install, configure, and operate the event captors to the pilot system.
- *CUMULUS*: The minimum disruption of the functionality of the main pilot hardware and software by the CyberSure monitor.

- *CUMULUS*: Ability to create a secure environment that will include authorization and authentication of different event captors before transmitting events to CUMULUS. This will prevent CUMULUS from receiving and analyzing events which were not transmitted from one of the Pilots.
- *RIS*: The RIS service relies on an Oracle Database and Oracle Application Express technology. The factors that must be considered in the validation of the process of risk assessment are: authentication and authorization mechanisms, reliability of input parameters, risk outcomes coherence and security.
- *RIS*: RIS's servers virtual infrastructure must be analyzed and evaluated.
- *RIS*: The RIS service must be provided in SaaS and the availability of the service must be analyzed and validated.
- *NESSOS*: Factors that need to be considered for the validation of the NESSOS tool are: Authentication and authorization, reliability of input parameters, risk outcomes coherence and security.
- *NESSOS*: For a reliable and secure execution of the NESSOS tool, it must be ensured that the infrastructure is reliable and secure, as well.
- *NESSOS*: Since the NESSOS tool must be integrated with other modules of the platform availability and correct integration with the other tools of the CyberSure platform, need to be validated, as well.
- *Pricing Module*: Regarding the software validation, some of the factors that must be considered are: authentication and authorization mechanisms, reliability of input parameters, reliability of products and prices of similar cyber insurance products, policy outcomes coherence and security.
- *Pricing Module*: Pricing Module's servers virtual infrastructure must be analyzed and evaluated.
- *Pricing Module*: The Pricing module must be integrated with other modules to receive inputs from the baseline and the comprehensive risk assessment, receive competitors' product and pricing intelligence from the market and must provide proper and adequate policies to the insurance company.

Business Criteria. The main objective of business criteria for validation is to assess the appeal of cyber insurance products and associated services in the market, as well as to define the value proposition of the platform that would allow us to capture enough market share to make the project financially viable. In addition, a very important goal is to be able to forecast the future market performance of the platform from the insurance point of view, and how the platform can be used to estimate the risk for cyber threats and, hence, adjust the pricing of insurance policies.

The key business factors for a successful cyber insurance business include the profitability of the underwriting models, the customer attractiveness of the cyber insurance products and the cuber risk score. The profitability of the underwriting models is defined as the total amount of insurance premiums collected from insured, subtracting the amounts claimed by the insured due to events that have affected the insured business as prescribed in the insurance agreement. The customer attractiveness of the cyber insurance products is based on a variety of factors, the main of which are the price, relatively to the competition and the insured value (sum assured), and the coverage of the insurance (i.e. under which events/circumstances would the cyber insurance reimburse the insured for their losses). Additional factors that contribute to the customer attractiveness is the ease of policy acquisition, the ease of the claims procedure and the availability and type of customer service (phone, chat, email, on-site, technical, 24-h). The CyberSure platform aims to aid the customer attractiveness process by estimating more accurately than the competition, and in a more robust and automated way, the cyber risks and expected economic value of the insured events, allowing the insurer to lower the insurance premiums. The cyber risk score, the main output of the CyberSure platform, will be calculated using semi-automated tools, developed by the CyberSure collaboration, and can be monitored by both the insurer and the insured continuously. Risks are taken into account depending on their economic value and their probability of occurrence, and are frequently re-evaluated to include new cyber risks or attacks that become possible as technology progresses. The insurance needs consist of the method to estimate the cyber risk of the customers, both in terms of the magnitude of the expected economic effect and of the expected frequency of each event. Utilizing the output from the CyberSure platform, and taking into account the cyber insurance market prices and the desire and prospect for growth of the company portfolio, the insurance company will price each prospective customer accordingly.

The evaluation of the key business criteria will be determined by two main factors: the market penetration and the profitability of the business. The market share of the cyber insurance products should be respectable, in order to have the cyber insurance line deemed successful. In addition, the brand awareness of the cyber insurance line should be such that potential that customers would consider this opportunity, even if they will not purchase in the end. The profitability of the business will be shown in the medium term, after cyber insurance claims have been filed and the cyber insurance line is profitable, after accounting for the claims, and the operating expenses, as well.

Legal Criteria. The main objective of legal criteria for validation is to verify that the platform CyberSure is compliant with all European and national laws and regulations, including GDPR. The development of the legal criteria includes the following steps: (i) the analysis of the legal landscape, in relevance to CyberSure, (ii) the awareness of the data and its nature and sensitivity, (iii) the application of certain principles on data quality, purpose specification, use limitation, security safeguards, practices and policies openness, individual participation and accountability. Finally, CyberSure takes its responsibilities under the GDPR and the requirement to treat personal information in an appropriate and lawful manner very seriously and as such, complies with the data protection principles.

4.2   Applications

To validate CyberSure, two different scenarios of cyber insurance will be used. The first validation scenario will be based in the e-health area, while the second scenario will be based in the cloud systems and services. These two scenarios involve different implementation platforms and critical security and privacy requirements to be insured. Successful deployment of CyberSure in these two distinct cyber ecosystems will validate the effectiveness of our framework. Moreover, during the deployment phase, CyberSure will be refined through the lessons learned during this process.

In the first scenario, we will use an IT software that is used in the healthcare domain. More specifically, this software focuses on integrated health-care solutions in the wider context of predictive, individualized, preventive and participatory medicine. The most major security, privacy and dependability requirements are: (i) the preservation of privacy, confidentiality and integrity of medical records in-transit and at-storage, (ii) the preservation of privacy, confidentiality and integrity of prescription and financial data in-transit and at-storage, and (iii) the preservation of a high degree of the e-health platform availability. In the second scenario, we will use the Datacenter Virtual Infrastructure (DVI) of Cablenet, an ISP that participates in the CyberSure project as member of the consortium. DVI is physically protected a number of protection measures focusing on physical access, power-related risks, air conditioning and fire suppression. The main security and privacy requirement for the cloud scenario is the fact that all data must be encrypted to remain confidential both in transit and at-storage. Furthermore, data integrity and privacy are highly required, while application integrity and availability need to be ensured. Thus, there must be mechanisms monitoring and reporting any abnormalities and breaches in the cloud services. Notifications of security breaches to system administrators and potentially the users should also be supported.

5   Conclusions

In this paper, we present the major objectives of the CyberSure project. CyberSure is a framework for liability based trust, supported by a platform of tools enabling an integrated risk cyber system security risk analysis, certification and cyber insurance, based on the analysis of objective evidence during the operation of such systems. The development of the CyberSure platform is driven by certification, risk analysis and cyber insurance scenarios for cyber system pilots providing cloud and e-health services. So far, the validation progress of the CyberSure project is in an initial state, as discussed in the corresponding section. As future work, we plan to publish the results and details of the validation progress, after its completion.

Acknowledgements. This work was supported by the European Commission through the project CONCORDIA Horizon 2020 Research and Innovation program under Grant Agreement No. 830927 and CYBERSURE Horizon 2020 research and innovation programme under the Marie Skłodowska-Curie Grant Agreement No. 734815.

References

1. Mehari 2010: risk analysis and treatment guide. club de la securite de l'information francias, August 2010. [cm03] C. Copeland J. Moteff, Science John Fischer Resources, and Industry Division
2. Amutio, M., Candau, J., Mañas, J.: Magerit-version 3, methodology for information systems risk analysis and management, book I-the method. Ministerio de Administraciones Públicas (2014)
3. Anisetti, M., Ardagna, C.A., Damiani, E.: A certification-based trust model for autonomic cloud computing systems. In: 2014 International Conference on Cloud and Autonomic Computing, pp. 212–219 (September 2014). https://doi.org/10.1109/ICCAC.2014.8
4. Böhme, R., Schwartz, G., et al.: Modeling cyber-insurance: towards a unifying framework. In: WEIS (2010)
5. Bolot, J., Lelarge, M.: Cyber insurance as an incentivefor internet security. In: Johnson, M.E. (ed.) Managing Information Risk and the Economics of Security, pp. 269–290. Springer, Boston (2009). https://doi.org/10.1007/978-0-387-09762-6_13
6. Calder, A., Watkins, S.: IT Governance: An International Guide to Data Security and ISO27001/ISO27002. Kogan Page Publishers, London (2012)
7. Caralli, R.A., Stevens, J.F., Young, L.R., Wilson, W.R.: Introducing OCTAVE Allegro: improving the information security risk assessment process. Technical report, Carnegie-Mellon Univ Pittsburgh PA Software Engineering Inst (2007)
8. CyberSure: Deliverable D2.2: CyberSurevalidation framework. http://www.cybersure.eu/m/filer_public/15/e4/15e47988-2b90-4828-ae63-4a4c4c9ccef3/cybersure_-_d22_final.pdf. Accessed 05 July 2019
9. Enisa: Incentives and barriers of the cyber insurance market in Europe. https://www.enisa.europa.eu/publications/incentives-and-barriers-of-the-cyber-insurance-market-in-europe. Accessed 05 June 2019
10. Fredriksen, R., Kristiansen, M., Gran, B.A., Stølen, K., Opperud, T.A., Dimitrakos, T.: The CORAS framework for a model-based risk management process. In: Anderson, S., Felici, M., Bologna, S. (eds.) SAFECOMP 2002. LNCS, vol. 2434, pp. 94–105. Springer, Heidelberg (2002). https://doi.org/10.1007/3-540-45732-1_11
11. Innerhofer-Oberperfler, F., Breu, R.: Potential rating indicators for cyberinsurance: an exploratory qualitative study. In: Moore, T., Pym, D., Ioannidis, C. (eds.) Economics of Information Security and Privacy, pp. 249–278. Springer, Boston (2010). https://doi.org/10.1007/978-1-4419-6967-5_13
12. Katopodis, S., Spanoudakis, G., Mahbub, K.: Towards hybrid cloud service certification models. In: 2014 IEEE International Conference on Services Computing, pp. 394–399, June 2014. https://doi.org/10.1109/SCC.2014.59
13. Kruger, R., Eloff, J.H.P.: A *Common Criteria* framework for the evaluation of information technology systems security. In: Yngström, L., Carlsen, J. (eds.) Information Security in Research and Business. ITIFIP, pp. 197–209. Springer, Boston (1997). https://doi.org/10.1007/978-0-387-35259-6_16
14. Lagazio, M., Barnard-Wills, D., Rodrigues, R., Wright, D.: Certification schemes for cloud computing. EU Commission report (2014)
15. Marotta, A., Martinelli, F., Nanni, S., Orlando, A., Yautsiukhin, A.: Cyber-insurance survey. Comput. Sci. Rev. **24**, 35–61 (2017). https://doi.org/10.1016/j.cosrev.2017.01.001. http://www.sciencedirect.com/science/article/pii/S1574013716301137

16. Nikolopoulou, A.: The directive on security of networks and information systems (NIS Directive) from a practical view (2019)
17. Podolak, G.D.: Insurance for cyber risks: a comprehensive analysis of the evolving exposure, today's litigation, and tomorrow's challenges. Quinnipiac L. Rev. **33**, 369 (2014)
18. Romanosky, S., Ablon, L., Kuehn, A., Jones, T.: Content analysis of cyber insurance policies: how do carriers price cyber risk? J. Cybersecur. **5**(1) (2019). https://doi.org/10.1093/cybsec/tyz002
19. Spanoudakis, G., Damiani, E., Mana, A.: Certifying services in cloud: the case for a hybrid, incremental and multi-layer approach. In: 2012 IEEE 14th International Symposium on High-Assurance Systems Engineering, pp. 175–176. IEEE (2012)

Deploying Fog-to-Cloud Towards a Security Architecture for Critical Infrastructure Scenarios

Sarang Kahvazadeh[✉], Xavi Masip-Bruin, Pau Marcer, and Eva Marín-Tordera

Advanced Network Architectures Lab (CRAAX), Universitat Politècnica de Catalunya (UPC),
Barcelona, Spain
{skahvaza,xmasip,pmarcer,eva}@ac.upc.edu

Abstract. Critical infrastructures are bringing security, and safety for people in terms of healthcare, water, electricity, industry, transportation, etc. The huge amount of data produced by CIs need to be aggregated, filtered, and stored. Cloud computing was merged into the CIs for utilizing cloud data centers as a pay-as-you-go online computing system for outsourcing services for data storage, filtering and aggregating. On the other hand, CIs need real-time processing for providing sophisticated services to people. Consequently, fog computing is merged into CIs aimed at providing services closer to the users, turning into a smooth real-time decision making and processing. When considering both, that is fog and cloud (for example, deploying the recently coined hierarchical fog-to-cloud F2C concept), new enriched features may be applied to the CIs. Security in CIs is one of the most essential challenges since any failure or attack can turn into a national wise disaster. Moreover, CIs also need to support quality of service (QoS) guarantees for users. Thus, bringing balanced QoS vs security is one of the main challenges for any CI infrastructure. In this paper, we illustrate the benefits of deploying an F2C system in CIs, particularly identifying specific F2C security requirements to be applied to CIs. Finally, we also introduce a decoupled security architecture specifically tailored to CIs that can bring security with reasonable QoS in terms of authentication and key distribution time delay.

Keywords: Critical infrastructure · Quality of service · Security · Fog-to-cloud · Fog computing · Cloud computing

1 Introduction and Motivation

Critical infrastructures (CIs) [1] play a vital role in the world impacting on the whole economy, security, and health provisioning. CIs are a set of assets, be it either physical or virtual, providing country's essential requirements and directions when any failure can cause a disaster in terms of security, economy or health. Nowadays, the Internet of Things (IoT) concept is merged into different CIs [1] such as hospitals, transport, nuclear plants, etc. Indeed, many sensors and actuators are utilized in CIs to facilitating the collection of distributed information from different locations to be analyzed for CIs. For example, a hospital uses distributed temperature sensors to collect temperature information for

© Springer Nature Switzerland AG 2020
A. P. Fournaris et al. (Eds.): ESORICS 2019 Workshops, LNCS 11981, pp. 35–48, 2020.
https://doi.org/10.1007/978-3-030-42051-2_3

providing comfortable environment for patients. A nuclear system uses sensors and actuators to collect information from a nuclear station to be checked aimed at preventing any nuclear radiation. However, the expected huge volume of data produced by IoT devices in CIs must be filtered, aggregated, and stored, thus requiring the right technology and infrastructure to do so. Cloud computing [2], as a pay-as-you-go online system provides datacenters for data processing, filtering, and storing. However, the conceptually far cloud cannot provide real-time processing, as required by CIs to provide services for people. Then, fog computing [3] appeared as a new concept which can be merged along with cloud to be used by CIs. Fog provides real-time processing, geo-distribution, security, etc., by handling services closer to the users. The fog computing concept was introduced as a complementary architecture leveraging cloud computing, rather than to compete with it. Inferred from this fog concept, the Fog-to-cloud (F2C) computing continuum system [4] recently emerged. This combined system allows services that demand real-time processing to use fog, and in parallel, services demanding huge volume of data processing to use cloud. The envisioned F2C hierarchical architecture can be merged into the CIs to facilitate their dependency interactions and services execution.

Certainly, it is widely accepted that a key challenge in the CIs world is security. Potentially, CIs are so dependable to bring safety and security for people. However, the larger the number of things (IoT devices) in CIs are, the larger the security and privacy risks will be. Indeed, IoT devices have limited computational power to handle cryptography and security provision by themselves. Therefore, IoT devices can be used by attackers to either launch the attack or get access to the collected information. These type of devices can be hacked or attacked in terms of passive and active attacks. The distributed nature of IoT devices brings a challengeable question, "can centralized cloud computing handle security requirements for the huge number of distributed devices at the edge of the network?". There are many positive answers: "yes, cloud computing by means of powerful data centers and virtualization can handle security". But then, the question is "why do CIs still suffer from attacks, such as the attacks to many hospitals, universities, transport systems in 2017?" Indeed, in 2017, one attack to a hospital in England stopped the hospital network system for 24 h. In this case, casualties might be so terrible due to human's life losses. On the other hand, there are also some negative answers: "Traditional, centralized and far away cloud computing is not suitable for handling the distributed devices security". Then a different question can arise: "How can this security be provided?". Some researchers rely on the emerging "fog computing" concept assuming that security can be handled closer to users (enhancing then the privacy as well) and in a distributed fashion. Nevertheless, in any case, centralized cloud and distributed fogs must be coordinated to deliver a safe and secure system.

Consequently, CIs must consider a new strategy for handling security in this distributed and hierarchical fashion, because the centralized cloud as a single point of failure cannot be sufficient for handling security in dependable CIs. In this paper, we identified most potential security requirement in a F2C system to be applied into CIs and propose a new security architecture. The proposed security architecture extends the work done in [5] by setting a transversal security architecture, decoupled from the underlying F2C system. To that aim, this paper is organized as follows. In Sect. 2, we briefly introduce the F2C concept. In Sect. 3, we revisit main security requirements in the cloud, fog and F2C domains, the proposed security architecture in Sect. 4, the security architecture in CIs in Sect. 5, evaluation and analysis Sect. 6, and finally, Sect. 7 concludes the paper.

2   F2C System

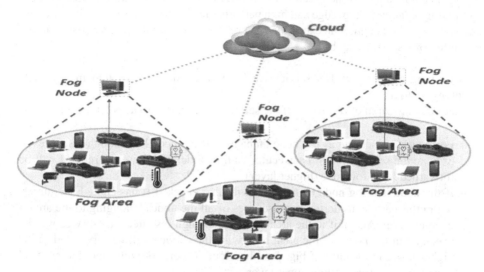

Fig. 1. F2C architecture

F2C is a hierarchical multi-layered architecture conceived to cover a broad area, from the edge up to the cloud with plenty of computing devices. The hierarchical distributed nature of this architecture puts together the advantages of both computing paradigms, i.e., proximity at the fog and high performance at the cloud, leading towards a coordinated management of the whole system, and enabling an optimal resource allocation intended to meet the expected service QoS requirements. The envisioned F2C ecosystem [7], as shown in Fig. 1, is organized into fog areas, each including its whole set of resources (nodes). The exact scope of an area and the individual allocation of resources into each area are topics of current research, certainly affecting the scalability of the system. One node at each area is selected to become the fog node as the manager of the fog area. The fog node as a manager, is a node with certain features, such as enough computing and networking capabilities to manage its area, and good network access, just to name a few. The responsibilities of such fog nodes are managing the devices inside the area as well as coordinating with higher level layers. In Fig. 1, the fog nodes as managers, are connected and managed by the Cloud layer, thus crafting the hierarchical architecture. Obviously, the cloud layer has enough capacity to perform a higher level management of the fog nodes set. Additionally, in a large scenario with millions of devices and spanning several squared kilometers, such architecture could increase the number of layers in order to facilitate an efficient coordination between nearby areas and, thus, becoming a multi-layered architecture. The multi-layered hierarchy guarantees the scalability of the system, as well as an efficient services management. Again, determining the number of layers for a specific ecosystem is a topic of current research and it is out of the scope of this paper, see [8]. The envisioned F2C scenario is enriched by considering users to play as both: (i) users share their resources to the F2C system; (ii) users become F2C clients requesting the execution of services or applications.

To take advantage of the execution of services in this combination of the different computing paradigms, fog, edge and high performance at cloud, it is necessary a system controlling and managing the execution of services. The outlined characteristics in the execution of a service may be:

- Launching the service: The service can be requested to the system in any node belonging to it.
- Hierarchical search of resources: If the service is requested to a specific node:

  - For nodes not serving as fog node managers: if the node has enough resources to execute the service, it will be executed in this node; otherwise the request will be forwarded to its fog node (higher layer).
  - If the node is a fog node manager, it will also check if it has enough resources, but in this case, considering the resources of all the nodes belonging to the area it is controlling. Again, if in the area there are enough resources the service will be executed in the nodes of the area; otherwise the service will be forwarded to the higher layer, in the case of Fig. 1 to the cloud leader, but with more hierarchical layers to the corresponding upper layer.

- Mapping of services and resources: The previous description about the hierarchical search of resources will be based on the smartness to map services into fog or cloud resources according to their capabilities, availability, expected QoS requirements, etc.
- Distributed and parallel execution: The F2C system must allow the distributed execution of services. Services can be either monolithic applications or services divided into subservices or task. When a service allows its division into tasks, the F2C system must perform the best division into tasks and also assign the tasks to the more suitable resources. Moreover, this distributed execution may be also parallel in some services. Taking advantage again of the large number of nodes, different tasks of a service can be executed in different nodes. The F2C management system must be endowed with a runtime controller responsible for controlling the synchronized execution of tasks.

Other main aspects of the F2C easing the distributed execution of services in this ecosystem are:

- Resource discovery: Nodes can be on the move in the city, such as mobile phones. A mechanism must exist to ease mutual discovery between leaders and normal nodes.
- Identification: Nodes participating in the system must be uniquely identified.
- Sharing model: users sharing their devices in the system should indicate the amount of resources they want to participate with (memory, storage, etc.).
- Handover: As mentioned, nodes can be on the move, first belonging to an area and after some time steeping away of it. Thus there should be a handover mechanism to reallocate tasks being executed in these on the move devices.

Critical infrastructure (CIs) can benefit from F2C system for providing hierarchical fog nodes in their system. It facilitates the services execution for CIs, without, or even increasing the security and the privacy of CIs' data. Data from sensors must be analyzed in CIs to detect possible risks. With the proposed deployment of fog nodes and fog areas, these data do not need to be sent to cloud through Internet to be processed. The cluster of devices in a fog area, under the control of a fog node manager, can handle the execution of sensitive services in CIs. In that sense, higher privacy is guaranteed. This is especially important in CIS, because data treated is particularly sensitive, both in terms of security (for example information about a nuclear station) and also in terms of privacy (for example patients' data in a hospital).

On the other hand, if data is processed close to the sources of data, real-time processing is also guaranteed, and finally, network traffic to cloud is also decreased.

Apart of the advantages of handling CIs services in a F2C system, the security itself should be managed by a distributed system instead of being managed by cloud. In this sense, in this paper we also propose a distributed and transversal security architecture, decoupled from the underlying F2C system to bring security with demanded quality of service (QoS) into the CIs. Next section will describe the specific requirements of this new proposed security architecture.

3   Security Requirements for Combined CIs-F2C

This section is aimed at describing the specific set of security requirements for F2C scenarios to be applied into CIs. Security requirements in CIs must be analyzed to establish a secure, robust and trustable environment for the people. In fact, we categorize most common security requirements in CIs as follows [8]: strong network security management, strong identification and authentication mechanism, firm security policy, data confidentiality, forensics analysis, operational technology (OT) protection, OT network protection, secure communication channel, anomaly behavior, detection mechanism, high network traffic detection mechanism (for DoS/DDoS attacks), security information and event management (SIEM), antimalware and antiviruses protection mechanism, hardware security, data privacy, data integrity, and IT network protection.

Therefore, most potential security requirements must be considered for applying F2C system into CIs can be shown as (see [1, 9–11], and [12]):

- Authentication: All components in a CIs system, such as users, edge devices, fog devices, gateways, services, and cloud service providers, must be authenticated not to allow access to unauthorized users. Thus, CIs systems need a new authentication mechanism to handle this hierarchical and distributed F2C system.
- Key management: a well-structured key management strategy must be applied for keys distribution, update and revocation in CIs to provide secure communication between components. Indeed, a hierarchical and distributed F2C system requires a distributed key management strategy to be applied.
- Identity management: all CIs components, such as edge devices, fog devices and cloud services must have a unique identity that might be updated or revoked.
- Data security: all data storage, processing, aggregation, and sharing must be secured and encrypted between edge-fog-cloud (F2C) in CIs.

- Network security: all communication in CIs components edge-fog-cloud (F2C) must happen in a secure way (i.e., encryption).
- Access control: A well-defined distributed and hierarchical access control must be defining in CIs due to hierarchical F2C systems.
- Devices and services discovery: edge devices, fog devices, and in parallel services for CIs must be discovered in a secure way to avoid attacks, such as eavesdropping, man-in-the-middle, and masquerade attacks.
- Security management: a well-defined security analysis and management must be applied into CIs due to hierarchical nature of F2C system.
- Distributed security architecture: Due to distributed nature of F2C systems, a new security architecture must be designed to handle a F2C system in a distributed and hierarchical way to be applied into CIs.
- Secure bootstrapping: all edge devices, fog devices, and other devices participating in CIs must bootstrap in secure way to avoid any alteration or modification in devices in hierarchical F2C.
- Integrity, confidentiality, and availability: Data and system in integrated CIs-F2C must be integrated, confidential and made available to all users and participants.
- Secure sharing computation: In a F2C system, edge devices might not be able to handle data processing, storage, and aggregation due to their low computational resources. Therefore, upper layers such as fog nodes or cloud resources must provide secure shareable computation to handle the required processing in CIs.
- Secure mobility: CIs components, such as fog nodes and edge devices, might be on the move (mobility) and have dynamic characteristic. Therefore, secure mobility and secure and fast handover are both needed in F2C systems.
- Intrusion detection: Intrusion detection mechanisms must be applied in cloud as centralized point and in parallel, distributed way for fog layers in F2C-CIs system.
- Privacy: In CIs such as healthcare, privacy is crucial security requirements. It means all the user's information must have kept private. In F2C-CIs system, data processing, aggregation, communication, storage must be done in secure way to not disclose any private information, data leakage, data eavesdropping, data modifications, and etc. All data in channels must be encrypted and access to data must not be disclosed to unauthorized users.
- Monitoring: A well-structure security monitoring in cloud and distributed security monitoring for distributed fogs must be applied in CIs-F2C system to analysis traffics and other variables and detect malicious activities.
- Security management: Well-defined security requirement, policies, security controls configuration, and etc. must be applied in CIs-F2C system. One of main challenges here is managing security in distributed fog layers and edge devices (IoT devices).

After illustrating security requirements in CIs for applying in an F2C system, we can conclude that the specific requirements and characteristics of combined CIs-F2C systems demand a novel architectural solution aimed at providing security. Next section describes a hierarchical security architecture suitable for security provisioning in CIsF2C systems.

4   Security Architecture for Combined CIs-F2C

In a previous work, a security architecture (Fig. 2) was proposed for handling a hierarchical F2C approach. The security architecture [5] includes a centralized F2C controller at cloud and distributed control-area-units (CAUs) at fog to provide security requirements in a hierarchical nature. The CAUs get authenticated and authorized from a F2C controller (at cloud) in an initialization phase. Then, CAUs can be trustable to act as distributed security controllers at fogs to provide security requirements for each corresponding areas. CAUs can provide security for fog devices, edge devices and even devices that do not have enough computational power to provide their security. This architecture eliminates single points of failure by deploying distributed CAUs. Other advantages of the envisioned architecture can be read as security management, distributed security provisioning, efficient key management, less-time delay authentication, hybrid cryptography using different keys, authentication mechanism in different layers, handling edge devices security with no computational power, secure mobility/handover, etc.

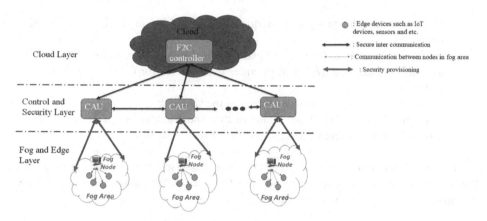

Fig. 2. Security architecture

The security architecture can be implemented as embedded inside of fog nodes or decoupled from fog nodes as transversal decoupled security architecture. The both scenario were tested in previous work [6]. The Decoupled CAUs F2C (DCF) scenario brings security with less impact on QoS as illustrated in Fig. 3.

In the proposed decoupled security architecture, all CAUs get authenticated and authorized from the F2C controller to handle security in their corresponding areas. In this case, security can be met with reasonable QoS and even CAUs are able to detect malicious fog nodes as they are not implemented inside of them.

In this paper, CAUs act as authenticator and key managers for distributed fog areas at the edge of the network as illustrated in Fig. 4. The implemented DCF workflow is described as following:

- Initialization phase: In this process, all distributed CAUs authenticated and establish secure channel with certificate authority (CA) in the cloud.

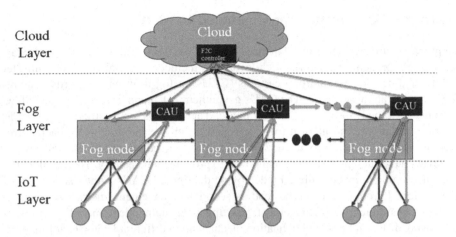

Fig. 3. Decoupled security architecture (DCF)

1- CAU sends certificate signature request (CSR) and its' id (CAU-id) to the F2C controller.
2- F2C controller checks the CAU-id existence in the list for validation if exists then, goes to the next step. (After id provider generate ids for CAU, it sends to F2C controller.).
3- F2C controller sends signed certificate to the CAU.
4- CAU and F2C controller are authenticated and transport layer security (TLS) establish for providing CAU-F2C controller secure channel.

It is worth mentioning the fact that after fog nodes selection in the fog areas, all the described processes will run to provide fog node-CAU authentication and TLS establishment in the initialization phase.

• Edge device authentication process:

5- Edge device is registered in cloud.
6- Id provider in the cloud, generates device-id.
7- The id-provider sends device-id to the edge device.
8- In parallel, the device-id is sent to the CAU by id-provider for local id validation.
9- The edge device comes to the fog area and discovered by fog node.
10- The edge device sends CSR and device-id to the CAU.
11- CAU check the device-id existence for validation. If the device-id exists and validates then, goes to the next step.
12- CAU signs certificate and send signed certificate to the edge device.
13- In parallel, CAU sends device id to the fog node.
14- Edge device and fog node are authenticated and establish TLS.

- Key distribution, generation and management:

15- Edge device sends request for keys.
16- CAU generates public key and private key.
17- CAU sends key pairs in secure channel.

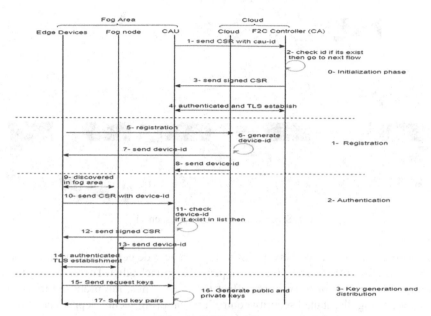

Fig. 4. DCF workflow

In the next section, we illustrate the decoupled security architecture in dependable CIs.

5 Decoupled Security Architecture in CIs

In a critical infrastructure scenario that includes different CIs such as, smart healthcare, smart factory, smart transportation, etc. (Fig. 5), the security architecture can be applied as a transversal architecture to provide security requirements in a distributed fashion. In this scenario and with the decoupled security architecture proposed, we can think on security controllers (which we have called CAUs) deployed in the different areas handling the security of all type of CIs; or in an even more decoupled architecture with specialized SCs for each one of the CIs.

In this second approach of specialized SCs, each smart component in each CI can use a certain number of specialized security controllers for each one of the CIs (smart Health, smart Transportation, etc.) as it is shown in Fig. 5. For example, smart healthcare might use security controllers for handling security according to the huge number of IoT devices in their environment. All distributed SCs have secure inter-communication. In case of a controller failing, being compromised or attacked, the security controller at cloud may substitute the nearest and safest security controller in that area till a new security controller will be selected.

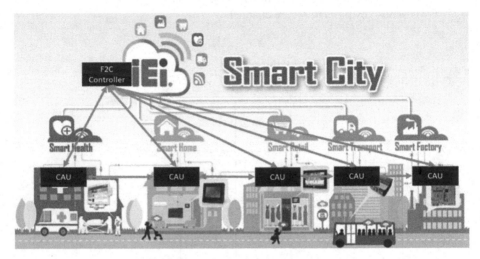

Fig. 5. Critical infrastructure scenario

This intercommunication between SCs can also help detect, counteract and react to possible cascading effects. The CIs are so dependable to each other. Therefore, any failure or compromise in one of them might affect the other. Thus, the proposed transversal architecture using distributed security controllers can bring secure dependency into the CIs (Fig. 6). Each one of the CIs might use different numbers of security controllers due to their infrastructure's needs. All SCs get authenticated and authorized from the F2C controller at cloud, therefore, they have secure inter-communication. This distributed SCs can bring trust into the CIs. For example, in case of an accident, a SC in healthcare can communicate with SC in transportation securely for getting patients information before patient arrives to hospital. Or in case of transportation accidents, SC in transportation system can securely communicate with emergency services to provide safety and security for people.

One of the critical infrastructure issues refers to how smart city related concepts are managed, considering all involved infrastructures, some of them highly critical (e.g. transportation, healthcare, etc.). When trying to deploy this security architecture in this smart city scenario with different CIs, the SCs might be embedded inside of different smart city's component with high computational power (similar to the scenario shown in Fig. 3). However, these components might have another critical responsibility, such as real-time service execution, real-time data processing with low-latency, data aggregation and storing. Therefore, SCs embedded into the smart city' devices might not be so suitable due to the high security processing usages which can impact on QoS in the smart city service to be executed. In this scenario, a decoupled transversal security architecture (similar to the scenario in Fig. 4) as another dimension with separated components from smart city may be applied into the system to bring safety and security with the demanded QoS.

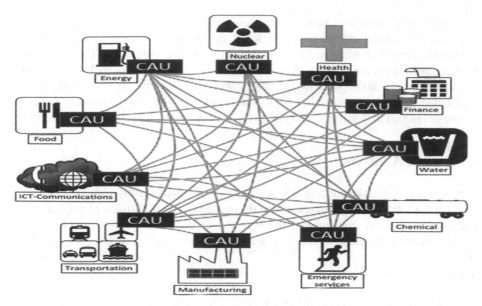

Fig. 6. Critical infrastructure scenario

This approach applied to a smart city scenario is shown in Fig. 7. The growth of IoT devices in a smart city for collecting information allows the execution of services aiming at easing people's lives. With this amount of IoT devices security is being a challenge. However, a key question is "How do we provide security requirements for IoT-devices with low computational power?". In our proposed architecture, we propose to distribute security controllers (SCs) into the city, hence each security controller is responsible for providing IoT-devices' security requirements in its area.

Fig. 7. Smart secured city

All security controllers have secure inter-communication with each other. In case of failing a SC, it is compromised, or attacked, the nearest safest SC is used as backup to provide security in that area till a new security controller is selected. The distributed security controllers are capable of providing security requirements such as key management, authentication, intrusion detection, abnormal behavior detection and etc. for distributed low-computational IoT devices in smart city. Therefore, smart city concept can be developed to "smart secured city" to ease people's lives with safety and security.

6 Results Analysis

In this paper, authentication and key distribution in two scenarios, such as traditional cloud authenticator and key manager and decoupled CAUs as distributed authenticator and key managers are implemented and analyzed as illustrated in Figs. 4 and 8.

The traditionally cloud workflow is described next (see also Fig. 8):

- Edge device registration:

    1- Edge device registers to the cloud.
    2- Identity provider in the cloud generates device-id.
    3- Cloud sends device-id to the edge device.

- Edge-cloud authentication:

    4- Edge device sends CSR and id to the cloud.
    5- Cloud checks device-id if exists then signs the certificate.
    6- Cloud sends signed certificate to the edge device.
    7- Edge device-cloud authenticated and establish TLS.

- Key distribution and management:

    8- Edge device sends key request to the cloud.
    9- Cloud generates public and private keys by elliptic curve.
    10- Cloud sends pair keys in secure channel to the edge device.

Both workflows (Figs. 4 and 8) are implemented in our smart city testbed. In traditional cloud, a Raspberry Pi 3 (RP3) is used as edge device and a server Fujitsu Primergy TX300 S8 acts as cloud and certificate authority (CA). In the cloud scenario, X.509 public key certificate is used for authentication and elliptic curve (ECC) is used for key generation. On the other hand, in the DCF workflow, a RP3 acts as edge device, a RP3 as CAU which is located at the edge of the network, and finally a Primergy TX300 S8 server as cloud and F2C controller. In this scenario, X.509 is implemented in the F2C controller and CAU. Therefore, once the F2C controller-CAU is authenticated, the CAU gets authorization to provide authentication and key distribution for edge devices. Elliptic curve is implemented in the CAU to provide key generation and distribution. In both scenarios, we compute the time for edge-device authentication, key generation and distribution to the edge devices. Obtained results are shown in Tables 1 and 2.

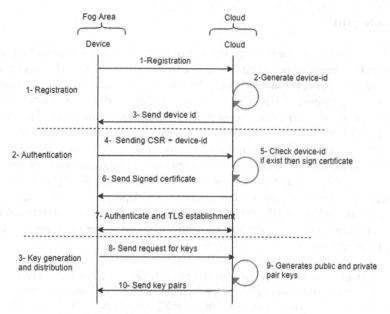

Fig. 8. Cloud authenticator and key manager workflow

Table 1. Authentication time delay

Scenario	Authentication time delay (MS)
Traditional cloud	86.567
DCF	8.288

Table 2. Key generation and distribution time delay

Scenario	Authentication time delay (MS)
Traditional cloud	59.613
DCF	8.009

As illustrated in the tables above, the DCF strategy can decrease authentication time delay almost 78 ms and for key generation and distribution can decrease almost 51 ms. In this case, we can claim that the DCF strategy is more suitable for critical infrastructures by bringing security with less impact on the QoS in terms of time delay.

7 Conclusion

In this paper, we illustrate the benefits of merging the F2C system into the critical infrastructures. F2C systems allow the execution of CI services close to the devices providing the sensitive data, but not competing with cloud but collaborating each other. However, the use of a F2C system in CIs brings security challenges due to its hierarchical and distributed nature. We identify the most potential security requirements for deploying a F2C solution into CIs. On the other hand, security must be provided based on these requirements. To this end, we also propose a transversal and distributed security architecture to bring security into the CIs, without impacting in the requested QoS, referred to as DCF. This architecture is based on distributed security controllers (SCs) specialized in different CIs. Some CI scenarios are described for deploying the proposed security architecture into the CIs. Finally, the DCF workflow is implemented, validated and compared with traditional cloud in terms of authentication, key generation and distribution, showing its main benefits.

Acknowledgment. This work has been supported by the Spanish Ministry of Science, Innovation and Universities and the European Regional Development Fund (FEDER) under contract RTI2018-094532-B-I00, and by the H2020 European Union mF2C project with reference 730929.

References

1. Simon, T.: Critical infrastructure and the internet of things. Cyber Security in a Volatile World (2017)
2. González-Martínez, J.A., et al.: Cloud computing and education: a state-of-the-art survey. Comput. Educ. **80**, 132–151 (2015)
3. Yi, S., et al.: A survey of fog computing: concepts, applications and issues. In: Workshop on Mobile Big Data (2015)
4. Masip-Bruin, X., et al.: Foggy clouds and cloudy fogs: a real need for coordinated management of fog-to-cloud computing systems. IEEE Wirel. Commun. **23**, 120–128 (2016)
5. Kahvazadeh, S., et al.: Securing combined fog-to-cloud system through SDN approach. In: Crosscloud (2017)
6. Kahvazadeh, S., et al.: Balancing security guarantees vs QoS provisioning in combined fog-to-cloud systems. In: 10th IFIP International Conference on New Technologies, Mobility & Security (NTMS) (2019)
7. mF2C project. http://www.mf2c-project.eu. Accessed Apr 2018
8. Barbosa, V., et al.: Towards a fog-to-cloud control topology for QoS aware end-to-end communications. In: IEEE/ACM International Symposium on Quality of Service, (IWQoS 2017), Vilanova i la Geltrú, Spain, June 2017
9. Cipsec project. http://www.cipsec.eu/
10. Ni, J., et al.: Securing fog computing for internet of things applications: challenges and solutions. IEEE Commun. Surv. Tutor. **20**, 601–628 (2017)
11. Martin, B.A., et al.: OpenFog security requirements and approaches. In: Fog World Congress (2017)
12. Kahvazadeh, S., Masip-Bruin, X., Marín-Tordera, E., Cárdenas, A.G.: Securing combined fog-to-cloud systems: challenges and directions. In: Arai, K., Bhatia, R., Kapoor, S. (eds.) FTC 2019. AISC, vol. 1069, pp. 877–892. Springer, Cham (2020). https://doi.org/10.1007/978-3-030-32520-6_63

Event-Based Remote Attacks
in HTML5-Based Mobile Apps

Phi Tuong Lau[✉]

Faculty of Computer Engineering, University of Information Technology,
Ho Chi Minh City, Vietnam
laulpt@gmail.com

Abstract. HTML5-based mobile apps become increasingly popular as they leverage standard web technologies such as HTML5, JavaScript, CSS for saving development cost. Like web apps, they are built using JavaScript frameworks (e.g. jQuery) for making mobile websites responsive, faster, etc. Attackers may fire the events integrated into the frameworks for reusing sensitive APIs included in apps. Once the internal functions are accessed successfully, it may cause serious consequences (e.g. resource access). Its main advantage is that it is not required to inject malicious payloads for accessing to the system resources into apps. We define this vector of attacks as event-based remote attacks.

In this paper, we present a systematic study about the event-based remote attacks. In addition, we introduce a static detection approach to detect vulnerable apps that can be exploited to launch such remote attacks. For the measurement, we performed the approach on a dataset of 2,536 HTML5-based mobile apps. It eventually flagged out 53 vulnerable apps, including 45 true positives.

Keywords: JavaScript framework · HTML5-based mobile app · Information flow analysis · PhoneGap

1 Introduction

HTML5-based mobile apps are increasing their popularity due to their advantages as reducing complexity and saving cost in development as compared with native mobile apps. Such hybrid mobile apps are developed using standard web technologies such as HTML5, JavaScript, CSS and JavaScript frameworks as web apps. JavaScript frameworks support a variety of custom events for building websites responsive, faster, etc. Adversaries may exploit the events of the frameworks used in apps for remotely accessing sensitive API gadgets contained in its event handlers for malicious purposes. The internal functions can be source APIs for retrieving sensitive data (e.g. contact, GPS) or sink APIs for sending the sensitive data outside. We call the attacks as event-based remote attacks.

The event-based remote attacks can be done by the following steps. First of all, an external attacker injects malicious triggering HTML/JavaScript code into the execution domain of a HTML5-based mobile app. The code injection can be achieved by XSS attacks [12], code injection attacks in hybrid mobile apps [15], etc. Afterwards, the

© Springer Nature Switzerland AG 2020
A. P. Fournaris et al. (Eds.): ESORICS 2019 Workshops, LNCS 11981, pp. 49–63, 2020.
https://doi.org/10.1007/978-3-030-42051-2_4

triggering code is executed on a mobile browser (e.g. WebView) to fire a framework event as an event gadget. Finally, its event handler is called for carrying out its internal sensitive APIs without requiring extra permission checks. Consequently, the adversary may attain malicious activities once the sensitive API gadgets are successfully called.

Hybrid mobile apps have received a little attention from researchers. Jin et al. [15], Lau et al. [18], Chen et al. [20] applied static analysis to detect code injection flaws in apps. Furthermore, permission-based mechanisms were proposed to limit invocations to the platform resources in apps [13, 14, 21]. However, such access control techniques may be unable to prevent our attacks. Yang et al. [23] introduced a new type of attacks through event-oriented exploits in Android hybrid apps. These attacks are executed by forcing WebView's event handlers as event handler gadgets. Meanwhile, our attacks rely on triggering JavaScript framework events as event gadgets.

Our Work. In this paper, we present event-based remote attacks that can remotely cause dangerous consequences. We consider two malicious purposes as follows. For resource access, the remote attacks are launched for accessing the platform resources. In the case of data leaks, an attacker deploys such attacks to leak the system resources out. Additionally, we propose an approach based on static data flow analysis to scan vulnerable apps.

Approach. The approach is implemented as follows. First of all, our approach performs slices of binding APIs that are used to register JavaScript framework events in apps. Typically, we pick up the custom events of jQuery Mobile, a mobile development framework ranked in top 2018–2019 [7–9]. More specifically, it receives a given HTML5-based app as an input and then parses its HTML files as well as its JavaScript files into a control flow graph. Eventually, it will give a collection of the binding APIs from the graph. Second, it performs data flow analysis to detect vulnerable apps. Loop through each binding API collected previously, it traces its callback function as an event handler, then enters into it. For the private data leakages, it scans data paths from source APIs to sink APIs inside the event handlers. In case of the system resource access, it tracks whether there are source APIs found in the callback function, and the retrieved data from the sources are saved into local storages, cookies, etc. as web contents. As a result, if any case is found, then it will flag the app as a vulnerable app.

Evaluation. We downloaded 2,536 HTML5-based mobile apps from Google Play stores and third-party stores for our evaluation. Eventually, it detected 53 vulnerable apps out of 2,536 apps. We conducted a manual code inspection of such 53 apps and found out 8 false positives. More specifically, there are 32 out of 45 true positives that can be exploited by the remote attacks in order to consequently raise the resource access. Meanwhile, 13 remaining vulnerable apps can be exploited for the data leaks.

Main Contribution. In this paper, we make the academic contributions as follows.

- We present a systematic study of the event-based remote attacks in HTML5-based mobile apps.
- We propose an approach to statically scan vulnerable apps that can be exploited for achieving the remote attacks.

- We show the evaluation of the approach on a dataset of 2,536 HTML5-based mobile apps. As a result, it scanned out 45 vulnerable apps.

The structure of the paper is organized as follows. Section 2 introduces the background. Section 3 presents our systematic study of the event-based remote attacks. Section 4 describes our approach. Section 5 shows the evaluation of our approach. Section 6 reviews the related work, and Sect. 7 concludes our research paper.

2 Background

2.1 Middleware Framework

The architecture of an HTML5-based mobile app includes native code (e.g. Java in Android) for accessing to the local system resources such as camera, contact, etc. and a mobile browser (e.g. WebView on Android). In the mobile browser, it leverages HTML5, CSS to display web contents, and a JavaScript engine for logic programming. HTML5-based mobile apps are characterized as hybrid mobile apps. To facilitate the communication between the native context and the web context for resource, it employs a middleware framework acted as a bridge between both sides. Because of using the standard web technologies as web apps, such type of apps can reduce development cost.

Middleware frameworks are implemented for building hybrid mobile apps and native mobile apps. The different frameworks have their own architecture and their own capabilities. For example, PhoneGap (Cordova) [1] is a well-known framework supporting for a wide range of platforms such as Android, iOS, WindowPhone, etc. Indeed, Phone-Gap is integrated with plugin APIs for resource interaction and is used as the core of other popular frameworks such as Ionic [2], React Native [3], Framework 7 [4], Onsen UI [5], Rhomobile [6]. Developers can freely add their own plugin APIs to PhoneGap for fulfilling app functionalities. Furthermore, PhoneGap has been investigated by the previous researches [13–15, 18]. Both middleware frameworks have their benefits and drawbacks, but most of them are powerful.

2.2 JavaScript Framework

JavaScript frameworks are used to create various functionalities (e.g. user interface, events, faster response, convenient) in mobile websites and web apps. There is a large number of JavaScript frameworks such as jQuery, React, Ember.js, Vue.js, Angular, etc., and they have their powerful features. HTML5-based mobile apps also employ JavaScript frameworks for its development like web apps. In particular, some typical frameworks are developed for building mobile websites (e.g. jQuery Mobile, Mobile Angular UI). jQuery Mobile is created by employing the powerful features of jQuery, while Mobile Angular UI is made by inheriting the full features of Angular. Furthermore, the middleware frameworks can be integrated with JavaScript frameworks. For example, Ionic middleware framework supports the features of Angular, whenever Framework 7 is fully integrated with Vue.js and React, or PhoneGap supports AngularJS and Bootstrap.

3 Event-Based Remote Attacks

3.1 Threat Model

Assuming an adversary can inject malicious triggering code (HTML/JavaScript code) into the execution domain of an app. Once the triggering code is run, it may force or reuse a JavaScript framework event included in the app. Then, it may remotely reuse the sensitive JavaScript APIs defined in its corresponding event handler without extra permission checks (e.g. Android permission). Once the APIs are successfully called, it may cause serious threats. We only consider resource access and private data leaks. An event-based remote attack is successfully done when such consequences occur.

System Resource Access. External attackers carry out the remote attacks for accessing to the resources. Then, the sensitive data can be saved into local storages, cookies, the text attribute of DOM elements, etc. as web contents. The attackers may need to perform an additional attack (e.g. XSS attacks) for collecting the saved web contents.

Private Data Leaks. Adversaries run the remote attacks for sending sensitive data to external servers. Internal sensitive functions include source APIs retrieving the sensitive data and sink APIs leaking the data to outside servers available in event handlers. The external servers may be controlled by the adversaries.

In practice, attackers can insert triggering code into app domain by various ways. For instance, it can be done by XSS attacks [12] or code injection attacks in hybrid mobile apps [15, 18].

XSS Attacks. An adversary can inject malicious code into trusted sites or benign sites. Client mobile browser actually has no ways to determine whether these sites are malicious or not, so the malicious triggering code inside the trusted websites can be loaded on victim's browser to be executed. This assumption is possible because XSS attacks are ranked in top common web attacks.

Code Injection Attacks in HTML5-Based Mobile Apps. An attacker may inject malicious triggering code into code injection channels such as camera, contact, etc. When the injected code are displayed using the vulnerable APIs of HTML pages like html() on a mobile browser, the malicious code can be activated.

3.2 Triggering JavaScript Framework Events

There are many frameworks, but we consider the jQuery-based, Ember-based, Angular-based frameworks as they are ranked in the top list 2018 [7–9]. We conducted an empirical evaluation on a dataset of 2,000 PhoneGap apps for measuring the frequency of using these frameworks. We choose PhoneGap apps since they can be integrated with many third-party tools [43] (e.g. Angular) and were leveraged by the previous researches [13–15, 18]. As a result, we found about 95% of the apps using the jQuery-based frameworks (e.g. jQuery UI, jQuery Mobile), around 5% of them leveraging the Angular-based frameworks, and nearly 0% developed by the Ember-based frameworks. From this analysis result, we aim at studying comprehensively the custom events of jQuery Mobile [11] built upon jQuery, a well-known framework in the top list 2018–2019 [7–9] for mobile development.

In Table 1, assuming that the event handler of the framework events is attached to a window object or a document object of a HTML page. We only collect the events of jQuery Mobile that can be fired through both HTML/JavaScript code. This is due to that injected JavaScript code used for triggering events can be sandboxed by a mobile browser. For example, the event *"scrollstart"* is one of the jQuery Mobile events, but we do not put it into the table. It is attached by *$(document).bind("scrollstart", function() {})*, and is forced using JavaScript code as *$("document").trigger("scrollstart")* or by a user action. In fact, there is no triggering HTML code for it. Thus, when JavaScript code are sandboxed to prevent malicious code, this type of events may not be fired to attain the remote attacks. We discover some interesting findings in the table as follows.

First of all, we found that almost events can be forced by the same triggering code via both JavaScript code [JS] and HTML code [HTML]. In practice, external attackers may create a variety of triggering code as malicious code, yet we just show some of them. For instance, adversaries can simply implement both the HTML code and the JavaScript code like *"<a href="http://....">"*, *window.location.reload()* for firing the events as shown in Table 1.

Second, the event *pageinit* fires after a page is loaded for the first time. Once the page is navigated back from another page, it will not fire since it is already initialized before. It is noting worth that this event cannot fire by reloading the previous pages using the JavaScript code *window.location.reload()* like the other ones. Instead, it can be just triggered when a new page is loaded using *window.location.href()*.

Table 1. Some triggering code for the events of jQuery Mobile.

Event	Description	Triggering code
pagebeforecreate	Trigger before a page is created. E.g. $(window).bind('pagebeforechange', function(e){…}	[HTML] <a href="http://..."> [JS] window.location.reload(), window.location.href = http://….
pagebeforechange	Trigger before a page is changed. E.g. $(window).bind('pagebeforechange', function(e){…}	[HTML] <a href="http://…."> [JS] window.location.reload(), window.location.href = http://….
pagebeforehide	Trigger before a page is transitioned from. E.g. $(window).bind('pagebeforehide', function(e){…}	[HTML] <a href="http://…."> [JS] window.location.reload(), window.location.href = http://….

(continued)

Table 1. (*continued*)

Event	Description	Triggering code
pagebeforeload	Trigger before a page is loaded. E.g. $(window).bind('pagebeforeload', function(e){…}	[HTML] <a href="http://…."> [JS] window.location.reload(), window.location.href = http://….
pagebeforeshow	Trigger before a page is transitioned to the next page. E.g. $(window).bind('pagebeforeshow', function(e){…}	[HTML] <a href="http://…."> [JS] window.location.reload(), window.location.href = http://….
pagechange	Trigger after a page is successfully changed. E.g. $(window).bind('pagechange', function(e){…}	[HTML] <a href="http://…."> [JS] window.location.reload()
pagechangefailed	Trigger when the request is failed to change a page. E.g. $(window).bind('pagechangefailed', function(e){…}	[HTML] <a href="http://invalid…."> [JS] window.location.href = "http://invalid…."
pagecreate	Trigger after a page is created. Similar to the event pageinit. E.g. $(window).bind('pagecreate', function(e){…}	[HTML] <a href="http://….."> [JS] window.location.reload()
pagehide	Trigger after a page is transitioned from. E.g. $(window).bind('pagehide', function(e){…}	[HTML] <a href="http://….."> [JS] window.location.reload()
pageinit	Trigger after a page is loaded for the first time. When the page is navigated back from another page, pageinit will not fire since it's already initialized. E.g. $(window).bind('pageinit', function(e){…}	[HTML] <a href="http://…."> [JS] window.location.href = http://….
pageload	Trigger after a page is loaded. E.g. $(window).bind('pageload', function(e){…}	[HTML] <a href="http://…."> [JS] window.location.reload()
pageloadfailed	Trigger when the request is failed to load a page. E.g. $(window).bind('pageloadfailed', function(e){…}	[HTML] <a href="http://invalid…."> [JS] window.location.href = "http://invalid…."
pageshow	Trigger after a page is transi-tioned to the next page. E.g. $(window).bind('pageshow', function(e){…}	[HTML] <a href="http://…."> [JS] window.location.reload()

3.3 Motivating Example

In this example, the event `pagebeforeshow` of jQuery Mobile fires before transitioning to the next page. This event is registered by using the short-hand jQuery API `.on()`, and its event handler is attached to a document object at line 3. When the app is ready to start, all device's APIs will be loaded on its mobile browser. First, an adversary may inject triggering code into the execution domain of the app through code injection attacks [15, 18]. The malicious JS triggering code (*window.location.reload()*) can be inserted into the contact. When the contact data are displayed at line 19 (`contacts[i].phoneName`), the event may be forced. Afterwards, its event handler as the callback function is called at line 3. In this handler function, it checks whether the

```
1. document.addEventListener('deviceready', onDeviceReady, false);
2. function onDeviceReady() {
3.    $(document).on('pagebeforeshow', function() {
4.       if(record.latitude == 0 || record.longitude == 0) {
5.          $('#new-record-latitude').val('');
6.          $('#new-record-longitude').val('');
7.          $('#new-record-altitude').val('');
8.          getCurrentLocation();
9.       } else {
10.         $('#new-record-latitude').val(record.latitude);
11.         $('#new-record-longitude').val(record.longitude);
12.      }
13.   });
         ........
14.   document.getElementById('myBtn').addEventListener('click',handler);
      }
15.function handler() {
16.   navigator.contacts.find(fields, sucessRead, onError, options);
17.   function sucessRead(contacts) {
18.      for(var i=0; i<contacts.length; i++)
19.         document.getElementById("div").innerHTML = con-
            tacts[i].phoneName;
20.      }
21.   }
      }
22.function getCurrentLocation() {
23.   if(navigator.geolocation) {
24.      navigator.geolocation.clearWatch(newRecordWatch);
25.      newRecordWatch = naviga-
         tor.geolocation.watchPosition(function(position) {
26.         $('#new-record-latitude').val(position.coords.latitude);
27.         $('#new-record-longitude').val(position.coords.longitude);
```

Fig. 1. Motivating example.

GPS data consisting of the longitude and the latitude are available at line 4. If not, it enters into the function call `getCurrentLocation()` at line 8 for carrying out its internal function API `navigator.geolocation.watchPosition` at line 25 so as to gather the latest GPS value. Such access may not need extra permission checks since the API gadget can be reused. These values are then saved to the text attribute of two DOM elements at line 15 and line 16 as web contents (Fig. 1).

To steal the web contents, the adversary may need to launch additional attacks such as XSS attacks, etc. In this case, the attacker can carry out code injection attacks by injecting other malicious payloads into the contact as reported by [15, 18]. When the contact data (`contacts[i].phoneName`) at line 19 is loaded on its browser, the malicious code can be fired for reading the GPS position of a target victim. Assuming that the web contents or the GPS data are resided in the *div* elements of its HTML pages. A possibly malicious payload for stealing it such as *<img src = "empty.gif" onerror = "var divs = document.getElementsByTagName("div"); for (let div of divs){ var content = div.childNodes[0]; window.location.href = 'http://stealer...'+content.nodeValue;}">*. Moreover, an attacker can write more malicious payloads to read web contents saved into other/all elements of a HTML page or cookies.

4 Approach

As the threat model in Sect. 3, adversaries may insert triggering code into the execution domain of an app through various ways of code injection. Our approach is not capable to track how code injection is done. Instead, we develop an approach to detect vulnerable apps that can be exploited for achieving the event-based remote attacks.

Information Flow Propagation. We define our problem as inter-procedural forward analysis extended from TAJS [40], a well-known framework for analyzing JavaScript-based programs. There are two main steps in our analysis as represented by Algorithm 1.

Algorithm 1: Detecting vulnerable apps

Input: A HTML5-based mobile app
Output: A Vulnerable app/not

```
1  CFG ← parseFiles(Input);
2  APIs ← collectBindingAPIs(CFG);
3  foreach API in APIs do
4      eventHandlers ← getEventHandlers(API);
5      foreach handler in eventHandlers do
6          sensitiveflow ← scanDataFlow(sourceAPIs, sinkAPIs);
7          resourceaccess ← scanResourceAccess(sourceAPIs);
8          if sensitiveflow!= empty || resourceaccess!=empty then
9              flagVulnerableApp(Input);
```

The first step parses HTML files and JavaScript files of a given app into a control flow graph at line 1, and then slices binding APIs used for registering the framework events on the graph at line 2 by *collectBindingAPIs(CFG)*. Such events are manually predefined as shown in Table 1. This step finally generates a collection of the binding APIs.

For the next step, traversing through each binding API, it collects its callback function as its event handler at line 4 as *getEventHandlers(API)*, and enters into the function at line 5. We handle two malicious purposes. In the case of the private data leaks, it monitors information paths from source APIs to sink APIs in event handlers at line 6 by *scanDataFlow(sourceAPIs, sinkAPIs)*. If there does exist any path, it will flag the app as a vulnerable app at line 9. In the scenario of the resource access, it tracks if source APIs are included in event handlers, and the sensitive data retrieved from the sources are passed to web contents as cookies, local storages, etc. at line 7 by *scanResourceAccess(sourceAPIs)*. If so, it will flag this app as a vulnerable app.

Source APIs. There is the vast number of source APIs integrated into middleware frameworks (e.g. PhoneGap APIs [41]). Our dataset is almost PhoneGap apps, so we preconfigured some of PhoneGap APIs for retrieving private data such as GPS, SMS, camera, etc. in our analysis. For example, the API *navigator.geolocation.getPosition()* is used to get the current GPS location (longitude, latitude).

Sink APIs. Sink APIs are used to send the sensitive information out. In practice, there are various forms of sink APIs, but we consider some following ones. First, an app can employ sink APIs from a middleware framework. As an example, the PhoneGap API *ft.upload(fileURL, "http://...+&longitude +&latitude....")* is used to upload a file to a server. In this case, the sensitive data can be leaked outside through injecting them into the URL. Additionally, an app can utilize HTML code for sending the data out as *<img src="http://...&longitude ....">* . Furthermore, sink APIs can be HTTP methods such as GET, POST, AJAX (e.g. $.ajax(), $.get) leveraged from JavaScript frameworks in communication with a server.

Binding APIs. We model the short-hand jQuery APIs as the binding APIs [42], including *.on()*, *.bind()*, *.one()*. Such APIs are designed for attaching/binding JavaScript framework events to a document/window object in HTML pages. As an example, *$(window).on("pageload", function(){})* binds the JS framework event *"pageload"* to a window object. The event handler of the binding APIs is defined as a callback function. Here, we model callback functions in term of anonymous and named callbacks for improving the soundness of our analysis approach.

5 Evaluation

In this evaluation, we measure the performance of the approach in term of how many vulnerable apps it detects. More specifically, we downloaded 2,536 HTML5-based mobile apps from Google Play Stores and third-party stores. In this dataset, the majority of the apps about 1,900 apps were taken from Lau et al. [18], and the others were downloaded by us. They are developed from 2013 to 2018 and are mainly built upon PhoneGap framework. This dataset was partially studied in Sect. 3.2, and they almost leveraged jQuery Mobile for their development. We implemented the approach in around 500 LOC written in Java. Additionally, we limit the average detection time per app by 50 s.

5.1 Performance

We carried out our approach on a dataset of 2,536 HTML5-based mobile apps. Eventually, it flagged out 53 vulnerable apps. Furthermore, we manually reviewed such 53 apps and found out 8 false positives. Such false alarms occur due to the imprecision of the data flow analysis. More specifically, we conducted a manual code inspection of such 45 true positives and discover some interesting facts as follows.

Distribution of Event Usages in the Dataset. We first examined the distribution of the jQuery Mobile events in the evaluated apps as shown in Fig. 2. As a result, the majority of the events is *pagecreate* that accounts for about 23% of the dataset, whenever the minority of the events is *pagebeforecreate* taking up at nearly 0% of all apps.

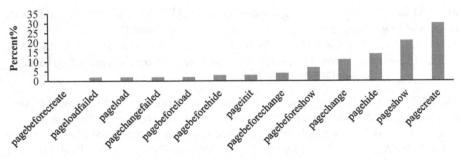

Fig. 2. The distribution of the framework events is examined in the dataset.

Distribution of Events Triggered in Vulnerable Apps. Such events can be fired to reach the event-based remote attacks. We picked out 45 vulnerable apps as shown in Fig. 3. In these vulnerable apps, there are totally 21 vulnerable apps that can be exploited by triggering the jQuery Mobile event *pagebeforeshow*, 15 apps by forcing the event *pageshow*, 8 apps by the event *pagebeforehide*, and one app by firing the event *pageinit*.

Fig. 3. The distribution of the events triggered in 45 vulnerable apps.

Vulnerability. As we presented in Sect. 3, attackers may launch the event-based remote attacks for reusing internal sensitive functions so as to eventually accomplish security threats. We take two malicious activities into account adversaries want, and the results are pointed out in Table 2.

For the system resource access, we discovered 32 of 45 vulnerable apps that can be exploited for the remote attacks and may consequently invoke to the resources. In these apps, most source APIs as internal sensitive APIs are once reused, they will return the GPS location. On the other hand, we investigated 13 remaining apps of 45 apps that can be exploited for the remote attacks resulting in finally the private data leaks. In such scenarios, most of source APIs retrieve the GPS position, and sink APIs leveraged from JavaScript frameworks are used to send the sensitive data to external servers.

Table 2. 45 vulnerable apps are classified into two scenarios.

Scenario	No. vulnerable apps
private data leaks	13
platform resource access	32

5.2 Soundness

Our approach currently aims at analyzing the custom events of top JavaScript frameworks, especially, jQuery Mobile. In practice, there is a large number of JavaScript frameworks which can be used in an app. In addition, analyzing JavaScript programs still remains many challenges due to its highly dynamic natures. Moreover, there may have various kinds of sensitive API gadgets used in an app, whenever we consider some of PhoneGap APIs (e.g. GPS APIs) as internal sensitive functions. Last but not least, the event-based remote attacks can cause more malicious activities, and we only consider two of them (e.g. resource access, data leaks) in this paper. Due to such limitations, it can create a major impact on its soundness, so there may exist potentially vulnerable apps in the dataset.

6 Related Work

Hybrid Mobile Apps. Hybrid mobile apps have various code injection channels which adversaries can carry out code injection attacks comparing with web apps. Choi et al. [25] provided a large-scale survey of code injection attacks in hybrid mobile apps. Mao et al. [16] proposed dynamic analysis to detect injected behaviors at runtime. Jin et al. [15], Lau et al. [18], Chen et al. [20] implemented static analysis to discover code injection flaws and reported new code injection channels. Our remote attacks can be considered as a variant of code injection attacks. Furthermore, there are permission-based techniques proposed to restrict invocations to the system resources [13, 14, 21]. Jin et al. [14] presented a novel mechanism to circumscribe invocations from JavaScript context to the mobile resources for different iframes in HTML pages. Phung et al. [21] developed a framework to enforce fine-grained access control. As we described in the threat model section, our remote attacks can reuse libraries used in apps, so it may bypass permission checks. Georgiev et al. [13] introduced fracking attacks that can break the same origin policy (SOP) in web-based mobile apps, and allow web contents from untrusted sites to communicate with the resources. Despite breaking SOP, this class of attacks may be unable to break app permissions for interacting with the native system features. Yang et al. [23] described event-oriented exploits by triggering the event handlers of WebView to call critical privileged APIs for interacting with the platform resources. Such attacks target to force WebView's event handlers, whenever our remote attacks focus on firing JavaScript framework events. Moreover, there are various vulnerabilities like surface attacks [17], web-to-app injection attacks [19], and origin stripping attacks [22]. Lau et al. [39] described event-based races in HTML5-based mobile apps that can occur by triggering middleware framework events. Yang et al. [24] proposed a scalable tool to find JavaScript security issues, yet this tool is unable to scan various kinds of attacks in hybrid mobile apps. In this paper, we present an attack vector so called event-based remote attacks that can be exploited by firing JavaScript framework events.

Native Android Apps. Native Android apps have received much attention from researchers. DroidSafe [32] and FlowDroid [26] are powerful techniques based on data flow analysis to scan out leaks of sensitive data in Android apps. Feng et al. [31] developed a static analysis approach, Apposcopy to detect malware based on semantic-based analysis. Li et al. [28] proposed an approach, ICCTA to scan private data leakages inter-components. Additionally, Android apps allow a repackaging mechanism, so it offers more opportunities for adversaries to inject malicious code in apps [29, 30]. Li et al. [29] presented a deep understanding about how piggybacked apps work and proposed an automated approach to locate malicious packages in the piggybacked apps. Zhou et al. [30] proposed an automated approach to discover Android piggybacked apps in a scalable and a precise manner. We aim at hybrid mobile apps using standard web technologies, especially, JavaScript framework events can be exploited to remotely invoke to the platform resources.

Web Apps. There are various classes of attacks in web apps such as XSS, SQL injection, phishing, DoS, etc. [12]. We only review advanced XSS attacks as they are in top common attacks in web apps [36], and our event-based remote attacks also can be seen as a variant of XSS attacks or a variant of HTML-injection attacks. Vogt et al. [33] and Stock et al. [35] introduced an automated approach to prevent XSS attacks. Lekies et al. [34] introduced a method to identify DOM-based XSS vulnerabilities in large scale analysis. Shar et al. [37] and Thomé et al. [38] proposed program analysis to detect vulnerabilities in web apps. The important point is that because web apps are protected by sandbox mechanisms, they are almost unable to communicate with local web resources. Meanwhile, hybrid mobile apps may not be absolutely prevented by sandbox mechanisms as they need to interact with the platform resources.

7   Conclusion and Future Work

HTML5-based mobile apps are developed by a variety of JavaScript frameworks (e.g. jQuery, Angular) and standard web technologies. Adversaries may trigger JavaScript frameworks events for remotely executing sensitive JavaScript APIs included in its corresponding event handlers. Consequently, it can raise serious threats (e.g. resource access). The main advantage of such attacks is that it is not required to insert malicious payloads for accessing to the resources (e.g. SMS, contact) into apps.

In this paper, we describe an attack vector so called the event-based remote attacks in HTML5-based mobile apps. Moreover, we introduce a static detection approach relying on data flow analysis to discover such type of vulnerabilities. In the evaluation, we conducted the experiments on a dataset of 2,536 HTML5-based mobile apps, and it eventually reported 53 vulnerable apps, including 8 false positives.

Our approach currently still remains some limitations. In the future work, we plan to implement a more effective way based on access control mechanisms to resolve the limitations.

References

1. Phone Gap: Build amazing mobile apps powered by open web tech. https://phonegap.com
2. Ionic: Ionic helps developers build and ship beautiful cross-platform hybrid apps. https://ionicframework.com/
3. React Native: React Native Build native mobile apps using JavaScript and React. https://facebook.github.io/react-native/
4. Framework 7: Full featured framework for building iOS & Android apps. https://framework7.io/
5. Onsen UI: The most beautiful and efficient way to develop HTML5 hybrid and mobile web apps. https://onsen.io/
6. Rhomobile. https://www.zebra.com/us/en/products/software/mobilecomputers/rhomobile-suite.html
7. Top JavaScript mobile frameworks 2018. https://www.redbytes.in/javascript-frameworks-for-mobile-app-development/
8. Top JavaScript mobile frameworks 2018. https://conceptainc.com/blog/best-javascript-frameworks-mobile-development/
9. Top JavaScript mobile frameworks 2019. https://www.mindinventory.com/blog/mobile-app-development-framework-2019/
10. AngularJS events. https://docs.angularjs.org/api/ng/directive
11. jQuery Mobile events. https://api.jquerymobile.com/category/events/
12. XSS attacks. https://www.owasp.org/index.php/Cross-site_Scripting_(XSS)
13. Georgiev, M., Jana, S., Shmatikov, V.: Breaking and fixing origin-based access control in hybrid web/mobile application frameworks. In: Network and Distributed System Security Symposium (NDSS) (2014)
14. Jin, X., Wang, L., Luo, T., Du, W.: Fine-grained access control for HTML5-based mobile applications in android. In: Desmedt, Y. (ed.) ISC 2013. LNCS, vol. 7807, pp. 309–318. Springer, Cham (2015). https://doi.org/10.1007/978-3-319-27659-5_22
15. Jin, X., et al.: Code injection attacks on HTML5-based mobile apps: characterization, detection, mitigation. In: Proceedings of the ACM SIGSAC Conference on Computer and Communications Security (CCS), pp. 66–77 (2014)
16. Mao, J., Wang, R., Chen, Y., Jia, Y.: Detecting injected behaviors in HTML5-based Android applications. J. High Speed Netw. 22(1), 15–34 (2016)
17. Shehab, M., AlJarrah, A.: Reducing attack surface on Cordova-based hybrid mobile apps. In: Proceedings of the 2nd International Workshop on Mobile Development Lifecycle, pp. 1–8 (2014)
18. Lau, P.T.: Scan code injection flaws in html5-based mobile applications. In: Proceedings of the 11th IEEE International Conference on Software Testing, Verification and Validation Workshops (ICSTW), pp. 81–88 (2018)

19. Hassanshahi, B., Jia, Y., Yap, R.H.C., Saxena, P., Liang, Z.: Web-to-application injection attacks on android: characterization and detection. In: Pernul, G., Ryan, P.Y.A., Weippl, E. (eds.) ESORICS 2015. LNCS, vol. 9327, pp. 577–598. Springer, Cham (2015). https://doi.org/10.1007/978-3-319-24177-7_29

20. Chen Y.L., Lee, H.M., Jeng, A.B., Wei, T.E.: DroidCIA: a novel detection method of code injection attacks on HTML5-based mobile apps. In: Trustcom/BigDataSE/ISPA, pp. 1014–1021 (2015)

21. Phung, P.H., Mohanty, A., Rachapalli, R., Sridhar, M.: HybridGuard: a principal-based permission and fine-grained policy enforcement framework for web-based mobile applications. In: Security and Privacy Workshops (SPW), pp. 147–156 (2017)

22. Yang, G., Huang, J., Gu, G., Mendoza, A.: Study and mitigation of origin stripping vulnerabilities in hybrid-postmessage enabled mobile applications. In: IEEE Symposium on Security and Privacy (SP), pp. 742–755 (2018)

23. Yang, G., Huang, J., Gu, G.: Automated generation of event-oriented exploits in android hybrid apps. In: Network and Distributed System Security Symposium (NDSS) (2018)

24. Yang, G., Mendoza, A., Zhang, J., Gu, G.: Precisely and scalably vetting javascript bridge in android hybrid apps. In: Dacier, M., Bailey, M., Polychronakis, M., Antonakakis, M. (eds.) RAID 2017. LNCS, vol. 10453, pp. 143–166. Springer, Cham (2017). https://doi.org/10.1007/978-3-319-66332-6_7

25. Choi, H., Kim, Y.: Large-Scale analysis of remote code injection attacks in Android apps. In: Security and Communication Networks (2018)

26. Arzt, S., et al.: FlowDroid: precise context, flow, field, object-sensitive and lifecycle-aware taint analysis for android apps. ACM Sigplan Not. **49**(6), 259–269 (2014)

27. Rasthofer, S., Arzt, S., Bodden, E.: A machine-learning approach for classifying and categorizing Android sources and sinks. In: Network and Distributed System Security Symposium (NDSS) (2014)

28. Li, L., et al.: IccTA: detecting inter-component privacy leaks in Android apps. In: Proceedings of the 37th International Conference on Software Engineering, pp. 280–291 (2015)

29. Li, L., et al.: Understanding android app piggybacking: a systematic study of malicious code grafting. IEEE Trans. Inform. Forensics Secur. **12**, 1269–1284 (2017)

30. Zhou, W., Zhou, Y., Grace, M., Jiang, X., Zou, S.: Fast, scalable detection of piggybacked mobile applications. In: Proceedings of the Third ACM Conference on Data and Application Security and Privacy, pp. 185–196 (2013)

31. Feng, Y., Anand, S., Dillig, I., Aiken, A.: Apposcopy: semantics-based detection of android malware through static analysis. In: Proceedings of the 22nd ACM SIGSOFT International Symposium on Foundations of Software Engineering, pp. 576–587 (2014)

32. Gordon, M.I., Kim, D., Perkins, J.H., Gilham, L., Nguyen, N., Rinard, M.C.: Information flow analysis of Android applications in DroidSafe. In: Network and Distributed System Security Symposium (NDSS) (2015)

33. Vogt, P., Nentwich, F., Jovanovic, N., Kirda, E., Kruegel, C., Vigna, G.: Cross site scripting prevention with dynamic data tainting and static analysis. In: Network and Distributed System Security Symposium (NDSS), p. 12 (2007)

34. Lekies, S., Stock, B., Johns, M.: 25 million flows later: large-scale detection of DOM-based XSS. In: Proceedings of the ACM SIGSAC Conference on Computer and Communications Security (CCS), pp. 1193–1204 (2013)

35. Stock B., Lekies S., Mueller T., Spiegel P., Johnss M.: Precise client-side protection against dom-based cross-site scripting. In: USENIX Security Symposium, pp. 655–670 (2014)

36. Son, S., McKinley, K., S., Shmatikov, V.: Diglossia: detecting code injection attacks with precision and efficiency. In: Proceedings of the ACM SIGSAC Conference on Computer and Communications Security, pp. 1181–1192 (2013)

37. Shar, L.K., Tan, H.B., K., Briand, L.C.: Mining SQL injection and cross site scripting vulnerabilities using hybrid program analysis. In: Proceedings of the International Conference on Software Engineering (ICSE), pp. 642–651 (2013)
38. Thomé, J., Shar, L.K., Bianculli, D., Briand, L.C.: An integrated approach for effective injection vulnerability analysis of web applications through security slicing and hybrid constraint solving. In: IEEE Transactions on Software Engineering (2018)
39. Lau, P.T.: Static detection of event-driven races in HTML5-based mobile apps. In: Ganty, P., Kaâniche, M. (eds.) VECoS 2019. LNCS, vol. 11847, pp. 32–46. Springer, Cham (2019). https://doi.org/10.1007/978-3-030-35092-5_3
40. TAJS framework. https://github.com/cs-au-dk/TAJS
41. PhoneGap APIs. https://cordova.apache.org/plugins/
42. jQuery binding APIs. https://api.jquery.com/category/events/event-handler-attachment/
43. Third-party tools in PhoneGap. https://phonegap.com/tool/page12/

Horizontal Attacks Against ECC: From Simulations to ASIC

Ievgen Kabin[(✉)], Zoya Dyka, Dan Klann, and Peter Langendoerfer

IHP – Leibniz-Institut für innovative Mikroelektronik, Frankfurt (Oder), Germany
{kabin,dyka,klann,langendoerfer}@ihp-microelectronics.com

Abstract. In this paper we analyse the impact of different compile options on the success rate of side channel analysis attacks. We run horizontal differential side channel attacks against simulated power traces for the same *kP* design synthesized using two different compile options after synthesis and after layout. As we are interested in the effect on the produced ASIC we also run the same attack against measured power traces after manufacturing the ASIC. We found that the *compile_ultra* option reduces the success rate significantly from 5 key candidates with a correctness of between 75 and 90% down to 3 key candidates with a maximum success rate of 72% compared to the simple *compile* option. Also the success rate after layout shows a very high correlation with the one obtained attacking the measured power and electromagnetic traces, i.e. the simulations are a good indicator of the resistance of the ASIC.

Keywords: Power traces · Side Channel Analysis (SCA) attacks · Horizontal attacks · ECC · ASIC

1 Introduction

The Internet of Things (IoT) is demanding of proper security features such confidentiality and integrity even for resource constraint devices such as embedded devices or wireless sensor nodes. Due to the scarce resources software implementations especially for asymmetric cryptographic approaches are not applicable, so hardware accelerators are becoming a must. It is also part of the very nature of IoT that some devices are deployed in the wild at difficult to access place and are connected wireless. This means potential attackers can gain physical access to those devices. If this happens they can measure parameters such as power consumption or electromagnetic emanation. The analysis of these measurements may reveal the used private key and by that render the deployed security solution useless.

In order to cope with the above mentioned issue implementations of cryptographic operations need to be side channel analysis attack (SCA) resistant. This is a very challenging task as the large amount of publications reporting on successful attacks impressively proofs. The best if not the only way to get an SCA resistant implementation is to run SCA attacks against your implementation at the earliest possible stage. This is kind of common sense and how to do it was discussed in several publications already. But to the best of our knowledge this paper is the first one presenting a thorough analysis of the

© Springer Nature Switzerland AG 2020
A. P. Fournaris et al. (Eds.): ESORICS 2019 Workshops, LNCS 11981, pp. 64–76, 2020.
https://doi.org/10.1007/978-3-030-42051-2_5

influence of design tool in the steps from a behavioural model down to an ASIC. The major contributions of this paper are:

- Discussion of the success rate of horizontal attacks against an ECC design after synthesis and layout for different design compiler options.
- Discussion and comparison of the success rate on simulated power traces with those measured on the ASIC manufactured using the more promising compile option.
- Discussion and comparison of the success rate on measured electromagnetic traces with the ones on simulated and measured power traces. The correlation between the clock cycles in which the success rate is high is pretty good which indicates that at least in this case the simulation after layout provides also some indication about potential issues when attacked using EM traces. This is of high importance as detailed EM simulations for that large designs are currently infeasible.
- Our results show that some compile options are helping to reduce side channel leakage while others don't. But be aware that compile options alone won't make a bad design SCA resistant.

The rest of this paper is structured as follows. In Sect. 2 we give a brief overview of different attacks classifications. In Sect. 3 we explain the implementation details of the investigated design. In Sect. 4 we present in detail how we performed the horizontal DPA attack on simulated power traces using *the comparison to the mean* [1] method. In Sect. 5 we give an information about produced ASIC. In Sect. 6 we discuss the results of the performed attacks using measured and simulated traces. The paper finishes with short conclusions.

2 Background: Vertical and Horizontal Attacks

One of most often used known classification of SCA attacks is the classification into simple and differential attacks, for example simple power analysis (SPA) and differential power analysis (DPA). If the secret (private) key can be successful revealed using a single power trace without any use of statistical methods the attack is classified as SPA attack. For DPA attacks [1] a lot of traces with different inputs are required for revealing the secret key using statistical analysis of the traces. If for revealing the key correlation coefficients are calculated the attack is usually classified as a correlation power analysis (CPA) attack [2]. Attacks known as collision attacks [3–5] need usually more than one trace for the analysis but not so many as the classical DPA attacks.

In 2010 Clavier et al. [6] applied the correlation analysis to reveal the secret exponent of an RSA implementation using a single power trace. They called this attack horizontal correlation analysis (HCA) attack. Due to the diversity of the attack classifications they introduced the simplified classification of SCA attacks into horizontal and vertical attacks. Corresponding to their classification horizontal attacks are single-trace attacks, for example SPA or HCA attacks. Practical examples of horizontal attacks

---

[1] we called this method in our earlier papers "the difference of the mean" as it differs from the well-known statistical method *"difference of means"*. To avoid confusions and/or misunderstandings due to the very similar names we call it from now on *the comparison to the mean*.

against asymmetric cryptographic approaches such RSA or ECC are the SPA described in [7], simple electromagnetic analysis (SEMA) attacks e.g. [8], the Big Mac attack [9], the localized EMA attack [10], horizontal collision correlation analysis (HCCA) attacks [11, 12], horizontal DPA and DEMA attacks [13, 14]. Vertical attacks corresponding to the new classification are "more than one trace" attacks i.e. classical DPA, CPA and collision-based attacks.

Vertical attacks exploit the fact that there is some kind of relation between the different inputs that are known by the attacker and the secret but constant key. The well-known countermeasures such as elliptic curve (EC) point blinding, randomization of projective coordinates of EC points or the key randomization proposed in [15] are effective against most vertical attacks because they resolve the knowledge of the attacker about the processed inputs or make the processed secret value no longer constant. But these countermeasures are not effective against horizontal attacks [6, 16] and against the vertical address bit DPA attack introduced in 2003 in [17]. This address bit DPA exploited key dependent addressing of registers in the Montgomery kP algorithm. 1000 traces were analysed to reveal the key. The horizontal address bit DPA reported in [13] successfully revealed the secret scalar analyzing only a single trace of a kP execution. Addressing of registers and other ECC design blocks caused the leakage exploited in the attack.

Most industrial authentication products such as NXP A1006 [18] and Infineon SLE95250 [19] are based on the Montgomery kP algorithm. So, countermeasures against the vertical and horizontal address bit DPA such as the randomized addressing of registers [17] or the randomization of the main loop of the Montgomery kP algorithm [20] or developing a regular schedule in which the blocks are addressed [21] are of high commercial interest and have to be implemented. The activity of the field multiplier can increase the inherent resistance of kP designs against SCA attacks. To exploit the field multiplier as a countermeasure different multiplication methods have to be combined [22]. We didn't find any information about the implementation of such a countermeasure in industrial chips. We found only classical countermeasures such as the randomization of coordinates of EC points were reported [23].

3   Investigated ECC Designs

3.1   Structure of the Implemented kP Designs

The implemented ECC design is a hardware accelerator for the multiplication of an elliptic curve point P with a scalar k. The operation is denoted as kP. The structure of the implemented kP-hardware accelerator is the same for designs investigated in this paper and it is shown on Fig. 1.

The kP accelerator obtains a scalar k and two affine coordinates x and y of a point P of the EC B-233 [24] as inputs for processing. The numbers x, y and k are up to 233 bit long binary numbers that represent elements of $GF(2^{233})$ with the irreducible polynomial $f(t) = t^{233} + t^{74} + 1$.

The hardware accelerator processes the scalar k bitwise according to the Montgomery kP algorithm using Lopez-Dahab projective coordinates [25]. Our implementations are based on Algorithm 2 presented in [26]. This implementation allows to perform all operations in parallel to the field multiplication.

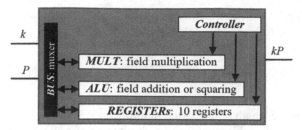

Fig. 1. Structure of the implemented kP-accelerator.

3.2 Field Multiplier

The multiplication is the most complex field operation in our designs. The polynomial multiplication (i.e. the first step of the multiplication of elements of in $GF(2^n)$) can be realized by applying a lot of multiplication methods e.g. the classical, Karatsuba [27], Winograd [28] or combinations of these [29].

We implemented the field multiplier using the 4-segment Karatsuba multiplication method according to a fixed calculation plan as described in [30]. The structure of our field multiplier is shown in Fig. 2.

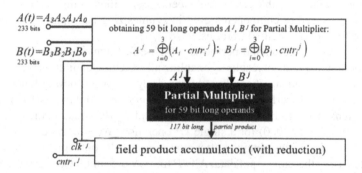

Fig. 2. Structure of the field multiplier.

Two up to 233 bit long operands $A(t)$ and $B(t)$ are segmented into four parts: A_3, A_2, A_1, A_0 and B_3, B_2, B_1, B_0 respectively. The parts A_3 and B_3 are 56 bit long. All other parts are 59 bit long. The field multiplier takes 9 clock cycles (clk^j, $j = 0,1,2,...,8$) to calculate the product of 233 bit long operands. In each clock cycle only one of 9 partial products of the 59 bit long operands is calculated accordingly to the 4 segment iterative Karatsuba multiplication method. The signals from Controller $cntr_i^j$ organize the calculation of operands for the Partial Multiplier clockwise. All partial products are accumulated in a register of the multiplier. The field product will be accumulated iteratively, step-by-step (or clock-by-clock), using the calculated partial products. The reduction could be performed only once, after all 9 partial multiplications, but the reduction consumes energy, i.e. it is a kind of "dummy operation" that hides partially the activity of other blocks of the kP design. Thus, performing of the reduction clockwise can increase the resistance of the kP design against SCA attacks. Even though we did not yet evaluate this effect, we perform the reduction in each clock cycle.

A partial multiplier was implemented using the classical multiplication formula only, i.e. it implements the following formula:

$$C = A \cdot B = \sum_{i=0}^{2n-2} c_i \cdot t^i, \text{ with } c_i = \bigoplus_{i=k+l} a_k \cdot b_l, \forall k, l < n \tag{1}$$

Here $n = 59$ is the length of the partial multiplicands.

The gate complexity of this multiplier, i.e. the amount of AND and XOR gates which are necessary to implement its functionality corresponding to formula (1) is n^2 of AND gates and $(n-1)^2$ of XOR gates, i.e.: $GC_{n=59} = 3481_{\&} + 3364_{XOR}$.

We synthesized the kP design using the gate library for our 250 nm technology for a clock cycle of 50 ns. We used two compilation techniques in the Synopsys Design Compiler (version K-2015.06-SP2) [31] to perform hardware optimizations: simple *compile* option and *compile_ultra* without clock gating, with *−no-autoungroup* option to preserve all hierarchies in the design. In the rest of paper the design obtained with a simple *compile* option is called as *D_noUltra*. The design obtained by using the *compile_ultra* option is called *D_ultra*.

The *compile* command performs logic-level and gate-level synthesis and optimization of the current design. The optimization process trades off timing and area constraints to provide the smallest possible circuit that meets the specified timing requirements. Values for area and speed of components used in synthesizing and optimizing the design are obtained from user-specified libraries.

The *compile_ultra* command performs a high-effort compilation on the design to achieve an optimum quality of results by enabling all DC Ultra features, therefore increasing the performance and significantly reducing design area and power consumption. It is targeted toward high-performance designs with very tight timing constraints.

Both designs investigated here, i.e. *D_noUltra* and *D_ultra*, require the same amount of clock cycles (about 13000) for a single kP operation. We simulated the power consumption of the kP designs obtained after syntheses and layout while the kP operation was executed using the same input data. All kP traces were simulated using the Synopsis PrimeTime suite [31].

Table 1 presents the parameters of the investigated kP designs. The goal is to show that the main parameters of the investigated kP designs after syntheses and after layout such as area and power are quite different.

Table 1. Parameters of investigated kP designs

	Investigated kP designs			Field multiplier			
	Name	Area, mm^2	Power, mW	Area		Power	
				Total, mm^2	Relative to kP design	Total, mW	Relative to kP design
Synthesis	D_noUltra	1.78	21.1	0.69	37.4%	14.6	69.2%
	D_ultra	1.68	13.7	0.62	36.8%	8.58	62.5%
Layout	D_noUltra	1.77	25.5	0.67	37.6%	16	62.7%
	D_ultra	1.70	16.6	0.63	37.0%	8.5	51.1%

4 Performed Attack Using the Comparison to the Mean

The simulated traces are noiseless. Due to this fact we compressed the simulated power trace, i.e. we represented each clock cycle using only one value – the average power value of the clock cycle. Figure 3(a) and (b) show compressed simulated traces obtained after syntheses and layout respectively. Power traces for $D\_noUltra$ are shown in red and power traces for D_ultra in blue. It can be seen that the design obtained using the *compile_ultra* technique consumes less power.

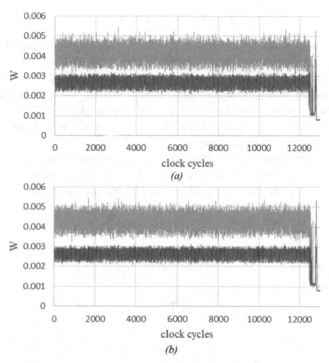

Fig. 3. Compressed simulated power traces for both designs: (a) the traces were simulated after synthesis; (b) the traces were simulated after layout. (Color figure online)

We applied *the comparison to the mean* for statistical analysis of the traces. To perform a horizontal DPA attack we fragmented the compressed trace into slots. The compressed trace consists of $l-2 = 230$ slots with similar profiles, where l is the length of the processed scalar k. Each slot corresponds to the processing of a key bit k_i with $0 \leq i \leq l - 3$ in the main loop of the implemented algorithm and consists of 54 values (one value per clock cycle). Thus, each value of the compressed trace can be represented as $v_i{}^j$, where i is the number of the slot and j is the number of the clock cycle within the slot, with $0 \leq i \leq l-3, 1 \leq j \leq 54$. We calculated the *mean* slot, i.e. the arithmetical mean of all values with the same number j and different number i: $\overline{v^j} = \frac{1}{l-2} \sum_{i=0}^{l-3} v_i^j$.

Thus, the 54 calculated values $\overline{v^j}$ define the *mean* slot. We obtained 54 key candidates – one per clock cycle j – using the following assumption: $k_{candidate}^j{}_i = 1$ if $\overline{v^j} \geq v_i^j$

else $k^j_{candidate}\,i = 0$. To evaluate the success of the attack we compared the extracted key candidates with the scalar k that was really processed. For each key candidate we calculated its relative correctness as follows:

$$\delta_1 = \frac{\#correct\_extracted\_bits(k^j_{candidate}\,i)}{l-2} \cdot 100\% \tag{2}$$

A correctness close to 0% means that our assumption is wrong and the opposite assumption will be correct. Taking this fact into account we can calculate the correctness as a value between 50 and 100% as follow:

$$\delta = 50\% + \left|50\% - \delta_1\right| \tag{3}$$

Figure 4 shows the calculated correctness of the key candidates obtained by analyzing all 4 simulated traces.

As a reference we defined the worst-case of the attack result from the attacker's point of view as 50% which means that the comparison to the mean method cannot even provide a slight hint whether the key bit processed is more likely a "1" or a "0", i.e. this means that the attack was not successful at all. The worst-case from the attacker's point of view is the ideal case from the designer's point of view.

Although we implemented our kP design strongly balanced and the field multiplier that is a kind of noise source is always active, the key was revealed with a correctness of 93 and 90% for the analysis of the synthesis and layout trace of the design $D\_noUltra$ respectively.

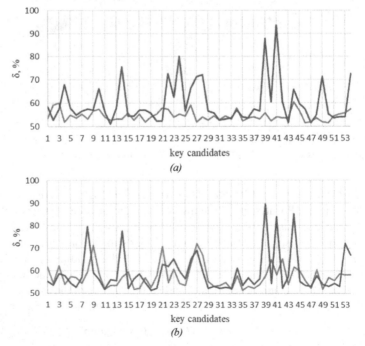

Fig. 4. Horizontal attack using *the comparison to the mean* method: the analysis results are obtained using traces after synthesis (a) and layout (b) of the kP designs $D\_noUltra$ (orange) and D_ultra (blue) synthesized for the 250 nm technology. (Color figure online)

The strong SCA leakage sources are the addressing of registers and the activity of the bus. Details are described in [21]. For the design *D_ultra*, i.e. for the same vhdl-code synthesized with option *compile_ultra* the best correctness for analysis of the power traces is 60 and 72% for synthesis and layout respectively. So, the optimization performed using the *compile_ultra* option hides information leakage significantly.

5 Produced ASIC

In order to understand how simulation results are comparable with results in real world, we produced the design *D_ultra* in the 250 nm technology for a working frequency of 20 MHz (50 ns clock cycle period as in the simulations) and bonded it to a printed circuit board (PCB). The PCB shown in Fig. 5(a) contains 4 different *kP* designs for the NIST B-233 EC. We are focusing on ASIC01 which is the first die from the left (see Fig. 5(b)). The die has dimensions of 2458.36 μm x 1086.12 μm.

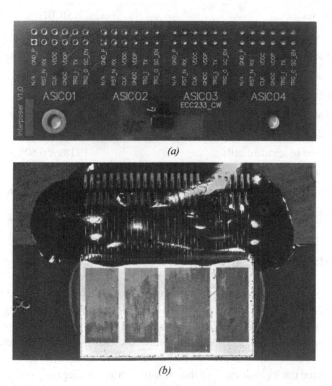

(a)

(b)

Fig. 5. A printed circuit board with produced ASIC (a) and a zoom of the unpackaged but bonded chips (b).

The layout is shown on Fig. 6. The highlighted area – white coloured right hand side of the layout – shows shape and placement of the multiplier. The main parameters of the produced ASIC are given in Table 2.

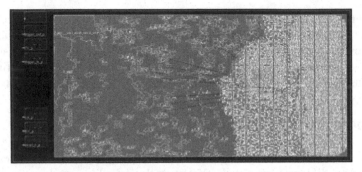

Fig. 6. Layout of ASIC01 obtained from Cadence Encounter. The white coloured area on the right hand side of the design corresponds to the multiplier block in the design.

Table 2. Parameters of the produced ASIC

Parameter	ASIC01
Used partial multiplier	Classical
Total area of chip	2670073.963 μm^2
Chip density (total)	91.345%
Chip density (subtracting physical cells)	73.145%
Total area of core	2198931.840 μm^2
Core density (total)	99.592%
Total area of standard cells	2189956.608 μm^2
Core density (subtracting physical cells)	77.493%
Total area of standard cells (subtracting physical cells)	1704016.94 μm^2
Total area of pad cells	249011.112 μm^2

6   Horizontal DPA/DEMA Attack Against the ASIC

We captured power and electromagnetic traces of the *kP* execution on ASIC01 with a LeCroy WavePro 254HD oscilloscope (with a 2.5 GS/s sampling rate) using the Riscure current probe [32] and MFA-R 0.2-75 [33] near-field micro probe. The input data were the same as those we used to obtain simulation traces. Our measurement setup is shown in Fig. 7.

We represented each clock cycle in the measured traces using only one value, that we calculated using all measured values (samples) within the clock cycle, i.e. we compressed the measured trace as follows:

$$v^{compressed} = \frac{1}{625} \cdot \sum_{l=1}^{625} \left(v_l^{measured}\right)^2 \tag{4}$$

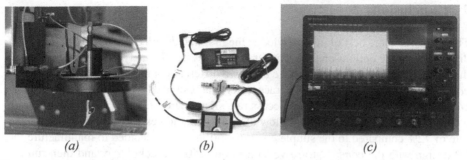

(a)   *(b)*   *(c)*

Fig. 7. Measurement setup: Riscure current probe (a), Langer FLS-106 IC Scanner equipped with MFA-R 0.2-75 near-field micro probe (b) and LeCroy WavePro oscilloscope *(c)*.

Here $v^{compressed}$ is the averaged squared amplitude value of all samples in a clock cycle; 625 is the number of measured values within the clock cycle. The squaring in (4) leads to the fact that the impact of the noise is significantly reduced. In addition the compression helps to reduce the complexity of the statistical analysis. The rest of attack is performed in the same way as described in Sect. 3.

Figure 8 shows the results of the attacks against the design *D_ultra* design analysing its power traces (measured and simulated after layout) as well as attacking a measured electromagnetic trace.

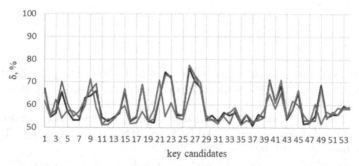

Fig. 8. Horizontal attacks using *the comparison to the mean* method: the *kP* design *D_ultra* produced in 250 nm technologie is attacked. (Color figure online)

Black line in Fig. 8 shows the attack results obtained analysing the measured power trace. The red line shows the attack results obtained analysing the measured electromagnetic trace. The blue line shows the attack results obtained analysing the simulated power trace obtained after layout.

7 Conclusions

This paper is to the best of our knowledge the first that detailed discussed the impact of different compile options on the success rate of side channel analysis attacks. In order to thoroughly investigate this impact we used two different compile options – *compile* and *compile_ultra*. We simulated power traces after synthesis and layout for both options. The *compile_ultra* option reduces the success rate significantly from 5 key candidates with a correctness between 75 and 90% down to 3 key candidates with a maximum success rate of 72% compared to the simple *compile* option. So we decided to manufacture the *kP* design with the *compile_ultra* version in our 250 nm technology and then run the same attack against measured traces after getting the ASIC.

Although the success rate after layout shows a very high correlation with the one obtained running the attack against measured traces, there are some key candidates that are revealed with a higher correctness than in the simulation after layout. But still the success rate is by far better from a designer's point of view than what we expect for an ASIC manufactured with the *compile* option.

We also run the same attack against a measured electromagnetic trace and here we got a pretty high correlation of the success rate with the success rate even for simulated power traces. This is of high importance as detailed EM simulations for that large designs are currently infeasible.

Please note even though our results show that some compile options are helping to reduce side channel leakage while others don't, compile options alone won't make a bad design SCA resistant.

References

1. Kocher, P., Jaffe, J., Jun, B.: Differential power analysis. In: Wiener, M. (ed.) CRYPTO 1999. LNCS, vol. 1666, pp. 388–397. Springer, Heidelberg (1999). https://doi.org/10.1007/3-540-48405-1_25
2. Brier, E., Clavier, C., Olivier, F.: Correlation power analysis with a leakage model. In: Joye, M., Quisquater, J.-J. (eds.) CHES 2004. LNCS, vol. 3156, pp. 16–29. Springer, Heidelberg (2004). https://doi.org/10.1007/978-3-540-28632-5_2
3. Homma, N., Miyamoto, A., Aoki, T., Satoh, A., Shamir, A.: Collision-based power analysis of modular exponentiation using chosen-message Pairs. In: Oswald, E., Rohatgi, P. (eds.) CHES 2008. LNCS, vol. 5154, pp. 15–29. Springer, Heidelberg (2008). https://doi.org/10.1007/978-3-540-85053-3_2
4. Fouque, P.-A., Valette, F.: The doubling attack – *why upwards is better than downwards*. In: Walter, Colin D., Koç, Ç.K., Paar, C. (eds.) CHES 2003. LNCS, vol. 2779, pp. 269–280. Springer, Heidelberg (2003). https://doi.org/10.1007/978-3-540-45238-6_22
5. Messerges, Thomas S., Dabbish, Ezzy A., Sloan, Robert H.: Power analysis attacks of modular exponentiation in smartcards. In: Koç, Ç.K., Paar, C. (eds.) CHES 1999. LNCS, vol. 1717, pp. 144–157. Springer, Heidelberg (1999). https://doi.org/10.1007/3-540-48059-5_14
6. Clavier, C., Feix, B., Gagnerot, G., Roussellet, M., Verneuil, V.: Horizontal correlation analysis on exponentiation. In: Soriano, M., Qing, S., López, J. (eds.) ICICS 2010. LNCS, vol. 6476, pp. 46–61. Springer, Heidelberg (2010). https://doi.org/10.1007/978-3-642-17650-0_5
7. Kadir, S.A., Sasongko, A., Zulkifli, M.: Simple power analysis attack against elliptic curve cryptography processor on FPGA implementation. In: Proceedings of the 2011 International Conference on Electrical Engineering and Informatics, pp. 1–4 (2011). https://doi.org/10.1109/ICEEI.2011.6021757

8. Mulder, E.D., et al.: Electromagnetic analysis attack on an FPGA implementation of an elliptic curve cryptosystem. In: EUROCON 2005 - The International Conference on "Computer as a Tool", pp. 1879–1882 (2005). https://doi.org/10.1109/EURCON.2005.1630348

9. Walter, C.D.: Sliding windows succumbs to big mac attack. In: Koç, Ç.K., Naccache, D., Paar, C. (eds.) CHES 2001. LNCS, vol. 2162, pp. 286–299. Springer, Heidelberg (2001). https://doi.org/10.1007/3-540-44709-1_24

10. Heyszl, J., Mangard, S., Heinz, B., Stumpf, F., Sigl, G.: Localized electromagnetic analysis of cryptographic implementations. In: Dunkelman, O. (ed.) CT-RSA 2012. LNCS, vol. 7178, pp. 231–244. Springer, Heidelberg (2012). https://doi.org/10.1007/978-3-642-27954-6_15

11. Bauer, A., Jaulmes, E., Prouff, E., Wild, J.: Horizontal collision correlation attack on elliptic curves. In: Lange, T., Lauter, K., Lisoněk, P. (eds.) SAC 2013. LNCS, vol. 8282, pp. 553–570. Springer, Heidelberg (2014). https://doi.org/10.1007/978-3-662-43414-7_28

12. Bauer, A., Jaulmes, E., Prouff, E., Wild, J.: Horizontal and vertical side-channel attacks against secure RSA implementations. In: Dawson, E. (ed.) CT-RSA 2013. LNCS, vol. 7779, pp. 1–17. Springer, Heidelberg (2013). https://doi.org/10.1007/978-3-642-36095-4_1

13. Kabin, I., Dyka, Z., Kreiser, D., Langendoerfer, P.: Horizontal address-bit DPA against montgomery kP implementation. In: 2017 International Conference on ReConFigurable Computing and FPGAs (ReConFig), pp. 1–8 (2017). https://doi.org/10.1109/RECONFIG.2017.8279800

14. Kabin, I., Dyka, Z., Kreiser, D., Langendoerfer, P.: Horizontal address-bit DEMA against ECDSA. In: 2018 9th IFIP International Conference on New Technologies, Mobility and Security (NTMS), pp. 1–7 (2018). https://doi.org/10.1109/NTMS.2018.8328695

15. Coron, J.-S.: Resistance against differential power analysis for elliptic curve cryptosystems. In: Koç, Ç.K., Paar, C. (eds.) CHES 1999. LNCS, vol. 1717, pp. 292–302. Springer, Heidelberg (1999). https://doi.org/10.1007/3-540-48059-5_25

16. Kabin, I., Dyka, Z., Kreiser, D., Langendoerfer, P.: Evaluation of resistance of ECC designs protected by different randomization countermeasures against horizontal DPA attacks. In: 2017 IEEE East-West Design Test Symposium (EWDTS), pp. 1–7 (2017). https://doi.org/10.1109/EWDTS.2017.8110037

17. Itoh, K., Izu, T., Takenaka, M.: A practical countermeasure against address-bit differential power analysis. In: Walter, C.D., Koç, Ç.K., Paar, C. (eds.) CHES 2003. LNCS, vol. 2779, pp. 382–396. Springer, Heidelberg (2003). https://doi.org/10.1007/978-3-540-45238-6_30

18. NXP A1006: Secure Authenticator IC. https://www.nxp.com/products/identification-and-security/authentication/secure-authenticator-ic-embedded-security-platform:A1006

19. Infineon OPTIGA™ Trust B SLE95250 Product Brief. https://www.infineon.com/dgdl/Infineon-OPTIGA_Trust_B_SLE95250-PB-v01_00-EN.pdf?fileId=5546d4625b04ae11015b0f3f7f1c332e

20. Izumi, M., Ikegami, J., Sakiyama, K., Ohta, K.: Improved countermeasure against address-bit DPA for ECC scalar multiplication. In: 2010 Design, Automation Test in Europe Conference Exhibition (DATE 2010), pp. 981–984 (2010). https://doi.org/10.1109/DATE.2010.5456907

21. Kabin, I., Kreiser, D., Dyka, Z., Langendoerfer, P.: FPGA implementation of ECC: low-cost countermeasure against horizontal bus and address-bit SCA. In: 2018 International Conference on ReConFigurable Computing and FPGAs (ReConFig), pp. 1–7 (2018). https://doi.org/10.1109/RECONFIG.2018.8641732

22. Kabin, I., Dyka, Z., Klann, D., Langendoerfer, P.: Horizontal DPA attacks against ECC: impact of implemented field multiplication formula. In: 2019 14th International Conference on Design Technology of Integrated Systems in Nanoscale Era (DTIS), pp. 1–6 (2019). https://doi.org/10.1109/DTIS.2019.8735011

23. NXP Application note AN11875: A1006 Host Reference Implementation for LPC1115

24. NIST Computer Security Division: Digital Signature Standard (DSS). FIPS 186-4. https://nvlpubs.nist.gov/nistpubs/FIPS/NIST.FIPS.186-4.pdf

25. Hankerson, D., López Hernandez, J., Menezes, A.: Software implementation of elliptic curve cryptography over binary fields. In: Koç, Çetin K., Paar, C. (eds.) CHES 2000. LNCS, vol. 1965, pp. 1–24. Springer, Heidelberg (2000). https://doi.org/10.1007/3-540-44499-8_1

26. Dyka, Z., Bock, E.A., Kabin, I., Langendoerfer, P.: Inherent resistance of efficient ECC designs against SCA attacks. In: 2016 8th IFIP International Conference on New Technologies, Mobility and Security (NTMS), pp. 1–5 (2016). https://doi.org/10.1109/NTMS.2016.7792457

27. Karatsuba, A., Ofman, Y.: Multiplication of many-digital numbers by automatic computers. Proc. USSR Acad. Sci. **145**, 293–294 (1962)

28. Winograd, S.: Arithmetic Complexity of Computations. Society for Industrial and Applied Mathematics (1980). https://doi.org/10.1137/1.9781611970364

29. Dyka, Z.: Analysis and prediction of area- and energy-consumption of optimized polynomial multipliers in hardware for arbitrary $GF(2^n)$ for elliptic curve cryptography. Dissertation (2012)

30. Dyka, Z., Langendoerfer, P.: Area efficient hardware implementation of elliptic curve cryptography by iteratively applying Karatsuba's method. In: Design, Automation and Test in Europe, vol. 3, pp. 70–75 (2005). https://doi.org/10.1109/DATE.2005.67

31. Synopsys: DC Compiler, PrimeTime. http://www.synopsys.com/Tools/

32. Riscure: Inspector data sheet. Current Probe. https://www.riscure.com/uploads/2017/07/datasheet_currentprobe1c1.pdf

33. LANGER EMV-Technik. MFA-R 0.2-75 datasheet. https://www.langer-emv.de/en/product/mfa-active-1mhz-6-ghz/32/mfa-02-set-micro-probes-1-mhz-up-to-1-ghz/618/mfa-r-0-2-75-near-field-micro-probe-1-mhz-up-to-1-ghz/854

Web Servers Protection Using Anomaly Detection for HTTP Requests

Paul Sătmărean[1,2] and Ciprian Oprişa[1,2(✉)]

[1] Bitdefender, 1, Cuza Vodă Street, City Business Center,
400107 Cluj-Napoca, Romania
{psatmarean,coprisa}@bitdefender.com
[2] Technical University of Cluj-Napoca, 28, Gh. Bariţiu Street, room M03,
400027 Cluj-Napoca, Romania

Abstract. Many web servers are vulnerable to HTTP attacks and patching is not always possible, especially against 0 day exploits. We propose a solution able to learn the normal patterns in HTTP requests and reject those requests that do not match these normal patterns. The solution is mainly oriented towards IoT devices. These devices usually support a limited range of requests. Performance and energy consumption considerations prevents the usage of an internal security solution, while the firmware may be difficult to upgrade. The proposed system was able to protect the test servers, by deflecting most of the incoming attacks.

Keywords: Anomaly detection · HTTP · IoT · Requests filtering

1 Introduction

We have entered a new digital age, and where there is progress there must be danger as well. Due to the fact that more and more services are using the Internet as a medium, either for use or advertising, the dangers of hacking and data loss are greater than ever. More vital systems such as healthcare monitor systems, and banking applications use the web as a means to reach every platform and because of that, they are exposed to new dangers, whether from lack of security to improper implementations of it to untrained staff, they are exposed to hacking and monitoring.

The web servers provide a medium for these applications but since the web is open, everyone can see them and interact with them. This is where security applications intervene, attempting to impede unwanted behavior but the attack patterns and methods are getting more complex as well. Too many resources allocated for security are not economically viable in most cases, which brings us to why this project exists.

This problem is not a new one, and many ways to counter it have been found. Next Generation Firewalls [6] are mostly used for small networks, which analyze traffic in real time, scan files, and even do traffic pattern matching trying to

© Springer Nature Switzerland AG 2020
A. P. Fournaris et al. (Eds.): ESORICS 2019 Workshops, LNCS 11981, pp. 77–90, 2020.
https://doi.org/10.1007/978-3-030-42051-2_6

detect malicious traffic before it reaches anything inside the protected network. These devices, although effective up to a point, are very expensive and limited by the hardware they incorporate and by the speed constraints when many devices are on the network. Either speed or security is compromised.

We need an easy to use and cheap method to protect smaller web applications from attacks. Endpoint security has long been around in the user market, where the anti-virus software solutions use different techniques to sniff out malicious behavior and protect the target machine, but this method was considered inefficient for servers, where modularity is desired for workloads [16].

Protection methods today for web applications include implementing security protocols such as the token authentication protocol used in Spring Security Framework [14], encrypting traffic using HTTPS protocols and using advanced, active protection methods such as active Next Gen Firewalls which can be very expensive and speed taxing. Smaller web applications have to rely on higher levels of protection provided by the hosting company or by implementing code-heavy and difficult protocols. These methods work, but they do not take into account human error and hardware limited resources which most small web applications have to contend with.

Using anomaly detection we can build a very easy to use framework that learns what normal traffic looks like for a particular web application from the server's standpoint and reports any anomaly it detects after the learning period is over. Due to the fact that a small web application does not contain many services and APIs there is not much difficulty in forming a working internal model of the expected traffic and detecting abnormal requests.

The application employs the use of multiple scanners, each of which focus on certain features extracted from traffic URL requests. The framework loads and maintains the scanner data integrity, logging, error detection and reporting, using dedicated components for each.

Using the framework should be very easy. After calibrating the storage and time-window size based on the type of web application which implements it the application will create a database which stores data learned in a certain time period. The user only has to validate a URL before decoding it and the application will evaluate it, and report it if it does not comply with the acquired dataset. The user can also view the event log, scanner status and other statistical data using a web interface which the framework will maintain.

The following section discusses some similar approaches for detecting anomalies in network traffic. Section 3 discusses common attacks against web servers, especially against the web servers hosted on IoT devices. We also provide some example, mostly produced by Nikto [17], a security scanning tool. The description of the anomaly detection system follows, along with experimental results and conclusions.

2   Related Work

The authors of [15] use the k-means clustering algorithm for anomaly detection in network traffic. The described method applies k-means with $k = 2$ aiming to classify the behavior into two clusters, normal and anomalous traffic. Outlier detection is used when encountering traffic which does not result in data nodes close to the normal or anomaly clusters. Combining the two methods overcomes the limitations of each individual method which greatly increases accuracy.

In [11] a feature-based approach using histograms is described. The histograms are created from features such as flows associated with destination ports. Data mining techniques are then used to identify the patterns. These patterns are finally compared to the online behavior of a network to identify anomalies. Ip address histograms are for a period of five consecutive days are also computed. The algorithm has 4 steps:

- Feature selection, which determines based on the current situation the best possible features
- Mapping into metric space, which groups together similar histograms
- Clustering and model extraction
- Classification

In our work, we only work with HTTP traffic, which restricts the usage of some traffic information.

In [12], the authors describe an anomaly detection approach which analyses HTTP requests from Apache server [7] logs. This method is very similar to the one described in this paper but only applies to URL strings contains queries. The approach uses different anomaly detection models each based on a feature extracted from a query string. These models assign a probability value to either a query or one of the query attributes. This probability value reflects the probability of the occurrence of the given feature with regards to the established profile. The assumption is that feature values with a sufficiently low probability indicate an anomaly. This is done by calculating an anomaly score individually for each query attribute and for the query as a whole. When one or more anomaly scores exceed the detection threshold we mark it as anomalous. The score is calculated using a weighted sum. Models operate in two phases, training and detection. The training phase involves creating profiles for each server side program and finding thresholds for each model. For each program and its attributes the highest anomaly score is stored and the threshold is then set to this value plus a certain percentage. After the profiles have been created the system switches to detection mode. Models used in this example rely on the following features: attribute length, attribute character distribution, structural inference, attribute presence or absence and attribute order.

Industrial projects, like the Cisco Traffic Anomaly Detector Module [4] also use anomaly detection to protect against network attacks. By constantly monitoring traffic destined for a protected device, this module compiles detailed profiles that indicate how individual devices should behave under *normal* operating conditions. If it detects any per-flow deviations from the profile, it considers the anomalous behavior alert. The anomaly detection technology eliminates the need to continually update string signatures while reducing the volume of alerts and false positives common with static signature-based approaches. In addition, the Cisco module comes preconfigured with default profiles for some devices for immediate operation.

3   Common Attacks Against Web Servers

The first task when designing a solution for protecting web servers is to analyze the most common attacks. This section will briefly describe them.

Directory traversal attacks [10] involve accessing resources that are not meant to be accessed, for example configuration files or sensitive data. These attacks are only viable when the web server is not properly configured.

```
http://192.168.1.106/query.idq?CiTemplate=../../../../../../winnt/win.ini
http://192.168.1.106/index.php?chemin=..%2F..%2F..%2F..%2F..%2F%2Fetc
```

Fig. 1. Example of directory traversal attacks produced by Nikto [17]

Figure 1 illustrates two example of directory traversal attacks. While the first example could be detected by searching for the pattern '../../', in the second example, some characters are escaped, for evading simple pattern matching methods.

Buffer overflow attacks [5,18] are attacks which exploit the implementation of argument parsing by a web server in which the constraints are not applied properly and more data ends up in a buffer than it should; that is, the rest of the data ends up where its not supposed to be. In the worst case this gives the attacker an entry point and eventually access to the system.

```
http://192.168.1.106/default.ida?NNNNNNNNNNNNNNNNNNNNNNNNNNNNNNNNNNNNNNNN
NNNNNNNNNNNNNNNNNNNNNNNNNNNNNNNNNNNNNNNNNNNNNNNNNNNNNNNNNNNNNNNNNNNNNNNNNN
NNNNNNNNNNNNNNNNNNNNNNNNNNNNNNNNNNNNNNNNNNNNNNNNNNNNNNNNNNNNNNNNNNNNNNNNNN
NNNNNNNNNNNNNNNNNNNNNNNNNNNNNNNNNNNNNNNNNNNNNNNNNNNNNNNNNNNNNNNNNNNNNNNNNN
NNNNNNNNNNNNNNNNNNNNNNNNNNNNNNNNNNNNNNNNNNNNNNNNNNNNNNNNNNNNNNNNNNNNNNNNNN
NNNNNNNNNNNNNNNNNNNNNNNNNNNNNNNN%u9090%u6858%ucbd3%u7801%u9090%u6858%uc
bd3%u7801%u9090%u6858%ucbd3%u7801%u9090%u9090%u8190%u00c3%u0003%u8b00%
u531b%u53ff%u0078%u0000%u00=a
```

Fig. 2. Example of buffer overflow attack [3]

The attack in Fig. 2 is characterized by a abnormal length (that triggers the buffer overflow) followed by encoded shellcode.

Brute force attacks [1] involve trying combinations of user and password strings until the login attempt is successful. Actually trying every letter and symbol is very rarely attempted but in the Internet of Things devices security is sometimes overlooked and in some cases we can find hard-coded values for user credentials which have administrative privileges. An attacker may collect a list of such credentials and attempt login on a huge number of devices with moderate success. An example of how frightening an attack like this can be was demonstrated by the malicious software known as Mirai [2] which managed to infect around 350.000 devices and attack major institutions (Fig. 3).

```
http://192.168.1.106/goform/CheckLogin?login=root&password=tslinux
http://192.168.1.106/proxy/ssllogin?user=administrator&password=administrator
http://192.168.1.106/proxy/ssllogin?user=administrator&password=operator
http://192.168.1.106/proxy/ssllogin?user=administrator&password=user
```

Fig. 3. Example of brute force attacks produced by Nikto [17]

Command injection attacks, as described in [13] take advantage of the lack of filtering and encoding information used as part of command. Most simple web servers use the system command and take an HTTP parameter as an argument. A router might take reboot commands like this for example. There are many ways to exploit a command injection: by injecting the command inside a backticks, for example **id**, by redirecting commands using pipes, running a second command if the first one success with the and operator, or by running another command if the first one fails (the or operator). Figure 4 illustrates two examples of commands injected into URLs.

```
http://192.168.1.106/cgi-bin/echo.bat?&dir+c:\\
http://192.168.1.106/cgi-bin/loadpage.cgi?user_id=1&file=|cat%20/etc/passwd|
```

Fig. 4. Example of command injection attacks produced by Nikto [17]

Another type of attacks make use of the *IFS* (Internal Field Separator) variable to avoid detection or to create complex commands in an environment where blank spaces are not allowed. These attacks are described in [8] and the usual syntax used in an attack involve ${IFS}. This is relevant, as one of our detection methods makes use of this information.

Cross-site scripting (XSS). Cross-site scripting [9] is an attack where some malicious client-side scrip (usually JavaScript) gets executed by the victim browser, through a vulnerable web server. Figure 5 shows some examples where the Nikto tool tries to inject the script `alert('Vulnerable')` which is benign (just displays an alert to the user) but if the attack is successful it will highlight the vulnerability in the web server.

```
http://192.168.1.106/index.php?dir=<script>alert('Vulnerable')</script>
http://192.168.1.106/<script>alert('Vulnerable')</script>.stm
```

Fig. 5. Example of XSS attacks produced by Nikto [17]

4   The Anomaly Detection System

4.1   Principle of Operation

The anomaly detector described in this paper has two operation modes. While it has insufficient data it learns, after which it switches to detection mode. The detection mode allows learning, but anomalies get reported. Every detection method is separately implemented and has its own constraints which means not all components may switch at the same time. Each component is initialized and is fed data as the program receives it. When enough data has been gathered for a component to be ready to switch it automatically switches to detection mode and emits signals for new detections.

Every component stores the data it learns by encoding it in a record format and using the data handling component to store it.

The data handling component saves every record with a timestamp. While in detection mode, old records are always being replaced with new ones so as to adapt to behavior changes. This is done in case a device changes behavior after an update for example. Every record has a maximum lifespan and is deleted when it reaches it. Record deletion and replacement is done in a transparent way by the data handling component.

Based on different features found in the URL of a HTTP Request we have a few detection methods: URL length based method, suspicious character based method, query string method, n-gram recording method and the pages method.

Each detection method is implemented as an algorithm with two parts: a LEARN() and a SCAN() procedure. Both procedures will receive an URL as input and will have access to $config$, a global configuration object and $data$, the data handling component. LEARN() will normally add information to the data handling component, while SCAN() will make use of it for triggering anomalies. Algorithms 1, 3 and 2 have the same structure and model the detection methods.

The detection methods described in this paper make use of the restrictions imposed by web server implementations on IoT devices, such as the limited functionality which implies a limited number of pages, a limited number of arguments. This gives us the information that the length of an average HTTP Request URL will not vary significantly, which brings us to the first detection method which is based on exactly that assumption.

4.2   Length Detection

Algorithm 1. LENGTH-DETECTOR

Global: *data*: the data handling component
Global: *config*: the configuration of the system
Require: *url*: input url for the protected server
 1: **procedure** LEARN(*url*)
 2:     **if** *url.length* < *data.minLen* **then**
 3:         *data.minLen* ← *url.length*
 4:     **end if**
 5:     **if** *url.length* > *data.maxLen* **then**
 6:         *data.maxLen* ← *url.length*
 7:     **end if**
 8: **end procedure**
 9: **procedure** SCAN(*url*)
10:     **if** *url.length* < *data.minLen* − *config.margin* **or**
11:             *url.length* > *data.maxLen* + *config.margin* **then**
12:         **return** $TRUE$
13:     **else**
14:         **return** $FALSE$
15:     **end if**
16: **end procedure**

The length detection method is simple, it only records every URL length while in the learning mode and obtains a maximum and minimum length value. The configuration allows the user to specify a margin that will be subtracted from the minimum and added to the maximum. All new URLs must be part of this interval, otherwise they will be detected as anomalies. The approach is similar with the one described in [12], which uses the length of query attributes as a feature and calculates a probability function for it. Given the relative simplicity of web applications found in IoT devices we will use a simpler solution. Most of the user input is configuration values so the usage of a query string is less common in this situation. Algorithm 1 present the learning and scanning steps for this approach.

4.3   *n*-grams Method

This method uses the extraction and matching of *n*-grams or contiguous sequences of characters from the given URL. The method described in this paper relies on the fact that given enough sample URLs the learning rate of new *n*-grams will eventually reach a satisfying enough value close to 0. That is, at a certain point in the learning process we will not see anymore new *n*-grams no matter how many samples are processed. It is at this point that the switch to detection mode is made. We use more than one value for so that our detection reporting is very precise.

During the scanning period, old records are replaced with new ones. If a n-gram is rediscovered however its timestamp is updated so as to avoid deletion. This also helps keep the size of the database to a minimum as we have no duplicate records.

This method is heavily dependable when the web application has simple functionality which usually means it does not require special URL syntax which might use the encoding of characters or special characters whatsoever. In a command injection attack there is usually a need for the use of special characters in order to achieve a success which in this case will most likely trigger a report.

Algorithm 2. N-GRAMS

Global: *data*: the data handling component
Global: *config*: the configuration of the system
Require: *url*: input url for the protected server
1: **procedure** LEARN(url)
2:      **for all** $n \in config.ngram\_sizes$ **do**
3:          **for** $i \leftarrow 0, url.length - n$ **do**
4:              $data.ngrams \leftarrow data.ngrams \cup \{url[i : i + n]\}$
5:          **end for**
6:      **end for**
7: **end procedure**
8: **procedure** SCAN(url)
9:      **for all** $n \in config.ngram\_sizes$ **do**
10:          **for** $i \leftarrow 0, url.length - n$ **do**
11:              **if** $url[i : i + n] \notin data.ngrams$ **then**
12:                  **return** $TRUE$
13:              **end if**
14:          **end for**
15:      **end for**
16:      **return** $FALSE$
17: **end procedure**

Algorithm 2 learns and stores all the n-grams of various sizes found in input URLs. In detection mode, new n-grams will trigger the detection. This detection method will only work if the number of input URLs is finite. For instance, if some web server received some unique identifier on every access, the unique identifier will span unique n-grams that will trigger false positives.

4.4   Suspicious Characters

This method relies on the usual characters present in a URL based attack. Most attacks, like directory traversal or command injection make use of certain characters which have special roles in the command line interface. Some examples include the semicolon and the plus sign, as well as the dollar sign which is widely used in the Bash command line. We store a local database with these characters and during the learning period we learn those which are used. For better speed we limit to groups of maximum length two so that we may store them in high speed structures for fast checking. We operate under the assumption that learning period traffic is of course non malicious and therefore we may be assured no gaps exist in our defense.

The ':' and '+' chars are used mostly with command injection attacks while '%2' is found in directory traversal attacks most often. In the URL encoding language characters may be represented by the '%' sign followed by their ASCII value written in hexadecimal form. Thus, '%2' is found in many characters used by this attack like '.' which is '%2e or '/' which is '%2f'. The '${' symbols together are mostly used in bash commands specifying command line variable values.

Algorithm 3 presents the learning and scanning steps for this approach. $config.single$ and $config.double$ contain the predefined list of suspicious characters and pairs of characters that are usually associated with attacks. $data.single$ and $data.double$ will store those characters or pairs that are found in normal URLs during the learning period, so the False Positives will be avoided.

4.5   Pages Method

http://server/component/subcomponent/page.html?p1=a&p2=b

Fig. 6. Example of URL for illustrating the pages method

This method finds and records every page accessed on the web server, that is every path taken while learning. For the URL in Fig. 6, the pages will be "component", "subcomponent", "page.html". The data handler component will also store this pages in a set, also in a similar manner with Algorithm 2.

4.6   Query String Method

Again, taking advantage of the limitations of IoT devices, we use this method in a simple way. All arguments and their values are recorded during the learning period. Most such devices feature very limited use of these arguments. Variable URL values are uncommon in this situation as most arguments are passed in a hard coded way through the URL by the client side web application. This application rarely has any dynamic components and mostly uses simple HTML forms. When a query string is detected by the special character '?', we parse the rest of the string and extract a tuple list with arguments and their value. This is stored using the data handling component and is later used when scanning. The key-value pairs found in the query string are stored in a set, in a similar manner with the n-grams method. The algorithm is very similar with Algorithm 2, but instead of keeping a set of n-grams, we keep a set of key-value pairs.

Algorithm 3. SUSPICIOUS-CHARACTERS

Global: $data$: the data handling component
Global: $config$: the configuration of the system
Require: url: input url for the protected server
1: **procedure** LEARN(url)
2:    **for** $i \leftarrow 0, url.length - 1$ **do**
3:       **if** $url[i] \in config.single$ **then**
4:          $data.single \leftarrow data.single \cup \{url[i]\}$
5:       **end if**
6:       **if** $i < url.length - 1$ **then**
7:          **if** $url[i : i + 2] \in config.double$ **then**
8:             $data.double \leftarrow data.double \cup \{url[i : i + 2]\}$
9:          **end if**
10:       **end if**
11:    **end for**
12: **end procedure**
13: **procedure** SCAN(url)
14:    **for** $i \leftarrow 0, url.length - 1$ **do**
15:       **if** $url[i] \in config.single$ **and**$url[i] \notin data.single$ **then**
16:          **return** $TRUE$
17:       **end if**
18:       **if** $i < url.length - 1$ **then**
19:          **if** $url[i : i + 2] \in config.double$ **and**$url[i : i + 2] \notin data.double$ **then**
20:             **return** $TRUE$
21:          **end if**
22:       **end if**
23:    **end for**
24:    **return** $FALSE$
25: **end procedure**

4.7 Solution Structure

Using a transparent proxy server we can redirect the traffic through the anomaly detector. We can of course use another type of proxy, however privacy and anonymity is not part of our end objectives for this project and the least disruptive proxy is the transparent one. This way anything else is untouched and the end user has a similar experience to normal browsing. Thus, our architecture implies having a web server, a proxy server which runs the filter before forwarding traffic, and a reporting server which is used by the anomaly detector to display status and additional information about the internal states and the detections so far.

5 Experimental Results

We tested our system by protecting two IP cameras, both using web servers for the user interaction. Both cameras used a limited range of distinct URLs, 84 for the first camera and 15 for the second one. These clean URLs are accessed in a random order, at every step, each URL having the same probability of being chosen (even if it has been chosen before).

We also built an attack URLs corpus, by using the Nikto tool on the two cameras.

After every group of 10 URLs, we simulated the fact that the learning period has ended and our system switched to detection mode. We computed the following indicators, for each detection method:

– False Positive Rate (*FRP*): the percentage of the clean URLs that would be detected by the given method
– True Positive Rate (*TPR*): the percentage of the attack URLs corpus detected by the given method

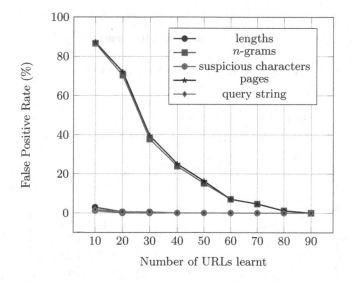

Fig. 7. False Positive Rate for the first camera

Figure 7 plots the False Positive Rate for the five detection methods. The lengths, suspicious characters and query string methods have low FP rates, all of them being below 3%. On the other hand, the n-grams and pages methods start with a high FP rate, above 80%, but they quickly drop to 0, while more data is fed into the system.

Figure 8 plots the True Positive Rate for the same methods. The n-grams and pages methods keep a high TP rate, above 95%, that doesn't drop as more data is added to the system. The query strings method also keeps a steady value, just above 40%. For the other two methods, the TPR drops as more data is fed into the system, but remains above 5%. For the lengths method, for instance, we will still detect very long URLs, that may correspond to given attack vectors, like buffer overflows or some command injections.

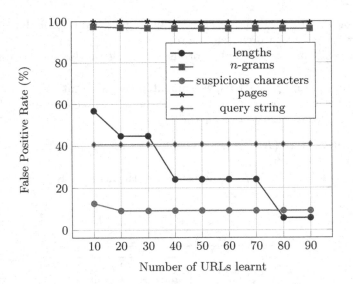

Fig. 8. True Positive Rate for the first camera

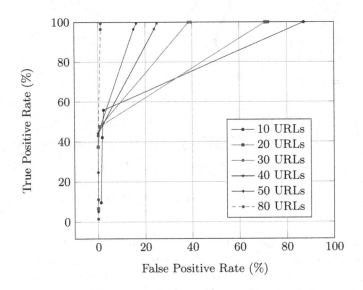

Fig. 9. ROC analysis

For the second webcam, where the range of distinct URLs is smaller (15), the results were similar, but the False Positive Rate dropped to 0 much quicker (after about 20 iterations).

The detection methods can also be combined using a voting system, where an URL is blocked only if at least k out of 5 methods detect it (k can take values from 1 to 5). After the system learned 10, 20, 30, 40, 50 and 80 URLs, we made a ROC analysis (*Receiver operating characteristic*), by varying k from 1 to 5. Figure 9 displays the ROC plot, where the perfect classifier is in the upper left corner (0% FPR and 100% TPR). After learning 80 URLs, the voting system gets close to this spot, for $k = 1$ and $k = 2$.

6   Conclusions

This paper aims to protect web servers used on IoT devices, by employing simple anomaly detection techniques. We started by analyzing the most common HTTP attacks on these servers, providing examples for each attack. The analysis showed that attack URLs differ from normal URLs by different characteristics, like length, n-grams, used characters, pages or query string parameters. Each characteristic was used in a different detection method.

The problem of protecting any web server is difficult, as normal URLs vary a lot, anomaly detection techniques being prone to false positives. However, for most IoT devices, normal usage involves only a limited range of URLs.

The experimental results performed on two different IP cameras showed that the presented detection methods quickly learn enough information to reach 0 false positives, while two of the five methods keep a very high detection rate.

As future work, we would like to explore more URL characteristics and test the detection methods on a wider range of IoT devices.

Acknowledgment. Research supported, in part, by EC H2020 SMESEC GA #740787 and EC H2020 CIPSEC GA #700378.

References

1. Adams, C., Jourdan, G.V., Levac, J.P., Prevost, F.: Lightweight protection against brute force login attacks on web applications. In: 2010 Eighth International Conference on Privacy, Security and Trust, pp. 181–188. IEEE (2010)
2. Antonakakis, M., et al.: Understanding the Mirai botnet. In: 26th {USENIX} Security Symposium {USENIX} Security 2017, pp. 1093–1110 (2017)
3. Boyce, R.: Malware FAQ: code red - ISS buffer overflow (2019). https://www.sans.org/security-resources/malwarefaq/code-red
4. Cisco: Cisco traffic anomaly detector module (2016). https://www.cisco.com/c/en/us/products/collateral/interfaces-modules/catalyst-6500-7600-router-traffic-anomaly-detector-module/product_data_sheet0900aecd80220a6e.html
5. Cowan, C., Beattie, S., Johansen, J., Wagle, P.: PointGuardTM: protecting pointers from buffer overflow vulnerabilities. In: Proceedings of the 12th conference on USENIX Security Symposium, vol. 12, pp. 91–104 (2003)
6. Dubrawsky, I.: Firewall evolution-deep packet inspection. Secur. Focus **29**, 1–5 (2003)
7. Fielding, R.T., Kaiser, G.: The Apache HTTP server project. IEEE Internet Comput. **1**(4), 88–90 (1997)
8. Garfinkel, S., Spafford, G., Schwartz, A.: Practical UNIX and Internet Security. O'Reilly Media Inc., Newton (2003)

9. Gupta, S., Gupta, B.B.: Cross-site scripting (XSS) attacks and defense mechanisms: classification and state-of-the-art. Int. J. Syst. Assur. Eng. Manag. **8**(1), 512–530 (2017)
10. Khan, S., Saxena, A.: Detecting input validation attacks in web application. Int. J. Comput. Appl. **109**(6), 1–4 (2015)
11. Kind, A., Stoecklin, M.P., Dimitropoulos, X.: Histogram-based traffic anomaly detection. IEEE Trans. Netw. Serv. Manag. **6**(2), 110–121 (2009)
12. Kruegel, C., Vigna, G.: Anomaly detection of web-based attacks. In: Proceedings of the 10th ACM Conference on Computer and Communications Security, pp. 251–261. ACM (2003)
13. Mahmood, O.: Command injection attacks: web for pentester (2016). https://securitytraning.com/command-injection-attacks-web-for-pentester/
14. Mularien, P.: Spring Security 3. Packt Publishing Ltd., Birmingham (2010)
15. Münz, G., Li, S., Carle, G.: Traffic anomaly detection using k-means clustering. In: GI/ITG Workshop MMBnet, pp. 13–14 (2007)
16. Roesch, M., et al.: Snort: lightweight intrusion detection for networks. In: LISA, vol. 99, pp. 229–238 (1999)
17. Sullo, C., Lodge, D.: Nikto - the manual (2019). https://cirt.net/nikto2-docs/
18. Wang, W., et al.: A combinatorial approach to detecting buffer overflow vulnerabilities. In: 2011 IEEE/IFIP 41st International Conference on Dependable Systems & Networks (DSN), pp. 269–278. IEEE (2011)

You Shall Not Register! Detecting Privacy Leaks Across Registration Forms

Manolis Chatzimpyrros[1]($\boxtimes$), Konstantinos Solomos[2], and Sotiris Ioannidis[1]

[1] FORTH, Heraklion, Greece
{machatz,sotiris}@ics.forth.gr
[2] University of Illinois at Chicago, Chicago, USA
ksolom6@uic.edu

Abstract. Most of the modern web services offer their users the ability to be registered on them via dedicated registration pages. Most of the times, they use this method so the users can profit by accessing more content or privileged items. In these pages, users are typically requested to provide their names, email addresses, phone numbers and other personal information in order to create an account. As the purpose of the tracking ecosystem is to collect as many information and data from the user, this kind of Personally Identifiable Information (PII) might leak on the 3rd-Parties, when the users fill in the registration forms. In this work, we conduct a large-scale measurement analysis of the PII leakage via registration pages of the 200,000 most popular websites. We design and implement a scalable and easily replicable methodology, for detecting and filling registration forms in an automated way. Our analysis shows that a number of websites ($\approx$5%) leak PIIs to 3rd-Party trackers without any user's consent, in a non-transparent fashion. Furthermore, we explore the techniques employed by 3rd-Parties in order to harvest user's data, and we highlight the implications on user's privacy.

Keywords: Privacy leakage · Personally Identifiable Information · Web tracking

1 Introduction

Web services are the building blocks of the synchronous Web, since they provide free content and services to online users. Their free of charge usage policy, is the main reason of their extreme popularity and the continuous daily usage by the users. Their financial business model is based on the *ad-ecosystem*, a set of complex technologies and entities (dubbed as *trackers*) present in most websites [1,2], whose goal is to deliver advertisements to end-users. Trackers are able to collect and share information about the user and her online activities, such us: online interests, sex, location, etc. The more information they retrieve and store about the user, the most efficient becomes the ad delivery by the highly personalized ads.

The vast majority of the ad-industry claims that tracking is based on non-Personally Identifiable Information (PII), but in the absence of user willingness

© Springer Nature Switzerland AG 2020
A. P. Fournaris et al. (Eds.): ESORICS 2019 Workshops, LNCS 11981, pp. 91–104, 2020.
https://doi.org/10.1007/978-3-030-42051-2_7

to pay for online services it seems unlikely, even though some of them find tracking privacy intrusive [3]. In a direction to conform user's needs, they also tend to offer a plurality of services in terms of content and user experience, by the option to opt-in (*register*) to their services. After users register to a website, they gain more benefits/privileges, easier or faster updates of the content, and access to hidden by the non-registered users content (e.g.: news,articles, forums, etc.). This process seems benign for a typical user who is unaware that the 3rd-party technologies constantly monitor her online activity, and have direct access on her PII when filling out a registration form. Also, most of the registration forms are being offered already implemented by different types of 3rd-party resources, and Web developers directly use their outsourced capabilities [4,5]. In regards to this fact, it is relatively easy for any 3rd-party which is present on a registration page and is the main controlling entity of the form, to access directly and store user's data without consent.

Personally Identifiable Information can be leaked through a variety of means, e.g., passing emails, names, addresses, as HTTP arguments when filling in Web forms. When such PII leakage occurs in a page hosting 3rd-party trackers, the trackers can associate the user's identity with online presence at any website,when a cookie or other type of deterministic data (tracking pixels, browser fingerprinting sequences, etc.) is observed. Trackers do not need the direct association between the PII and the cookie, they just require a constant identifier(e.g., a user ID or a username) to confirm that a user who has been active at one website is the same s now visiting another. Having such information they are not only able to reconstruct the browsing history, but also to correlate any of the user's PII with another user's devices [6] or with previous browsing activities (e.g.: correlate IP and geolocation with Zip Code).

As previous studies report [3,7], PII leakage is categorized as accidental or intentional. On the first case, the leakage occurs "by accident" when the Web script passes the -leaked- values through the HTTP requests. On the second case, the website owner intentionally leaks the user's data to 3rd-party trackers. Also, according to a recent report [8], there have been also cases of malicious trackers, that tried to harvest sensitive user data (e.g.: Credit Card info, SSN) from registration forms.

Based on these facts, as well as on previous studies on leakage of user information in different devices, online platforms, and social networks [7,9–11], on this paper we focus on 3rd-party tracking and PII leakage occurring on the Registration pages of the Web services. We design and implement a methodology, and we also conduct large scale analysis, in order to investigate how the 3rd-parties interact with the specific kind of forms, how they try to harvest the user information during the time which the user fills in the form, and how the PII leakage occurs even before users submit their data. Since the different types of leakages have been thoroughly analyzed in previous works, our focus is to explore the tracking ecosystem of the registration services. Overall, the main contributions of this work are:

- The design of an easily replicable methodology for online tracking measurements. Our methodology is able to identify and fill in registration forms with high accuracy at scale.
- A set of findings, when applying the methodology on the Top-200K most popular websites. Specifically:
  - 6% of registration forms leak email addresses directly to 3rd-parties without any encryption used.
  - The most common identifiers which are more valuable and possible to leak are user's email address, username, and location/address.
  - We found a specific type of trackers (*session-replicate*) which is mainly active on web forms and is responsible for the reported incidents of Privacy leakage.

Our analysis reflects a lower bound threshold of the actual PII leakage occurring on the wild. We plan to expand our methodology, in order to cover more and different types of websites, web forms, tracking techniques and devices. We believe that our initial study is going to raise awareness of Internet Users, by highlighting the privacy violations triggered by Web services.

2   Related Work

In this section we examine how the tracking ecosystem works and its causation with the leakage of user's information. We also provide the necessary terminology to understand the technical contributions of our work, while in parallel we present various mechanisms and technologies proposed in previous works on the area.

2.1   Web Tracking

As the purpose of online advertising is to increase the market share of the companies by promoting their products and services, the advertising industry continuously designs new mechanisms to deliver more effective and highly targeted ads. In order to serve highly targeted ads, advertisers employ various, often questionable and privacy intrusive, techniques for collecting and inferring users' personal information. They typically employ techniques, both stateful and stateless, for tracking users visits across different websites, which allow them to collect user's data, and reconstruct parts of their browsing history.

One of the first studies about tracking [12], investigated which information is collected by third parties and how users can be identified. Roesner et al. [13] measured the prevalence of trackers and different tracking behaviors in the web. Many works investigated stateful tracking techniques, their converge as well as their evolution through time [14–18], and also stateless techniques such as browser fingerprinting [1,19–23]. Moreover, Olejnik et al. [14] investigated "cookie syncing", a technique that enables trackers to have a more completed view on the users' browsing history by synchronizing their cookies, and found that this technique is employed by a large number of 3rd-parties. Acar et al. [1]

investigated the prevalence of "evercookies" and the effects of cookie respawning in combination with cookie syncing. Englehardt and Narayanan [15] conducted a large scale measurement study to quantify stateful and stateless tracking in the web, and cookie syncing.

With regards to stateless tracking, Nikiforakis et al. [21] investigated various fingerprinting techniques employed by popular trackers and measured the adoption of fingerprinting in the web. Acar et al. [20] proposed a framework to detect fingerprinting by identifying and analyzing specific events such as the loading of fonts, or accessing specific browser properties. In another work, Nikiforakis et al. [22] proposed a tool that employs randomization to make fingerprints non-deterministic, in order to make it harder for trackers to link user fingerprints across websites. Also, in a recent work, Cao et al. [24] proposed a fingerprinting technique that utilizes OS and hardware level features, for enabling user tracking not only within a single browser, but also across different browsers on the same machine.

2.2   Leakage of Personal Information

In one of the earliest works Krishnamurthy et al. [25], identified and measured the PII leakage occuring when users interact with popular OSNs. On their followup work [11] the authors also investigated the PII leakage on popular web services. They discovered that 48% of these sites leaked a user identifier to a 3rd-party website. Using a similar methodology, Mayer et al. [26] signed-up and interacted with 250 websites,finding out that 61% of the tested websites leaked a user's PII to third parties In the closest to our work, Starov et al. [7] identified and measured the potential PII leakage occurring on the "Contact Forms" of the 100K popular websites. Similarly Englehardt et al. [3], discovered the PII leakage and prevalence of tracking in various emails received by users, after they sign up on a service.

Furthermore, many works investigated privacy leakage in mobile devices and the different factors influencing mobile advertising [9, 27–31]. A recent study by Papadopoulos et al. [9] compared privacy leakage when visiting mobile websites and using mobile apps. Meng et al. [30] studied the accuracy of personalized ads served by mobile applications based on the information collected by the ad-networks. Also, Razaghpanah et al. [28] developed a technique that detects 3rd-party advertising and tracking services in the mobile ecosystem and uncovers unknown relationships between these services.

Finally, a large number of works also developed mechanisms and techniques in order to disassembly the ad-ecosystem and its internal technologies. ln a recent work, Papadopoulos et al. [10] developed a methodology that enables users to estimate the actual price advertisers pay for serving them ads. The range of these prices can indicate which personal information of the user is exposed to the advertiser and the sensitivity of this information. Liu et al. [32] proposed *AdReveal*, a tool for characterizing ads, and found that advertisers frequently target users based on their interests and browsing behavior. Lecuyer et al. [33] proposed *XRay*, a data tracking system that allows users to identify which data is being used for targeting, by comparing and correlating outputs from different accounts with similar data.

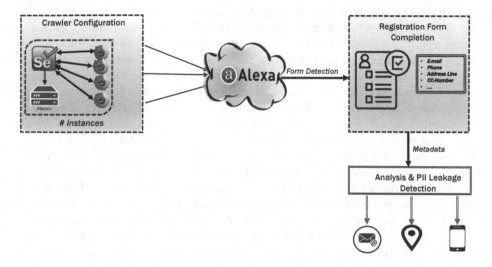

Fig. 1. High level representation of our methodology.

3   Methodology

Conducting large scale measurements on the online tracking ecosystem is a non-trivial task, due to the complex structure of the modern websites. For this reason, we design and implement a scalable methodology, to measure the potential PII leakage in registration forms. Our methodology is based on widely used by the previous works components (e.g.: automated browsers, HTTP(s) Proxies, etc.), that are able to replicate realistic browsing activity and to log and store the generated data. An overview of our methodology is illustrated in Fig. 1.

3.1   Crawler Configuration

Since we want to achieve scale, we use an automated approach to emulate a user visiting multiple websites and registering to their services on parallel. We create a web crawler based on the Selenium framework [34], that offers an API suitable for interacting with websites and locating nested and hidden elements. For our methodology, we chose to automate Firefox Web Browser since it is fully compatible with Selenium framework and also easily deployable. For capturing the HTTP(s) requests that are being triggered by the browser, we also use the BrowserMob Proxy plugin [35]. The plugin captures the generated HTTP(s) traffic, and stores it in JSON format for later analysis. The aforementioned tools enable us to successfully discover, identify and fill in registration forms, while on parallel they provide efficiency and performance by supporting multiple parallel crawling instances.

3.2 Form Detection

Preprocessing and Initial Step. Since we do not know a priori which websites contain valid registration forms, we perform an initial proccess, in order to collect a satisfying number of keywords and terms that are the common identifiers of the web forms. These sets of terms will be used by our crawlers for the discovery and identification of registration forms. A main component for this initial step, as well as for the rest of our study, is Alexa list [36]. Alexa list is a popular source for many studies, since it maintains a public list of the Top 1 million popular websites based on monthly traffic statistics, as well as rankings of the Top 500 websites by category, country, popularity, etc. At first, we crawl the Alexa Top 500 sites and extract from the DOM tree (rendered HTML) of each site, all the <a> tags that contain the inner pages of the website, where the registration forms are usually stored. Afterwards, we collect only the URLs that their title contains one of the common registration keywords, such us:"*{ Register, Sign Up, Login, Subscribe, Create Account, Join,...}* ". If a link with a matching title is found, the browser visits it and search for any < input > and < textarea > elements. These elements, as well as all the JavaScript elements, have a unique ID that is often used for describing their functionality. We collect the retrieved IDs, and store only those that loosely match with any of the values: "*{ name,surname,email,street-address,..}*". Those values are suggested by the Firefox Browser [37] to web developers when they build web forms, and are a guidance regarding the type of information expected in the fields. Afterwards, we manually filter the collected keywords and store only those that are potentially related with the registration process. We also store the translations of the previous set of keywords to various languages with the use of WordNet library [38], for covering as many as possible from the non-english domains of the Alexa list. Finally, we crawl the Alexa Top 500 popular sites by country, in order to (1) validate that our method is able to identify registration forms in different EU/Non EU languages, and (2) expand the sets of keywords for collecting as many as possible registration form and input keywords. Performing the previous steps, we retrieve $\sim$ 2500 keywords containing all the potential registration related keywords and their translations.

Large Scale Form Detection. The large scale form detection is mainly based on the previous initial step and is detailed in the Algorithm 1. Similarly to the previous step, we visit a webpage and search for the tag elements. If a tag element contains any valid registration term (or any of its translations) we visit its inner URL. We consider a valid registration form, a web form that contains at least two input elements (e.g.: an email, and a name/surname/other field) and a submit button. If any of the above conditions is met, we label the URL as a valid registration form and proceed on the next step.

3.3 Registration Form Completion

Once a form is found, the crawler must fill in the input fields with valid text and user's information. The crawler interacts with all visible form fields including:

Input: URL // a URL of the corpus
Output: Boolean:True-False // if the URL contains a form
get_URL()
all_Links ← Collect_All_innerLinks(URL)
for *link in all_Links* **do**
    if *title contains Registration_Term()* **then**
        visit_link(link)
        Text_Inputs ← Collect_All_Inputs(link)
        if *size(Text_Inputs) ≥ 2 and contains submit()* **then**
          | **return** *True* // a valid Form is found
        end
    end
end
return *False* //the URL does not contains a Form

Algorithm 1. Registration Form Discovery.

$< input >$, $< select >$, $< type >$ and also with the submit $< button >$ tags. From the previous initial step where we surveyed a number of top websites to determine common naming practices for the input fields, at this stage we fill the fields with the data of the expected and/or recommended type(s). For example, input names were filled a realistic first and last name, email fields with real emails that we created for the purposes of our study, dates and zipcodes with real values and IDs matching with our location. Moreover, we also used a valid Paypal account when the registration service needed credit-related values. For easier PII leakage, when possible, we provided the same input data. A detailed description of the most frequent input fields, is given in Table 1.

During the completion process, if a field is unknown (e.g.: a special code from the site is required, a 2FA token) or a CAPTCHA protects the form, we discard the completion of the form, since we want to capture the more accurate data from the input that we control without breaking any of the functionalities of the site. When all the data are filled, our crawler either submits the form with the provided data, or continues to the next site of the collections and performs the previous steps respectively. In both cases we are logging all the HTTP(s) requests, the type of input data that we provided, the rendered HTML and other browsing metadata. This option of the crawler for submitting or not a registration form enables us to identify easier the different types of PII leakage as will be discussed later.

3.4 Analysis and PII Leakage Detection

As we mentioned earlier, any information from a user input that will potentially leak through remote resources requests (3rd-party requests for scripts, content, etc.) is considered as a PII leakage. Thus, we consider PII to be leaked when it is sent to a 3rd-party entity, which is a domain other than the one which the

Table 1. Most frequent input fields and their HTML attributes

Field	HTML attribute
Name	name
Surname	family-name
Email address	e-mail
Telephone number	tel
Company/Organization	organization
Address	street-address
Country name/Code	country, country-name
Zip code	postal-code
Credit card fields	cc-number, cc-name cc-exp, cc-type

user visited. Detecting such leaks is not as simple as searching for substrings inside larger strings, since any input field might be hashed and/or encoded multiple times. To detect this kind of leakage we design a method that needs three different sources of inputs:

1. A set of encodings and hashes
2. A plaintext input field (name, email, address, phone, etc.)
3. A string URL token

Handling these values, our method is able to determine if the URL contains any transformation of the PI. First we check whether a PII is sent directly through a network request without the use of any encryption or encoding. Since this is a non frequent scenario, we follow the previous works on this topic [3,7] and we employ a similar method. We start with the plaintext value and we compute a candidate set of tokens by applying various hashes and encodings which are typically used on the network requests. More specifically, we iteratively use *md5, gzip, base64, sha1,sha256*. As previous works direct [3], the encryption or hashing of those values, is no deeper than three nested layers, and thus we follow similar direction.

We then take the URL token and search for the specific substring. In order to eliminate the False Positives, since any hashed/encrypted string might match with a subset of the input, we also apply the supported decodings to the URL and check whether the result contains any of the input values. We are able to apply this method in the collected network *Metadata* (as illustrated in Fig. 1), that contain crawl-related data (i.e.: rendered HTML pages, Network Traffic) as well as various log files which are used for the syncing of the components. Finally, the described method covers a lower bound threshold in detecting PII leakage in encrypted traffic, since any other transformation or custom algorithm that is not known to us, might be applied by any kind of website.

The aforementioned kind of leakage, might occur "*accidentally*" or "*on purpose*". For the former, we describe those websites which by accident or by bad developing practices, are responsible for leaking user's PII to 3rd-parties through the HTTP referrer header. For the latter, we label those websites that intentionally leak the PII to trackers, typically through the outsourcing of contact forms to 3rd-parties, enabling them to indirectly harvest user's identity. More specifically, every JavaScript library present on a registration form can access the user's PII at the time of typing, through the use of appropriate key-pressed event handlers, and even before the user submits their input. On our analysis we mainly focus on this type of trackers, as well as other similar scripts, and we measure their frequency of inclusion by taking advantage of the option which we described earlier.

Dataset. Finally from the 200,000 visited websites, we identified 66764 registration forms ($\approx$33%). On total, from this set of websites we were able to successfully complete $\approx$80% of the registration forms. The crawls were executed on a 8-core server located in the EU, between February and April of 2019.

4   PII Leakage Analysis

On this section we apply the analysis of Sect. 3.4, in order to quantify and measure the PII leakage on the collected data. We evaluate our methodology on the intentional PII leakage occuring during "before submit" process, while we analyze other aspects regarding the behavior and prevalence of 3rd-Party Trackers.

4.1   On Purpose PII Leakage

Plaintext Data. On the first level of our analysis, we check whether any PII is sent as a plaintext directly to trackers, via an HTTP(s) request. We found that in 6% (3557) of the webpages of the corpus[1], the email address is directly sent to the network destination without any encoding or hash. By applying our method we did not found any other instances of HTTP(s) requests containing other values different than the email. Figure 2, represents the 3rd-Party trackers receiving the HTTP(s) requests, along with their percentage of coverage. Interestingly Google and AdRoll, which are well-known entities of the tracking ecosystem, are highly present in this set of websites and potentially responsible for any leakage. As we mentioned earlier, most of the registration forms are outsourced, and for this reason the outsourced services have direct access on the user's input. Thus, they might check for the validity of an email, or if the user already exists by sending this type of requests to their backend servers. It is inherently difficult to validate the purposes of the 3rd-Party, and even if the percentage is relative low, we consider this first preliminary result as prominent, since it is still possible for a user to visit those sites that belong to the 200K most popular sites of Alexa.

Hashes and Encodings. We apply the methods introduced in Sect. 3, and we create nested encrypted/encoded tokens of our input values (as reported

---

[1] By corpus we describe the set of sites that we succesully visited, identified and filled in the registration forms.

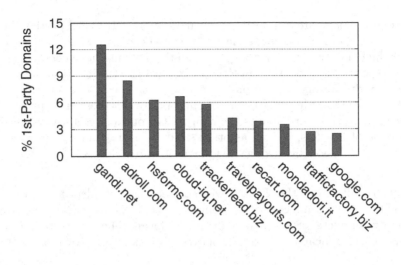

3rd-Party Domain

Fig. 2. Top-10 most frequent trackers and their coverage in the set of websites that send e-mail address as a plaintext through HTTP(s) requests.

in Table 1). In total, we found that 8% websites of our dataset, leak at least one identifier to a 3rd-party. The most common values that leak are: **email address(50%), username(25%), location-city-country (8%)**. Those PIIs are sufficient for correlating any user along with her browsing activity. Email address is a strong identifier, and on parallel with the username (users tend to register with the same username in multiple services) and the IP address, can reveal the user's identity. Considering that 3rd-parties collect large amounts of data for a user daily, indeed these types of information are valuable for the tracking ecosystem, and create new privacy risks for the individual users. Figure 3 illustrates the CDF of websites and the total number of 3rd-party requests to tracking domains. Overall, 50% of the 1st-party domains, generate at least 5 tracking requests, and less than 5% generate more traffic in terms of load, totalling in more than 20 requests directed to one or multiple trackers. If we focus more on those tracking domains, we observe that the most frequent ones, are self-identified as "session-replicate" trackers[2]. These scripts record and store users keystrokes, mouse movements, and scrolling behavior, along with the entire contents of the pages that one visits. Unlike typical analytics services that provide aggregate statistics, these scripts are intended for the recording and playback of individual browsing sessions. We found that 3 major well-known session replicate trackers (Hotjar [39], Inspectlet [40] and Mouseflow [41]), cover more than 40% of the registration pages of our corpus, and specifically most of the pages that we found potential leakage.

---

[2] The description on their site contains the terms: visual way to understand your users, scrolling heatmaps, eye tracking, scroll heatmaps, replicate.

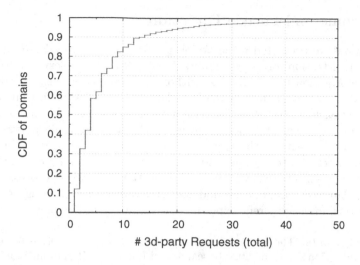

Fig. 3. Total number of 3rd-Party requests per registration website.

Even though that these marketing services claim that they are privacy preserving and GDPR compliant, we consider these actions as highly privacy intrusive,that violate an individual user's online privacy. The session recording scripts can extract information different than the "typical" tracking information, and are uniquely connected with the user's behavior, e.g.: scrolling rate, typing rate, mouse clicks, etc. Advertisers can use this information and identify users without the need of traditional tracking data (cookies, IP address, etc.) across multiple websites, reconstruct their browsing history, extract their interests, and finally serve them (re)targeted ads.

4.2   Email Notifications

During the time that we conducted our experiments, the test emails started to receive email notifications from the domains that we visited, without submitting any of the input values. The template was similar across the emails, and they were mainly trying to remind us to finish our registration, or they were offering a type of discount. In total 60 web services send us more than 700 emails, with the most "aggressive" one sending us more than 20 emails either with discounts, offers, or other content-related material. Similarly to Englehardt et al. [3] that analysed web tracking occurring via emails, we found that approximately 17% of the received emails contained tracking pixels. By sending those pixels to clients, 3rd-parties are able to check whether a receiver has opened the email and returned to the webpage to finalize the registration. This behavior might be a side effect of the session-replicate trackers, or other types of trackers and still are use cases of privacy violations by 3rd-Parties.

5 Outcome and Future Directions

On this paper we presented a methodology for identifying and measuring PII leakage in registration forms. We found that 5–10% of web services leak user's personal information to 3rd-Parties, without the user's consent. We also measured the presence of the new type of trackers(session replicate), that have not been studied exclusively before. Moreover, in theory we should have studied in depth the privacy rules and cookie consest both for first and 3d-party domains and correlate the leakage with such terms, but this was out of scope of our paper. Our initial effort was to explore one step further the tracking ecosystem, and highlight the potential privacy issues related to the registration processes. In the future, we plan to expand our methodology in a direction to investigate different kinds of forms, under different experimental scenarios and emulated users.

Acknowledgments. The research leading to these results has received funding from the European Union's Horizon 2020 Research and Innovation Programme under grand agreement No. 786669 (project CONCORDIA). The paper reflects only the authors' views and the Agency and the Commission are not responsible for any use that may be made of the information it contains.

References

1. Acar, G., Eubank, C., Englehardt, S., Juarez, M., Narayanan, A., Diaz, C.: The web never forgets: persistent tracking mechanisms in the wild. In: Proceedings of the 2014 ACM SIGSAC Conference on Computer and Communications Security. CCS 2014, pp. 674–689. ACM, New York (2014)
2. Englehardt, S., et al.: Cookies that give you away: the surveillance implications of web tracking. In: Proceedings of the 24th International Conference on World Wide Web. WWW 2015, Republic and Canton of Geneva, Switzerland, International World Wide Web Conferences Steering Committee, pp. 289–299 (2015)
3. Englehardt, S., Han, J., Narayanan, A.: I never signed up for this! privacy implications of email tracking. Proc. Priv. Enhanc. Technol. **2018**(1), 109–126 (2018)
4. Jay, M.: Top 9 Trending Web Development Technologies 2018 (2018). https://www.ipraxa.com/blog/web-development-technologies/
5. Flatword Solutions: Forms Processing Services (2018). https://www.flatworldsolutions.com/data-management/forms-processing.php
6. Solomos, K., Ilia, P., Ioannidis, S., Kourtellis, N.: {TALON}: an automated framework for cross-device tracking detection. In: 22nd International Symposium on Research in Attacks, Intrusions and Defenses ({RAID} 2019). (2020)
7. Starov, O., Gill, P., Nikiforakis, N.: Are you sure you want to contact us? Quantifying the leakage of pii via website contact forms. Proc. Priv. Enhanc. Technol. **2016**(1), 20–33 (2016)
8. Privacy team: The Trackers Who Steal (2018). https://whotracks.me/blog/trackers-who-steal.html
9. Papadopoulos, E.P., Diamantaris, M., Papadopoulos, P., Petsas, T., Ioannidis, S., Markatos, E.P.: The long-standing privacy debate: mobile websites vs mobile apps. In: Proceedings of the 26th International Conference on World Wide Web, WWW 2017, pp. 153–162. International World Wide Web Conferences Steering Committee, Republic and Canton of Geneva (2017)

10. Papadopoulos, P., Rodriguez, P.R., Kourtellis, N., Laoutaris, N.: If you are not paying for it, you are the product: how much do advertisers pay to reach you? In: Proceedings of the 2017 Internet Measurement Conference, IMC 2017, pp. 142–156. ACM, New York (2017)
11. Krishnamurthy, B., Naryshkin, K., Wills, C.: Privacy leakage vs. protection measures: the growing disconnect. In: Proceedings of the Web, vol. 2, pp. 1–10 (2011)
12. Mayer, J.R., Mitchell, J.C.: Third-party web tracking: policy and technology. In: Proceedings of the 2012 IEEE Symposium on Security and Privacy, SP 2012, pp. 413–427. IEEE Computer Society, Washington, DC (2012)
13. Roesner, F., Kohno, T., Wetherall, D.: Detecting and defending against third-party tracking on the web. In: Proceedings of the 9th USENIX Conference on Networked Systems Design and Implementation, NSDI 2012, p. 12. USENIX Association, Berkeley (2012)
14. Olejnik, L., Minh-Dung, T., Castelluccia, C.: Selling off privacy at auction. In: Network and Distributed System Security Symposium (NDSS) (2014)
15. Englehardt, S., Narayanan, A.: Online tracking: A 1-million-site measurement and analysis. In: Proceedings of the 2016 ACM SIGSAC Conference on Computer and Communications Security, CCS 2016, pp. 1388–1401. ACM, New York (2016)
16. Yu, Z., Macbeth, S., Modi, K., Pujol, J.M.: Tracking the trackers. In: Proceedings of the 25th International Conference on World Wide Web. WWW 2016, pp. 121–132. International World Wide Web Conferences Steering Committee, Republic and Canton of Geneva (2016)
17. Lerner, A., Simpson, A.K., Kohno, T., Roesner, F.: Internet jones and the raiders of the lost trackers: an archaeological study of web tracking from 1996 to 2016. In: 25th USENIX Security Symposium (USENIX Security 2016). USENIX Association, Austin (2016)
18. Solomos, K., Ilia, P., Ioannidis, S., Kourtellis, N.: Clash of the trackers: measuring the evolution of the online tracking ecosystem. arXiv preprint arXiv:1907.12860 (2019)
19. Eckersley, P.: How unique is your web browser? In: Atallah, M.J., Hopper, N.J. (eds.) PETS 2010. LNCS, vol. 6205, pp. 1–18. Springer, Heidelberg (2010). https://doi.org/10.1007/978-3-642-14527-8_1
20. Acar, G., et al.: FPDetective: dusting the web for fingerprinters. In: Proceedings of the 2013 ACM SIGSAC Conference on Computer & #38; Communications Security, CCS 2013, pp. 1129–1140. ACM, New York (2013)
21. Nikiforakis, N., Kapravelos, A., Joosen, W., Kruegel, C., Piessens, F., Vigna, G.: Cookieless monster: exploring the ecosystem of web-based device fingerprinting. In: Proceedings of the 2013 IEEE Symposium on Security and Privacy, SP 2013, pp. 541–555. IEEE Computer Society, Washington, DC (2013)
22. Nikiforakis, N., Joosen, W., Livshits, B.: Privaricator: deceiving fingerprinters with little white lies. In: Proceedings of the 24th International Conference on World Wide Web, WWW 2015, pp. 820–830. International World Wide Web Conferences Steering Committee, Republic and Canton of Geneva (2015)
23. Panchenko, A., et al.: Website fingerprinting at internet scale. In: NDSS (2016)
24. Cao, Y., Li, S., Wijmans, E.: (Cross-)browser fingerprinting via OS and hardware level features. In: Proceedings of Network & Distributed System Security Symposium (NDSS), Internet Society (2017)
25. Krishnamurthy, B., Wills, C.E.: On the leakage of personally identifiable information via online social networks. In: Proceedings of the 2nd ACM workshop on Online social networks, pp. 7–12. ACM (2009)

26. Mayer, J.: Tracking the trackers: where everybody knows your username. The Center for Internet and Society (2011)
27. Terkki, E., Rao, A., Tarkoma, S.: Spying on android users through targeted ads. In: 2017 9th International Conference on Communication Systems and Networks (COMSNETS), pp. 87–94 (2017)
28. Razaghpanah, A., et al.: Apps, trackers, privacy and regulators: a global study of the mobile tracking ecosystem. In: Proceedings of NDSS, NDSS 2018 (2018)
29. Grace, M.C., Zhou, W., Jiang, X., Sadeghi, A.R.: Unsafe exposure analysis of mobile in-app advertisements. In: Proceedings of the Fifth ACM Conference on Security and Privacy in Wireless and Mobile Networks, WISEC 2012, pp. 101–112. ACM, New York (2012)
30. Meng, W., Ding, R., Chung, S.P., Han, S., Lee, W.: The price of free: privacy leakage in personalized mobile in-apps ads. In: NDSS (2016)
31. Ren, J., Rao, A., Lindorfer, M., Legout, A., Choffnes, D.: Recon: revealing and controlling pii leaks in mobile network traffic. In: Proceedings of the 14th Annual International Conference on Mobile Systems, Applications, and Services, pp. 361–374. ACM (2016)
32. Liu, B., Sheth, A., Weinsberg, U., Chandrashekar, J., Govindan, R.: Adreveal: improving transparency into online targeted advertising. In: Proceedings of the Twelfth ACM Workshop on Hot Topics in Networks, HotNets-XII, pp. 12:1–12:7. ACM, New York (2013)
33. Lécuyer, M., et al.: Xray: enhancing the web's transparency with differential correlation. In: USENIX Security Symposium, pp. 49–64 (2014)
34. Selenium browser automation. https://www.seleniumhq.org/
35. Browsermob proxy. a free utility to help web developers watch and manipulate network traffic from their ajax applications. https://bmp.lightbody.net/
36. Alexa: The top 500 sites on the web (2018). https://www.alexa.com/topsites/category/Top/
37. Mozilla: The HTML autocomplete attribute (2018). https://developer.mozilla.org/en-US/docs/Web/HTML/Attributes/autocomplete
38. Princeton university: a lexical database for English (2018). https://wordnet.princeton.edu/
39. Hotjar: The fast & visual way to understand your users (2018). https://www.hotjar.com/
40. Inspectlet: stop guessing what your visitors want (2018). https://www.inspectlet.com/
41. Mouseflow: Mouseflow reveals why your visitors aren't converting into customers (2018). https://mouseflow.com/

MSTEC Workshop

A Model Driven Approach for Cyber Security Scenarios Deployment

Chiara Braghin[1](✉), Stelvio Cimato[1], Ernesto Damiani[1,2], Fulvio Frati[1],
Lara Mauri[1], and Elvinia Riccobene[1]

[1] Computer Science Department, Università degli Studi di Milano, Milan, Italy
{chiara.braghin,stelvio.cimato,ernesto.damiani,
lara.mauri,elvinia.riccobene}@unimi.it
[2] EBTIC Laboratory, Khalifa University,
Abu Dhabi Campus, PO Box 127788, Abu Dhabi, UAE

Abstract. Cyber ranges for training in threat scenarios are nowadays highly demanded in order to improve people ability to detect vulnerabilities and to react to cyber-threats. Among the other components, scenarios deployment requires a modeling language to express the (software and hardware) architecture of the underlying system, and an emulation platform.

In this paper, we exploit a model-driven engineering approach to develop a framework for cyber security scenarios deployment. We develop a domain specific language for scenarios construction, which allows the description of the architectural setting of the system under analysis, and a mechanism to deploy scenarios on the OpenStack cloud infrastructure by means of HEAT templates. On the scenario model, we also show how it is possible to detect network configuration problems and structural vulnerabilities. The presented results are part of our ongoing research work towards the definition of a training cyber range within the EU H2020 project THREAT-ARREST.

1 Introduction

Detecting and responding effectively to cyber attacks is a challenge for companies and industries whose businesses nowadays are more and more related to IT and thus exposed to a large number of threats. According to different reports, the annual cost of cyber-attacks amounts to 9.5$ millions and is increasing at an annual rate of 21% [7].

Advanced security training has indeed gained importance in order to mitigate cyber attacks. In this context, cyber ranges have been introduced as environments where staff people can practice skills and improve the ability to respond to attacks and defend company's business. In analogy to military ranges, cyber ranges consist of interactive simulations of organizations local systems and software applications, connected to a simulated networked environment.

Currently, there are a number of initatives focused on the design of cyber ranges, including national and international projects, academic environments

A. P. Fournaris et al. (Eds.): ESORICS 2019 Workshops, LNCS 11981, pp. 107–122, 2020.
https://doi.org/10.1007/978-3-030-42051-2_8

for training students, and commercial tools offered to private companies. The National Cyber Range (NCR) [10] is a program led by the Defense Advanced Research Projects Agency (DARPA) and started in 2008, whose goal is realistic cyberspace security testing, supporting also training and rehearsal exercises. CYBERWISER [2] is a European H2020 project focused on the development of an independent cyber range platform devoted to the professional training of both students and IT professionals. CyRIS (Cyber Range Instantiation System) is an academic platform [16] that provides a mechanism to automatically prepare and manage cyber ranges for cybersecurity education. Other commercial platforms have been developed by companies involved in IT security and networking, such as Cisco Cyber Range [1], whose goal is to improve security staff skills and train them to face modern cyber threats, using synthetic war-gaming environment.

The provision of realistic cyber-security threat scenarios is a challenging activity, requiring expert skills, a lot of effort, time and resource consuming, and is also error-prone, since a large number of features need to be specified for having complex and realistic simulated environments.

In this paper, we propose a model-driven approach to engineering a framework for the description and deployment of cyber security threat scenarios. We started with the definition of a domain specific language, the *Cybersecurity Training Language* (CTL), able to describe, in terms of scenarios, the architectural setting of the cyber system under analysis. On scenario models, it is possible to guarantee structural and semantic correctness by checking a number of model validation rules. Such a mechanism can be exploited to reveal network configuration problems and structural misconfiguration. Then, we developed a software component able to translate CTL scenarios into HEAT templates, the input programs for the OpenStack cloud infrastructure. Such a mechanism allows to deploy CTL scenarios on the OpenStack and use it, in the future, for scenarios emulation. We show the use of our platform for scenarios definition and deployment by means of a simple case study.

The paper is organized as follows. The background section presents a short introduction to model-driven development of Domain Specific Languages (Sects. 2.1 and 2.2), and to the OpenStack cloud infrastructure with HEAT templates for orchestration (Sect. 2.3), respectively. Section 3 gives a general overview of our framework for scenarios definition and deployment, whereas Sect. 4 gives a detailed description of each specific phase of the process of defining a cyber range scenario, starting from the description of the CTL language to the translation of a scenario into HEAT. Section 5 gives an overview of related work, while Sect. 6 concludes the paper and underlines future directions of our ongoing research.

2 Background

2.1 Model Driven Development of Domain Specific Languages

In the context of language and software development, model-based approaches consider models as first-class entities that, depending on the specific needs, can

be mapped into programs and/or other models by automatic model transforma-
tions. In contrast to *general-purpose* modelling languages (like the UML) that
are used for a wide range of domains, *domain-specific languages* (DSL) are tailored to a particular problem domain and offer designers concepts and notations
to capture structural and behavioural aspects of their applications, and DSLs
themselves can be seen as artifacts of the model-based approach for language
engineering.

In a model-based language definition, the *abstract syntax* of a DSL is defined
in terms of an object-oriented model, called *metamodel*, that characterizes syntax elements and their relationships, thus separating the abstract syntax and
semantics of the language constructs from their different concrete notations.
The latter ones can be of different forms depending on the purpose: *machine-
readable* notation, as XML, allows model exchange and facilitates automatic
model transformation; *human-readable* notation makes easy human comprehen-
sion of the model and avoids writing pain, verbosity and syntactical noise of
using machine-readable notation such as XML.

The definition of a DSL abstract syntax by a metamodel is well mastered and
supported by a number of metamodelling environments [12]. However, currently,
the most exploited approach to define and develop a DSL is the grammarware
approach of Xtext [8] combined with the modelware approach of EMF (Eclipse
Metamodeling Framework) [19].

Xtext is a framework for languages development. The user gets a full infrastructure to define a new language by using a powerful grammar language, to
parse a written program, process it, and then possibly interpret it or generate
code in another language. A fully featured IDE (Integrated Development Environment) based on Eclipse allows for an easy editor development of the new
language and a language validator. In the following, we briefly describe the main
steps of a DSL development.

2.2   Developing Steps of a DSL

An Xtext-based process developement of a DSL consists of the following main
steps:

1. Definition of an abstract and one or more concrete syntaxes (textual, graphical, mixed);
2. Development of an editing environment for models/programs;
3. Serialization/Deserialization for models;
4. Static semantics definition (mostly based on type checking);
5. Dynamic semantics definition (interpreter, model compiler, code generator).

Xtext-based development is a grammarware approach, i.e., the grammar of
the DSL is specified by means of a textual language (a DSL) provided by Xtext.
Due to the tight integration of Xtext with EMF, an EMF Ecore model (the
metamodel of the new DSL, i.e., the classes typing the objects and their relationships) is automatically inferred from the DSL grammar definition; it is then

used as the in-memory representation of any parsed text file. Note that, depending on the community, this in-memory object graph is called the abstract syntax tree (AST) or document object graph (DOM) or model instance of a metamodel. We use here the term (meta)model and AST interchangeably to denote the DSL abstract syntax that abstracts over syntactical information.

The DSL metamodel can be used by later processing steps in Xtext, such as validation, compilation or interpretation or artifacts/code generation. The DSL *parser* is generated automatically by Xtext and can be then complemented by a *validator* to perform static analysis of DSL models and give informative feedback to the users. Standard Xtext validation works by checking precise constraints on the metamodeling elements expressed in terms of OCL (Object Constraint Language) formulas.

Once the grammar has been defined, an Eclipse *editor* can be automatically generated within Xtext. The editor provides a framework for a human-readable way to specify a program in the new DSL and supports nice user feature such as context assist. The code generation is done with Xtend, a general purpose programming language that has complete interoperability with Java and is entirely developed within Xtext. A serialization of a DSL model is possible in a textual format. An XML file can be automatically generated from a program in the DSL by exploiting Xtext facilities.

Semantics of a DSL is usually given by natural language with all the consequences of ambiguities and incompleteness that derive from it. However, a number of approaches exist to provide metamodel-based language semantics in a rigorous way by means of the use of formal methods [11].

2.3   OpenStack and Heat

OpenStack [15] is an open source cloud computing platform. It consists of a collection of interrelated software tools that control pools of processing, storage and networking resources, that can be accessed through RESTful APIs with different language bindings (e.g., Python, and Java) and with common authentication mechanisms. The core software components are: Nova, provisioning and managing computer resources and virtual machines; Neutron, the virtual network manager; Keystone, the identity manager; Horizon, providing a GUI for both administrator and end users; and Heat, the orchestration component.

Heat [14] implements an orchestration engine allowing users to launch multiple composite cloud applications (called *stacks*) based on templates (Heat Orchestration Templates - HOTs) in the form of text files readable and writable by humans that can be treated like code by the system. A HOT template allows the creation of most OpenStack resource types (such as instances, networks and subnets, floating IPs, volumes, security groups, users, etc), as well as some more advanced functionalities such as the possibility to configure software installed on the launched VMs.

HOT templates are defined in YAML, and follow the structure outlined in Code 1.1. More in detail, each HOT template has to include at least the *heat_template_version* key with a valid version of HOT, and the *resources* section,

Code 1.1. The basic structure of a HOT template file

```
heat_template_version: 2016-10-14

description:
  # explanation of the template

parameters:
  # declaration of each input parameter

resources:
  # resource list and property specification
```

Code 1.2. An example of a HOT template

```
heat_template_version: 2015-04-30

description: >
  Simple template to deploy a single compute instance

resources:
  my_instance:
    type: OS::Nova::Server
    properties:
      name: test1_v3_svr
      key_name: chiara
      image: cirros-0.4.0-x86_64-disk
      flavor: m1.small
      networks:
        - network: private
```

with the declaration of the resources to be deployed, selected from the *OpenStack Resource Types* [13] list that specifies the complete list of possible resources. Both the *description* and the *parameters* sections are optional, the latter being used to define a set of input parameters in place of hard-coding such values in order to have a more easily reusable template.

The most basic template that can be defined contains only a single compute instance. An example is depicted in Code 1.2, where a single resource is specified. Each resource has a name, a type, and a set of properties. Resource types are organized in packages, e.g., *OS::Nova::Server*, where it is specified the type of component (*Server*) and the OpenStack software component that will instantiate and manage the resource (*Nova*).

Some of the properties of a server must be specified in order to produce a valid template, they are:

- *image*: specifying the image ID of the virtual machine the system will deploy;
- *flavor*: describing the specific properties of a VM (memory and disk size, virtual CPUs, ...);
- *key*: the public SSH key to be injected into the instance on launch, in order to access it by connecting via SSH using the private key;
- *security groups*: a named collection of network access rules that are used to limit the types of traffic that have access to instances (both inbound to

instances and outbound from instances). The rules can specify the operations and protocols this VM is allowed to apply on a specific network;

– *network*: the VM must be connected at least to a network. In general, it is possible to configure richer network topologies, by creating and configuring multiple networks and subnets, and attaching virtual devices to ports on these networks.

Notice that some special objects such as VMs images and key pairs must be defined in advance within the overall OpenStack infrastructure in order to be then referenced in the HOT template by the unique ID (UUID) assigned by the system.

3 Platform Architecture

The framework we propose enables the development of high quality cyber ranges having the characteristics of being rapidly reconfigurable and easily deployable. A completely manual configuration process is a complex activity often leading to errors, not always representing the target operating environment, with unpredictable timing [17].

For this reason, our proposal, as depicted in Fig. 1, includes semi-automatic steps that make it very easy to pass from the model of a scenario to a running environment where the training can be performed. In particular, the first module includes an editor that allows the modeler to provide a description of the simulated system using a DSL, in our case the Cybersecurity Training Language. A validator gives also the possibility to introduce some constraints and rules against which it is possible to test the correctness of the description. The model is then automatically translated into an intermediate description (using XML) that is translated into a HEAT template and then provided as input to the HEAT engine. Such description is finally used to start the training environment as OpenStack cloud infrastructure, where the different VMs and their configurations are effectively deployed.

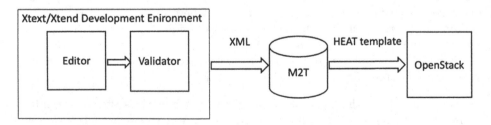

Fig. 1. The platform architecture: from a CTL scenario to an OpenStack environment

4   CTL as Domain Specific Language

In this section, we describe in detail the framework we propose for cyber security scenarios deployment. First, we present the process we have followed to develop the Cybersecurity Training Language (CTL), i.e., the language used to specify the input model for a cyber range. To this aim, we exploited the Xtext-based approach for a DSL definition, that offers a full infrastructure, including parser, linker, typechecker, compiler as well as editing support for Eclipse. Then, we describe how a CTL scenario is translated into a HEAT template to be used to deploy the scenario on OpenStack.

4.1   CTL Description

Starting from the grammar definition, Xtext automatically infers an EMF meta-model for the specified language. EMF provides tools and runtime support to produce a set of Java classes for the model, along with a set of adapter classes that enable viewing of the model. In particular, an essential part of EMF is Ecore, which provides language constructs that enable the definition of an abstract syntax of a model and its representation with a graphical notation following conventions similar to UML class diagrams.

In Fig. 2 we provide the Ecore class diagram derived from CTL, and below, we describe the different classes that give shape to the structured hierarchy represented in the diagram itself.

The *model* is designed as an *asset* composition. An asset acts as a generalized superclass of three subclasses representing the key elements of a typical network configuration, i.e. *nodes, networking devices* and *connections* among them. A node, in turn, is a generalization of two other subclasses which are represented by *virtual machines* (VMs) and *any device* which needs to be modeled separately as it presents features that cannot be captured by a generic VM (e.g., a web cam or a sensor). A custom VM represents a specialized form of virtual machine modeled as a subclass of the generic VM base-class with the image of the VM itself as an attribute.

For each VM it is possible to specify zero or more properties expressed in terms of *software/hardware characteristics* and *vulnerabilities* associated to a specific component of the system under consideration. More in detail, the software properties can be of three different types according to the aspects of software considered: operating system (system software coordinating and controlling all the processing activities of the computer), programming language (i.e, the specific language used to create computer programs) and applications (software performing tasks for specific purposes). The latter type of software allows the completion of several tasks such as creating spreadsheets and databases, doing online research, sending emails and so on. On the other hand, the hardware properties represent the main physical characteristics of a computer, i.e. the system unit containing CPU, hard disk and RAM.

A network infrastructure comprises different hardware components, i.e., *networking devices*, which contribute as a whole to the overall functioning of the

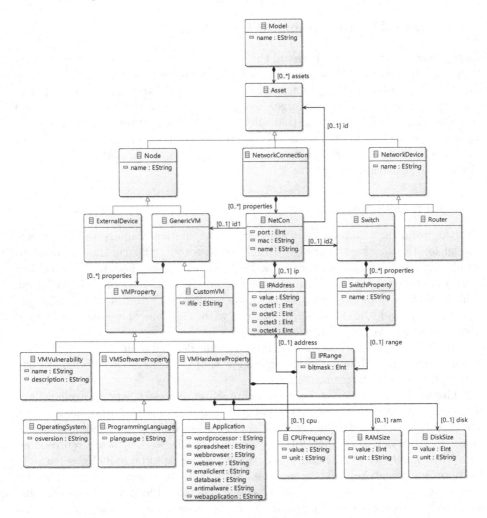

Fig. 2. Ecore class diagram of the CTL language

network system and are responsible for transmitting information. The basic types of networking devices required for communication and interaction among nodes within the network are switches and routers. The class modeling the *network connections* has associated the parameters necessary to make possible the communication between the system components (e.g. MAC addresses, ports and IP addresses).

4.2   CTL Development

In Fig. 3, we report a fragment of the grammar specification for CTL. As previously mentioned, in order to implement the language, we used the open source Xtext Eclipse framework. The generated grammar is composed of a series of rules defining the individual elements of the desired language. The first rule defines the root element of the model of the CTL. Specifically, it declares that a Cyber-security Training Language model is a collection of asset elements, whilst in the subsequent rule it is specified that an asset can be of three different types. From these two rules it is easy to understand that the specification of the grammar immediately reflects the structure of the class diagram provided in Fig. 2.

```
 5⊖Model:
 6       'emulation' name=ID '{' assets+=Asset* '}';
 7
 8⊖Asset:
 9       Node | NetworkDevice | NetworkConnection;
10
11⊖Node:
12       GenericVM | ExternalDevice;
13
14⊖GenericVM:
15       CustomVM | 'VM' name=ID '{' properties += VMProperty* '}';
16
17⊖VMProperty:
18       VMHardwareProperty ';' |
19       VMSoftwareProperty ';' |
20       VMVulnerability ';';
```

Fig. 3. Fragment of the CTL grammar definition: scenario's basic components.

Figure 4 shows another fragment of the grammar specification necessary to define the connection between the different components of the system.

```
71⊖NetCon:
72      'VM' id1=[GenericVM] 'is' 'connected' 'to' 'switch' id2=[Switch]
73          'with' 'IP' ip=IPAddress 'via' 'port' 'name' port=INT
74          'and' 'MAC' 'address' 'name' mac=ID ';' |
75      'Router' id=[Router] 'is' 'connected' 'to' 'subnet' name=ID ';' |
76      'Router' id=[Router] 'is' 'connected' 'to' 'ext' ';' |
77      'VM' id=[GenericVM] 'has' 'the' ip=IPAddress ';';
```

Fig. 4. Fragment of the CTL grammar definition: network connections.

After creating all the artefacts deriving from the grammar, Xtext automatically generates a textual editor and a parser. In Fig. 5, we provide an example of a model defined with CTL. In particular, we modeled a scenario where there are two virtual machines: one representing a LAMP system with a web application exposed to a SQL injection vulnerability and the other used by a client to browse the web application. The parser performs syntax validation based on the grammar of the language. For example, thanks to the definition of network connections in terms of cross references between nodes, the parser is able to check that the VMs on the network have already been defined as nodes.

```
emulation emulation_scenario {
    VM server {
        RAM_size: 16 GB;
        CPU_speed: 2.5 GHz;
        Disk_size: 250 GB;
        Web_server: "Apache HTTP Server";
        Operating_System: "Linux";
        Database: "MySQL";
        Programming_language: "PHP"
        Web_application: "https://www.homebanking.com";
        Vulnerability SQLi: "SQL injection";
    }
    VM client {
        Operating_System: "Ubuntu";
        Web_browser: "Mozilla Firefox";
    }

    Network_connection {
        VM server has this public IP ...
        ...
    }
}
```

Fig. 5. Xtext editor for the client/server example.

4.3 CTL Model Validation

To check model correctness in terms of satisfiability of given syntactic and semantic rules expressing relations that must exist among elements of the model, the Xtext framework provides an embedded validator. It allows to perform static analysis and get informative feedback while typing.

The definition of a list of static properties that must hold on a CTL model is still under development. However, at the moment we have started to define syntactic rules able to guarantee simple network configuration properties such as: absence of isolated nodes, correct definition of subnets, and absence of IP address duplication.

To give a hint of such rules, we report in the following an example of two validation rules written as OCL rules:

- the first rule checks the validity of IP addresses, i.e., that an IP address has valid octets values in the 0–255 range:
  Context IPAddress inv:
  (self.octect1 >= 0 and self.octect1 <= 255) and
  (self.octect2 >= 0 and self.octect2 <= 255) and
  (self.octect3 >= 0 and self.octect3 <= 255) and
  (self.octect4 >= 0 and self.octect4 <= 255)
- the second rule checks that the IP address of a VM that has been specified as public does not fall in the private IP address range (note that the standard RFC 1918 reserves the following three subnets to private addresses: 10.0.0.0/8, 172.16.0.0/12, 192.168.0.0/16):
  Context IPAddress inv:
  value='public' implies ((octect1 <> 10) and (octect1 <> 172 and
  forAll (ip : IPAddress | ip.octect2 < 16 or ip.octect2 > 31))
  and (octect1 <> 192 and octect2 <> 168))

4.4   From CTL Models to Heat Templates

The translation from CTL to HEAT cannot be treated just as a one-to-one mapping from the CTL concepts, described as XML tags and properties in the input file, to HEAT parameters and resources, specified in the output YAML template file.

The CTL model covers only a subset of resource types that will be necessary to actually deploy the scenario. Some default objects dealing with the internal OpenStack representation of the network, like for instance the outbound network and routers, or floating IPs, are included in the output YAML file without being specified in the input CTL file. In this case, those special objects will be defined by default within the overall OpenStack infrastructure and referenced in the YAML template by their unique ID (UUID).

More specifically, the process of translating the cyber security scenario from XML to HEAT consists of the following steps:

1. Create an object of type *OS::Neutron::Router* associated to the public network to give Internet access.
2. Create an object of type *OS::Neutron::RouterInterface* to connect to the public network the router created at the previous step.
3. For each *customVM* object in the input XML file, specify an object of type *OS::Nova::Server* in the resources section of the HOT output template file. Each server must be characterized by a name, an image, a flavor, and a key, as specified in the XML file.
4. For each network associated to a *customVM* in the XML file:
   (a) Create a new resource of type *OS::Neutron::Net* defining a new virtual network.
   (b) Define an object *OS::Neutron::Subnet* defining a specific subnet associated to the network and to the gateway listed among the properties.
   (c) Create an object of type *OS::Neutron::Port* defining a network interface that will connect the VM/server to a particular network and subnet. A security group will be included, specifying the operations and protocols allowed in the network.
   (d) Associate the port created in the previous step to the VM created at step 3 by adding an item *-port* in the *networks* field of the server object properties.
   (e) If the scenario requires the VM to be reachable from outside the network, create an object of type *OS::Neutron::FloatingIP* to associate an Open-Stack Floating IP address to a specific port and to the public network by means of the virtual router created at step 1.

The compiling procedure described above creates a HOT template file ready to be deployed in OpenStack by the HEAT engine.

In the following, as an example, we provide both a fragment of the XML file (Code 1.3) containing the definition of the client virtual machine the client/server example with a SQL injection vulnerability of Fig. 5, and a fragment of the resulting HOT template (Code 1.4).

Code 1.3. XML input file - Specification of a VM

```xml
<CustomVM name="vm2">
    <ram val="2048"></ram>
    <vcpus val="1"></vcpus>
    <disk val="80"></disk>
    <image name="img2" val="Ubuntu-16.04-LTS-Xenial-Xerus"></image>
    <Network idref="net2" />
</CustomVM>
<Networks>
    <Network id="net2" >
        <gateway name="gateway2" val="10.10.10.1"></gateway>
        <cidr name="cidr2" val="10.10.10.0/24"></cidr>
    </Network>
</Networks>
```

In the HOT template, for the sake of brevity, we omitted the details of the *parameters* section containing the references to objects that have already been created in OpenStack and are used in the *resources* section. The commands *get_param* and *get_resource*, get the value of the indicated object specified in the *parameters* and in the *resources* sections, respectively.

Code 1.4. HEAT Orchestration Template - Definition of the client VM

```yaml
parameters:
  [...]
resources:
  vm2:
    properties:
      flavor: get_param: flavor-vm2
      image: get_param: img2
      key_name: get_param: key2
      name: Threat-Arrest_vm2
      networks:
      - port: get_resource: Threat-Arrest_vm2_portnet2
    type: OS::Nova::Server

  vm2_floating_ip:
    properties:
      floating_network_id: get_param: public_net1
      port_id: get_resource: vm1_portnet1
    type: OS::Neutron::FloatingIP

  vm2_portnet1:
    properties:
      fixed_ips:
      - subnet_id: get_resource: private_subnetnet2
      network_id: get_resource: private_net2
      security_groups:
      - get_param: secgroup2
    type: OS::Neutron::Port

  private_net2:
    properties:
      name: private_net2
    type: OS::Neutron::Net

  private_subnetnet2:
    properties:
      cidr: get_param: cidr2
      gateway_ip: get_param: gateway2
      network_id: get_resource: private_net2
    type: OS::Neutron::Subnet

  router_interfacenet2:
    properties:
```

```
    router_id: get_resource: router_net2
    subnet_id: get_resource: private_subnetnet2
    type: OS::Neutron::RouterInterface

router_net2:
  properties:
    external_gateway_info:
      network: get_param: public_net2
    type: OS::Neutron::Router
```

In Code 1.4, the details specific to the scenario are defined by using the following parameters:

- *cidr2, gateway2:* the CIDR and the gateway as specified in the XML input file;
- *flavor-vm2:* the flavor describing the specific properties of a VM (memory and disk size, virtual CPUs, ...). If needed, flavors are dynamically created using OpenStack APIs during the translation process, starting from the values specified in the XML file, and referenced as parameters;
- *public_net2:* the reference to the outbound network connected to the Internet. This network is used by the system to give access to Internet to the client VM, and is connected to the VM virtual network by a virtual router defined in the *resources* section. Figure 6, extracted from the OpenStack Horizon interface, shows the two networks created by the YAML template connecting the VM and the virtual router.

Fig. 6. Example of network deployed by Heat in OpenStack

5 Related Work

Interest in cyber ranges is increasing and a number of research projects and papers have been published recently. The National Cyber Range (NCR) program is guided by the Defence Advanced Research Project Agency (DARPA) in USA, and it has the goal to create general purpose test ranges where cyber technologies or architectures can be evaluated in the same way other test systems support the test and diagnostics of electronic and electro-mechanical devices [10]. The supported framework should address different issues, such as scalability, security, easy reconfiguration to rapidly test large scale cyber systems [17].

A technique for model based verification for cyber range scenario has been presented in [9] enabling the detection of misconfiguration and then reducing costs and time to the deployment. The technique relies on an Common Cyber Environment Representation (CCER) ontology and a method for the specification of verification rules and corresponding error messages. A more didactic approach has been described in [18], where a Security Scenario Generator has been designed to automatically build random scenarios where a number of VMs can interact considering different use-cases, such as correct configuration of networks, vulnerable networks to be tested, till more complex Capture The Flag challenges. The framework has been used for teaching purposes and to organize national CTF competitions.

However, most existing cyber challenge platforms are either restricted to use by government only or are too expensive to be purchased and maintained by high schools and universities. Born out of the idea of creating a cyber challenge platform usable at the educational level in schools, the University of Rhode Island Open Cyber Challenge Platform (OCCP) [6] is a project supported by the U.S. National Science Foundation which proposes to develop a cyber challenge platform with low cost hardware requirements. The OCCP is a configurable and virtual controlled teaching environment that is freely distributed to high schools and colleges. In order to bridge together government, industry and academia knowledge to advance the foundation of cyber science in the context of Army networks, in 2013 the U.S. Army Research Laboratory (ARL) established a Cyber Security Collaborative Research Alliance (CSCRA) [3] led by Pennsylvania State University. The CSCRA is expected to be applicable to a broad array of Army domains and applications, and its ultimate goal is to enhance cyber threat detection, autonomous planning and control of cyber maneuvers, and adaptive reasoning for deception in complex, adversarial, and uncertain environments. One of the most widely used training and simulation platform is Cyberbit Range [4], which provides a hyper-realistic training environment and advanced training tools including highly customizable dynamic range modeling and simulated attack scenarios, whilst the KYPO platform [5] is an innovative cyber range solution developed using a requirements-driven development process. Specifically, it was designated as a flexible and scalable system based on cloud platforms OpenNebula and OpenStack with the goal to guarantee cost-effective and time-efficient simulation, as well as provide transparent access to the environment itself. Indeed, the proposed platform is offered as a service with access through a web browser, so it inherits the benefits deriving from PaaS, such as efficiency, agility and productivity. Moreover, it supports multiple use cases and provides monitoring infrastructure for experiments.

6   Conclusion and Future Work

In this paper, we presented some results of our ongoing research work towards the definition of a cyber security training environment. To this aim, we defined a language to specify cyber range scenarios and to automatically build an environment, based on the OpenStack platform, to deploy and emulate such scenarios. Our work is at a preliminary stage and we plan to extend and improve it in several directions.

First, we need to provide an alternative way to future trainees to access the training scenario once it has been deployed. Currently, we allow user to access the VMs by means of SSH or by creating a virtual cloud desktop using Apache Guacamole, but we would like to provide a more interactive dashboard. Then, we want to exploit the validation mechanism of Xtext to check and guarantee other semantic properties. We also want to supply the CTL with a formal semantics and to improve the verification mechanism on CTL models. Finally, in order to help trainers to define different configurations, we would like to automatize the generation of different scenarios based on a list of common threats or attacks, such as the OWASP Top 10, addressing the most impactful web application security risks currently faced by organizations.

Acknowledgment. This work has been partly funded by the European Union's Horizon 2020 research and innovation programme under the project THREAT-ARREST (Grant Agreement No. 786890).

References

1. Cisco Cyber Range. https://www.cisco.com/c/dam/en_us/about/doing_business/legal/service_descriptions/docs/asf-cyber-range-large.pdf?dtid=osscdc000283
2. Civil Cyber Range Platform for a novel approach to cybersecurity threats simulation and professional training. https://cyberwiser.eu/
3. Cyber Security Research Alliance. https://www.arl.army.mil/www/default.cfm?page=1417
4. Cyberbit Range. https://www.cyberbit.com/solutions/cyber-range/platform/
5. KYPO Cyber Range. https://www.kypo.cz/en
6. Open Cyber Challenge Platform. https://opencyberchallenge.net/
7. Ponemon Institute: 2016 cost of cyber crime study & the risk of business innovation (2016). https://www.ponemon.org/local/upload/file/2016%20HPE%20CCC%20GLOBAL%20REPORT%20FINAL%203.pdf
8. Bettini, L.: Implementing Domain Specific Languages with Xtext and Xtend, 2nd edn. Packt Publishing, Birmingham (2016)
9. Damodaran, S.K., Tidmarsh, D.: Model based verification of cyber range event environments. In: Proceedings of the Modeling and Simulation of Complexity in Intelligent, Adaptive and Autonomous Systems 2016 (MSCIAAS 2016) and Space Simulation for Planetary Space Exploration (SPACE 2016), MSCIAAS 2016, Society for Computer Simulation International, San Diego, CA, USA, pp. 5:1–5:8 (2016). http://dl.acm.org/citation.cfm?id=2962664.2962669
10. Ferguson, B., Tall, A., Olsen, D.: National cyber range overview. In: 2014 IEEE Military Communications Conference, pp. 123–128, October 2014. https://doi.org/10.1109/MILCOM.2014.27
11. Gargantini, A., Riccobene, E., Scandurra, P.: A semantic framework for metamodel-based languages (2009). https://doi.org/10.1007/s10515-009-0053-0

12. Kleppe, A.: A language description is more than a metamodel. In: Fourth International Workshop on Software Language Engineering, vol. 1. megaplanet. org (2007)
13. OpenStack: Openstack docs: openstack resource types (2018), https://docs. openstack.org/heat/stein/template_guide/openstack.html
14. OpenStack: Heat orchestration template (HOT) guide (2019). https://docs. openstack.org/heat/latest/template_guide/hot_guide.html
15. OpenStack: Open source software for creating private and public clouds (2019). https://www.openstack.org/
16. Pham, C., Tang, D., Chinen, K., Beuran, R.: CyRIS: a cyber range instantiation system for facilitating security training. In: SoICT (2016)
17. Pridmore, L., Lardieri, P., Hollister, .R.: National Cyber Range (NCR) automated test tools: implications and application to network-centric support tools. In: 2010 IEEE AUTOTESTCON, pp. 1–4, September 2010. https://doi.org/10. 1109/AUTEST.2010.5613581
18. Schreuders, Z.C., Shaw, T., Shan-A-Khuda, M., Ravichandran, G., Keighley, J., Ordean, M.: Security scenario generator (SecGen): a framework for generating randomly vulnerable rich-scenario VMs for learning computer security and hosting CTF events. In: 2017 USENIX Workshop on Advances in Security Education ASE 17. USENIX Association, Vancouver (2017). https://www.usenix.org/conference/ ase17/workshop-program/presentation/schreuders
19. Steinberg, D., Budinsky, F., Paternostro, M., Merks, E.: EMF: Eclipse Modeling Framework, 2nd edn. Addison-Wesley Professional, Boston (2008)

Difficult XSS Code Patterns for Static Code Analysis Tools

Felix Schuckert[1,2]([✉]), Basel Katt[2], and Hanno Langweg[1,2]

[1] Department of Computer Science, HTWG Konstanz,
Alfred-Wachtel-Straße 8, 78462 Konstanz, Germany
{felix.schuckert,hanno.langweg}@htwg-konstanz.de
[2] Department of Information Security and Communication Technology,
Faculty of Information Technology and Electrical Engineering,
NTNU, Norwegian University of Science and Technology,
Teknologivegen 22, 2815 Gjøvik, Norway
{felix.m.schuckert,basel.katt,hanno.langweg}@ntnu.no

Abstract. We present source code patterns that are difficult for modern static code analysis tools. Our study comprises 50 different open source projects in both a vulnerable and a fixed version for XSS vulnerabilities reported with CVE IDs over a period of seven years. We used three commercial and two open source static code analysis tools. Based on the reported vulnerabilities we discovered code patterns that appear to be difficult to classify by static analysis. The results show that code analysis tools are helpful, but still have problems with specific source code patterns. These patterns should be a focus in training for developers.

Keywords: Static code analysis · Source code patterns · Cross site scripting · Vulnerabilities · PHP

1 Introduction

Static code analysis tools exist for a long time now. Nevertheless, looking into OWASP top 10 and CWE top 25 lists shows that the same vulnerability types occur all the time. Are modern static code analysis tools sufficient to detect recent vulnerabilities which occurred in recent years? Another problem might be that the tools have too many false positive reports that discourage developers from using them? Are there patterns that are not detectable with state of the art static code analysis tools? False positives are vulnerability reports that are actually no vulnerabilities. Accordingly, these patterns should either not be mitigated by developers or should be taught to developers that they know what are critical parts for manual security reviews. Our goal of this study is to find problems and limitations of static code analysis tools. Is it possible to create small source code samples which have a high probability to create false positive or false negative reports? False negatives are vulnerabilities that are not reported by the tool. We focus on cross site scripting vulnerabilities because it is

© Springer Nature Switzerland AG 2020
A. P. Fournaris et al. (Eds.): ESORICS 2019 Workshops, LNCS 11981, pp. 123–139, 2020.
https://doi.org/10.1007/978-3-030-42051-2_9

a widespread vulnerability. Source code from open source projects is used to find false positives and false negatives. These reports are then reviewed to find the corresponding problematic source code patterns. These patterns are evaluated using the initial static code analysis tools and two open source tools.

2   Related Work

Many research projects exist that evaluate static code analysers. Goseva-Popstojanova and Perhinschi [14] evaluated three commercial static code analysis tools. They calculated a G-score that used the detection and the false positive rate. This score was used to compare the different static code analysis tools. They scanned the Juliet database [1] to evaluate different permutations of security issues. They used three open source projects with known vulnerabilities for their evaluation. These projects were chosen based on CVE reports. The research showed that none of the tools detected all security issues. They stated that relying only on static code analysis for detecting security vulnerabilities will leave a large number of vulnerabilities undiscovered (false negatives). Our research also uses open source projects with known vulnerabilities. Instead of just scanning these projects to evaluate the tools, we identified different source code patterns based on the source code that are problematic for the tools.

Delaitre et al. [12] researched about effectiveness measurement from static code analysis tools based on significance, ground truth and relevance metrics. They used three different types of source code for their data set. The production software type did not have any known security vulnerabilities. Then they used source code related to CVE reports as their second type. Their last type was small samples where small source code samples were created specifically. They used these data sets to evaluate 14 static code analysis tools and presented the results from four tools. The results showed that the tools detect specific issues, but not a single tool detected all kinds of issues. Our work has very similar results. None of our evaluated tools could detect all vulnerabilities from our created data sets.

The research from Díaz and Bermejo [13] evaluated different open source and commercial static code analysis tools. They focused on the detection rate and the false positive rate. They used the SAMATE database to evaluate the tools. From the SAMATE database they used the test suite 45 that contains security vulnerabilities and the test suite 46 that has the vulnerabilities fixed. For the evaluation the F-measure from Van Rijsbergen [17] was calculated.

Another article from AlBreiki and Mahmoud [10] evaluated three open source tools. The tools have different approaches. One tool analyzes source code (OWASP Yasca), the next one analyzes byte-code (FindBugs) and the last one analyzes binary code (Microsoft Code Analysis Tool .NET). The evaluation test cases are based on top security issues from OWASP/CWE/SANS. False positives were not included in the evaluation. Basso et al. [11] researched about how software fault injection will affect static code analysis tools. They showed that software fault injection affects the detection rate of the tested static code analysis tools. Primarily, it created false positive reports and the existing vulnerabilities were not detected. Zhioua et al. [18] evaluated four static code analysis tools. They described how security issues and security properties are related to each other. Their focus is more on how the tools detect vulnerabilities and what techniques the tools use. Khare et al. [15] also evaluated static code analysis tools. Their approach was based on large samples with more than 10 million lines of code. Their test showed that less than 10% of vulnerabilities were detected. Even some simple vulnerabilities were not detected.

3 Methodology

We use multiple static code analysis tools to find and evaluate problematic source code patterns. Problematic patterns result in false negative and false positive reports. This section provides background knowledge, explains what commercial and open source static code analysis tools were chosen and how the problematic patterns are examined.

3.1 Background

False negative (FN) reports mean that a tool did not report a vulnerability that actually exists. To find source code patterns that create such false negative reports, initial source code is required that contains such patterns. In contrast false positive (FP) reports mean that a tool reports a vulnerability that actually is no vulnerability. To find such patterns, source code is required that might look like there is a vulnerability, but one can be sure that the program is secure.

3.2 Selected Static Code Analysis Tools and Data Set

We selected three commercial static code analysis tools. These tools are called Tool A, Tool B and Tool C. Our licences do not allow to publish the name of the tools. Our primary goal is not to evaluate the tools against each other. Instead we want to identify source code patterns that are problematic for state of the art static code analysis tools. All of these tools support data flow analysis and use it for their analysis. The tools were all up to date when the scans were started in September 2018.

For the evaluation of specific patterns two open source static code analysis tools (Exakat [4] and Sonarcloud [9]) were added. To find relevant open source static code analysis tools a collection of open source static code analysis tools [2] was reviewed. First of all, all tools that do not scan for security issues or are not maintained anymore (last update >1 year) were filtered out. The remaining tools were checked, if they can detect cross site scripting vulnerabilities. Only Exakat and Sonarcloud were found to be suitable for the validation.

We used the CVE data set from the work [16]. These samples are source code from open source projects that are related to CVE reports from 2010 until 2016 (seven years) focusing on cross site scripting vulnerabilities. Those reports are old enough to provide the static code analysis tool developers enough time to adapt their algorithms. We use the corresponding vulnerable and fixed versions. The data set contains 50 vulnerable and 50 fixed samples.

3.3 Vulnerability Analysis

The vulnerability analysis process is shown in Fig. 1. The commercial tools are used to scan the related source code. Because of previous investigation we already know where the corresponding sinks are located. This information is used to **automatically check** if the vulnerability is not found (false negative) or if the fixed version still is reported as a vulnerability (false positive). Because our previous work was a manual review, the false positive and false negative reports are checked if these are really false positive or false negative reports. After that check all interesting samples are identified and manually reviewed to find the problematic source code patterns.

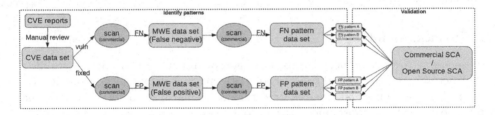

Fig. 1. XSS vulnerability analysis process.

The **manual review** is done by checking the data flow from the source to the corresponding sink. A source is a function or method where data is provided by a user. Such data can be potentially dangerous if it reaches critical functions. Such critical functions are called sinks. It is reviewed for code patterns which might be problematic for static code analysis tools. Because each of the reviewed samples are either a false positive or a false negative report, there must be something in the data flow which might interrupt the data flow algorithm or confuses the static code analysis algorithm. Based on the review results a minimal working example (MWE) data set is created that contains simple source code samples that imitate the vulnerabilities. The corresponding sink is noted down for further scans. To ensure that the samples are still vulnerable, exploits are written that result in a cross site scripting vulnerability.

The next step is to check if problematic source code patterns are found. The simple samples are **scanned again** by the three commercial static code analysis tools. Again the results can be automatically checked because the corresponding sinks are known. All simple samples that created false positive and false negative reports are then designated as problematic patterns for static code analysis tools. These samples are in the FN pattern and FP pattern data set. The results from the scans and the identified problematic patterns are presented in this article.

Because these samples can contain multiple source code patterns at once, further scans are required to **validate** which of these patterns are problematic. For each source code pattern a specific sample is created that just contains that pattern. These samples are scanned by the commercial and open source tools again to evaluate which of these patterns are problematic.

4   Static Code Analysis Results

As described in the previous chapter, our data set for the first scan contains source code of 50 vulnerable and 50 fixed projects. For this work that data set is labeled as "CVE data set" because it is the source code related to CVE reports. Accordingly, each tool scanned 100 projects. For our work only false positive and false negative reports are important. Figure 2 shows how many false positive and false negative reports the three tools issued on the CVE data set. It shows that tool C has a lot more false positive reports but it has the lowest false negative reports. This is an issue static code analysis tools have, if they want to detect more vulnerabilities this usually also means more false positive reports. Accordingly, tool C is more noisy than tools A and B. Investigating the false reports of tool C shows that common sanitization methods like *htmlspecialchars()* are reported as a possible cross site scripting vulnerability. Tool C rates reports with such sanitization functions not as critical as without such functions. Nevertheless, if such functions are used in the correct context, they are sufficient to prevent cross site scripting attacks. Depending on the context it also might not be sufficient. The tools have to check the context of the sink to successfully decide if it is a vulnerability or not. In the CVE data set we assume all of the fixed samples use sufficient sanitization methods for their context. Table 1 shows the computed metrics of the results. As stated, tool C has a higher probability of a false alarm (false report). If we look into these metrics the recall rate indicates how many of the existing vulnerabilities will be reported. Only one tool is below 50%. Nevertheless, there are still vulnerabilities

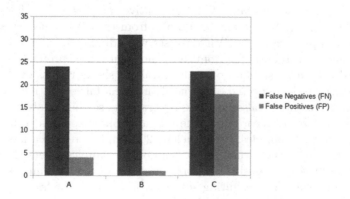

Fig. 2. False positive and false negatives reports on the CVE data set.

Table 1. Overview of metrics for the commercial tools.

Metric	Tool A	Tool B	Tool C
Number of projects	50	50	50
True Positive	26	19	27
False Negative	24	31	23
Number of fixed	50	50	50
True Negative	46	49	32
False Positive	4	1	18
Accuracy	72%	68%	59%
Recall	52%	38%	54%
False Alarm Prob.	8%	2%	36%

that are not detected by the other tools as well. Also the accuracy metric results are in a good range. The accuracy shows how accurate the reports are related to be a true positive or true negative report. These metrics are interesting to see, but for a comparison our data set does not contain enough samples. From the vulnerable CVE samples there were 35 samples that got from at least one tool a false negative report. In the fixed CVE samples, 18 samples produced a false positive report from at least one tool.

5   Minimal Working Example Data Set

We reviewed the source code of the false positive and false negative reports from the CVE data set. We created a data set that imitates the source code with minimal required lines of code. Some samples of the CVE data set contained the same relevant source code patterns. We only created one sample if the same source code patterns were found because the minimal working examples would be the same. In this work that data set is called minimal working example "MWE data set". The data set contains 25 false negative samples and 12 false positive samples. Accordingly, 13 vulnerable samples from the CVE data set and 6 out of the fixed samples from the CVE data set were duplicates. A reason for this was that, some CVE reports are from the same open source project but different versions and they used similar code parts. Table 2 shows results of the scan on the samples where the expected outcome should be a false negative report. Five samples did not create a false negative report because the count of false negative reports were zero. Accordingly, the relevant source code patterns were not examined for these 5 samples. Nevertheless, 20 samples created a false negative report. Table 3 shows the results of the scan of the samples where the expected outcome should be false positive reports. Ten out of twelve samples provoked false positive reports. The resulting source code patterns for false positive and false negative reports are presented in Sect. 7.

Table 2. Scan results from false negative MWE data set with 25 samples.

CVE related	Patterns	Tool A	Tool B	Tool C	Count of FN	Type
CVE-2015-7777	$_SERVER	✓	FN	✓	1	Reflected
CVE-2014-3544	Inheritance DB Implementation Class variable assignment by string SQL DAO List assignment - list()	FN	FN	FN	3	Stored
CVE-2015-1347	-	✓	✓	✓	0	Reflected
CVE-2011-2938	Unc. function call - call_user_func_array Unserialize	FN	FN	FN	3	Stored
CVE-2015-1562	-	✓	✓	✓	0	Reflected
CVE-2012-2331	*Foreach* on super global variable Scope global Return value by reference	✓	FN	✓	1	Reflected
CVE-2012-5608	Sink print_r	FN	FN	✓	2	Reflected
CVE-2013-7275	Template XML file	FN	FN	FN	3	Reflected
CVE-2014-3774	-	✓	✓	✓	0	Reflected
CVE-2014-4954	DB wrapper List assignment - list()	FN	FN	FN	3	Stored
CVE-2014-9270	SQL DAO	✓	FN	✓	1	Stored
CVE-2015-5076	-	✓	✓	✓	0	Reflected
CVE-2011-3358	Unc. function call - call_user_func_array	FN	FN	FN	3	Reflected
CVE-2012-5339	DB Source Unc. function call - string	✓	FN	FN	2	Stored
CVE-2011-4814	Conditional sanitiziation - disabled	✓	FN	✓	1	Reflected
CVE-2013-1937	Input valid type check	FN	FN	✓	2	Reflected
CVE-2012-2129	Keyword global	FN	FN	✓	2	Reflected
CVE-2012-4395	Template output buffering	FN	FN	FN	3	Reflected
CVE-2014-9219	Input valid type check	FN	FN	✓	2	Reflected
CVE-2015-7348	Replacement	✓	FN	✓	1	Reflected
CVE-2014-9271	Sink - header	FN	FN	FN	3	Stored
CVE-2013-0807	-	✓	✓	✓	0	Reflected
CVE-2014-9281	Stripslashes	✓	FN	✓	1	Reflected
CVE-2014-9269	$_COOKIE Stripslashes	✓	FN	✓	1	Reflected
CVE-2012-5163	Conditional sanitization - disabled	FN	FN	✓	2	Reflected
Summary (FN)		12	20	10		

6   Stored Cross Site Scripting

Cross site scripting vulnerabilities are categorized into reflected and stored. Static code analysis tool can simply find reflected cross site scripting vulnerability by doing a data flow analysis and see if tainted data will reach a possible sink. Tainted data is data can be manipulated by the user/attacker. Stored cross site scripting is a bit more difficult to be successfully detected.

Table 3. Scan results from false positive MWE data set with 12 samples.

CVE related	Patterns	Tool A	Tool B	Tool C	Count of FP	Type
CVE-2013-0201	Standard - specialchars	✓	✓	FP	1	Reflected
CVE-2011-4814	Custom - preg_replace	FP	✓	FP	2	Reflected
CVE-2014-8352	Custom - reset if not valid	✓	FP	FP	2	Reflected
CVE-2013-0275	Standard - specialchars	✓	✓	FP	1	Reflected
CVE-2014-9571	Standard - specialchars Custom - preg_replace	✓	✓	FP	1	Reflected
CVE-2015-5356	Standard - htmlentities	✓	✓	FP	1	Reflected
CVE-2012-5163	Library - HTMLPurifier	✓	✓	FP	1	Reflected
CVE-2011-2938	-	✓	✓	✓	0	Stored
CVE-2014-9269	-	✓	✓	✓	0	Reflected
CVE-2014-2570	Standard - htmlentities	✓	✓	FP	1	Reflected
CVE-2013-4880	Standard - specialchars	✓	✓	FP	1	Reflected
CVE-2011-3371	Standard - specialchars	✓	✓	FP	1	Reflected
Summary (FN)		1	1	10		

Figure 3 shows an overview of stored cross site scripting. It is split into two main parts. The insert part (1, 2, 3) uses a common source like $_GET. Then a SQL statement will be created that will store the tainted data in the database. In another source code location a database source exists. These are functions that allow getting data from a database. A SQL statement will get the tainted data out of the database. Then it will be shown on a webpage. If no sanitization is used, a stored cross site scripting vulnerability would exist. As seen in Fig. 3, sanitization can be done in two different steps, (2) and (6). Either before inserting tainted data it can be sanitized (2) or it can be sanitized before the data will be displayed on the webpage (6). Static code analysis tools have to know the relation between the SQL statements (3) and (5) to successfully detect stored cross site scripting vulnerabilities without any false reports.

Samples were created to check if the tools can detect the different scenarios. Table 4 shows the result of the scans on the samples. The two open source tools were tested as well. Tool B and the open source tools did not even detect the simple stored cross site scripting sample, and consequently they will not report

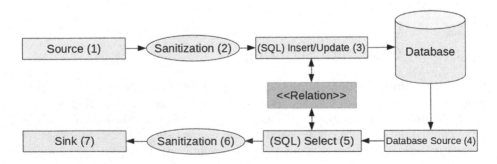

Fig. 3. Overview of an stored XSS vulnerability.

any vulnerabilities in the fixed versions. Tool A detects all samples correctly. Accordingly, it knows the relations between the INSERT and SELECT SQL statements. Tool C does at least detect the sample where the sanitization happens before the data reaches a sink. To detect stored cross site scripting, the tools have to define database functions as a possible sources for tainted data. To reduce false positive reports, the relation between the SQL statements are important.

Table 4. Scan results on the different stored and reflected XSS samples.

False negative pattern	Tool A	Tool B	Tool C	Exakat	Sonarcloud
Reflected XSS sample	✓	✓	✓	✓	✓
Stored XSS vulnerable	✓	FN	✓	FN	FN
Stored XSS sanitization insert (2)	✓	✓	FP	✓	✓
Stored XSS sanitization view (6)	✓	✓	✓	✓	✓

7   Difficult Source Code Patterns

The review process required to look for suspected source code patterns which might be problematic for static code analysis tools. This section describes what suspected source code patterns were used to create the MWE data set. Only patterns are presented which are related to samples which created false positive or false negative reports.

7.1   Sources

Three sources were considered to be problematic for static code analysis tools.

$_SERVER. The super global variable $_SERVER is a special variable that contains some entries that are just controllable by the server. Nevertheless, it also has some entries which can be modified by the users. In our data $_SERVER['PHP_SELF'] was used. This can be easily modified by inserting the payload in the url.

Foreach on Super Global Variable. Most samples used super global variables by directly accessing the required key. For example, $_GET['id'] is a commonly seen source. One sample did not access them directly instead it used a *foreach* loop to access all keys with the corresponding values.

$_COOKIE. One sample in our data set had the cookies as source. It uses the super global variable $_COOKIE.

7.2   Stored XSS Sources

As already described in Sect. 6 stored cross site scripting vulnerabilities have two different sources. This section focus on the database sources and what source code patterns occurred in the data set.

Inheritance DB Implementation. One sample used an inheritance database implementation. That implementation does execute the query depending on the inherited database.

SQL DAO. Two samples used a database access object (DAO). Such an object stores the relevant information as class variables. It provides a function to create a SQL statement using the class variables as parameters.

DB Wrapper. One sample used an database wrapper object. It wrapped the database object which is used to access the database. The wrapped object is depending on the configuration of the project. Different databases require different database objects. This samples used a *switch case* based on a String variable to choose the database implementation. The database wrapper is defined as a global variable.

7.3   Data Flow

The main focus of this research is about source code patterns that might interrupt or confuse the data flow analysis. Nowadays the sources and sinks are well known. Accordingly, not many specific source or sinks are identified as problematic source code patterns. It is getting difficult for static code analysis tools to follow all kinds of data flows that are possible. This section will describe different source code patterns that cause problems for our evaluated static code analysis tools.

Unconventionally Function Call. The programming language PHP offers a lot of different features. One feature is to call functions in a unconventional way using other functions. Such functions allow to call a function that might not be known at the implementation time. In our CVE data set, multiple function call via the function *call_user_func_array* were found. Calling a function using a string variable was found in our data set as well. (E.g. *$functionName($param1, $param2)*.)

Global Variables. Global variables are very common in programming language. Also PHP allows to define global variables. This happens either by simply defining a variable in a PHP file without being inside a scope like a function or class. Another possibility is by defining a variable using the *global* keyword. This can be used inside a scope and is still a global variable.

Return Value by Reference. In the programming language C it is common to use function parameters to return values. This requires a copy by reference parameter. PHP also allows to pass a reference as a parameter. In our data set one samples used such copy by reference to pass the tainted data.

List Assignment. Another language concept from PHP allows to assign values from a list to variables. This can either be used by using *[ ]* brackets or using the *list()* function.

Singleton. Another well known source code pattern is the singleton. This is a class where only one instance is allowed to exists. This is usually archived by defining the constructor of a class private. A static method has to be added which return the single instance of the class. This allows similar to a global variable to assign and access data from anywhere.

Class Variable Assignment by String. Similar to a function call, using a String allows PHP to assign class variables to determine which class variable should be used. For example, if you want to assign the class variable with the name *foo* you can use following code:

```
$varName = 'foo ';
$this->$varName = 'value ';
```

Unserialize. A serialization framework is already included in PHP. Before PHP 7.1 the function *unserilize()* was very dangerous to use. Since PHP 7.1, it does only allow to unserialize an array or boolean [6]. Nevertheless, this function can be used to assign tainted values to an array.

7.4   Failed Sanitization

Another way of provoking false negative report is by having functions that look like sanitization functions, but are insufficient or simply disabled by a conditional variable. The patterns we found in our samples are described in this section.

Conditional Sanitization - Disabled. Three samples had sanitization methods which were disabled by a conditional variable.

Input Valid Type Check. Three samples had a method to check, if the input is a valid type. In our sample it was checked, if the input is an array. This does not prevent any cross site scripting issues.

Replacement. One sample used *str_replace* for replacing some characters in the tainted string. This can also let the static code analysis tools think, that the input is sanitized.

Stripslashes. Two samples used the *stripslashes* function. This is insufficient depending on the context where the tainted data will be shown.

7.5 Sink

Two sinks were found which created a false negative report. One is the *header* function. Since PHP version 5.1.2, this is not considered as a sink anymore. Since then it was exploitable by inserting new line characters to do a header injection attack. Accordingly, this sink will not be relevant anymore as long up to date PHP is used. The other sink in the data set was the function *print_r* this is a function which prints data well formated. This is a exploitable sink for cross site scripting attacks.

7.6 Template

Modern web pages are commonly developed by using frameworks which are using templates. Different template implementations were found in our data set.

Template Output Buffering. Templates can be archived by using the output buffering feature. This allows to write the outputs from the template into a buffer. That buffer can be printed later on. This can result in a cross site scripting vulnerability.

Template XML File. Two samples used a XML file for the templates. A template file can be used to define multiple output pages. Each entry is put into a *CDATA* field. The PHP functions *simplexml_load_file* and *xpath* are used to get the related *CDATA* field. Then the *eval* function is used. This allows the templates to use variables like it was a normal PHP file. This also opens up more dangerous attacks as cross site scripting. But this is not the focus of this work.

7.7 Sanitization Methods

Some false positive reports were found. This section will describe what patterns were found that sanitized the tainted input sufficient, but the static code analysis tools reported a vulnerability.

Standard. There are some standard sanitization methods which can be used to sanitize the tainted input. These are just sufficient enough, if the context of the sink fits to the sanitization method. In our data set 7 samples used the *htmlspecialchars* and two samples used the *htmlentities* function.

Library - HTMLPurifier. One sample used the HTMLPurifier [5] library to defend any cross site scripting attacks. This prevents any attacks, but it is very difficult for static code analysis tools to know that such a library will sanitize against cross site scripting attacks.

Custom - preg_replace. One sample sanitized the input using the *preg_replace* function. This allows to successfully prevent any cross site scripting attacks. For example, all characters instead of numerics will be replaced with a whitespace. This prevents any cross site scripting attacks depending on the context. Static code analysis tools have to analyze the regular expression to validate, if the sanitization is sufficient.

Custom - Reset if Not Valid. A simple solution to prevent against any attacks is to only allow numbers as inputs. This can be archived by casting a variable to integer. In one sample, the solution was to use the *is_numeric* function from PHP to check, if the input is numeric. If it is not numeric, the input will be reset to an empty string. Static code analysis tool have to check the condition and see that only numbers will be passed. This is another difficulty for static code analysis tools.

7.8   Validation

The different patterns were identified. Without further scans there would be no validation which of these patterns are really problematic. Specific samples were created which contain only one problematic pattern. The corresponding samples can be found in a GitHub repository [8]. To validate that the sink and source we used in our samples are known by the tools a simple XSS sample was created. It uses *$_GET* as source and *echo* as sink. Table 4 shows that each tool detected the simple reflected XSS vulnerability.

Table 5 shows the result for the patterns which expected to create false positive reports. The two open source static code analysis tools were added to the validation. Two samples were problematic for each of the five static code analysis tools. Of 25 patterns, one (Input valid type check - string) did not result in any false negative reports. Accordingly, that pattern is not problematic for state of the art static code analysis tools. Six patterns were not problematic for the commercial tools. There are three patterns (SQL DAO, Inheritance DB Implementation, DB wrapper) related to a database source. As previous seen, the three tools Tool B, Exakat and Sonarcloud did not even detect samples with a simple database source. These tools cannot detect the more specific samples. The specified samples even tricked Tool A which performed best at the simple samples. Only Tool C detects two of these samples. This might be because they simply define database methods as possible sources without even checking if it is user provided data.

We looked up if our source code samples are already defined in the Common Weakness Enumeration [3] (CWE) data-base. For Cross Site Scripting there are no different patterns defined as CWE cases. We also looked up if our samples are present in the PHP Vulnerability Test Suite [7] from NIST. Table 5 shows that two of our samples were found in the test suite.

The false positive patterns were only five samples. Table 6 shows the scan results. The sample using the *HTMLPurifier* library did not create any false

Table 5. Scan results on the different false negative patterns.

False negative pattern	Tool A	Tool B	Tool C	Exakat	Sonarcloud	Count of FN	PHP Test suite
Class variable assignment by string	FN	✓	FN	FN	FN	4	-
SQL DAO	FN	FN	✓	FN	FN	4	-
Inheritance DB Implementation	FN	FN	✓	FN	FN	4	-
DB wrapper	FN	FN	FN	FN	FN	5	-
Conditional sanitization - disabled	✓	FN	✓	FN	FN	3	✓
Input valid type check - array	✓	FN	✓	FN	✓	2	-
Input valid type check - string	✓	✓	✓	✓	✓	0	-
Replacement	✓	FN	✓	✓	FN	2	-
Stripslashes	✓	FN	✓	✓	FN	2	-
Keyword global	✓	✓	✓	FN	FN	2	-
Scope global	✓	✓	✓	FN	FN	2	-
List assignment - brackets	✓	✓	✓	FN	FN	2	-
List assignment - list()	✓	✓	✓	FN	FN	3	-
Return value by reference	✓	FN	✓	FN	FN	3	-
Singleton	FN	✓	FN	FN	FN	4	-
Sink print_r	FN	✓	✓	✓	✓	1	-
$_COOKIE	✓	FN	✓	✓	✓	1	-
Foreach on super global variable	✓	✓	✓	FN	FN	2	-
$_SERVER	✓	FN	✓	FN	FN	3	-
Template output buffering	FN	✓	✓	FN	FN	3	-
Template XML file	FN	FN	FN	FN	FN	5	-
Unc. function call - call_user_func_array	✓	FN	FN	FN	FN	4	-
Unc. function call - call_user_func	✓	FN	FN	FN	FN	4	-
Unc. function call - string	✓	FN	FN	FN	FN	4	-
Unserialize	FN	FN	✓	FN	FN	4	✓
Summary (FN)	9	15	7	20	21		

positive reports. It may either be that the tools saw the library as a sanitization method or the data flow was interrupted by the library. As already stated tool C reports cross site scripting vulnerabilities at a lower risk even when sanitize functions are correctly used. The *Custom - reset if not valid* sample also reported a false positive in tool B. Our samples were not able to produce a false positive report for tool A.

If a combination of the different reports is used, only the two problematic patterns (DB wrapper, Template XML file) would not be detected. On the other hand, that would also increase the false positive rate.

8   Discussion

Our results show that two commercial tools in our data set had an above 50% recall rate. Accordingly, if all projects related to the data set would have used one of the two tools it could have prevented at least 50% of the vulnerabilities. The tools are useful for software developers to get an idea where a vulnerability might be. Nevertheless, one cannot be sure that scanned source code is free of vulnerabilities, even if the tools did not report any vulnerabilities. Each tool has advantages and disadvantages, and all of them have problems with specific source

Table 6. Scan results on the different false positive patterns.

False positive pattern	Tool A	Tool B	Tool C	Exakat	Sonarcloud	Count of FP
Standard - htmlentities	✓	✓	FP	✓	✓	1
Library - HTMLPurifier	✓	✓	✓	✓	✓	0
Standard - specialchars	✓	✓	FP	✓	✓	1
Custom - preg_replace	✓	✓	FP	FP	✓	2
Custom - reset if not valid	✓	FP	FP	FP	✓	3
Summary (FP)	0	1	4	2	0	

code patterns. Some patterns were difficult for all of our tested tools. We cannot specify special patterns that could be declared as problematic for static code analysis tools because of technical reasons. All of the tools have specific patterns that are problematic for them. Also the open source tools did not perform better on the source code patterns. The static code analysis tools also allow some configurations for specific projects. For example, custom sanitization methods can be declared. This can help in some of our patterns, but most of our patterns are more based on programming language features like specific *if* conditions.

Some patterns are not the best practice in programming. For example, using a return value by reference. Modern tools should detect such coding variants. Nevertheless, developers could prevent such unconventional programming methods to make the static code analysis tools results more precise. On the contrary, the use of templates is very common and useful. Tools have to be able to scan templates as well. In our data set there was one sample which used *tpl* files for templates. That sample was ignored because these templates use a custom language. Nevertheless, the samples using an output buffer that uses normal PHP files for the templates should be detected by all tools. The XML sample is bit more difficult because it uses a different file format and an *eval* function is used. Altogether developers can mitigate some patterns, but the static code analysis tools still can improve their algorithms.

Our researched patterns can be used as teaching examples. These are very interesting because these patterns are not detected by all static code analysis tools. Future work could research if today's learning examples cover such patterns. For example, do today's capture the flag events use such patterns or do they just use vulnerabilities that can be easily detected by static code analysis tools? Teaching the vulnerabilities that can be detected by tools is useful for basic understanding. Problematic patterns should be taught as advanced skill set. Our results show that focus on stored cross site scripting would be beneficial. Only one Tool A reported correctly the simple stored XSS samples and still had problems with our stored XSS source code patterns. Stored XSS is still difficult for state of the art static code analysis tools because of the required relation between the SQL statements.

Our data set is not very large, we used 50 samples with a vulnerable and patched version. The data set is not sufficient to compare tools against each other. It was sufficient to find some source code patterns which are problematic for static code analysis tools. Further research using a data set with other CVE reports might reveal more problematic patterns. Our patterns are also very specific to the static code analysis tools we used. For example, the *print_r* function which created a false negative report on tool A is probably just a missing sink in the analyzing part. It could be researched why these patterns are problematic for static code analysis tools. This would require access to the algorithm of the static code analysis tools or at least a documentation about how the algorithms work. We do not have access to such documentation. Our test was a black box test of static code analysis tools.

Our results do not reveal a lot of problematic patterns for false positive reports. One reason might be that tools have to detect a vulnerability correctly in the vulnerable sample. If they do not detect the vulnerability in the vulnerable version, it cannot create a false positive report in the patched version. This reduces the samples we could use for the review process.

9   Conclusion

Our goal was to find patterns that are problematic for static code analysis tools. The analysis of the source code from open source projects related to CVE reports revealed 19 source code patterns which led to false negative reports. The commercial tools provided better results than the open source tools. Nevertheless, the commercial tools also had problems with our identified patterns. Some can be mitigated by the software developers of the scanned projects. Others should be correctly detected by the static code analysis tools. The patterns can be used to improve static code analysis tools. For example, the patterns can be used as a test suite like the "PHP Vulnerability Test Suite" from SARD [7]. Overall, our results show that there are still a lot of source code patterns that are problematic for static code analysis tools. Developers who use static code analysis should know that there still might be undetectable vulnerabilities in their projects. Accordingly, developers should get taught those problematic patterns. Training of developers could be targeted to identifying and avoiding especially those patterns that are hard to flag by static analysis.

References

1. Juliet Test Suite. http://samate.nist.gov/SRD/testsuite.php
2. PHP static code analysis tools list. https://github.com/exakat/php-static-analysis-tools
3. CWE - Common Weakness Enumeration (2015). http://cwe.mitre.org/
4. Exakat (2019). https://www.exakat.io/
5. HTMLPurifier (2019). http://htmlpurifier.org/
6. PHP manual (2019). https://www.php.net/manual/de/function.unserialize.php
7. Software assurance reference dataset Testsuite (2019). https://samate.nist.gov/SARD/testsuite.php
8. Difficult source code patterns (2019). https://github.com/fschuckert/sca_patterns

9. Sonarcloud (2019). https://sonarcloud.io
10. AlBreiki, H.H., Mahmoud, Q.H.: Evaluation of static analysis tools for software security. In: 2014 10th International Conference on Innovations in Information Technology (IIT), pp. 93–98 (2014). https://doi.org/10.1109/INNOVATIONS.2014.6987569
11. Basso, T., Fernandes, P.C.S., Jino, M., Moraes, R.: Analysis of the effect of Java software faults on security vulnerabilities and their detection by commercial web vulnerability scanner tool. In: Proceedings of the International Conference on Dependable Systems and Networks, pp. 150–155 (2010). https://doi.org/10.1109/DSNW.2010.5542602
12. Delaitre, A., Stivalet, B., Fong, E., Okun, V.: Evaluating bug finders - test and measurement of static code analyzers. In: 2015 IEEE/ACM 1st International Workshop on Complex Faults and Failures in Large Software Systems (COUFLESS), pp. 14–20 (2015). https://doi.org/10.1109/COUFLESS.2015.10
13. Díaz, G., Bermejo, J.R.: Static analysis of source code security: assessment of tools against SAMATE tests. Inf. Softw. Technol. **55**(8), 1462–1476 (2013). https://doi.org/10.1016/j.infsof.2013.02.005. ISSN 09505849
14. Goseva-Popstojanova, K., Perhinschi, A.: On the capability of static code analysis to detect security vulnerabilities. Inf. Softw. Technol. **68**, 18–33 (2015). ISSN 09505849
15. Khare, S., Saraswat, S., Kumar, S.: Static program analysis of large embedded code base: an experience. In: Proceedings of the 4th India Software Engineering Conference 2011, pp. 99–102 (2011)
16. Schuckert, F., Hildner, M., Katt, B., Langweg, H.: Source code patterns of cross site scripting in PHP open source projects. In: Proceedings of the 11th Norwegian Information Security Conference (2018)
17. Van Rijsbergen, C.J.: Information Retrieval, 2nd edn. Butterworth, London (1979)
18. Zhioua, Z., Short, S., Roudier, Y.: Static code analysis for software security verification: problems and approaches. In: 2014 IEEE 38th International Computer Software and Applications Conference Workshops (COMPSACW), pp. 102–109 (2014)

An Open and Flexible CyberSecurity Training Laboratory in IT/OT Infrastructures

Umberto Morelli$^{(\boxtimes)}$ ⓘ, Lorenzo Nicolodi$^{(\boxtimes)}$ ⓘ, and Silvio Ranise$^{(\boxtimes)}$ ⓘ

Security & Trust, Fondazione Bruno Kessler, Via Sommarive 18,
38123 Trento, Italy
{umorelli,ranise}@fbk.eu, lo@microlab.red
https://st.fbk.eu

Abstract. There are significant concerns regarding the lack of proficient cybersecurity professionals with a background in both Information Technology (IT) and Operational Technology (OT). To alleviate this problem, we propose an open and flexible laboratory for experimenting with an IT/OT infrastructure and the related cybersecurity problems, such as emulating attacks and understanding how they work and how they could be identified and mitigated. We also report our experience in using the laboratory during a one-week training event with 24 students from 7 different high-schools at the mechatronics prototyping facility ProM in Rovereto (Italy).

Keywords: Education · CyberSecurity · Laboratory · Operational Technology · Information Technology

1 Introduction

During the last few years, it became harder for companies to find technically proficient cybersecurity professionals for their open positions: in the *State of Cybersecurity* survey [6], ISACA reports that in 2019 the 69% of participating enterprises (1,576 worldwide organisations) have understaffed cybersecurity teams and 58% have unfilled (open) cybersecurity positions. Figure 1 compares the results of the ISACA survey in 2019 and 2018 (based on 2,300 worldwide cybersecurity and information security practitioners and managers).

To reduce the cybersecurity gap, schools and universities started to provide courses and training in information security (also via shared testbed facilities for conducting hands-on experiments, such as the DETER Lab[1]), while non-academic events proposed talks on bleeding edge technologies and contests (e.g., Kaspersky's promoted *Capture-The-Flag* [7]). Most of these initiatives focus on information security and only marginally consider the security issues arising at the convergence of Information Technology (IT) and Operational Technology

---

[1] https://deter-project.org/about_deterlab.

© Springer Nature Switzerland AG 2020
A. P. Fournaris et al. (Eds.): ESORICS 2019 Workshops, LNCS 11981, pp. 140–155, 2020.
https://doi.org/10.1007/978-3-030-42051-2_10

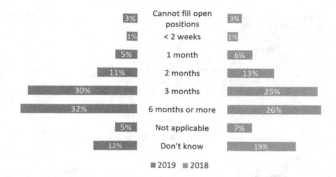

Fig. 1. Time to find technically proficient cybersecurity professionals (derived from ISACA reports in 2019 [6] and 2018 [5]).

(OT), that is the cornerstone of Industry 4.0. In this context, IT security issues are still relevant but are augmented with OT security problems that are typical of protocols and standards used in OT. To make the situation even more critical, novel attacks are enabled by the connection between IT and OT networks. Given the complexity of the situation, it is not surprising that students and schools struggle with finding test environments to investigate the attack scenarios and mitigation measures belonging to Industry 4.0. As a consequence, the cybersecurity gap is widening because of the lack of professionals able to evaluate the risks and secure IT/OT infrastructures by considering the distinguishing features of OT and their interplays with IT.

Our contribution to alleviate this problem is an open and flexible laboratory for experimenting with an IT/OT infrastructure and the related cybersecurity problems, such as emulating attacks and understanding how they work and how they could be identified and mitigated. The laboratory is open because it is freely accessible and allows to plug in new components and protocols of interest. It is flexible as it can be customized by instructors to support different use case scenarios from basic to more advanced (e.g., on top of the laboratory, we were able to deploy a solution for predictive maintenance, which is fundamental to many Industry 4.0 solutions). One customization relates to the optional cloud components: instructors decide if and where to deploy the database and a monitoring dashboard (and which type); if to have a local or remote messaging broker.

Finally, the laboratory is cheap in terms of hardware and software requirements; this makes its adoption possible even in schools with restricted budgets.

The theoretical lectures and the hands-on workshops that form the laboratory[2] help instructors to illustrate the most common cybersecurity issues and best practices in IT/OT infrastructures, and to train students over the problems "hidden" in the hands-on sessions.

Plan of the Paper. In Sect. 2 we present the requirements and the goals of the proposed laboratory. In Sect. 3 the current state of the laboratory is presented,

---

[2] All the material is available at https://sites.google.com/fbk.eu/itotlab.

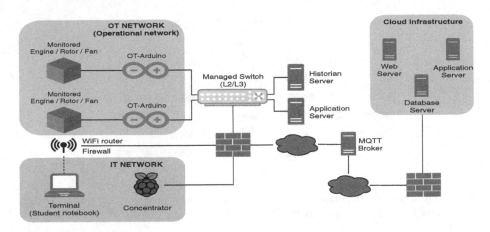

Fig. 2. Architecture of the IT/OT infrastructure used by our laboratory. (Color figure online)

while in Sect. 4 we report our experience on how it was used during a training event held at the mechatronics prototyping facility in Rovereto (Italy) during February 2019 (called *ProM Camp* - henceforth *ProM*) with high-school students.[3] Finally, in Sect. 5 we draw some conclusions and present possible improvements.

2   Architecture, Design Choices, and Goals

In order to identify the technical solutions to adopt in our laboratory and deploy a realistic IT/OT infrastructure, we reviewed current literature and integrated the study with our field experience.[4] The result of this activity is the reference architecture shown in Fig. 2. It is composed of three main blocks: an OT network (yellow area in the top left corner), an IT network (yellow area in the bottom left corner), and a cloud infrastructure (yellow area in the top right corner). The components on the right of the OT network are optional and used to log and elaborate data close to where they are produced. The components between the IT and OT networks are a WiFi router and a firewall; they are optional and can be used to segment the two networks and avoid certain types of attacks. The components connecting the IT/OT networks (on the left) with the cloud infrastructure (on the right) are the communication protocols, the broker, and the firewall that can be used to transmit data to the cloud where algorithms (typically based on machine learning) implement the application logic; e.g., one

---

[3] The solution developed by students is available at: https://gitlab.fbk.eu/promcamp/promcamp-2019.

[4] One of the author owns a company performing offensive security activities, especially on IT/OT infrastructures; another is the head of the Security&Trust Research Unit at Fondazione Bruno Kessler in Trento (Italy).

can think of predictive maintenance solutions in Industry 4.0 scenarios that
collect and process large amounts of data and then transmit various types of
feedbacks to the actuators while keeping a monitoring dashboard updated.

Below, we describe the various blocks of the architecture in Fig. 2, together
with the design choices; then, we identify the goals we want to achieve with our
laboratory.

2.1 Description and Design Choices

As a first step, we identified the most common technologies in use in this specific field: the Spanish National Cybersecurity Institute (INCIBE) describes
ModbusTCP [9] as one of the most widely used industrial communication protocol [12], something that is aligned to our experience. Developed in 1999, it is
a well-documented, royalty-free protocol based on the master/slave model: contrary to the client-server model of Interned-oriented networks, in ModbusTCP a
node called master initiates the communication and requests a resource to one
or more slave.[5] Requested data, named *registers* or *coils*, can be read or written,
both individually or as a group. As also reported by [4], ModbusTCP does not
support any native authentication mechanisms or data encryption. This makes
it an ideal candidate to demonstrate the vulnerabilities in the OT component of
our infrastructure and investigate common attack vectors.

Another protocol we decided to include is MQTT (Message Queuing Telemetry
Transport), one of the most popular IoT messaging protocols [13]. It is developed
for resource-constrained devices, standardized by OASIS (v.3.1.1 [3] in 2014 and
v.5 [2] in 2019) and based on the publish-subscribe pattern: messages sent by
publishing clients to transitory messaging queues, called topics, are received and
(possibly) routed by an *MQTT Broker* to topics-subscribed clients. A recent
review on the state of (in)security of MQTT deployments [10] reveals that the
majority (∼60%) of the Internet-facing brokers indexed by Shodan[6] put data
confidentiality and integrity at risk by allowing anyone to connect, publish and
receive messages. According to the authors, this is typically due to the difficulties
in configuring adequate security measures. To alleviate this problem, a part of the
laboratory focuses on enforcing the most secure authentication and authorization
mechanisms in Mosquitto,[7] one of the most widely used MQTT implementations.

While choosing the devices to employ, we decided to use *Arduino*, an open-
source project that offers an affordable set of microcontroller developing boards
and a cross-platform IDE; its mission is to *"make technology accessible to everyone, and into the hands of every student and educator"*.[8] Over the years, *Arduino*
has been used as a learning tool (e.g., in the field of robotics) and for the rapid
prototyping of many different applications [1]: the project hub,[9] maintained by

---

[5] This misalignment derives from the original Modbus protocol (of which ModbusTCP is
a direct evolution).

[6] A search engine for Internet-connected devices at https://www.shodan.io.

[7] https://www.mosquitto.org.

[8] https://www.arduino.cc/en/Main/Education.

[9] https://create.arduino.cc/projecthub.

the community of users, hosts more than 4,000 solutions of increasing complexity. By considering a trade-off between costs, functionalities and ease of development, we integrated two *Arduino Mega 2560* (currently Rev.3) as part of the OT section. The choice of two boards is to allow multiple sensors to interact and emulate more complex scenarios. In addition, by using two devices students can dedicate one to reading the measures and the other to interact with the environment as an actuator; e.g., cutting off power in case an alarm signal is received.

To simplify the interaction with sensors and actuators, we decided to adopt the Grove[10] prototyping system: a base shield to be mounted on top of each *Arduino Mega 2560* (that enables the interaction with Grove sensors), and analog and digital Grove sensors. In particular, an accelerometer and temperature sensors were used to acquire data while two actuators were used to receive feedback on measures: a led and a buzzer. The decision of adopting the Grove environment was made to allow students to focus on the Industrial Control System (ICS) related topics rather than spend time and effort against the difficulties of using embedded devices and sensors for the first time.

In addition to *Arduino* boards, we decided to include a *Raspberry Pi* in the IT section of the laboratory to enable more sophisticated interactions: send controlling commands to *Arduino* boards (e.g., to reset alarms) and collect their measurements, act as MQTT client and present the health status of the OT components through a dashboard (hosted either locally or in the cloud). The *Raspberry Pi* acts as an edge computing node and reduces the workload on more resource-constrained devices (here the *Arduino* boards) and possibly the data exchanged with the cloud infrastructure over the Internet.

It is important to highlight that the laboratory enables the interaction of cloud services with the OT network components (and the communication of data over the Internet) to investigate the risks and security issues. This is typically avoided in robust OT infrastructures.

Ancillary systems that could be optionally added to the infrastructure are the *Historian Server* and the *Application Server*. Those reside in a separated network and enable the laboratory to simulate an Industrial-DMZ. Similarly, the use of a cloud service provider (e.g., Amazon AWS) enables the exchange of messages between the systems residing in the OT/IT infrastructure and the ones that (from an external network) monitor the status and allow remote interaction. In Fig. 2 it is possible to see three different servers residing in the cloud: a *Database Server*, storing the acquired information, an *Application server* running the algorithms that examine the data and a *Web Server* that visualize the elaboration through a dashboard.

The IT and OT components in Fig. 2 are connected by a consumer-oriented *WiFi router*, that also acts as a firewall to protect the Internet-facing uplink. An additional *Managed switch* at layers 2 and 3 (of the ISO/OSI model) simulates a segmented network by leveraging VLANs and similar technologies.

---

[10] http://wiki.seeedstudio.com/Grove_System.

2.2 Goals

By creating the laboratory we aim at offering an affordable and easy to reproduce training environment to emulate realistic scenarios and bridge the skill gaps in IT/OT cybersecurity. Below, we discuss these aspects in more details.

G1: Inexpensive and Easy to Reproduce. The main reason for building an affordable and simple laboratory was the possibility to reach a broader audience and to be deployed by small communities (e.g., rural schools or independent groups of students). Table 1 provides the costs to deploy all the components of the laboratory: we were able to create it by spending around 300 euro. To improve the hands-on experience with *Arduino*, the sensors and the actuators, we advise to provide an *Arduino* board, a Grove Base Shield, one actuator and an analog or digital sensor for each group of 3/4 students (~30 euro each new group). The remaining components do not need to scale according to the number of students or may require a minor upgrade.

It is possible to achieve considerable savings by refurbishing an old router and install OpenWRT[11] to provide the necessary features. Even if OpenWRT might be considered a complex system, no special knowledge of the firmware is needed for configuring the laboratory. Another opportunity to bring down costs, at the expense of realism, is to use just one *Arduino Mega 2560* and one *Raspberry Pi*. We also observe that sensors can be directly connected to the *Arduino* board; indeed, this increases complexity as it requires the management of the direct interaction with sensors.

To provide the necessary background knowledge to operate and assess each component of the infrastructure, in addition to detailed tutorials, we are now in the process of creating Jupyter[12] notebooks. Those will complement and integrate the lectures provided by instructors.

Table 1. Breakdown of the costs of the hardware for the laboratory (prices in euros).

Component	Quantity	Unit price	Total price
Arduino Mega 2560 (Rev. 3)	2	15	30
Seeed Grove Base Shield v2	2	5	10
Seeed Grove Sensors (various)	5	8	40
Raspberry Pi 3 Model B+	1	30	30
MicroSD 16 GB Class 10	1	10	10
WiFi Router	1	70	70
Managed switch L2/L3	1	60	60
Miscellaneous (e.g., cables)	–	50	50
Total			300

---

[11] https://openwrt.org.
[12] https://jupyter.org.

G2: Real-Word Scenarios. One of the main motivation underlying our laboratory is to work with realistic use case scenarios on top of a well-tailored IT/OT infrastructure. For this purpose we decided to implement the following:

- multiple interconnected networks, to show the network flows and to demonstrate possible vulnerabilities and attack vectors;
- real ICS protocols, such as `ModbusTCP` and `MQTT`;
- layered technologies and a flexible infrastructure. These allow the laboratory to be easily tuned according to the skill level and capabilities of the students, to improve their competences by gradually integrating new components and to propose an evolving environment, stimulating them to adapt accordingly;
- hardware devices, to improve the student dexterity and to recreate all the problems and the conditions experienced in real deployments that are difficult (if possible at all) to reproduce in virtual environments.

3   Teaching with the Laboratory

We describe how the architecture in Fig. 2 can be used to develop three scenarios of increasing complexity (Sect. 3.2): the first introduces the use of sensors, the developing boards and the communication of data over the network; the second focuses on the role of actuators while the third discusses how cloud-based applications could be integrated. In each scenario, a specific set of vulnerabilities is identified, discussed and mitigated with guidelines (Sect. 3.3). Preliminary, we discuss how the basic notions underlying IT/OT infrastructures are introduced to students and detail their deployment (Sect. 3.1).

3.1   Introducing IT/OT

The IT block in Fig. 2 includes the terminal used to interact with the scenarios (e.g., a student notebook), the concentrator (a RaspberryPi 3 ModelB+ with the latest Raspbian Lite OS) and a WiFi router with OpenWRT. OpenWRT enables the Internet connectivity (as uplink) and it is configured to support two linked subnets: one for the IT network (via wireless connectivity) and one dedicated to the OT (via Ethernet). In both cases, the DHCP server facilitates the management of the network and no particular firewall rule is required. In more complex scenarios, by leveraging an L2/L3 managed switch it is also possible to configure in addition different VLANs in the OT network.

Terminal. By using their device, students are initially instructed to program the *Arduino Mega 2560* boards via USB and master the interaction with Grove sensors. A lecture introduces the *Arduino* project, the available boards and the software IDE; if necessary, insights are provided on the basics of C++ programming[13] and specific concepts: e.g., the difference between a micro-controller and a computer, or between digital and analog signal processing. Once completed,

---

[13] In particular the program structure, data types, functions, *waits* and loops.

students are instructed to connect the Grove base shield with one or more sensors according to the official documentation.[14] To test the connectivity, they have to first understand the characteristics of each sensor;[15] once done, they can run and enhance some of the base examples provided directly by Grove. If no errors occurred, the next step for the students is to combine the interaction of two or more sensors; e.g., blink a led if the accelerometer measures a value that exceeds a threshold.

Another lecture introduces the students to the basics of Python programming (see footnote 13) (if necessary) and to the MQTT protocol; during the same lecture, *Eclipse Paho*,[16] a simple and straightforward Python library that can be used to develop an MQTT client, is presented. Students initially connect and interact with the MQTT broker provided by the Eclipse Foundation: iot.eclipse.org; later in the laboratory, we introduce Mosquitto and its capabilities in terms of authentication and authorization mechanisms in order to deploy a secure instance running either locally (on the *Raspberry Pi*) or in the cloud.

While proposing the use of two different languages may only seem to increase the complexity, it is in line with the goals of the project: be a learning (and training) environment for its users; moreover, some implementations (e.g., the MQTT client and the ModbusTCP master) are significantly easier to deploy in Python than in C++.

Concentrator. The name of this component, physically interpreted by the *Raspberry Pi*, comes from the fact that it is where the data coming from the *Arduino* devices and the one acquired by MQTT broker are concentrated and it is one of the most "critical" systems in the infrastructure, also from a security point of view. During the implementation of the laboratory, students are guided in installing the Raspbian Lite OS on the *Raspberry Pi*, configure it to enable SSH communication, to connect it to the WiFi router (either through WiFi or Ethernet) and to control it through SSH. Once done, they can install the required software and libraries (e.g., Mosquitto) and interact with the other systems (*Arduino* and the MQTT broker) through Python scripts.

WiFi Router. Multiple guides can be used to understand how the WiFi router has to be configured. The most suitable depends on the scenario being deployed and students expertise on the device operating system; the same applies to the managed switch (if deployed in the scenario). Considering that almost any WiFi router provides also Ethernet connectivity, it is possible to use it also as a managed switch (if the software provides this feature).

The **OT block** in Fig. 2 contains dedicated devices, sensors and other systems with the goal of interfacing the industrial plant with the outside world. Those components allow the students to experience the technologies in use and the problems that have to be solved in OT environments. One of the challenge while preparing this part of the laboratory was to balance the need of demonstrating

---

[14] http://wiki.seeedstudio.com.

[15] In particular the working voltage and if analog or digital.

[16] https://www.eclipse.org/paho/clients/python.

the complexity and the quantity of ad-hoc solutions (e.g., protocols) used in ICS with the need to facilitate their understanding and management by students. We decided to employ both the ModbusTCP and MQTT protocols.

To speed up the development of the OT network and have intermediate working prototypes (e.g., configuring components might need additional time), our strategy is to divide the deployment in different "versions", from the simplest to the most complex and articulated.

3.2 Scenarios

We describe three scenarios deployed on the architecture of Fig. 2 in increasing order of complexity. Such scenarios have been presented to students as refined versions of the same deployment according to the strategy hinted above.

Scenario I - Simple IT/OT. Once introduced to all the mandatory components of the laboratory, students are guided in enabling the flow of information between the OT and IT: the *Arduino Mega 2560* boards collect the measures from the Grove sensors[17] and provide the value via LAN to the *Concentrator* using ModbusTCP. The *Concentrator* is used to acquire these values via ModbusTCP and, with the use of Paho, communicate the data to a local/remote broker via MQTT messages. In this scenario, no feedback is sent by the MQTT broker and no *Historian Server* or similar ancillary systems are required in the OT.

The WiFi router provides connectivity to the OT and IT network with no segmentation (the same subnet is used) and students can connect to the scenario through WiFi or Ethernet.

From a security perspective, this scenario allows to test different attacks on the physical media and on the network (ModbusTCP) and application layers (MQTT); moreover, students can understand the importance of segregating the OT and the IT networks in real deployments, by experiencing how easy it is to intercept communications and subvert protocols.

Scenario II - IT/OT with Feedback. The second scenario introduces an alarm buzzer and a led to signal a critical condition in the monitored devices: for instance, if the accelerometer measures a value that bypasses the threshold (set according to past measurements). Here, an attacker has the ability to raise false alarms by sending or re-publishing well-tailored MQTT messages or even worse: to prevent a real signal to reach the alarm sensors.

Scenario III - Extended IT/OT. In the third scenario, the infrastructure includes the cloud servers and one or more ancillary services. The goal is to segment the network in order to assess and secure each step of the data flow; new protocols and technologies will be used in both the IT and the OT. An example is the OPC protocols framework[18] or the REST interfaces that connect the additional servers.

---

[17] That will either sample analog signals or provide digital measures.

[18] https://opcfoundation.org.

From a network perspective, some VLANs should be created and also the routing and the firewalling rules running on the WiFi router have to be changed accordingly.

The (optional) **cloud** components in Fig. 2 requires the instructors to provide access to an instance of a cloud service provider (e.g., accessing an Amazon AWS free subscription). If using Amazon AWS, they are guided in configuring an instance of the AWS RDS (relational DB) or DocumentDB (MongoDB-compatible) service for the *Database Server*. Then, deploy a Virtual Machine (VM) in a Infrastructure-as-a-Service environment (IaaS, such as AWS EC2), that will interact with the database and run an Internet-facing status dashboard (as a *Web Server*): if needed, to simulate a more complex infrastructure, the *Application Server* and the *Web Server* can be deployed as Platform-as-a-Service (PaaS) services instead of running within the VM. Instructors are guided in creating a VM for the *Application Server*, configure the SSH access and install the necessary software. To provide the students with maximum flexibility, we support two types of *Database Server*: relational or no-SQL. Instructors will accordingly install MariaDB or MongoDB in the VM, or use specific PaaS solutions.[19]

A lecture introduces the students to the basics of data processing with Machine-Learning (ML) algorithms and how to fetch and visualize the data with a dashboard (e.g., use Thingboard or Node-RED). Examples and code snippets are provided as part of an interactive tutorial. An important part of the lecture focuses on the shared responsibility model typically offered by cloud service providers and the accountability of developers.

3.3   Attacks and Mitigations

By leveraging the weaknesses of the various scenarios it is possible to investigate different kind of flaws and vulnerabilities in the IT, OT and cloud components.

Code Flaws and Physical Attacks. When providing the basics of C++, students are presented typical code flaws: missing input validation, memory mismanagement and code snippets that force them to reset the Arduino boards (e.g., buffer overflows conditions). Similarly, when using the Python Paho library they will be shown the consequences of bad error handling. In scenario III, similar concepts are applied to the code that runs the dashboard in the cloud.

Particular attention is given to the physical isolation of the devices: no authentication and authorisation mechanisms at the application layer is able to protect against physical tampering and insider attackers. According to the Ponemon Institute *Cost of Insider Threats* [11], in 2018 insider incidents cost the surveyed 159 worldwide organizations an average of 8.76 million dollars in a year.

Network-Related Attacks. Typical network-based attacks can be replicated thanks to the different technologies and protocols in place. With the more basic

---

[19] A guide will help them in using AWS RDS or DocumentDB, and connect them to the VM via AWS VPN.

configurations, it is possible to test attacks on open and weakly protected wireless networks (easily spotted in real life scenarios where the ICS devices are not capable of dealing with WPA encrypted WiFi) and to execute network scans and analysis on physical devices. On more advanced scenarios, it is also possible to test good and bad firewall rules, pivoting and exploiting more complex protocols, like the ones belonging to the OPC framework. To replicate the danger of using IT tools (e.g., network scanners) on OT infrastructure, broken network stacks could also be implemented, to demonstrate to the students the effects.

Data Leakage - ModbusTCP. This attack can be shown by using a technique called *port mirroring*,[20] that supports the replication of all the traffic that flows through a port of a switch to another port where the attacker is sniffing. In this case, all the traffic that is not encrypted (or that can be decrypted) can be analyzed and exploited by a threat actor to mount additional attacks. Alternatively, if the devices are made to communicate through an open WiFi, the sniffing can be done on that media, without using any *port mirroring*. It is important to note, however, that the highest risk derives from the missing encryption of the ModbusTCP protocol.

Data Tampering - ModbusTCP. Even though there are some extensions of this protocol that allows the authentication through X509 certificates,[21] their adoption is far from common; this happens because dealing with certificates is normally quite complex and also due to their missing support by legacy devices that are still widely used in OT networks. An attacker could leverage this condition by impersonating the Modbus slave, for instance through ARP poisoning attacks[22] (their use have to be carefully guided by instructors as they could strongly impact OT networks with denial-of-service attacks). Alternatively, it could be possible to mangle with the switch/access point configuration in order to make the real slave unreachable and by getting the same IP address: from that moment, all the requests coming from the Modbus master (i.e., the *Concentrator*) are received by the system managed by the attacker.

Data Leakage and Tampering - MQTT. If the MQTT service does not enforce TLS or adequate authentication and authorization mechanisms, it is possible to intercept and tamper with the data exchanged between the *Concentrator* and the MQTT broker; including device usernames and passwords. Students are guided in the use of *MQTTSA* [10] to incrementally protect the MQTT component: initially, the instructors run the MQTT broker as downloaded (out-of-the-box configuration). This allows the students to intercept the MQTT packets (on the network) and the MQTT messages (on topics), and to perform data tampering and denial-of-service attacks: damage the service by issuing a considerable amount of heavy MQTT messages to the MQTT broker or send well-tailored data (according to the format of intercepted packets) to raise false alarms

---

[20] https://en.wikipedia.org/wiki/Port_mirroring.
[21] http://www.modbus.org/docs/MB-TCP-Security-v21_2018-07-24.pdf.
[22] https://security.radware.com/ddos-knowledge-center/ddospedia/arp-poisoning.

(via the buzzer) or even crash the MQTT broker.[23] Students are then shown that the sole enforcement of password-based authentication is not sufficient to protect data if using weak passwords or not enforcing TLS: they will use *MQTTSA* to intercept and exploit a valid set of credentials. Finally, after students are guided in supporting certificate-based authentication and access control lists (to authorise specific MQTT clients with respect to specific topics), the MQTT component of the infrastructure is sufficiently protected.

Cloud-Enabled Attacks. Students are shown the consequences of exposing the *Database Server* to the Internet (with no authentication or a simple password) instead of creating a VPN. A simple case of MQTT-based SQL injection is also presented (inspired by [8]).

4   ProM Camp: An Instance of the Laboratory

We now discuss our experience of using the laboratory during an event held on February 2019 at the mechatronics prototyping facility in Rovereto (Italy).[24] The event was organized over 5 days, with 24 students from 7 different local high schools.[25] The goal was to build a predictive maintenance solution to detect and signal the malfunctioning of a DC motor or a 12V DC fan. Critical situations have been simulated by unbalancing the motor shaft with a small weight (increases temperature and vibrations) and removing one of the fan blades (increases vibrations).

When building the OT infrastructure, most of the difficulties generated from the heterogeneous background knowledge: some students already had experience with C++ and Python programming, while others were introduced to the basics. Similarly, microcontroller development boards were only part of some school curricula; in only one case, students had prior knowledge of ModbusTCP (no one of MQTT). To better manage those situations, we plan to provide introductory notes on programming, boards and protocols as part of the next *ProM* event.

During *ProM*, we initially divided students into 8 small groups to support each other and collaborate during the hands-on training; then we created two teams to develop the predictive maintenance solution, with the possibility to integrate and use different technologies (e.g., MongoDB instead of MariaDB) according to their experience. The strict schedule and the necessary insights (provided as part of the lectures) prevented us to introduce and enable the integration of some ancillary systems (e.g., the *Historian Server*) and the interaction with cloud components. Figure 3 provides the components deployed by both teams.

---

[23] During the *ProM* 2019 event, an old version of Mosquitto was deployed to exploit a known vulnerability (CVE-2018-12543).

[24] http://www.polomeccatronica.it/en.

[25] https://fbkjunior.fbk.eu/prom-camp-2019-participants.

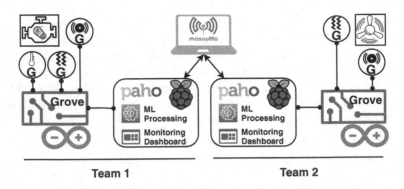

Fig. 3. Predictive maintenance solution developed by the ProM teams.

Team 1, responsible to monitor the temperature and the vibration of the motor, acquired the measures through the Grove 3-Axis Digital Accelerometer and the Temperature (v1.2) sensors connected to the Grove shield; mounted with the Ethernet shield on top of the *Arduino Mega 2560*. Then, measures were acquired via LAN (from the *Concentrator* through ModbusTCP) and published as MQTT messages to a Mosquitto server using Paho. Paho was also used as a receiver to collect the measures from an MQTT topic and store their value in a MongoDB database (run on the *Concentrator*). A Python script was responsible to train the Machine Learning algorithm (a K-Nearest Neighbors Classifier[26]) and, by continuously reading new measures form the database, monitor the measures through a simple NodeJS dashboard and signal the malfunctioning of the motor (via a Grove Buzzer). Team 2, responsible to monitor the vibration of the DC fan, adopted a similar approach but using a MariaDB database and a NodeRED dashboard.

As expected, it was fundamental to take a step by step approach to develop the solution: a part of the students was losing interest by not having sufficient experience with sensors and the configuration of the dashboard, sometimes re-using code snippets without the necessary modifications. We believe to address both problems by creating interactive Jupyter notebooks to guide the incremental learning during the laboratory.

With respect to the OT infrastructure and the specific technologies in use, we were quite surprised by the fact that different groups were faster than expected in implementing the code needed to interact with the *Arduino Mega 2560* through ModbusTCP and to leverage it to subvert how the slaves were acting. On the other hand, we had to put additional effort in explaining the differences between the standard IT world and the peculiarities related to the industrial control systems; in this case, we succeeded by proposing some real stories, related to cases we personally experienced, providing pictures and videos (of course, any connection to specific companies and public entities was previously removed).

---

[26] https://scikit-learn.org/stable/modules/generated/sklearn.neighbors.
KNeighborsClassifier.html.

During these sessions, we explained also some key differences, such as the safety needs and the use of custom hardware and software, to provide them with some hints about these particular topics.

In the context of protecting the OT infrastructure, it was possible to explain typical code flaws and the importance of static and dynamic code analysis. Network-related analysis and attacks have been executed using typical tools (e.g., *nmap*[27] and *Wireshark*[28]) or by implementing ad-hoc scripts with powerful frameworks, like *Scapy*.[29]

Regarding the technologies and the components belonging to the IT infrastructure, students were initially instructed to generate a self-signed certificate for the MQTT client (on the *Concentrator*) in order to enforce the certificate-based authentication (by modifying the configuration of Mosquitto); then, they get informed on how to proceed with (more secure) *Let's Encrypt* certificates. The topics used by the *Concentrator* to interact with the broker have been correctly protected with access control lists. Although no student exploited the vulnerabilities reported by [10], the use of MQTTSA was fundamental in demonstrating the effectiveness of the implemented security mechanisms: for instance, the interception of credentials in the configuration that implement password-based authentication without TLS.

Given the focus on protecting IT/OT infrastructures, we expected the teams to silently attempt the shown attacks to tamper each other projects (e.g., the Mosquitto CVE-2018-12543). To the best of our knowledge, this was not the case as no malfunctioning or strange behaviour was reported by the participants. In our opinion, suggesting (or even encouraging) this kind of offensive behaviour in the next *ProM* event (to be held around February or March 2020) will create more awareness and a deeper understanding about the implementation of adequate security measures.

During the closing event of the *ProM* 2019 camp, we had the chance to spoke informally with the students to get feedback, criticisms and ideas. All the students were satisfied by the experience and the new topics they discovered but sometimes found hard to deal with all of them fitted into the tight schedule of the event. The effort everyone could put in shaping the group project was also based on the different backgrounds and curricula, becoming a negative side of the experience for those students with weaker technical experience (it was hard for them to be supportive in the group). We took in great consideration these feedbacks and decided to put a particular effort in improving both the material provided to the students and the structure of the events, to understand what can be possibly removed or made lighter to relax the schedule.

We have also agreed with a high-school in Trento (Italy) to experiment with the laboratory for around 3 months starting in January 2020. This will allow us to investigate more complex use cases with students having a more heterogeneous background.

---

27 https://nmap.org.
28 https://www.wireshark.org.
29 https://scapy.net.

5   Conclusions and Future Work

We have presented a cybersecurity training laboratory to teach and learn the security best practices in IT/OT infrastructures. In the OT, we provide the means to secure the acquisition of data from sensors and their communication via Modbus; one of the most widely used industrial communication protocol. In the IT, we guide the students to enforce secure authentication and authorisation mechanisms for MQTT; one of the most popular messaging protocols for the Internet of Things. In both cases, we exploit known vulnerabilities related to data at rest and in transit, and explain how to mitigate them.

The laboratory is open and consists of theoretical lectures and practical hands-on sessions: students are introduced to the basics of C++ and Python programming, and their correct use with the Arduino and Raspberry Pi development boards; they are then guided in enabling and securing the flow of information between the OT and IT via ModbusTCP and MQTT. To foster an incremental approach to problem solving, we provide three scenarios of increasing complexity with the possibility to adapt the number of components and security tests according to the specific requirements: one that introduces a basic set of components to emulate and assess a real ICS; another that integrate all the ancillary systems to provide analytics on measures (via a dashboard) and raise alarms in case of critical situations; finally, one that extends the communication and data processing to the servers of a cloud service provider to investigate security issues and risks. Each scenario allows the student to develop a different set of skills and the awareness on specific classes of vulnerabilities.

The laboratory has been proficiently used in the ProM Camp event held in Rovereto (Italy) in February 2019. Even though we were quite satisfied with how the laboratory performed during the event, there are different aspects that we plan to improve along the lines discussed below.

Use of Different Protocols. As commonly known in the ICS area, the industrial infrastructures are using hundreds of different protocols, some of which are very specific for some fields (e.g., energy) while others are emerging solutions trying to solve problems like the interconnection of different devices with different technologies. One of the interesting possible evolution of our laboratory is the addition of some of the OPC-related protocols (e.g., OPC-UA), (See footnote 18) that would allow students to gain some experience with one of the core framework used today.

Improve Documentation. We are working to improve the documentation that comes with the laboratory for both students and instructors. In particular, we are evaluating the adoption of Jupyter notebooks, that would allow students to try out different snippets of code without the need of configuring a whole development environment. For instructors, we believe that we need to improve the material concerning attacks and mitigations. The current version of our laboratory requires instructors to have an understanding of different strategies and methodologies normally used by attackers and defenders. While we are convinced that every instructor has to master a topic before starting to teach it, the learning environments are sometimes different from a typical school lesson: in those cases, having readily available attacks and mitigation evidence (such as network captures) would be probably helpful. In this respect, we found particularly useful during the *ProM* 2019 event the use of MQTTSA for both identifying and mitigating MQTT vulnerabilities. We plan to investigate how similar tools can be integrated into our laboratory for other protocols and components.

References

1. Galadima, A.A.: Arduino as a learning tool. In: 2014 11th International Conference on Electronics, Computer and Computation (ICECCO), September 2014. https://doi.org/10.1109/ICECCO.2014.6997577
2. Banks, A., Briggs, E., Borgendale, K., Gupta, R.: MQTT Version 5, March 2019. https://docs.oasis-open.org/mqtt/mqtt/v5.0/mqtt-v5.0.pdf
3. Banks, A., Gupta, R.: MQTT Version 3.1.1, December 2015. http://docs.oasis-open.org/mqtt/mqtt/v3.1.1/mqtt-v3.1.1.pdf
4. Hu, Y., Yang, A., Li, H., Sun, Y., Sun, L.: A survey of intrusion detection on industrial control systems. Int. J. Distrib. Sens. Netw. **14**(8) (2018). https://doi.org/10.1177/1550147718794615
5. Information Systems Audit and Control Association: State of cybersecurity 2018. Survey, ISACA, October 2017. https://cybersecurity.isaca.org/csx-resources/state-of-cybersecurity-2018
6. Information Systems Audit and Control Association: State of cybersecurity 2019. Survey, ISACA, November 2018. https://www.isaca.org/info/state-of-cybersecurity-2019/index.html
7. Kaspersky Lab ICS CERT: Industrial CTF. https://ics-cert.kaspersky.com/tag/industrial-ctf/. Accessed 30 June 2019
8. Lundgren, L., Hindocha, N.: Light Weight Protocol: Critical Implications. https://www.youtube.com/watch?v=o7qDVZr0t2c. Accessed 30 June 2019
9. Modbus-IDA: MODBUS TCP/IP Implementation Guide, October 2006. http://www.modbus.org/docs/Modbus_Messaging_Implementation_Guide_V1_0b.pdf
10. Palmieri, A., Prem, P., Ranise, S., Morelli, U., Ahmad, T.: MQTTSA: a tool for automatically assisting the secure deployments of MQTT brokers. In: 2019 IEEE World Congress on Services (SERVICES), vol. 2642–939X, pp. 47–53, July 2019. https://doi.org/10.1109/SERVICES.2019.00023
11. Ponemon Institute LLC: 2018 Cost of Insider Threats: Global. https://www.observeit.com/ponemon-report-cost-of-insider-threats
12. Spanish National Cybesecurity Institute: Protocols and Network Security in ICS Infrastructure, February 2017. https://www.incibe-cert.es/sites/default/files/contenidos/guias/doc/incibe_protocol_net_security_ics.pdf
13. Yassein, M.B., Shatnawi, M.Q., Aljwarneh, S., Al-Hatmi, R.: Internet of Things: survey and open issues of MQTT protocol. In: 2017 International Conference on Engineering MIS (ICEMIS), pp. 1–6, May 2017. https://doi.org/10.1109/ICEMIS.2017.8273112

PROTECT – An Easy Configurable Serious Game to Train Employees Against Social Engineering Attacks

Ludger Goeke[1], Alejandro Quintanar[1], Kristian Beckers[1], and Sebastian Pape[1,2(✉)]

[1] Social Engineering Academy (SEA) GmbH, Eschersheimer Landstrasse 42, 60322 Frankfurt am Main, Germany
[2] Faculty of Economics and Business Administration, Goethe University Frankfurt, Theodor-W.-Adorno-Platz 4, 60323 Frankfurt am Main, Germany
sebastian.pape@m-chair.de

Abstract. Social engineering is the clever manipulation of human trust. While most security protection focuses on technical aspects, organisations remain vulnerable to social engineers. Approaches employed in social engineering do not differ significantly from the ones used in common fraud. This implies defence mechanisms against the fraud are useful to prevent social engineering, as well. We tackle this problem using and enhancing an existing online serious game to train employees to use defence mechanisms of social psychology. The game has shown promising tendencies towards raising awareness for social engineering in an entertaining way. Training is highly effective when it is adapted to the players context. Our contribution focuses on enhancing the game with highly configurable game settings and content to allow the adaption to the player's context as well as the integration into training platforms. We discuss the resulting game with practitioners in the field of security awareness to gather some qualitative feedback.

Keywords: Security controls · Social psychology · Serious games · Fraud prevention · Security training

1 Introduction

Kevin Mitnick a most famous social engineer was interviewed over 15 years ago and stated the following. "The biggest threat to the security of a company is not a computer virus, an unpatched hole in a key program or a badly installed firewall. In fact, the biggest threat could be you [...] What I found personally to be true was that it's easier to manipulate people rather than technology [...] Most of the time organizations overlook that human element" [3]. Today this is as true as it was back than as various current studies confirm [6,15].

Serious games have established a reputation for getting employees of companies involved in security activities in an enjoyable and sustainable way.

© Springer Nature Switzerland AG 2020
A. P. Fournaris et al. (Eds.): ESORICS 2019 Workshops, LNCS 11981, pp. 156–171, 2020.
https://doi.org/10.1007/978-3-030-42051-2_11

Moreover, serious games are designed for a primary purpose other than pure entertainment, e.g. education, awareness training or social change, but they preserve a playful character. Williams et al. [20] introduced the protection poker game to prioritise risks in software engineering projects. Shostack [18] from Microsoft presented his Elevation of Privileges card game to practice threat analysis with software engineers. Furthermore, games are used as part of security awareness campaigns [8] and particularly as a part of social engineering threat analysis [4].

Another game called *PERSUADED* specifically trains people to withstand social engineering attacks [1]. The game works as follows. Employees get confronted with a possible social engineering threat and have to select a defence mechanism. This correct defence mechanism is a pattern of behaviour ensuring a secure outcome. For example, an employee gets a phishing mail and is asked to open its attachment. Afterwards the player selects a countermeasure: "Do not open the email and inform the information security department immediately". The player gets immediate feedback whether the chosen defence is correct. In this paper, we describe how we built on the concept of PERSUADED and developed a new family of games called *PROTECT*.

Our contribution in this paper is the serious game PROTECT, which entails the following novelties:

- The game contains new scenarios for automated shipping and electronic cancer register domains.
- The game can be configured to serve various game settings to allow a progression between difficulty levels and various other challenges to keep the players playing.
- A discussion with five security practitioners to assess the potential of the game for security trainings.

Our paper is organised as follows. Section 2 presents background and related work, while Sect. 3 contains the design methodology applied for creating our game. Section 4 describes the serious game PROTECT in detail. Section 5 documents the feedback for the game from practitioners and Sect. 6 concludes.

2   Background and Related Work

As security is usually a secondary task, computer security training has often been perceived to be an uninteresting enforcement to users and managers. The approach of developing serious games has therefore been adopted to provide knowledge and training in that field.

CyberCIEGE is a role playing video game, where a player acts as an information security decision maker in an enterprise. Players' main responsibilities are to minimize the risk to the enterprise while allowing users to accomplish their goals. Similar to Persuaded, the game offers a simulation of the reality particularly portraying the need to maintain the balance between productivity and security. As decision makers, players get to make choices concerning users (i.e. How extensive will background checks be?), computers (i.e. How will computers be networked?) and physical security (i.e. Who is allowed to enter a zone?) while monitoring the consequences of their choices. When compared to Persuaded, we recognized CyberCIEGE offered several advantages common to those offered by Persuaded. For instance, players are in a defensive mode and they get to make decisions and experience their consequences. CyberCIEGE even incorporates assets and resources in the game, which is a missing element in Protect. On the other hand, the game requires longer time to learn and to play [10].

PlayingSafe is a serious game in the domain of social engineering. It consists of multiple choice questions which are wrapped in typical mechanics of a board game. Since questions provided are exclusive to social engineering, the game is very similar to ours. The main difference lies however in the focus in the topic of social engineering. PlayingSafe asks questions in the fields of Phishing, advanced fee fraud, spam and others, being a category that covers less common attacks. Our game on the other hand covers a broader field without offering depth in each topic. Additionally, our game incorporates strategy favouring the entertainment element, in order to enhance the game experience the game provides [13].

SEAG is a serious game designed to raise awareness of social engineering. The game utilizes levels that tackle different cognitive aspects and hence provide an effective learning experience. The first level consists of quiz-like questions to build a knowledge base for the players. The second level is a match game where players have to match social engineering terms with respective pictures. Finally, the players are presented real life scenarios to analyse pertaining to threat. This simulation of real life application of the learnt lesson should test players ability to detect attacks- an approach very similar to inoculation [14]. Due to the construction with the different levels, the game seems to be more suitable for a one-time approach. In contrast, our game is based on one basic principle, but the configuration allows to raise the game's difficulty.

HATCH is a serious game for teaching employees about social engineering attacks [4]. The employees are guided by the game to elicit social engineering threats for their context. An extension of the game provides various scenarios e.g. for energy providers and personas to allow players to understand attacks of other contexts [5]. HATCH is a physical table top game that requires at least three players and a game master. Our game does not need a game master, and thus can be played by individual players at any time alone.

3   Methodology

PROTECT is based on the game concept of PERSUADED [1]. In this paper, Aladawy et al. discuss design goals and game concepts for a serious card game for the sensitization of people against social engineering attacks. To evaluate PERSUADED, a prototype implementation of the game has been developed.

It realizes the following improvements:

In this section, we describe the concepts for building PROTECT.

3.1 New Implementation with Enhanced Configuration

PROTECT is a complete new implementation of the design goals and game concepts of PERSUADED. While taking the findings from the case study into account, the focus was on the configuration of the game. By offering a lot of configuration options, i.e. for the game play, PROTECT can be seen as a family of games with PERSUADED just being a specific member of the game family. The aim is to allow an easy adaption to specific scenarios as well as to the player's skills. This can be particularly important if an employee changes the department and faces new threats in his/her new department.

By making the configuration options accessible via an application programming interface (API), PROTECT can not only serve as a stand-alone application but also be easily embedded into a training platform. In this case a training platform could control the difficulty of the game by changing the game configuration depending on the player's achievement in previous games. It would also be possible that the external training platform considers various other inputs such as the player's reaction to phishing mails, the results from other games or trainings.

In particular, we implemented an additional algorithm for the appearance of attacks in the game to make it easier for beginners to get started in the game. We introduced new cards that can defend any attack (jokers). We provided new algorithms for handling attacks which are not defended correctly and a special treatment for attacks that have not been defended correctly in previous games. The corresponding configuration parameters can be changed independently, allowing a number of (slightly) different games. The different configuration options are explained in detail in Sect. 4.2.

3.2 Game Concept

As for PERSUADED, the scientific foundation of this game are findings from Schaab et al. [16,17]. The authors analysed social psychology methods of training against persuasion and mapped them to trainings in IT security. One identified gap was the lack of using *inoculation*, the repeated confrontation of people with a challenging situation in order to trigger an appropriate response. In particular, inoculation is incorporated into the game mechanics to trigger resistance to social engineering attacks through exposing people to realistic attack scenarios. In order to provide the validity of the attack scenarios, we took all of them from scientific publications [2,7,11,12,15,19]. The game enables employees to learn about social engineering, while practising simultaneously. This immediate application of learned knowledge has proven to have lasting effects [9]. The enhanced configuration allows to adapt the game better to the player's needs. This is not only important to keep players motivated but also to adapt the game in a way that fits to the concept of inoculation. In versions for beginners the player's focus is mainly on matching different threats with the correct defences. In the more challenging versions for advanced players in order to be successful, the player is forced to think ahead. As a consequence, matching the different threats with the correct defences is still necessary but happens more unconsciously.

4   PROTECT

PROTECT is a serious card game that implements a training for the subject of social engineering. Its primary goal is the inoculation of people against social engineering attacks. This inoculation shall be achieved by confronting people repeatedly with social engineering scenarios in order to trigger an appropriate response.

PROTECT is implemented as an online game.

This chapter is divided into the following subsections:

- Section 4.1 describes game concepts and game mechanisms of PROTECT.
- Section 4.2 considers the configuration of PROTECT. In that respect, the configuration options regarding to (a) card decks, (b) instantiations of PRO-TECT and (c) properties for a game of PROTECT are discussed.
- Section 4.3 considers the implementation of PROTECT. It comprises the Graphical User Interface of PROTECT and its future provision as a web service.

4.1   Game Concepts and Game Mechanisms

This section considers the game concepts and mechanisms of PROTECT.

It is designed to achieve the following goals:

1. increasing awareness for social engineering,
2. training resistance to persuasion and
3. addressing the general population.

Regarding its main game concepts, PROTECT is designed as a single player card game that realizes a patience and solitaire game approach. As usual with this type of card games, the cards can be contained in the card deck or on the player's hand. In every turn of the game, a player can either draw a card from the deck or play a card from his/her hand. The implementation of these easy rules by PROTECT keep the complexity of the game low. This leads to a quite low initial barrier for playing the game and a focus on the actual content of teaching. Because the deck of cards is always shuffled before a game starts, each game is different from the previous game(s) (cf. [1], chap. 3, p. 5). This fact shall motivate players to play the game repetitively. The solitary approach enables players to play the game at any time, independently from other persons.

During a game of PROTECT, a player is confronted with different social engineering attacks. The task of the player is to select an appropriate defense mechanism for an attack. In this context, a defense mechanism represents a pattern of behaviour that prevents a successful conduct of a social engineering attack (cf. [1], chap. 1, p. 2). For the implementation of this game concept, PROTECT provides the following types of cards:

1. *Attack cards* represent scenarios for social engineering attacks in textual form.

2. *Defense cards* describe a pattern of behaviour for preventing the success of a certain attack. For each Attack card exists one corresponding Defense card. The contents of Defense cards are also represented in textual form.
3. *See The Future cards* allow the player to take a look on the three upper cards on the top of the card deck.
4. *Skip turn cards* allow the player to skip the top card of the deck and put this card to the bottom of the deck. It is only allowed to play a Skip turn card at the beginning of a turn when the top card of the deck is still hidden (cf. [1], Chap. 1, p. 4).
5. *Joker cards* are wildcards that can be selected by the player as a defence mechanism for every Attack card.

At the beginning of a game all cards are contained in the shuffled card deck. The game starts when the player draws the first card from the deck.

In the following, the game mechanisms of PROTECT are described.

At the beginning of a turn, a player can perform ONE of the following actions:

1. Draw a card from the top of the card deck.
2. Playing a See the future card or Skip turn card if such a card is on the player's hand.

Any drawn card that is NOT an Attack card, is put to the hand of the player. After that, the turn is over.

When an Attack card has been drawn, the player has to select the appropriate Defense card. If he/she

1. selects the correct Defense card, the score is increased.
2. selects an incorrect Defense card, the score is decreased and the player loses a life.
3. has no Defense card on the hand, a life is lost.

A player can also play a Joker card to defend every Attack card. In this case, the score is also increased. By playing Joker cards, players can achieve a good score, even if they do not know the appropriate defenses for some attacks. This shall keep up the motivation of the players high, to play the game repeatedly.

When the card deck is empty, the game is won. The game is lost if

1. the game time is up before finishing the deck or
2. a player has lost all his/her lives.

The following description considers the special function of See the future and Skip turn cards. As previously mentioned, it may be the case that a player has no appropriate Defense card or no Defense card at all on the hand to defend a drawn Attack card. If the player's hand does also not include a Joker card, he/she has no direct chance to prevent the loss of a life. This fact shall encourage the player to use See the future and Skip turn cards in the following way.

The player can play a See the future card to peek the upper three cards on top of the card deck. If these cards include any Attack cards, he/she can check if the appropriate Defense cards are

– on his/her hand or
– contained in the future cards itself at the right position.

If the future cards should contain any Attack cards for which no corresponding Defense card is available, the player can remember the order of these Attack cards and play a Skip turn card to skip such an Attack card when it is on the top of the deck. In this way, the loss of a life can be prevented. The provision of this game strategy increases the learning effect because the player studies the content of any Attack cards included in the future cards more carefully. This also applies for the content of the current Defense cards on his/her hand. Furthermore, he/she matches Attack cards partly against defense mechanisms that are not represented by Defense cards on the player's hand.

The provision of the strategy, mentioned before, requires an increased understanding of the game from the player. Additionally, it has a random factor because of the random order of the cards in the deck.

The study of [1] has shown that a considerable amount of players rated the above mentioned concept for the appearance of Attack cards on the top of the deck, as negative. Thus, PROTECT provides additionally a further concept for the appearance of Attack cards on the top of the deck. The implementation of this concept ensures that only such Attack cards can appear on the top of the deck for which an appropriate Defense card is currently on the player's hand. In this scenario the player can use the See the future cards and Skip turn cards to skip Attack cards for which he/she is not able to identify the appropriate Defense card on the hand. Because the additional concept for the appearance of Attack cards make the playing of PROTECT easier it shall be used for players on the beginner level.

PROTECT also provides two different concepts for the handling of Attack cards that have been solved incorrectly. In that regard, such an Attack card is

1. removed from the game or
2. is put back to the bottom of the card deck.

The second alternative represents the more easier variant because the player gets more chances to solve an attack correctly. Compared to the first variant, the player could still reach a good score, even with some incorrect solutions of attacks.

Example Scenario. We have extended the game PROTECT with various real scenarios from the EU project Threat Arrest[1]. One of these scenarios concerns automatic shipping. Digitalisation has increased the use of industrial control systems in the shipping domain. The increased use of computers and their interface exposes the systems that control vital systems and steer the ship itself to the risk of cyberattacks. The captain and crew are on their ship, while a back office provides IT-support. We elicited possible attacks that could be mitigated with awareness training such as the following. The crew is in contact with the back

---

[1] Threat Arrest homepage: https://www.threat-arrest.eu.

office on land in some intervals. If there is a problem with the onboard computer system the back office provides advice for maintenance to the crew. A social engineer pretends to be a back office employee and asks them to provide their credentials for maintenance. Another possible scenario would be that the crew is in ports all over the world. Maintenance is done on ports during stays outside of the home harbour. A social engineer pretends to be a maintenance worker and distributes usb sticks on the harbour with the hope that one of the crews picks one up and connects it to the computer system of the ship. We elicited totally over 20 plausible attacks for the game PROTECT.

4.2   Configuration Options

In this Section the options for the configuration of PROTECT are discussed. This discussion considers the following configuration aspects:

1. Configurations of card decks
2. Configurations during an instantiation of PROTECT
3. Internal configuration parameters of PROTECT

Configuration of Card Decks. Within PROTECT, the content of the cards of a deck are defined in a JSON format. Each card is defined by a single JSON file. The graphical representation of a drawn card in the GUI is generated on the fly during a game, based on the content of the corresponding JSON file. The definition of cards based on JSON files enables easy and fast

- creations of new card decks and
- modifications of existing card decks

to cover more specific social engineering scenarios.

Each card deck in PROTECT is identified by an unique identifier. These identifiers are used to configure which card deck shall be played within an instantiation of PROTECT (see Sect. 4.2).

Standard Card Decks. The standard card deck of PROTECT contains pairs of Attack and Defense cards for typical social engineering scenarios. It includes the following types off attacks (cf. [1], chap. 1, p. 4):

- baiting,
- phishing,
- tailgating
- mail attachment,
- physical impersonation,
- virtual impersonation,
- voice of Authority and
- popup window.

Additionally, the standard card deck contains action cards in form of Joker, See the future and Skip turn cards. The number of action cards of each type in the card deck can be configured when PROTECT is instantiated (see Sect. 4.2).

Adapted Card Decks. The game PROTECT can be also used to verify that a company's security policy is understood and followed by its employees. This works by describing the possible attacks against a company that the rules of the policies try to prevent. For example, the policy might contain a rule to shredder all confidential documents. We provide a card in which a person takes the shredder for maintenance and tells the staff that in the absence of the shredder they should throw the documents in the regular trash bin and that is not necessary to use the shredder on the next floor. The right behaviour would be to object and use the other shredder and inform the security staff of this incident.

Instantiation Parameters. PROTECT provides the hand over of information that is necessary for a game, during its instantiation. This information is represented by so-called *instantiation parameters* that are listed in Table 1.

The instantiation parameters *player ID* and *player name* provide information about the player of the game. The time that a game can take the longest is represented by the parameter *game time*. Because of their logical connection the instantiation parameters *card deck ID* and *difficulty level* shall be considered in more detail. The *card deck ID* and *difficulty level* enable the definition which card deck shall be played with which level of difficulty. Within PROTECT, a value for a difficulty level is mapped to a certain configuration of PROTECT regarding the selected card deck. This means, that a level of difficulty results from the particular values of the configuration parameters. These configuration parameters are specified in Table 2.

The parameter *special practice* defines if Attack cards that have been solved incorrectly in previous rounds of the game and there corresponding Defense cards shall be included multiple times in the card deck. If this is the case, the number of occurrences for such pairs of cards is defined by the appropriate configuration parameter (see Table 2).

Table 1. Instantiation parameters of PROTECT

Parameter	Description
player ID	Unique identifier of the player
player name	Name of the player
game time	Game time in minutes
card deck ID	Unique identifier of the card deck that shall be played
difficulty level	Level of difficulty with which the game shall be played. The value of the difficulty level corresponds to a certain internal configuration of PROTECT
special practice	Defines if Attack cards that have been solved incorrectly in previous games of PROTECT and the appropriate Defense cards shall occur multiple times in the card deck

Internal Configuration Parameters. *Internal configuration parameters* enable a configuration of properties for a game of PROTECT. The different internal configuration parameters are described in Table 2. A set of internal configuration parameters with the appropriate value is contained in a *configuration*. Configurations specify certain levels of difficulty for a game of PROTECT by the values of their parameters. For example, the level of difficulty decreases

- the more Joker cards a card deck includes,
- the more lives a player has,
- when only such Attack cards can be drawn for which the corresponding Defense card is on the player's hand,
- when incorrectly solved Attack cards are put back into the card deck and
- when the score can not have a value less than zero.

A configuration is associated to a certain difficulty level for a play of PROTECT with a particular card deck. The information according to the card deck and difficulty level are passed during the instantiation of PROTECT (see Table 1).

Table 2. Internal configuration parameters of PROTECT

Parameter	Description
number of lives	Defines the numbers of lives that a player has
number Joker cards	Defines the number of Joker cards in the card deck
number See the future cards	Specifies the number of See the future cards in the card deck
number Skip turn cards	Defines the number of Skip turn cards in the card deck
score increase	Defines the number of points added to the score when the CORRECT Defense card or a Joker card has been selected for an Attack card
score decrease	Defines the number of points removed from the score when an INCORRECT Defense card has been selected for an Attack card
range of score	Specifies if the score can be less than zero or if the lowest score is zero
appearance of Attack cards	Defines if (a) ANY Attack card can appear on the top of the deck, even if the corresponding Defense card is not on the hand of the player. (b) ONLY those Attack cards can appear on the top of the card deck for which the corresponding Defense card is on the player's hand
handling of incorrectly solved Attack cards	Specifies if an Attack card that has been solved incorrectly is (a) put back to the bottom of the card deck or (b) removed from the game

Fig. 1. GUI of PROTECT at the beginning of a game

4.3   Implementation

This Section discusses the implementation of game concepts and mechanisms that are described in Sect. 4.1 by PROTECT. The discussion considers the Graphical User Interface of PROTECT and a concept for its future provision as a web service.

Graphical User Interface. The Graphical User Interface (GUI) of PROTECT is executed in a web browser. It is implemented in JavaScript by using the JavaScript library *jQuery* and the framework *Bootstrap*. The GUI is especially designed to be displayed on mobile devices. Nonetheless, it can be displayed on PC monitors and laptop screens without any problems.

The Fig. 1 shows an execution of the PROTECT GUI in a web browser at the beginning of a game. The dialog for changing the language of the game is displayed. The card deck, including the Attack, Defense and action cards (e.g See the future cards), is positioned in the top right corner. It is shuffled automatically before each game. A player can draw a card by double-clicking on the card deck. The game score and the remaining game time are represented in the bottom right corner. It is also possible to pause a game with help of the *Pause*-button in the bottom left corner of the GUI. A game can also be cancelled and restarted. The corresponding *Restart*-button is positioned next to the *Pause*-button. The remaining lives of a player during a game are displayed by the pink heart symbols.

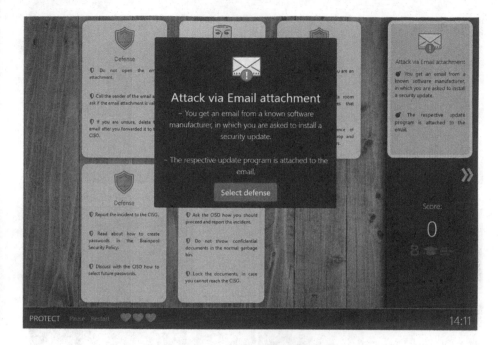

Fig. 2. Dialog after an Attack card has been drawn

The GUI supports the player in the game flow with appropriate dialogs. For example, the dialog in Fig. 2 is shown after the player has drawn an Attack card. It requests the player to select a defense card after clicking on the *Select defense*-button. The Fig. 3b displays the dialog after the selection of the correct Defense card. The game continues, after the player has pressed the *Continue*-button.

For example, the dialog in Fig. 3a is shown after the player has drawn an Attack card. It requests the player to select a defense card after clicking on the *Select defense*-button. The Fig. 3c displays the dialog after the selection of an incorrect Defense card. When the player clicks on the *Show the right answer*-button, the subsequent dialog represents the correct defense mechanism for the drawn Attack card (see Fig. 3d). The game continues, after the player has pressed the *Continue*-button.

Provision of PROTECT as a Web Service. The content of this section describes a concept for the provision of PROTECT as a web service. This type of provision has the following advantages:

1. Companies that want to use PROTECT for training their employees do not need to set up an own infrastructure for the deployment of PROTECT.
2. PROTECT can be integrated easily into other training platforms. This is achieved by the use of standardized application protocols that enable a loose coupling between different systems. Such an approach will be realized within

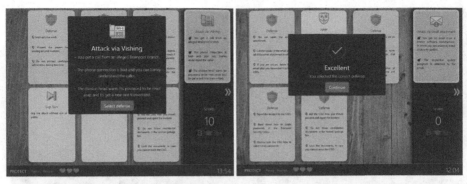

(a) Attack card has been drawn   (b) Selection of the correct Defense card

(c) Selection of an incorrect defense card   (d) Correct defense mechanism

Fig. 3. Different dialogs within the game

the research project *Threat-Arrest*[2], where PROTECT will be integrated into the *Threat-Arrest training platform*.

PROTECT shall be provided as a cloud computing service in form of *Software as a Service (SaaS)*. For the deployment of PROTECT, an appropriate cloud infrastructure, deployment environment and database shall be used in form of cloud services. The usage of these services shall be supplied by a third party cloud service provider.

The architecture of the PROTECT web service is represented in Fig. 4 in an abstract way. It shows that the PROTECT web service will use

- a deployment environment for the deployment of PROTECT and
- a data base service for storing data that is related to played games of PROTECT.

The selection of a certain deployment environment (e.g. virtual server, container service) is currently in the state of development.

---

[2] https://www.threat-arrest.eu/.

The external functionality of the PROTECT web service is provided via a REST API (see Fig. 4). A client can use a certain function by sending the appropriate HTTP request to the PROTECT web service. The web service sends the result of the function back to the client via an HTTP response. In the following, the basic functionality of the PROTECT REST API will be considered:

1. Instantiation of PROTECT with the specified instantiation parameters (see Table 1). The PROTECT web service returns the created PROTECT instance to the client.
2. Query of results regarding to games of PROTECT. The set of the returned results can be defined by filter parameters that are contained in the content data of the appropriate HTTP requests.

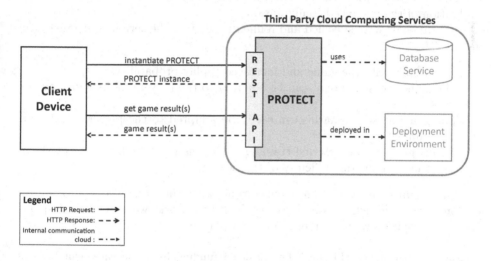

Fig. 4. Abstract architecture of the PROTECT web service

5   Discussion

We showed our game to 5 practitioners from different domains (from the information technology, cybersecurity, smart homes, and automotive) and gathered the following feedback. The general perceptions during game play provided feedback that conforms with our design goals. One participant stated, that for them the game simulates the reality. The player further explained, that in real life, it is rather difficult to expect social engineering attacks and always be ready for them, which they found was mapped through the random factor. Furthermore, the player mentioned that usually even the most cautious people might fall victim for social engineering when not constantly reminded of this threat. The player stated that the game does a good of job of doing that. Moreover, being able to defend themselves against social engineering in the game gave confidence the same could be achieved in real life. Another participant provided feedback on the challenge level in the game saying that "one has to think". For this player, the game was also "easy to understand", reflecting the modesty of the trade-off between those two conflicting elements. Finally, the player emphasised the importance of the game being single player for the replay value, saying that he can "play the game another 3 times just right now".

6   Conclusion

We designed, implemented and evaluated a serious game family for training social engineering defence mechanisms, called PROTECT. Since the basic concept of the game has already been evaluated for PERSUADED [1], we focused on the evaluation of the enhanced configuration.

Several goals were specified and refined to achieve the serious purpose of the game:

- Easier start into the game and increased replay probability.
- The game, i.e. game play, can be adapted to the player's skills and previous game results.
- The game attack scenarios can easily be adapted to the player's skills and environment.
- An integration into external training platforms is allowed, i.e. the platform can decide about the difficulty of the next games.

Our qualitative evaluation showed that with the enhanced configuration options, we could achieve our purpose. In future work, we aim to do a quantitative evaluation with a larger number of players.

Acknowledgements. This work has received funding from the European Union's Horizon 2020 research and innovation programme under grant agreement No 786890 (THREAT-ARREST).

References

1. Aladawy, D., Beckers, K., Pape, S.: PERSUADED: fighting social engineering attacks with a serious game. In: Furnell, S., Mouratidis, H., Pernul, G. (eds.) TrustBus 2018. LNCS, vol. 11033, pp. 103–118. Springer, Cham (2018). https://doi.org/10.1007/978-3-319-98385-1_8. ISBN 978-3-319-98384-4
2. Bakhshi, T., Papadaki, M., Furnell, S.: A practical assessment of social engineering vulnerabilities. In: HAISA, pp. 12–23 (2008)
3. BBC: How to hack people (2002). news.bbc.co.uk/2/hi/technology/2320121.stm
4. Beckers, K., Pape, S.: A serious game for eliciting social engineering security requirements. In: Proceedings of the 24th IEEE International Conference on Requirements Engineering (RE 2016). IEEE Computer Society (2016). https://doi.org/10.1109/RE.2016.39

5. Beckers, K., Pape, S., Fries, V.: HATCH: hack and trick capricious humans - a serious game on social engineering. In: Proceedings of the 2016 British HCI Conference, 11–15 July 2016, Bournemouth, United Kingdom (2016). http://ewic.bcs. org/content/ConWebDoc/56973

6. Dimensional Research: The Risk of Social Engineering on Information Security: A Survey of IT Profesionals (2011). http://docplayer.net/11092603-The-risk-of-social-engineering-on-information-security.html

7. Ferreira, A., Coventry, L., Lenzini, G.: Principles of persuasion in social engineering and their use in phishing. In: Tryfonas, T., Askoxylakis, I. (eds.) HAS 2015. LNCS, vol. 9190, pp. 36–47. Springer, Cham (2015). https://doi.org/10.1007/978-3-319-20376-8_4

8. Gondree, M., Peterson, Z.N.J., Denning, T.: Security through play. IEEE Secur. Priv. **11**(3), 64–67 (2013)

9. Greitzer, F.L., Kuchar, O.A., Huston, K.: Cognitive science implications for enhancing training effectiveness in a serious gaming context. J. Educ. Resour. Comput. **7**(3), 2 (2007)

10. Irvine, C.E., Thompson, M.F., Allen, K.: CyberCIEGE: gaming for information assurance. IEEE Secur. Priv. **3**(3), 61–64 (2005)

11. Manske, K.: An introduction to social engineering. Inf. Syst. Secur. **9**(5), 1–7 (2000)

12. Mitnick, K.D., Simon, W.L.: The Art of Deception: Controlling the Human Element of Security. Wiley, Hoboken (2011)

13. Newbould, M., Furnell, S.: Playing safe: a prototype game for raising awareness of social engineering. In: Australian Information Security Management Conference, p. 4 (2009)

14. Olanrewaju, A.S.T., Zakaria, N.H.: Social engineering awareness game (SEAG): an empirical evaluation of using game towards improving information security awareness. In: Proceedings of the 5th International Conference on Computing and Informatics (ICOCI 2015) (2015)

15. SANS: Social Engineering Threats (2003). http://www.sans.org/reading-room/ whitepapers/engineering/threat-social-engineering-defense-1232

16. Schaab, P., Beckers, K., Pape, S.: A systematic gap analysis of social engineering defence mechanisms considering social psychology. In: Proceedings of the 10th International Symposium on Human Aspects of Information Security & Assurance (HAISA 2016), 19–21 July 2016, Frankfurt, Germany (2016). http://www.cscan. org/openaccess/?paperid=301

17. Schaab, P., Beckers, K., Pape, S.: Social engineering defence mechanisms and counteracting training strategies. Inf. Comput. Secur. **25**(2), 206–222 (2017). https:// doi.org/10.1108/ICS-04-2017-0022

18. Shostack, A.: Threat Modeling: Designing for Security, 1st edn. Wiley, Hoboken (2014)

19. Stajano, F., Wilson, P.: Understanding scam victims: seven principles for systems security. Commun. ACM **54**(3), 70–75 (2011). https://doi.org/10.1145/1897852. 1897872. http://doi.acm.org/10.1145/1897852.1897872

20. Williams, L., Meneely, A., Shipley, G.: Protection poker: the new software security "game". IEEE Secur. Priv. **8**(3), 14–20 (2010)

Model-Driven Cyber Range Training: A Cyber Security Assurance Perspective

Iason Somarakis(✉) [ID], Michail Smyrlis [ID], Konstantinos Fysarakis [ID],
and George Spanoudakis [ID]

Sphynx Technology Solutions AG, Zug, Switzerland
{somarakis,smyrlis,fysarakis,spanoudakis}@sphynx.ch
http://www.sphynx.ch

Abstract. Security demands are increasing for all types of organisations, due to the ever-closer integration of computing infrastructures and smart devices into all aspects of the organisational operations. Consequently, the need for security-aware employees in every role of an organisation increases in accordance. Cyber Range training emerges as a promising solution, allowing employees to train in both realistic environments and scenarios and gaining hands-on experience in security aspects of varied complexity, depending on their role and level of expertise. To that end, this work introduces a model-driven approach for Cyber Range training that facilitates the generation of tailor-made training scenarios based on a comprehensive model-based description of the organisation and its security posture. Additionally, our approach facilitates the automated deployment of such training environments, tailored to each defined scenario, through simulation and emulation means. To further highlight the usability of the proposed approach, this work also presents scenarios focusing on phishing threats, with increasing level of complexity and difficulty.

Keywords: Cyber Range training · Model driven engineering ·
Security assurance

1 Introduction

The insufficient knowledge of security procedures and the lack of security awareness across different types of employees within an organisation, combined with the rapid technological advancements (e.g., 5G, the Internet of Things - IoT) [1] that transform various domains (e.g., energy, health-care), provide fertile ground for various threat actors (sophisticated or otherwise) to carry out successful attacks that may significantly damage tangible and intangible assets [2]. Organisations own or access a vast number of cyber systems that can be exposed through numerous known and unknown attack vectors; as organisations advance technologically, the complexity of their systems and their security

© Springer Nature Switzerland AG 2020
A. P. Fournaris et al. (Eds.): ESORICS 2019 Workshops, LNCS 11981, pp. 172–184, 2020.
https://doi.org/10.1007/978-3-030-42051-2_12

further increase. Nevertheless, the security awareness and security expertise of employees typically, does not increase at the same pace. This is especially critical for organisations that handle sensitive data (e.g., hospitals [3]) or are part of critical infrastructures (e.g., smart energy grids [4]). Therefore, to protect their assets and mitigate potential attacks, such organisations need to train their employees to appropriately respond to the security challenges of this era. This includes, educating them with the latest learning resources that will allow them to comprehend the security related changes introduced by the new technologies and giving them access to training scenarios that realistically represent situations that may occur in their organisation. In this manner, Cyber Security training that is not explicitly designed to fit the requirements of an organisation and does not have the ability to easily adapt to the rapidly changing landscape, is insufficient and quickly becomes obsolete. Thus, the importance for a dynamic and continuously up-to-date cyber security training environment emerges.

Motivated by the above, this work aims to highlight the potential of model-driven Cyber-Range training that: (i) is applicable to any type of a system; (ii) is able to represent the actual assets of an organisation and generate training scenarios based on them; (iii) offers scalability and adaptability, by enabling adjustments to the model as the organisation evolves; (iv) is up-to-date regarding threat intelligence, considering new vulnerabilities discovered [5]) or changes to the organisation's setup (e.g., adding new systems that may introduce new vulnerabilities).

The remainder of this paper is organised as follows: Sect. 2 presents an overview of the background, related works and how the proposed approach overcomes the limitations of current commercial solutions; Sect. 3 describes the adopted security assurance methodology; Sect. 4 provides a detailed model of an example scenario and two variations; and finally, Sect. 5 summarises the paper and sets future goals.

2   Background and Related Work

This work is based on the definition of a security assurance model, adopting and extending state of the art approaches in model-driven cyber assurance and certification, simulation, emulation, and e-training cyber range tools and platforms.

The security assurance's focus is to evaluate ICT systems, products and services with regard to security standards and security properties [6]. To achieve this, the proposed approach follows certification schemes such as CUMULUS [7], an open source model driven framework, capable of executing automatically different types of certification schemes for cloud services. It was introduced to close the gap of automation that other certification frameworks lacked (STAR [8], ECSTA [9]). In this work, cyber training leverages the continuous security assurance enabled by the assurance model to use its elements (e.g., Threats, Security Controls, monitoring evidence) and create realistic simulations for CyberRange training programmes, while monitoring the assurance schemes to measure the performance of the trainees following training.

To cover the needs for the implementation of the training environment several tools for simulation and emulation can be considered to support automatic deployment of the emulated components and facilitate the communication across simulated and real assets (see Sect. 3.2). Regarding the simulation requirements, the Cyber-Range sub-model needs to be able to accommodate a detailed representation of simulation environments and its components in order to support automatic generation of the simulation demands of the training programme; thus, several open source discrete event-driven simulators were examined. The NS-3 [10] provides support of TCP, routing and multicast protocols over wired and wireless networks and has the ability to run software on simulated models. GNS3 [11] is an open source network simulator mainly focuses on Cisco and Jupiter software. Netkit [12] is a command-line based simulator tool that uses user-mode linux to create network nodes. Finally, OMNet++ [13] is another open source discrete event simulator that offers a highly scalable and modular framework primarily for building any-kind of network (e.g., wired, wireless, on-chip) simulators. OMNet's community is vast providing domain-specific support for sensor networks, wireless ad-hoc networks, internet protocols, performance modelling, photonic networks etc. Considering the emulation requirements, two major virtualisation tools are OpenStack [14] that features deployment and management of virtual machines and Docker [15] that uses an engine to host containers of virtualised software.

Considering external sources for keeping the security assurance model up to date with changes in the threat landscape, various established cyber security threat and vulnerability lists can be considered; e.g., OWASP [16], ENISA [17], NIST [5]. Additionally, state of the art research efforts such as project CIPSEC [18] can provide valuable insights on personnel training courses, know-how on forensics analysis tools and education for protection against cascading effects.

Furthermore, various products established in the market of Cyber Training must be considered in order to identify gaps and needs in the domain. Kaspersky Interactive Protection Simulation (KIPS) [19] targets senior managers and decision makers to increase their security awareness by offering 6 scenarios (i.e., Corporation, Bank, eGovernment, Transport, Power Station, Water Plant) with related types of attacks. The Adaptive Awareness Portal [20] offers modular means for building your own training programmes but it emphasises on security awareness training, social engineering scenarios and e-learning management. Sophos Phish Threat [21] is another phishing training solution that utilises phishing simulations to educate and tests its end users. Inspired e-learning's Security Awareness Training [22] is a role-based solution educating against phishing scenario via a combination of videos and immersive situation-based role-playing scenarios. Finally, literature [23,24] indicates that the gamification of cyber range training offers promising results. This approach is followed by PwC's Game of Threats [25]; a solution that simulates cyber security breaches and uses gamification and game theory to provide a realistic game environment for an interactive blue team/red team experience. While there are various solutions in the market, most offer a fixed number of scenarios, role/domain specific limitations, minimal automation, and often lack the interaction with actual emulated cyber environments, thus lacking in realism.

3   Security Assurance Modelling

The proposed model-driven approach to Cyber-Range training is based on the definition of a Security Assurance Model that enables the systematic representation of the target organisation, its assets and their relations, and, ultimately, its security posture. This comprehensive approach allows us to identify and describe the assets of the system, their relations and their corresponding threats; the sequence of events that leads to the manifestation of these threats, alongside the responsible threat actor/s; the actions that trainees are expected to take against these attacks and the tools that may be used for this purpose; targets regarding the preparedness and effectiveness level that the trainees targeted by a Cyber-Range training programme are expected to achieve and how these levels may be measured in different stages of the delivery of the programme; and, finally, information on how the system can simulate and emulate the components necessary for its implementation. Additionally, it supports the effortless integration of potential changes in the composition of the organisation to the model (e.g., hiring a person, introducing a different job role, acquiring a software or hardware, removing old hardware, the disclosure of new vulnerabilities etc.); and enabling the generation of updated or brand-new Cyber Range training scenarios driven by these changes. To support the training, the core model is extended with the Cyber-Range sub-model that provides training relevant information; this allows it to build custom training scenarios for known cyber-attacks; new cyber-attacks; learning how to effectively and systematically utilise different security tools; learning the procedure for various types of actions (e.g., preparedness, detection and analysis, incident response, post incident response) and security processes in the target organisations and availability for different types of users of the system (e.g., end-user, administrator, technician, security engineer, blue/red team). This approach allows us to provide automated means for generation of tailored Cyber-Range training programmes that align with the organisation's composition and security requirements. The core assurance model and the Cyber-Range sub-model will be described in the following sections.

3.1   The Security Assurance Model

The core of the defined security assurance model are the organisations' assets (i.e., anything of value to the organisation), as well as the interplay between threats, vulnerabilities, security properties and security controls. For the sake of brevity, a view of the assurance model depicting the above is shown in Fig. 1. In the above, an asset can be a software asset (Software Architecture Layer (SAL) or Physical Architecture Layer (PAL)), a hardware asset, a physical infrastructure asset, data, person or a process. An asset inherits a number of attributes that are grouped into a single element namely the SecurityAssuranceModelElement.

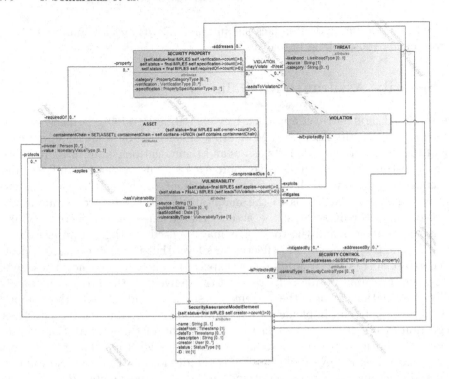

Fig. 1. Cyber Range sub-model UML diagram

The status of this element must be equal to final in order for an asset to have all its attributes/interconnections set. An asset may have security properties and be subject to vulnerabilities. A security property can be of type (a) integrity, (b) confidentiality, (c) availability; it also contains a verification attribute which describes the way a security property is verified and a specification of it; a security property is addressed by security control and may be required by assets. Threat is any circumstance or event with the potential to adversary impact an asset through unauthorised access, destruction, disclosure, modification of data, and/or denial of services; a threat exploits a number of vulnerabilities and violates a number of security properties. Vulnerability is a weakness an adversary could take advantage of to comprise the security properties of a resources; a vulnerability applies to a number of assets and is exploited by a threat which may lead to the violation of a security property if a security control is not in place or properly set up; a vulnerability can either be of physical or computational type. The latter applies to a computational asset (i.e., a Software or Hardware asset) and (mostly) follows the structure provided by National Vulnerability Database (NVD) while the former applies to a physical asset. Finally, a security control protects assets, address security properties and mitigates vulnerabilities. For the sake of brevity, a view of the assurance model depicting the above is shown in Fig. 1.

3.2   Cyber-Range Sub-model

The Cyber-Range sub-model is developed to provide essential information for the specification and implementation of the Cyber-Range training programmes. To accomplish this, the Cyber-Range sub-model extends the security assurance core model in the sense of utilising certain elements from it. Specifically, to generate training scenarios tailored to a target cyber system the cyber range sub-model considers the system's assets, threats, security properties and security controls; information provided by the core security assurance model. For example, if a system isn't prone to phishing attacks, then the cyber range sub-model will not generate a phishing training scenario. Furthermore, to generate different types of difficulty and execution steps of a training scenario, the cyber-range sub model considers information about a person asset (i.e., its role within the organisation). For instance, if an organisation doesn't have any security experts then scenarios targeting this role will not be generated. Additionally, the core security assurance model defines the sequence of events that lead to the manifestation of the threats which is utilised by the Cyber-Range sub- model to drive the different phases of the training scenario. Subsequently the Cyber-Range sub-model defines the threat actors (e.g., external attacker, insider) that cause the aforementioned sequence of events, as it is important for the purposes of the training. The Cyber-Range sub-model extends the network module of the core security assurance model to support virtual networking required for the communication between the emulation's Virtual Machines' (VM); this information (i.e., as a class) can also be of use to the security assurance model to support interactions between virtual systems within the actual cyber-system. Finally, Cyber-Range sub-model uses the organisations software assets to describe the components of the emulation and makes use of the inheritance and other associations with the asset. For example, the containment relationship between assets is utilised by the emulation to describe the link between a VM and its operating system. The diagram of the model is provided in the form of a Unified Modelling Language (UML) class diagram (see Fig. 2) together with a detailed description below.

The Training Programme is specified by a brief **description** of the programme; a measurable **goal** for the training (e.g., in a phishing scenario, the trainee has to identify at least 50% of the phishing emails); **roles** that the programme aims to train (e.g., end-user, administrator, technician, security engineer); **types** of training (e.g., analysis, detection, preparedness, security awareness); **legal frameworks** that align with the programme (e.g., GDPR compliance scenario); a **difficulty** value that indicates the difficulty rating (e.g., a phishing training scenario could be represented very simply to considerably complex).

The training programme covers one or more **Assets**, **Threats** and **Security Properties**; zero or more **Security Controls**. For example, a phishing scenario concerns an end-user asset, covers a phishing specific threat, that involves the confidentiality security property and involve a spam filter as a security control. In this example, if the target organization doesn't employ a spam filter, then it won't be included in the training.

The training programme records zero or more **actual trace** evidence for debugging or training reasons, including system and traffic logs; The training programme sets one or more expected trace to track the progress of a user during its training. For example, an end-user examines a malicious email, the email contains a link, the expected trace is to monitor if the user presses the link or not. In this example, the training programme isn't concerned with any actual trace; however, if this scenario involved a security expert (instead of an end-user) that needs to investigate the origins of the aforementioned link, then the training programme will need to monitor actual trace to follow the user's investigation path (e.g., packets send).

The training programme supports one more **training programme executions**. This class defines the actions enabled for the training programme considering the role of the account undergoing the training (e.g., in a phishing scenario the end user wouldn't have the same actions enabled versus a security engineer or administrator). The **account** class is utilised by one or more **person**, for example, a red team/blue team might have a single account for training their team members. Another example, an account can be used by a security engineer that wants to train on different positions, like system admin, forensics, blue/red team etc. A person can belong to zero or more groups.

The training programme consists of **phases**, that are the stages the programme is deployed; in some cases this class is driven by a **sequence of events** that lead to the specific manifestation of a threat generated by zero or more **threat actors** or in other cases this represent stages of the training scenario (e.g., for example on a blue/red team scenario, on phase 1 the blue team secures the system and on phases 2 the red team tries to exploit it and blue team defends it).

The implementation of the Cyber Range training will be accomplished through emulation and simulation of the components and the interactions among them. In some cases where the training requires an additional level of realism interactions with real assets (e.g., specialised devices like Global Position System (GPS), or actual devices like an email server), will be accommodated as well. The Cyber range model will provide the necessary information and links to resources to support the automated deployment of the playable training programmes via various simulation (e.g., OMNet++) and emulation tools (e.g., OpenStack). This information is described in the simulation and emulation sub-models. A training programme may involve more than one simulation and emulation sub-models, considering its deployment phases. For example, a training programme may deploy one virtual machine with a set of configurations for the implementation of its first phase and an additional virtual machine with different configurations for its second phase, or more than one virtual machines for its third phase. Similarly, the simulation model of training programme may deploy a simulation environment on one phase and a different simulation environment on another phase.

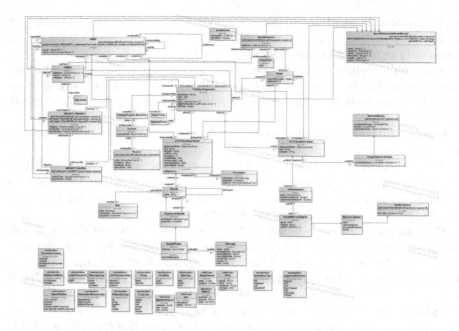

Fig. 2. Phishing scenario emulated and simulated components

Simulation Sub-model. The Simulation Sub-Model is responsible for indicating if a component can be simulated and is describing the simulation environment and its individual components. The simulation model specifies: if an asset can be simulated; the deployment mode for the simulated component (e.g., build from scratch or by using a template); which tool is used to realise the simulation (e.g., OMNet++, NS3); the required, initialisation operations (e.g., instantiation scripts); the time and date that the simulation started and ended; the current simulation and date time; the execution speed that describes how fast the simulation is passing; the random seed value that influences the random operations of the simulation in order to have reproducible randomness; the list of messages that are exchanged among the simulation's modules (e.g., events, commands, packets) during the simulation; Additionally, the simulation model facilitates different simulation environments if required by different phases of the training programme. To describe the composition, the model follows the paradigm of the Network Description (NED) language that is used by the discrete simulator OMNet++ which describes the simulation environment as topology of modules and connections between them. A module is a node in the composition of the simulation; it has a distinctive name, it can be either a simple or compound module and supports communication with other modules via Gates. A **module** is a node in the composition of the simulation; it has a distinctive name, it can be either a simple or compound module and supports communication with other modules via **Gates**.

A **compound module** consists of modules (i.e., simple or compound); it has one or more gates that enable the communication across modules in the compound system and the modules outside of it.

A **simple module** contains source code, specifying the behaviour of a simulated component (e.g., hardware, software), it involves one or more gates to enable the communication with other modules and, it uses operations to handle messages.

Gates can be either input, output and in-out and serve as a connection points between two modules.

A **connection** links two gates and has a specific behaviour, which is defined by characteristics; a variety of characteristics are supported but two main are the data-rate and the delay. All objects of the simulation model can be further specified by a set of parameters and properties.

Parameters are variables that further define an object; variables can hold different simple values (e.g., int, double, boolean, string) or even complex ones (e.g., XML). For example, for a simple module simulating an Application, a set of parameters may define the communication protocol (e.g., UDP, TCP, ICMP), destination address, packet length of message etc.

Properties are various meta-data that can be attached to objects of the simulation model. For example, properties can be statistics that are needed to track the progress of a trainee, such as end-to-end delay, jitter etc. Properties can also be rendering information of the specific object for the GUI.

Emulation Sub-model. The emulation sub-model indicates if a component can be emulated and is responsible for defining the information required by the training programme to emulate components and facilitate connections between them, with simulated components and possibly external real assets (e.g., external email server via the internet). Thus, the emulation sub-model includes information about the resources for instantiating and configuring the various emulated components, the deployment mode for them (e.g., from scratch, template) and the tool that will carry out the emulation (e.g., OpenStack). The resources involve images (i.e., software and OS settings), hardware characteristics (e.g., memory, Central Processing Unit (CPU) cores, storage) and connections details (e.g., internal connection of OpenStack resources or external communication).

The emulation sub-model describes the emulation environment as a structure of one or more software assets and zero or more virtual network modules.

Software assets are a set of programs used to operate computers and execute specific tasks; software can either be SAL or a PAL. SAL is an application later software module (e.g., the sources code of a software implemented within the organisation). PAL is platform level software, which describes an abstract software platform (e.g., a virtual machine, web server, OpenStack). Software asset inherits from asset the containment association; this indicates that an asset can contain or be managed by another asset. A containment can illustrate a deployment relation if an asset is contained in another asset and it operates within the containment. For instance, a software asset can be contained in a hardware asset, a software (SAL) operates in a virtual machine (PAL) and an Operating System (OS) controls the virtual machine.

The **virtual network module**, specifies the network configuration information necessary to support the communication between the emulated nodes, such as IP address, netmask, protocol and routing.

Finally, the emulation sub-model supports one or more phases, supporting the capability to modify the emulated components throughout the training scenario, according to the different phases that the training programme consists of.

4   Sample Scenario

In this section, three variants of training focused around phishing attacks are used to demonstrate the use of the proposed approach. The first is a simple phishing scenario where the trainee analyses a sequence of emails, to identify their legitimacy or malicious intent. The second is more complex, deployed on a realistic environment where the trainee uses their email client to identify and quarantine (i.e., isolate in the spam folder) phishing emails. The third is a capture the flag scenario. This involves the red and blue team and adds another level of complexity. More specifically, the trainer places vulnerabilities on a emulated smart home system, where the blue team tries to secure it and the red team tries to infiltrate it, scoring flags for each vulnerability exploited.

4.1   Simple Phishing Scenario

This is a social engineering scenario that targets trainees with low security expertise. In this simple scenario the user is trained on identifying phishing email attempts. The user logs into the Cyber Range application and is presented with a sequence of emails; their target is to select which of them are legitimate or malicious.

Scenario Modelling. By using the Cyber-Range sub-model the above scenario is specified below. The **Training Programme** class includes a description (i.e., Simple Phishing Scenario), a goal (i.e., identify 50% of the malicious emails), a type (i.e., preparedness), role (i.e., low privilege end-user), difficulty (i.e., 1). The **actual trace** that the training programme records include, system logs, traffic logs and the fake emails that were generated during this scenario. The **expected trace** that the training programme sets include the correct and wrong answers of the user. The **Training Programme Execution** class defines that the only actions allowed to the user is to indicate, via the Cyber Range software, if an email is legitimate or malicious. This scenario has only one **phase**, that is the presentation of the email sequence; when that phase concludes the scenario completed. The **Simulation Model** defines that the deployment mode for this scenario is "from scratch"; the tool that is used to implement the simulation is "Omnet"; the simulation timer starts with 0; messages that contain events; specifically the event that starts the simulation, 10 emails with varying states (i.e., legitimate or malicious), and the event that concludes the simulation; the randomness seed is set to 1; execution speed is set to 1; the starting time and date of the simulation is 20:00 25/8/2019; the end time and date of the simulation is 21:00 25/8/2019. The simulation topology consists of a simple module, an email generator application. The **Emulation Model** defines that the deployment mode for this scenario is "preset"; the tool that is used to implement the emulation is "Open-Stack"; and also provides a path to the preset template "/path/simplePhishingVM". The emulation sub-model consists of one Software-PAL asset (virtual machine) that will contain two Software-SAL assets (1) the operating system "Linux" (2) the simulation software. The scenario's emulated and simulated components are displayed in Fig. 3, while the populated model for this scenario is displayed in Fig. 4.

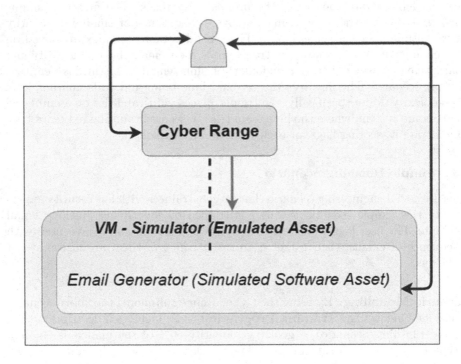

Fig. 3. Cyber Range sub-model Object diagram

Besides the aforementioned simplistic scenario, the Cyber-Range sub-model can facilitate more complex and advanced scenarios that will be explored as part of our future work.

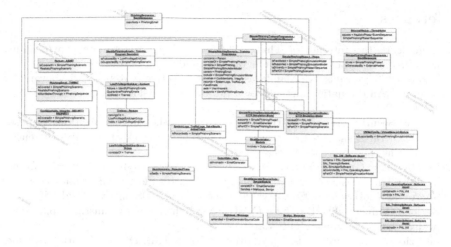

Fig. 4. Cyber-Range sub-model

5   Conclusions and Future Work

This paper presented a model-driven approach to Cyber-Range training based on the definition of a security assurance model, extending it to facilitate the definition of Cyber-Range training programmes, via the Cyber-Range sub-model. The Cyber-Range sub-model is developed with applicability and scalability in mind, so to offer realistic training scenarios via a hybrid approach of simulation and emulation, which satisfy the security training demands tailored to any specific organisation. While the security assurance model is used to model the organisation as a whole, the Cyber-Range sub-model facilitates the specification, implementation and automatic generation of Cyber-Range training programmes. To this end, the Cyber-Range sub-model links the Assets, Security Properties, Security Controls, and Threats covered in the scenario and defines it, in terms of training information (e.g., description of the scenario, goal), simulation (e.g., simulation tool, components) and emulation (e.g., emulation tool, components). This approach, along with the integration of state of the art simulation and emulation solutions, enables the automated deployment of cyber range training programmes tailored the specific organisation, in realistic environments, while also considering changes in the threat landscape (as encompassed in the assurance model).

Next steps will focus on further refining the Cyber-Range sub-model, testing its applicability in more complex and advanced scenarios, clearly defining the goal and scoring functions supported by the model for trainee performance evaluation. Special focus will be given on improving the simulation and emulation sub-models and integrating additional simulation and emulation tools [26] design. Moreover, the aim is to develop and demonstrate a proof of concept converting a Cyber-Range sub-model to a playable training scenario. Finally, the applicability of the proposed approach will be investigated in different domains, covering smart home, health-care, smart shipping environments.

References

1. A guide to the Internet of Things (2015). https://www-ssl.intel.com/content/www/us/en/internet-of-things/infographics/guide-to-iot.html
2. Rantos, K., Fysarakis, K., Manifavas, C.: How effective is your security awareness program? An evaluation methodology. Inf. Secur. J.: Glob. Perspect. **21**(6), 328–345 (2012)
3. Lack of Security Awareness Training Leaves Healthcare Organizations Exposed to Cyberattacks. https://www.hipaajournal.com/lack-of-security-awareness-training-healthcare-cyberattacks/
4. ENISA Smart Grid Security. https://www.enisa.europa.eu/topics/critical-information-infrastructures-and-services/smart-grids/smart-grids-and-smart-metering/ENISA_Annex%20II%20-%20Security%20Aspects%20of%20Smart%20Grid.pdf
5. National Vulnerability Database (NVD). NIST. https://www.nist.gov/programs-projects/national-vulnerability-database-nvd
6. Lagazio, M., Barnard-Wills, D., Rodrigues, R., Wright, D.: Certification Schemes for Cloud Computing. EU Commission Report, Digital Agenta for Europe (2014)
7. CUMULUS Project. Certification infrastructure for multi-layer cloud services project. D2.2 Certification models (2012). http://cordis.europa.eu/docs/projects/cnect/0/318580/080/deliverables/001-D22Certificationmodelsv1.pdf
8. Cloud Security Alliance, CSA Security, Trust and Assurance Registry (STAR). https://cloudsecurityalliance.org/star/
9. EuroCloud Start Audit. https://resilience.enisa.europa.eu/cloud-computing-certification/list-of-cloud-certification-schemes/eurocloud-star-audit
10. NS-3. https://www.nsnam.org/overview/what-is-ns-3/
11. GNS3. https://www.gns3.com/
12. Netkit. http://wiki.netkit.org/
13. OMNet++ Discrete Event Simulator. http://www.omnetpp.org
14. OpenStack. https://www.openstack.org/
15. Docker. https://www.docker.com/
16. OWASP Attack Categories. OWASP. https://www.owasp.org/index.php/Category:Attack
17. ENISA. https://www.enisa.europa.eu/
18. CIPSEC-EU Project. http://www.cipsec.eu/
19. Kaspersky Interactive Protection Simulation (KIPS). https://www.kaspersky.com/enterprise-security/security-awareness
20. MediaPro's Adaptive Awareness Portal. http://www.mediapro.com/adaptive-awareness-framework/adaptive-awareness-portal
21. Sophos Phish Threat. https://www.sophos.com/en-us/products/phish-threat.aspx
22. Inspired eLearning's Security Awareness Training. https://inspiredelearning.com/security-awareness/
23. Amorim, J.A., et al.: Gamified Training for Cyber Defence: Methods and Automated Tools for Situation and Threat Assessment (2013)
24. Boopathi, K., et al.: Learning Cyber Security Through Gamification (2015)
25. PwC's Game of Threats. https://www.pwc.co.uk/issues/cyber-security-data-privacy/services/game-of-threats.html
26. Jasima Discrete Event Simulator. https://www.simplan.de/en/software-2/jasima/

Towards the Insurance of Healthcare Systems

George Hatzivasilis[1]([✉]), Panos Chatziadam[1], Andreas Miaoudakis[1], Eftychia Lakka[1],
Sotiris Ioannidis[1], Alessia Alessio[2], Michail Smyrlis[3], George Spanoudakis[3],
Artsiom Yautsiukhin[4], Michalis Antoniou[5], and Nikos Stathiakis[6]

[1] Foundation for Research and Technology, Vassilika Vouton, Greece
{hatzivas,panosc,miaoudak,elakka,sotiris}@ics.forth.gr
[2] Network Integration and Solutions (NIS) Srl., Genoa, Italy
alessia.alessio@dgsgroup.it
[3] City, University of London, London, UK
{Michail.Smyrlis,G.E.Spanoudakis}@city.ac.uk
[4] Italian National Research Council (CNR), Naples, Italy
artsiom.yautsiukhin@iit.cnr.it
[5] HD Insurance (HDI) Ltd., Athens, Greece
michalis.antoniou@hellasdirect.gr
[6] Center for eHealth Applications and Sevices (CeHA), Heraklion, Greece
statiaki@ics.forth.gr

Abstract. Insurance of digital assets is becoming an important aspect nowadays, in order to reduce the investment risks in modern businesses. GDPR and other legal initiatives makes this necessity even more demanding as an organization is now accountable for the usage of its client data. In this paper, we present a cyber insurance framework, called CyberSure. The main contribution is the runtime integration of certification, risk management, and cyber insurance of cyber systems. Thus, the framework determines the current level of compliance with the acquired policies and provide early notifications for potential violations of them. CyberSure develops CUMULUS certification models for this purpose and, based on automated (or semi-automated) certification carried out using them, it develops ways of dynamically adjusting risk estimates, insurance policies and premiums. In particular, it considers the case of dynamic certification, based on continuous monitoring, dynamic testing and hybrid combinations of them, to adapt cyber insurance policies as the conditions of cyber system operation evolve and new data become available for adjusting to the associated risk. The applicability of the whole approach is demonstrated in the healthcare sector, for insuring an e-health software suite that is provided by an IT company to public and private hospitals in Greece. The overall approach can reduce the potential security incidents and the related economic loss, as the beneficiary deploys adequate protection mechanisms, whose proper operation is continually assessed, benefiting both the insured and the insurer.

Keywords: Insurance · Security · Risk analysis · Certification · E-Health · CyberSure

© Springer Nature Switzerland AG 2020
A. P. Fournaris et al. (Eds.): ESORICS 2019 Workshops, LNCS 11981, pp. 185–198, 2020.
https://doi.org/10.1007/978-3-030-42051-2_13

1 Introduction

Cyber insurance and security certification are two instruments to mitigate risk and establish trust in the provision of a wide spectrum of services and industries [1, 2], including healthcare, constructions, information and communications technology, transportation, hospitality, and banking operations (e.g. [3–6]). For several types of them, insurance and certification are also required by current legislation and regulations. From an insurance perspective, having cyber security certifications is a way to demonstrate that certain security controls have been implemented according to appropriate standards. Therefore, some insurance companies require reduced premiums for certified products [3, 7]. Another positive effect of certification and insurance is the enhanced trustworthiness for the services by the consumers. The increasing importance of the digital insurance market worldwide and in Europe and the challenges arising in it are indicated by several studies [1, 2, 8, 9].

Moreover, the use of health data has massive implications for how healthcare is delivered and how we manage our health [4]. The whole healthcare industry is undergoing a huge reformation, whereby access and utilization of vast amounts of data is becoming more and more accessible. How we manage data has enormous potential along with some large challenges for healthcare professionals, organizations that deliver healthcare, patients, and consumers of information.

The challenge with digitization in health is how to do it safely. Last year was a significant one for health plans when it came to data breaches and breach settlements. For example, the largest health data breach settlement in history was paid out in 2018, when Anthem, surrendered $16 million in fines to the Office for Civil Rights (OCR) for the breach of 79 million patient records in 2014–2015 [10].

And at the end of the last year, OCR named three health plans among the top 10 breaches it was investigating, including one involving the alleged unauthorized access or disclosure of 1.2 million records by the Employees Retirement System of Texas Health Plan [11]. Also, under investigation was the CNO Financial Group for allegedly exposing more than half a million records, by unauthorized access and disclosure. Those health plan breaches are increasing introspection about current vulnerabilities of protected health information. Figure 1 summarizes the security-related incidents for e-health that have been recorded by ENISA [12].

The overall aim of CyberSure is to develop an innovative framework, supporting the creation and management of cyber insurance policies, and offering a sound liability basis for establishing trust in cyber systems and services. Based on a comprehensive risk analysis prior the certification, the evaluated organization is given advices to improve its security. The system is certified and the insurance contracts are established. Then, monitoring controls are deployed in the system that assess the runtime protection status. The beneficiaries are timely notified in real operational time for potential violations in order to take the designated actions. In case of a security-related incident, the framework can justify in a short period what has happened, who is accountable, and which is the compensation amount. The overall operation reduces the security breaches and the related economic loss as the organization improves its security level in order to be certified and can be warned proactively when the adequate policies are not followed, benefitting the insurer as well.

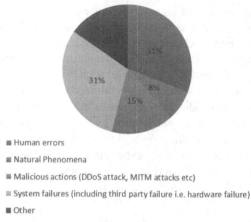

■ Human errors

■ Natural Phenomena

■ Malicious actions (DDoS attack, MITM attacks etc)

▩ System failures (including third party failure i.e. hardware failure)

■ Other

Fig. 1. Security incidents in e-health, by ENISA [12]

The rest paper is structured as follows: Sect. 2 outlines the related solutions of cyber insurance and their limitations. The evaluated healthcare system is sketched in Sect. 3. Section 4 details the proposed CyberSure framework and its underlying components. The assessment of the e-health system by CyberSure is detailed in Sect. 5. Finally, Sect. 6 concludes the results of this work.

2 Background Theory

Several studies have analyzed different types of markets (competitive, monopolistic and oligopolistic) for cyber insurance (e.g., [13, 14]), concluding that in most cases cyber insurance is a profitable option. However, it does not necessarily lead to improvement of security in cases of information asymmetry and interdependency among stakeholders [13, 15], although its positive influence on cyber protection has been shown in other cases in practice [3, 9, 14].

Cyber insurance is special with respect to other types of insurance [2, 8] and faces challenges related to its low maturity. The first of these challenges is the lack of statistical data about the assessment of cyber security incidents [16]. One of the reasons for this is that data about cyber security accidents are highly sensitive and, thus, organizations avoid their disclosure. However, this issue is increasingly mitigated by the introduction of incident notification schemes and regulations, such as the ones in EU by ENISA[1] and in USA by US-CERT[2].

Technological challenges for the cyber insurance market relate to the fast evolution of systems and attacks, difficulties in identifying occurrences and impact of security breaches, complex interdependencies amongst security properties, and information asymmetry [2, 3, 8]. In order to enable the market achieve higher maturity, other challenges to enable the market achieve higher maturity as well [8, 9], such as the limited

---

[1] ENISA – Incident report: https://www.enisa.europa.eu/topics/incident-reporting.

[2] US-CERT – National cyber incident response plan: https://www.us-cert.gov/sites/default/files/ncirp/National_Cyber_Incident_Response_Plan.pdf.

clarity of insurance coverage, the high amount of exceptions, and the correctness of policy languages which are of a legal (rather than technological) nature. On the other hand, despite these challenges cyber risks can still be insured [17, 18].

By relying on automated or semi-automated security certification and risk assessment, the CyberSure project will develop a novel framework for cyber insurance. In this framework, insurance policies can drive certification processes and be based on the outcomes of such processes, demanding specific attention to risks to be covered and relaxing the assessment of the risks that are not covered by the policy. The interaction between cyber insurance and security certification will also reduce the information asymmetry between insurers and clients. Automating cyber insurance management will also enable the generation of statistical data about risk assessment and rates of accidents, which will improve the maturity of the cyber insurance market.

3   The E-Health Pilot

For the e-health pilot validation, CyberSure will evaluate the Integrated Care Solutions – Medical (ICS-M) software suite[3]. In brief, the software suite is implemented by the Center for eHealth Applications & Services (CeHA), which operates in the context of Foundation for Research and Technology – Hellas (FORTH). The software is based upon an open, evolvable, and scalable architecture with a modular and robust infrastructure, comprising a series of IT services and applications. It constitutes an innovative service platform providing e-health functionality across heterogeneous networks, focusing on a patient-centered, clinically-driven, healthcare delivery system. High quality international trends are applied for the structure of the Electronic Health Record (EHR), as well as for the integration with third party systems by utilizing internationally acclaimed standards and protocols (like, e.g. HL7, DICOM etc.). Through its various applications and tools, ICS contributes to the treatment planning and the clinical decision support for disease management. The ICS suite is installed in 20 health service providers in Greece, including regional health authorities, hospitals, and primary care centers.

3.1   ICS-M Architecture

CyberSure assesses the protection level that is provided by the ICS-M software suite. Three available ICS-M services are examined:

- **Ward Management:** supports the placement of patients in specific clinic beds and the monitoring of the medical and nursing operations.
- **Supply Management:** the nursing personnel of each clinic orders specific medical and nutrition products, which are automatically recorded in the patient's healthcare history. ICS-M exchanges relevant information with the hospital's storage department (another third-party application).

---

[3] CeHA's ISC-M software suite: https://www.ics.forth.gr/ceha/FlipbookV1/CeHA.pdf.

– **EHR:** the medical and nursing personnel can access the health-records of each patient that is currently nursing at the specific clinic. As EHR contains sensitive personal data, role-based access control (RBAC) is imposed where each user accesses the subset of information that is absolutely necessary for the requested action, with medical personnel gaining higher degree of interaction.

The system architecture is depicted in Fig. 2. The medical records for all patients are maintained in the Data Base server. The data is accessed via the Application Server that implements the core backend functionality for the ICS-M services. The services can exchange information with third-party applications (e.g. the Laboratory Information System (LIS)) through the MS Rhapsody broker.

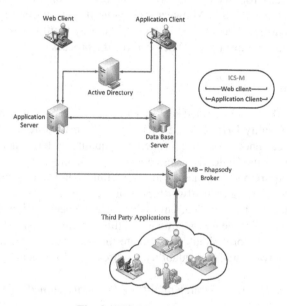

Fig. 2. ICS-M architecture

The Active Directory is utilized for the user authentication. Two interfaces are available. The *web client* communicates directly only with the Application Server, which then exchange information with the rest components (i.e. the Active Directory, the Data Base server, and the MS broker). On the other hand, the *application client* communicates directly with the Active Directory, the database, and the broker. The same functionality is offered by both interfaces.

3.2 Legislation

For the e-health pilot system, legal compliance must be assured by the following procedures: (i) informed consent and voluntary participation, (ii) confidentiality, (iii) anonymity and privacy, (iv) data usage/control/destruction, (v) minimal risk, (vi) transfer of data to third parties, and (vii) feedback.

Moreover, we have identified two main points that require special attention and focus from an ethical point of view:

- Ensure personal data protection and anonymity for the ICS-M components, which are deployed in Greece
- Ensure compliance with legislation and directives on both the European but also the national levels of Greece where the examined healthcare system is applied

These actions include a special effort to conform to the new European data protection legislation, labelled as General Data Protection Regulation (GDPR), which becomes enforceable in May 2018.

All collected data from the e-health systems must be anonymized in order to avoid any law violation. Also, the ICS-M owner must grant its permission regarding the integration of the monitoring mechanisms with the CyberSure platform. If it is required, the healthcare organization must be also informed for the process.

3.3 Certification

CeHA is an ISO27001:2013 certified center [19]. In 2011, ICS-M was certified with the EuroRec Seal of Quality EHR Level 2 by the European Institute for Health Records EuroRec[4]. The Seal encompasses 50 functional quality criteria, addressing various essential functions of the EHR: (i) access and security management of the system, (ii) basic functional requirements on medication, (iii) clinical data management, and (iv) the generic statements focusing on trustworthiness of the clinical data.

The nursing and medical applications of ICS-M have been designed for health care professionals who require the use of software within a medical context. The integration with the CyberSure platform should not violate the provided protection mechanisms. The key security, privacy, and dependability requirements for e-health pilot include:

1. the preservation of privacy, confidentiality and integrity of medical records in-transit and at-storage
2. the preservation of privacy, confidentiality and integrity of prescription and financial data in-transit and at-storage
3. and the preservation of a high degree of the e-health platform availability.

Thus, the integration of ICS-M and CyberSure's platform must comply with these technical criteria. The CyberSure platform does not have access to confidential information and EHR data. Additionally, the monitoring components at the pilot-end do not collect information regarding the patients' personal identifiable information (PII) and are compliant with the GDPR.

---

[4] EuroRec: www.eurorec.org.

3.4 Potential Insurance Scenarios

3.4.1 Contract 1 – Insurance of the IT Company that Provides a System to the Hospital

In case where the contract insures the availability of the main hospital's server during the working hours for the public, the CyberSure platform should inform the hospital about the potential violation of the contract before event really occurs (the server has not been maintained for some period and the possibility of malfunctioning during the next few days is high).

3.4.2 Contract 2 – Insurance of the Hospital (Direct PII Processor) Against GDPR Violations

The hospital's management sector needs to issue an insurance contract between the hospital and the IT Company in order to comply with the GDPR [20], regarding the privacy preservation and the prevention of unauthorized disclosure of health-related information. The company must guarantee that the role-based access to the sensitive personal data is enforced in all cases and the access rights are properly handled.

The monitoring controls on the pilot system should capture the personnel's login behavior (e.g. [21]) and inform the organization if the compliance with the security policy is not adhered (i.e. the password strength is not sufficient, the passwords are not changed regularly, there many failed login connections, etc.).

4 Risk Analysis, Certification, and Insurance with CyberSure

This section describes the deployment infrastructure of CyberSure. The various components of the CyberSure platform are installed in the relevant host companies with on-line monitoring controls being deployed on the healthcare organization.

CyberSure consists of four core components: the risk assessment tools (RIS[5] and NESSOS[6]), the insurance tool (HELLAS DIRECT[7]), the certification tool (CUMULUS [22, 23]), and the e-health system (ICS-M). The various systems are integrated and common interfaces are implemented in order to enable the exchange of information. The overall architecture and data flows are depicted in Fig. 3.

The two risk assessment tools that perform the baseline and comprehensive risk analysis are installed in the two host companies (the RIS tool in NIS and NESSOS in CNR). Security experts from these two companies interview the employees of the evaluated system, sequentially. For both tools, questionnaires and other information are completed on-line by the employees. The tools process the received data and the security experts finalize the risk assessment report. In the first iteration, the whole system is analyzed by the RIS tool. This initial universal documentation forms the baseline analysis, as illustrated in the next figure, is provided to the evaluated organization along with a set of suggested system upgrades. Then, a comprehensive risk analysis is conducted with

---

[5] RIS: https://dgsspa.com/pagine/15/ris.

[6] NESSOS: http://www.nessos-project.eu/.

[7] HDI tool: https://www.hellasdirect.gr/en/.

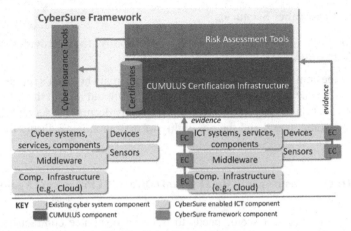

Fig. 3. CyberSure architecture

the NESSOS tool, which concentrates in the assets that exhibit the highest risk and takes into account real incidents in the examined organization and attack trends in the related business sector. Figure 4 depicts the overall risk analysis procedure. The process can be repeated for a more thorough analysis that examines the final compliance of the pilot system.

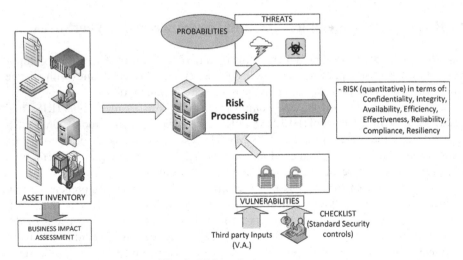

Fig. 4. Risk analysis processes

Then, the final risk assessment outcomes, which reflect the current cyber security status, are parsed by the insurance tool that runs in HELLAS DIRECT. Classified historical data regarding the considered risks are aggregated in the model together with other parameters, like discounts or penalizations. The insurance experts estimate the economic parameters of the potential insurance contract. The result is a set of contract offers that cover specific operational aspects and risks, providing several options from basic to full coverage of the economic loss. Each evaluated organization chooses one of the possible options based on its needs and financial capabilities.

Finally, the on-line certification model and the underlying controls must be established. These are the CyberSure's components that continuously monitor the pilot system, issue the CUMULUS certificate, and detect potential violations. The reasoning procedures are modelled in the Event Calculus (EC) [16]. Continuous monitoring is one of the main novelties of the framework and is detailed in the next section.

5   Assessment of the ICS-M with CyberSure

5.1   Real Case Scenario – Database and Application Servers' Up-Time

For the CyberSure framework, we will evaluate the protection level and the potential risks for the underlying assets of the three aforementioned ICS-M services. For real-time monitoring, the CyberSure platform will inspect parameters that are described in the Service License Agreement (SLA) for the fair use between the hospital and the ICS-M provider, such as the servers' up-time, the EHR availability, and the volume of concurrently supported clients.

The back-end infrastructure for the service (i.e. applications and database servers) is located in the private company's premises in Athens. The hospital in Heraklion runs a terminal application at the front office (i.e. for arranging rendezvous regarding the available medical services).

The company operations start at 9:00 a.m. The hospital operations for the public start at 8:00 a.m. If the server is out of service, the hospital has to wait for at least 1.5–2 h until the company's personnel reach the company, get informed, and fix the problem.

The hospital's management sector needs to issue an insurance contract between the hospital and the IT company, regarding the availability of the service. The company must guarantee a minimum delay in responding to availability issues for the front office applications. The delay cannot exceed the half hour during the working period where the hospital is open for the public (i.e. 8:00 a.m. – 4:00 p.m.).

Nevertheless, except from the availability of the service and the dependability of the provided solution, the authorized access to the data must be also ensured. Thus, the company must verify that the RBAC is enforced in all cases.

5.2   Risk Analysis and Evaluation

Figure 5 illustrates the evaluation results of the baseline risk assessment analysis for the examined ICS-M suite. As ICS-M was already a certified product (i.e. EuroRec), only minor improvements regarding the operational aspects in the examined hospital where made by RIS and NESSOS. Then, we proceed by deploying CUMULUS certification models and monitoring controls for the assets that are related with the aforementioned insurance scenarios and exhibit the highest risk.

Fig. 5. The baseline risk assessment result of the e-health pilot, made by the RIS tool

5.3   Insurance and CUMULUS Certification

The hospital's management sector needs to issue an insurance contract between the hospital and the IT company, regarding the availability of the service. The company must guarantee a minimum delay in responding to availability issues for the front office applications. The delay cannot exceed the half hour during the working period where the hospital is open for the public (i.e. 8:00 a.m.–4:00 p.m.).

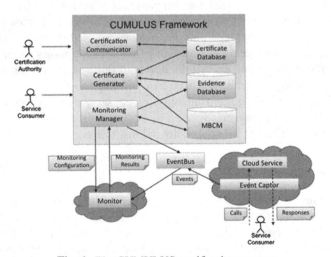

Fig. 6. The CUMULUS certification process

Figure 6 illustrates the CUMULUS certification process. The two organizations will issue a contract utilizing the extended version of CUMULUS [22, 23] via CyberSure.

The initial evaluation life-cycle is for one year and the contract can be renewed in an annual basis. Every day from Monday to Friday, the system must monitor the availability of the system every half hour during the working period 8:00 a.m.–4:00 p.m. The relevant SLA certification model (CM) is defined as:

```
<ns1:CertificationModel xmlns:xsi='http://www.w3.org/2001/XMLSchemainstance'
    xmlns:ns3='http://slasoi.org/monitoring/citymonitor/xmlrule'
    xmlns:ns2='http://assert4soa.eu/schema/Assert_SQL'
    xmlns:ns1='http://www.cumulus.org/certificate/model'
    xsi:schemaLocation='http://www.cumulus.org/certificate/model
CertificationModel-v2.xsd'>
    <CASignature></CASignature>
    <AbstractSecurityProperty
        expression="http://www.slaatsoi.org/commonTerms#availability"/>
    <AssessmentScheme>
        <EvidenceFrequency checkingPeriod="0.5" periodUnit="hours"
            minNoOfEvents ="1"></EvidenceFrequency>
        <SufficientEvidence minMonitoredPeriod="30" periodUnit="days"
            minNoOfEvents="350"></SufficientEvidence>
    </AssessmentScheme>
    <ValidityTests negated="false" certificateScope="SINGLE">
        <ns2:Condition negated="false" relation="EQUAL-TO">
            <ns2:Operand1>
                <ns2:AssertOperand facetName="Assert" facetType="Assert">
                    //ASSERTCore/SecurityProperty/@PropertyAbstractCategory
                </ns2:AssertOperand>
            </ns2:Operand1>
            <ns2:Operand2>
                <ns2:Constant type="STRING">
                    http://www.assert4soa.eu/ontology/security/security#Integrity
                </ns2:Constant>
            </ns2:Operand2>
        </ns2:Condition>
    </ValidityTests>
    <MonitoringConfigurations>
        <MonitoringConfiguration>
            <Component type="REASONER">
                <EndPoint>http://localhost:8888/...</EndPoint>
            </Component>
            ... ... ... ...
        </MonitoringConfiguration>
    </MonitoringConfigurations>
</ns1:CertificationModel>
```

The two entities request a certificate from the CyberSure's certification authority (CA) based on this CM. The CA submits it to the certificate generator (CG). The CG configures the monitoring infrastructure for starting the incremental certification process. CG calls the Service MonitorAbility Reporting Tool (SMART) and finds the monitoring infrastructure in the hospital's terminal devices (JAVA program that periodically checks the HTTP request status).

- The monitoring component is has a unique identifier $<CaseId>$
- Its type is SENSOR: It checks if the server is down or not
- The front office application is a web service $<\_SrvId>$. Technically, the availability is checked by examining periodically the HTTP request of the service's home page. If the status '404 Not Found' is returned, the service is unavailable. If the problem has not been fixed until the next try (i.e. half an hour), the assertion $<\_AssertId>$ has been violated.

The relevant EC-Assertion+ for the EVEnt REaSoning Tollkit (EVEREST) is defined as:

```
Event _eId = unavailable service – HTTP '404 Not Found' is returned
Rule r1:
            Happens(e(_eId, _SrvId, CaseId), _ti) =>
            HoldsAt(Unavailable(_SrvId), _ti)
Rule r2:
            Happens(e(_eId, _SrvId, CaseId), _ti) ∧ HoldsAt(Unavailable(_SrvId), _ti-1)=>
            HoldsAt(AssertionViolation(_AssertId, _SrvId), _ti)
```

If the problem is fixed, the monitoring status is restored.

```
Event _eId2 = problem fixed
Rule r3:
            Happens(e(_eId2, _SrvId), _ti) =>
            Terminate(Unavailable(_SrvId), _ti) AND
            Terminate(AssertionViolation(_AssertId, _SrvId), _ti)
```

As it concerns the authorization perspective, the IT company needs to insure its RBAC service. A similar procedure is followed, with monitoring controls assessing the access to the databases. The controls examine every access attempt to the data through the database's log file and, in case of violation, the framework is informed accordingly (as in the server's availability case above).

5.4 Accomplishments

This comprehensive approach, including the real-time contribution of CUMULUS, allows us to determine a more reliable picture of the service to insure. In this case, CyberSure achieves to:

- Provide information of historical data/incident to evaluate the actual probability a threat can occur
- Give a real-time evidence of a violation in a security control (e.g. availability and authorization)

The corresponding, potential, vulnerabilities might be evaluated immediately and objectively, and not "off-line" with the subjective contribution of the checklist. This can be applied to some technical controls of the ISO27002:2013 [19]. On the other side, if some specific security controls are managed by CUMULUS and are meaningful for the assessment, they can be included in the configuration or the risk analysis tools.

6   Conclusions

The digitalization of insurance procedures and the coverage of cyber assets has now become an emerging necessity. The European GDPR further stresses the need towards cyber insurance, especially for the healthcare organizations that process high volumes of personal sensitive data. This article proposes a novel cyber insurance framework, called CyberSure. It tackles several limitations of the current solutions by deploying continuous certification and real-time assessment of risk and the contracted insurance policies. As a case study, CyberSure is applied in order to assess the system of a medium-size public hospital in Greece. The overall approach is effective and efficient, and reduces the possibility of potential security events, benefiting both the insurer and the insured organizations.

Acknowledgements. This work has received funding from the European Union Horizon's 2020 research and innovation programme under the grant agreements No. 786890 (THREAT-ARREST) and No. 830927 (CONCORDIA), and the Marie Skodowska-Curie grant agreement No. 734815 (Cyber-Sure).

References

1. Pritchett, W.: Insurtech 10: Trends for 2019. The Digital Insurer, KPMG, March 2019, pp. 1–36 (2019)
2. Matouschek, G.: InsturTechs – Reshaping insurance today. In: 27th congress of the International Association of Legal Protection Insurance (RIAD), 5–6 October 2017, Ireland, Dublin, pp. 1–29 (2017)
3. Millaire, P., et al.: Latest industry trends in cyber security and cyber insurance. CyberCube, pp. 1–10, May 2018
4. Hatzivasilis, G., et al.: Review of security and privacy for the Internet of Medical Things (IoMT). In: IEEE DCOSS, 29–31 May 2019, Santorini Island, Greece, pp. 8–15 (2019)
5. Hatzivasilis, G., et al.: The CE-IoT framework for green ICT organizations. In: IEEE DCOSS, 29–31 May 2019, Santorini Island, Greece, pp. 1–7 (2019)
6. Hatzivasilis, G., et al.: Real-time management of railway CPS. In: IEEE ECYPS, 11–15 June 2017, Bar Montenegro, pp. 1–4 (2017)
7. Woods, D., Simpson, A.: Policy measures and cyber insurance: a framework. J. Cyber Policy **2**(2), 209–226 (2017)
8. Marotta, A., et al.: Cyber-insurance survey. Comput. Sci. Rev. **24**, 35–61 (2017)
9. Meland, P.H., Tøndel, I.A., Solhaug, B.: Mitigating risk with cyberinsurance. IEEE Secur. Privacy **13**(6), 38–43 (2015)
10. U.S. Department of Health & Human Services (HHS), "Anthem pays OCR $16 million in record HIPAA settlement following largest U.S. health data breach in history," HHS Press Office, 15 October 2018
11. Largest healthcare data breaches of 2018. HIPPA J. (2018). https://www.hipaajournal.com/largest-healthcare-data-breaches-of-2018/
12. Liveri, D., Sarri, A., Skouloudi, C.: Security and resilience in eHealth. ENISA reports, 15 March 2016, pp. 1–48 (2016)
13. Pal, R., Golubchik, L., Psounis, K., Hui, P.: Will cyber-insurance improve network security? A market analysis. In: IEEE INFOCOM, 27 April–2 May 2014, Toronto, Canada, pp. 235–243 (2014)
14. Pal, R., Golubchik, L., Psounis, K., Hui, P.: Security pricing as enabler of cyber-insurance a first look at differentiated pricing markets. IEEE Trans. Dependable Secure Comput. **16**(2), 358–372 (2019)
15. Martinelli, F., et al.: Preventing the drop in security investments for non-competitive cyber-insurance market. In: Cuppens, N., Cuppens, F., Lanet, J.L., Legay, A., Garcia-Alfaro, J. (eds.) CRiSIS 2017. LNCS, vol. 10694, pp. 1–16. Springer, Heidelberg (2017). https://doi.org/10.1007/978-3-319-76687-4_11

16. Hatzivasilis, G., et al.: AmbISPDM: managing embedded systems in ambient environment and disaster mitigation planning. Appl. Intell. **48**(6), 1623–1643 (2017)
17. Meland, P.H., Seehusen, F.: When to treat security risks with cyber insurance. Int. J. Cyber Situational Awareness, C-MRiC **3**(1), 39–60 (2018)
18. Romanosky, S., et al.: Content analysis of cyber insurance policies: how to carriers price cyber risk? J. Cybersecurity **5**(1), 1–38 (2019)
19. Information security management systems, ISO/IEC 27001 (2013). https://www.iso.org/isoiec-27001-information-security.html
20. Directive 95/46/EC – General Data Protection Regulation (GDPR), European Parliament and European Council (2016). https://eur-lex.europa.eu/legal-content/EN/ALL/?uri=celex%3A32016R0679
21. Hatzivasilis, G.: Password-hashing status. Cryptography. J. **1**(2), 1–31 (2017)
22. Krotsiani, M., Spanoudakis, G., Kloukinas, C.: Monitoring-based certification of cloud service security. In: Debruyne, C., et al. (eds.) OTM 2015. LNCS, vol. 9415, pp. 644–659. Springer, Heidelberg (2015). https://doi.org/10.1007/978-3-319-26148-5_44
23. Krotsiani, M., Kloukinas, C., Spanoudakis, G.: Cloud certification process validation using formal methods. In: Maximilien, M., Vallecillo, A., Wang, J., Oriol, M. (eds.) ICSOC 2017. LNCS, vol. 10601, pp. 65–79. Springer, Heidelberg (2017). https://doi.org/10.1007/978-3-319-69035-3_5

The THREAT-ARREST Cyber-Security Training Platform

Othonas Soultatos[1,9](✉), Konstantinos Fysarakis[2], George Spanoudakis[9],
Hristo Koshutanski[3], Ernesto Damiani[4], Kristian Beckers[5], Dirk Wortmann[6],
George Bravos[7], and Menelaos Ioannidis[8]

[1] Foundation for Research and Technology, Vassilika Vouton, 70013 Heraklion, Greece
sultatos@ics.forth.gr
[2] Sphynx Technology Solutions AG, 6300 Zug, Switzerland
fysarakis@sphynx.ch
[3] ATOS Spain SA, 28037 Madrid, Spain
hristo.koshutanski@atos.net
[4] University of Milan, 20122 Milan, Italy
ernesto.damiani@unimi.it
[5] Social Engineering Academy (SEA), 60322 Frankfurt, Germany
kristian.beckers@social-engineering.academy
[6] SimPlan AG, 63452 Hanau, Germany
dirkwortmann@simplan.de
[7] Information Technology for Market Leadership (ITML), 11525 Athens, Greece
gebravos@itml.gr
[8] Lightsource Labs Limited (LSE), Dublin D06C8X4, Ireland
menelaos@lightsourcelabs.com
[9] Department of Computer Science, City, University of London, London, UK
{othonas.soultatos,G.E.Spanoudakis}@city.ac.uk

Abstract. Cyber security is always a main concern for critical infrastructures and nation-wide safety and sustainability. Thus, advanced cyber ranges and security training is becoming imperative for the involved organizations. This paper presets a cyber security training platform, called THREAT-ARREST. The various platform modules can analyze an organization's system, identify the most critical threats, and tailor a training program to its personnel needs. Then, different training programmes are created based on the trainee types (i.e. administrator, simple operator, etc.), providing several teaching procedures and accomplishing diverse learning goals. One of the main novelties of THREAT-ARREST is the modelling of these programmes along with the runtime monitoring, management, and evaluation operations. The platform is generic. Nevertheless, its applicability in a smart energy case study is detailed.

Keywords: Security training · Cyber range · Training programmes · Training exercises · Dynamic adaptation · CTTP · Smart grid · Smart energy

© Springer Nature Switzerland AG 2020
A. P. Fournaris et al. (Eds.): ESORICS 2019 Workshops, LNCS 11981, pp. 199–214, 2020.
https://doi.org/10.1007/978-3-030-42051-2_14

1 Introduction

Massive advancements in computer technologies have given rise to a cyber-infrastructure enabling the acquisition, storage, sharing, integration, and processing of data, through distributed software services cutting across organizational and national boundaries. It is estimated that up to 200 billion devices will be connected to the Internet by 2020 (i.e. 26 connected objects per person [1]), while 5.5 million new "things" were being connected every day in 2016 alone. This cyber infrastructure has facilitated the development of complex interconnected cyber systems, supporting an ever-increasing spectrum of everyday personal, societal and business activities, making modern society and enterprise increasingly dependent on them.

The unprecedented levels of data sharing and cyber systems interoperability, and the complex compositional structures of cyber systems have also led to increasingly sophisticated, stealthy, targeted, and multi-faceted cyberattacks. The "cyber-war" against essential infrastructures around the globe has already been underway. Examples include attacks in airports and airlines [2, 3] government services (U.S. Office of Personnel Management [4]), health insurance companies and health providers [5].

Preserving the security of cyber systems is a particularly challenging problem [6–8]. This is due to the inherent difficulty of: (i) identifying vulnerabilities in the complex end-to-end compositions of heterogeneous components and devices of such systems, (ii) selecting appropriate security controls for them, and (iii) preserving end-to-end security when dynamic changes occur in the components, the compositional structures and the infrastructures that they deploy.

However, despite the importance of security training, the initiatives to "educate" enterprise personnel (particularly of SMEs) and make it realize the importance cybersecurity are limited [9, 10]. The provision of effective and comprehensive security training in organizations and enterprises is becoming even more important due to the sheer complexity of cyber systems that need to be secured and the ever-increasing number and level of sophistication of cyber-attacks [11, 12].

Even though at a first glance, the existence of a wide spectrum of security tools appears to provide a comprehensive machinery for detecting and responding effectively to cyber-attacks (e.g. [13, 14]), in reality the very existence of several alternative tools, targeting different aspects and layers of modern cyber systems and having different capabilities, makes it difficult to establish effective tool usage strategies and processes for addressing the ever-expanding landscape of cyber-attacks. Moreover, the advent of more "intelligent" cyber-security solutions [8, 13], which make use of technologies, like machine learning, statistical analysis and user behavior analysis, requires sophisticated and hands-on training of the key personnel of organizations, who have responsibility for security, for the latter to be able to master them.

Overcoming the above difficulties requires the development of advanced security training frameworks to adequately prepare stakeholders with responsibility in defending high-risk computer systems and organizations to counter advanced cyber-attacks. A framework of this type must be able to accommodate and cover emerging security controls and tool innovations from different providers in a scalable manner (i.e. [7, 15]). It should also be supported by experience sharing [16, 17] and put emphasis on the human aspects of security. In this direction, technologies, such as serious gaming (e.g.

[18–20]), whose aim is to address security attacks launched through social engineering, get an important role, as one of the most effective ways to defend systems against attacks and train humans to resist social-engineering.

In response to these needs, the overall aim of THREAT-ARREST is to develop an advanced training platform incorporating emulation, simulation, serious gaming, and visualization capabilities to adequately prepare stakeholders with different types of responsibility and levels of expertise in defending high-risk cyber systems, and organizations to counter advanced, known, and new cyber-attacks. The THREAT-ARREST platform will deliver security training, based on a model-driven approach where **cyber threat and training preparation (CTTP)** models, specifying the potential attacks, the security controls of cyber systems against them, and the tools that may be used to assess the effectiveness of these controls, will drive the training process, and align it (where possible) with operational cyber system security assurance mechanisms to ensure the relevance of training. The platform will also support trainee performance evaluation and training programme evaluation, and adapt training programmes based on them. The effectiveness of the framework will be validated on a real pilot system in the area of smart energy.

The rest paper is structured as follows: Sect. 2 presents the related work in cyber security training landscape along with a qualitative comparison. Section 3 defines the CTTP modeling and its application on a smart energy scenario. Section 4 details the platform architecture and the underlying modules for hybrid training, gamification, emulation, simulation, and visualization. Finally, Sect. 5 concludes this work.

2 Related Work and Comparison

Today, there are several research and commercial solutions for cyber security training for organizations or individuals. The most representative of them are reviewed below.

Apart from the general-purpose online training platforms (e.g. Coursera Udacity, edX, etc.) that can provide main educational courses on cyber security, there are also specialized platforms, like the SANS [21], CyberInternAcademy [22], StationX [23], Cybrary [24], and AwareGO [25]. In most cases, they target individual students/trainees whose goal is to develop/sharpen new skills. Nevertheless, these approaches fail when it comes to hands-on experience on real systems or cyber ranges.

The German company BeOne Development has implement its own solution of security awareness training [26]. It includes e-learning modules, awareness videos, and simulation tools. For the former, the BePhished simulator is utilized, which is focused on phishing attacks. To facilitate the process for establishing new training exercises, they have also developed the Security Awareness Library which contains 28 learning topics. Multinational working environments and cultural differences are taken into account, as the training becomes more effective when used examples are recognized by employees from their own daily jobs. The product can offer pre-packaged and generic programs, organization-specific look and feel, or tailor-made programs that have been developed in close consultation with the customer. The overall approach supports general teaching processes for the main training, while the more advanced simulation-centric training targets phishing attempts.

ISACA developed the CyberSecurity Nexus (CSX) training platform [27]. It provides instructional lectures and hands-on lab works on real equipment. The trainee gets experience in applying basic concepts and industry-leading methods. Capture-the-flag scenarios are also supported, advancing the trainee's technical skills. The users are assessed and the goal is to earn a relevant professional certification. This would assist an organization's chief information security officer (CISO) to hire employees with the right skills.

Kaspersky offers advanced computer-based training programs for all organizational levels [28]. Except from online training, the platform supports benchmarking against world/industry averages, robust simulation, and true gamification. It builds an educational schedule and internal learning with constant reinforcement, offered automatically through a blend of training formats, including learning modules, email reinforcement, tests, and simulated phishing attacks. It follows the trainees' progress via a user-friendly dashboard, supporting live data tracking, trends, and forecasts.

CyberBit was founded in 2015 and its cyber security training platform provides a realistic simulation of cyber-attacks in an environment that mirrors a real-life network and a security operations center (SOC) [29]. This cyber range solution is consisted of a virtual network (mirror of an actual system), an attack engine (malicious traffic), a traffic generator (legitimate data), and a virtual SOC (trainee's viewpoint). The goal is to simulate hyper-realistic cyber ranges. The platform provides a high variety of training scenarios, such as incident response and pentesting. The trainers set up the training session which includes debriefing, session recording, trainee ranking, and scenario management. Scenario customization is also supported via a graphical interface.

On the other hand, the THREAT-ARREST platform offers training on known and/or new advanced cyber-attack scenarios, taking different types of actions against them, including: preparedness, detection and analysis, incident response, and post incident response actions. The THREAT-ARREST platform supports the use of security testing, monitoring and assessment tools at different layers in the implementation stack, including:

- Network layer tools (e.g. intrusion detection systems, firewalls, honeypots/honeynet)
- Infrastructure layer tools (e.g. security monitors, passive and active penetration testing tools (e.g. configuration testing, SSL/TLS testing)
- Application layer tools (e.g. security monitors, code analysis, as well as passive and active penetration testing tools such as authentication testing, database testing, session management testing, data validation & injection testing)

The procedure begins by analyzing the organization's system. An assurance tool evaluates the current security level and reports the most significant security issues that must drive the following training process. Then, hybrid training programmes are produced, tailored to the organization needs and the trainee types. This includes the main training material along with serious games, as well as, the simulation and emulation of the cyber range system. THREAT-ARREST also provides continuous evaluation of: (a) the performance of individual trainees in specific training programmes; and (b) the effectiveness of training programmes across sub-groups of trainees or the entire organization. These evaluations will be used to tailor programmes to the needs of individual trainees or alter them at a more macroscopic level.

The qualitative comparison results are summarized in Table 1. THREAT-ARREST combines all modern training aspects of serious gaming, emulation, and simulation in a concrete manner, and offers continuous security assurance and programme adaptation based on the trainee's performance and skills.

Table 1. Cyber-security training platforms: (A) THREAT-ARREST, (B) BeOne, (C) Kaspersky, (D) ISACA CSX, (E) CyberBit, (F) online training platforms. The following notations are utilized for (Y)es, (N)o, and (P)arial.

Feature	A	B	C	D	E	F
Automatic security vulnerability analysis of a pilot system	Y	N	N	N	N	N
Multi-layer modelling	Y	P	Y	Y	Y	P
Continuous security assurance	Y	N	N	Y	Y	N
Serious gaming	Y	N	Y	Y	N	P
Realistic simulation of cyber systems	Y	P	Y	Y	Y	N
Combination of emulated and real equipment	Y	N	P	Y	N	N
Programme runtime evaluation	Y	N	N	Y	Y	Y
Programme runtime adaptation	Y	N	Y	Y	N	P

3 CTTP Modelling

3.1 Pilot System Modelling and Continuous Security Assurance

One of the main novelties of the THREAT-ARREST approach is the modelling of the training process, the real-time assessment of the security features for an examined system, and the continuous evaluation of the trainer.

The development of the THREAT-ARREST framework will be based on a model-driven approach in which the delivery of cyber-threat training and preparation (CTTP) programmes will be driven by CTTP models. A CTTP model will define the structure and automate the development of a CTTP programme by determining:

1. the components of a cyber-system, their relations and the cyber threats covered by the CTTP programme
2. the ways in which these components should be simulated and emulated
3. the ways in which cyber-attacks against the cyber system may manifest themselves
4. the actions that trainees are expected to take against these attacks and the tools that may be used for this purpose, and
5. targets regarding the preparedness and effectiveness level that the trainees targeted by a CTTP programme are expected to achieve and how these levels may be measured in different stages of the delivery of the programme.

A CTTP model covers two key layers in the implementation of a cyber-system, i.e., the software architecture layer (SAL) and the physical architecture layer (PAL). It also covers dependencies between components in SAL & PAL. The SAL part of the CTTP model is an application-level model of the cyber system, specifying the different software components of it (e.g. data repositories and servers, client facing dashboards, clients and drivers running on external devices, etc.). SAL is specified by a SAL sub-model having the form of a typed directed graph. The nodes of this graph represent the software components of the cyber system and specify: (i) the type of the software component, (ii) any implementation dependencies that the component may have (e.g., on libraries and operating systems), and (iii) the key responses that the component produces upon input stimuli. Part (ii) is important for emulating the component and part (iii) is important for simulating the component. The edges of the SAL model represent call, data and resource dependencies between components (e.g., data flows, access to shared memories).

The PAL part of the CTTP model covers the network and the computational infrastructure used by the cyber system. PAL is specified by a PAL sub-model, which is also a typed directed graph. The nodes of this graph represent the physical components of the cyber system including, for example, computer servers, terminals, network routers and controllers and other telecommunication components, surveillance equipment, sensors and devices that may be used by the system (e.g., external mobile devices, special hardware of industrial automation platforms, healthcare equipment or geolocation devices). PAL model nodes hold information about the properties of the physical component they represent. They describe, for example, the type of the physical component (e.g. desktop, server, routing device, etc.), the key responses that it produces upon input stimuli, and other general capabilities (e.g. number of CPU-cores, storage and memory capabilities). The edges connecting the nodes of the PAL model represent the network-level topology of the cyber system and describe the connection's type and properties such as IP address space, link rate, type of linkage (e.g. wireless, Ethernet, etc.).

The CTTP model includes also specifications of two more important aspects that are necessary for the delivery of a CTTP programme. These are:

(a) A deployment model specifying the allocation of the software (SAL) components of the cyber system onto its physical (PAL) components.
(b) An assurance model specifying known threats that may affect the physical or software components of the system; assumptions regarding the external environment of the cyber system and the behavior of agents (human- or system-agents) related to it that can affect it (i.e., prevent or enable threats); and security controls used to mitigate the risks arising from the threats. The assurance sub-model also specifies assessment measures, determining how to detect attacks arising from the threats and assess the effectiveness of the security controls. It also specifies the assessment tools that should be used to realize these measures prior to the deployment of the system (e.g., static analysis and testing tools) or during the operation of the system (monitoring and dynamic testing tools). It will also specify parameters determining how the attacks may manifest themselves, how the security controls may respond to

them (e.g., the attack manifestation events captured and detection time, the undertaken response actions) and the outputs that the deployed assessment tools will generate for the situation.

3.2 Motivating Example – Smart Energy Home

We demonstrate the application of CTTP modeling on a smart energy scenario, where energy is collected by solar panels installed in houses. The solution is provided by the Lightsource company in Ireland. Figure 1 depicts the main application modules.

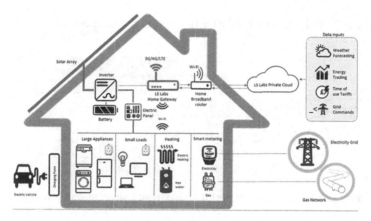

Fig. 1. Smart energy system architecture

Figures 2 and 3 show the PAL and SAL parts of the CTTP model of a smart energy metering cyber system for smart homes. As shown in Fig. 2, at the PAL layer, this cyber system consists of a number of smart-meters (i.e., SM-1, ..., SM-n), and a number of photovoltaic sensor devices (i.e., Sensor-1, ..., Sensor-n). The smart-meters are connected to the Smart Meter Server while the sensors are connected to the Sensor Server for monitoring and management purposes. The two servers are connected to the Main Server (Gateway), which is equipped with a hardware Security Device (i.e., trusted platform module (TPM) enabled host). The entire system is connected to the internet via firewall equipment.

As shown in Fig. 3, the SAL layer of the smart metering system consists of an external communication service, used by third party operators, and an internal communication service. The two services are connected and share a set of software security tools offering authentication and security monitoring. The external communication service interfaces with an Intrusion Detection System (IDS), connecting the entire system to the Internet. The internal communication application is used for interconnecting the smart-meter monitoring and command service with the sensor monitoring and command service. The two monitoring and command services are used in order to collect information from the smart-meters and photovoltaic sensors, issue control commands and act as dashboards for data visualization. They also interface with the appropriate software

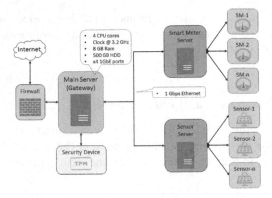

Fig. 2. PAL sub-model of the CTTP model of a smart metering system.

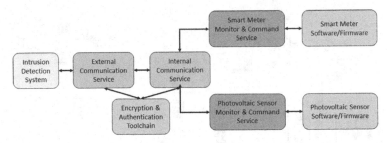

Fig. 3. SAL sub-model of the CTTP model of a smart metering system.

and firmware solutions, driving the various sensors and smart-meters, towards data and command exchange. Figure 3 depicts the SAL layer as graph.

The deployment of SAL components onto PAL components is shown in Fig. 4. In particular, we can see that some PAL components are used in order to host a single SAL component, such as the firewall solution. Multiple software services are hosted on a single device, such as the two communication services, while on the other hand software components depend on multiple PAL components, such as the smart-meter and sensor software/firmware components. As we can see, the deployment sub model is conceptualized as a three-dimensional graph, indicating the relation between the PAL and SAL sub-models, where a node of each level may have dependencies to one or multiple nodes of the same or different level.

A part of the assurance model of the smart metering system in our example is shown in Fig. 5. This model specifies threats for system components, assumptions affecting the manifestation of them, and the security controls that are used to mitigate the threats. The model shown in Fig. 5 is based on the protection profile for smart gateways specified in [30]. According to the part of the model shown in the figure, the smart metering system gateway is threatened by Time Modification, Local Data Disclosure, Resident Data and Privacy threats. For each of these threats, the model specifies: (a) assumptions regarding the behavior of system components and actors that affect the manifestation of the threat (e.g. the assumption that system administrators are trusted - A.TrustedAdmins)

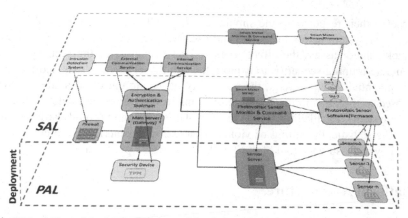

Fig. 4. PAL, SAL and deployment sub-models of the CTTP model of a smart metering system.

- and (b) the security controls which are used to mitigate the threats (e.g. the use of user authentication before any action - i.e. FIA. UAU. 2). CTTP models of the form described above will provide the basis for generating training scenarios involving the simulation and/or emulation of cyber system components, attacks launched upon them, and the use of assessment and response tools.

Based on the threats and parameters of the assurance model, for example, it will be possible to generate synthetic system events corresponding to the manifestation of attacks, feed them onto the emulated or simulated physical or software security controls

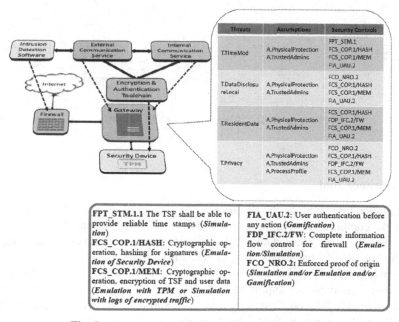

Fig. 5. Assurance model of a smart metering system.

and observe their response to the simulated attacks. It will also be possible to check the ability of system actors to initiate and use the assessment tools in order to detect the attacks and/or assess the effectiveness of the responses of the security controls, and generate training scenarios to explore the validity of assumptions and the impact of their potential violation (e.g., the possibility of having untrusted admin personnel, as opposed to the assumption A.TrustedAdmins in the assurance model of the smart metering system). The likelihood of a violation of this assumption could also be estimated through the statistical profiling of violation indicators (events) that are collected and analyzed by the assurance tool of the THREAT-ARREST platform.

4 Platform Architecture

An initial conceptualization of the platform is shown in Fig. 6. As shown in the figure, the envisaged platform will comprise the following key components.

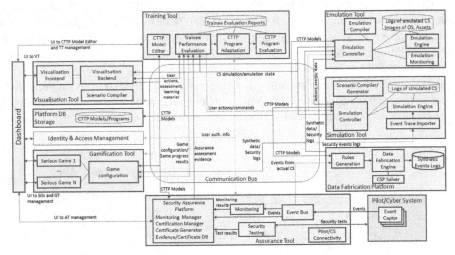

Fig. 6. The THREAT-ARREST platform.

4.1 Assurance Tool

The assurance tool supports the continuous assessment of the cyber system's security through the combination of runtime monitoring and dynamic testing in order to provide information about the actual status. It also collects runtime system events and generates alerts that provide the basis for setting up realistic simulations.

The assurance tool carries out a continuous runtime assessment of the aspects of the target cyber system that are important for CTTP training programme. These aspects are defined by the CTTP model (security assurance sub model). For example, the CTTP model defines the components of the cyber system that should be monitored, the events of these components that are of importance (e.g. operating system calls, external service calls, user actions, etc.), and the conditions that should be satisfied by them. It also defines dynamic system tests that should be executed at runtime and should be combined with monitoring to form hybrid assessments of security [31, 32]. The collected monitoring events and testing outcomes form the operational system evidence that is passed over to simulation component to enable statistical profiling and thereby the generation of realistic simulations.

4.2 Hybrid Training

The CTTP models enable training scenarios based on hybrid combinations of simulation and emulation training. In these scenarios, some of the components of the cyber system will be emulated and the rest will be simulated. This hybrid training mode is useful when emulating the entire system is not needed or is not feasible but hands-on experience is required for certain system components. In hybrid training scenarios, trainees will in general be expected to monitor, test and take actions on emulated components, and observe the effects of these actions to the rest of the cyber system following the propagation of these effects through simulation. Hybrid training scenarios will also be useful in cases where the training process is divided in consecutive related parts. Each part may require that specific components should be emulated and the rest could be simulated in order to preserve system resources. Using a hybrid approach, the training platform will be able to terminate the emulation of specific components and proceed with their simulation, as they will not be required for a certain part of the training, or choose to emulate components that used to me simulated in a previous part of the training phase. Overall, the training scenarios that will be supported by THREAT-ARREST will vary with respect to:

– The extent of *system coverage*: With regards to this criterion, scenarios may be distinguished into those involving attacks targeted to: (a) single components of a cyber-system, (b) clusters (i.e., subsets of interconnected) of components of a cyber-system, or (c) the whole set of components of a cyber-system.
– The *type of attacks*: With regards to this criterion, scenarios may be distinguished into those involving: (a) historic attacks, or (b) live attacks unfolding as the scenario is simulated by the platform.
– The *type of response* required: With regards to this criterion, scenarios may be distinguished with regards to the type of response to a security incident that they are aimed to train people for. Different types of response are typically defined in reference to the phase in the life cycle of an incident that they focus on. These, according to [33], are: (a) preparation/preventive responses (i.e., actions whose aim is to prepare organizations for incident handling and/or prevention), (b) detection and analysis responses, (c) containment, eradication and recovery responses, or (d) post-incident responses.
– The *trainee's profile*: With regards this criterion, scenarios may be distinguished with regards to the initial cognitive profile of the trainee, as obtained from the security games and the performance of the trainee in the training scenarios that he/she has been exposed so far.

The allowed forms of variability along the above factors will be defined as part of scenarios forming a CTTP programme. The training tool will support the definition of CTTP models and programmes, the presentation of learning materials/exercises of CTTP programmes, enable trainee actions in response to cyber threats, interactions with simulated and/or emulated cyber system components, trainee performance evaluation, CTTP programme evaluation and adaptation.

Beyond supporting the definition of CTTP models and programmes, the training tool will also ensure a high level of interactivity with the trainees and deliver the training scenarios, enabling them to respond, sending the appropriate commands to the emulated and simulated components. Also, it will continuously receive information about the status of the emulation and simulation, evaluating in real time the state of progress based on user's responses and their effects on the components and will determine the overall performance of the trainees. The tool will also be responsible for validating the assumptions of the assurance model based on the trainees' responses to the training scenarios and generate warnings in case these assumptions are violated. It will also be able to assess the performance of trainees and evaluate and adapt CTTP programmes. Finally, the tool will collaborate with the visualization tool for the effective delivery of training.

4.3 Gamification

Beyond simulation, emulation and hybrid-based training, the CTTP model will also drive training based on games. This form of training will focus on developing skills to prevent attacks based on exploiting human factors (i.e., the users) of a cyber-system. The delivery of games based training will be driven by the assumptions of the assurance sub-model, particular those that have to do with human users. Games will be used to test whether the assumptions made in an assurance model are plausible and to gradually improve the ability of human users to behave according to them. For instance, if the target cyber system is equipped with a two-factor user authentication system, using passwords and security tokens, we can assume that the users will change the passwords frequently and abstain from sharing the security tokens. A possible game scenario will pose questions to the users based on these assumptions and their decisions will drive the training procedure. For example, users will be asked if they would share the security token in order to favor a person that gained their trust, simulating a phishing attack. Games will also be used to perform an initial profiling of trainees in order to establish the form and level of additional types of training (and their difficulty) that would be beneficial for them. For example, a game may be used to test the familiarity of trainees with access controls and depending on it steer any follow up training towards, for example, emulation in order to give trainees a more hands-on exposure to access control.

The gamification tool will host various serious games, scenarios and training evaluation mechanisms, which will enable trainees to develop skills in being resilient to and preventing social engineering attacks (e.g., phishing, impersonation attacks etc.). The games to be provided will be driven by the threats and assumptions specified in CTTP models (security assurance).

Beyond providing serious games, the gamification will also support an initial cognitive profiling of trainees and measure their familiarity with various security issues.

This profile will be used in order to adjust the type and level of difficulty of the training process. Moreover, it will prompt the trainees to take part in serious games which test whether they behave according to the security assumptions and policies provided by the security assurance model of CTTP models. Their performance at these games will determine the unfolding of the scenarios and will have impact on the status of the emulated and simulated components. Furthermore, the tool will support post training assessments of trainee awareness (in terms of knowledge, attitudes and behavior) of these types of attacks that will be useful in tailoring other forms of CTTP training.

4.4 Emulation

Based on the CTTP model, it will be possible to emulate SAL and PAL components. Emulation will involve creating live instances of SAL and PAL components such as virtual machines, executing the services/operations available for them, and enabling data and stimuli flows using the network and deployment links connecting them in the SAL, PAL and deployment sub-models. In the smart metering system, for example, components that could be emulated in a CTTP programme include the Smart Meter command service and the security controls shown in Fig. 5. Emulation enables training scenarios where the behavior of certain SAL/PAL components cannot be described in sufficient detail to enable the simulation of their behavior, or when hands-on experience of trainees in observing and controlling components is necessary.

In emulations, there will also be emulated clients of the cyber system requesting services from it and trainees will be required to interact with the emulated components (e.g. log in the VMs) and perform certain operations in order to protect the relevant components and through them wider parts of or the entire emulated cyber system. For example, after logging onto a VM they will be able to use testing or monitoring tools to detect an attack, analyze it and respond to it (e.g. deactivating some functionality, strengthening access restrictions, etc.) in real time. Trainees may also be allocated to groups with responsibility of defending specific system components or even be given the role attackers to insight on how attacks can be launched.

4.5 Simulation

The CTTP model will also enable the simulation of the propagation of the effects that attacks on some cyber system components would have on other parts of the system. For instance, the information provided by the CTTP model can be used for the simulation of the propagation of a DDoS attack, targeting the smart gateway on our previous example, and its effects on the simulated hardware and software components. The propagation of such effects will be controlled by simulating the response mechanisms specified for SAL and PAL components and their capabilities and enabling data and other stimuli (e.g. calls) flow across components through the links of the SAL and the PAL sub-models. The effects of attacks may also be propagated from the PAL to the SAL layer (and vice versa) based on component links specified in the deployment model of the CTTP model. Simulations will vary with regards to the level of difficulty that they present to trainees. This level can be controlled by reducing the degree of information that is available for an attack, the time at which this information becomes available following an attack, and the consistency of information generated by the different cyber system security controls and the external assessment tools used.

To ensure the provision of realistic simulations, the THREAT-ARREST framework will continually monitor the real cyber system and log any events of importance related to it. The events to monitor and the types of analysis that will be applied to them will be defined by the assessment measures of the assurance sub-model. The captured assurance related events will be statistically profiled. Statistical profiling will cover event meta data (e.g. the timing of their occurrence and other characteristics such as their sender and receiver) and – where allowable by the applicable security policies – the actual event payload (e.g. data passed between components, parameter values of component operation calls, size of files read or written, etc.).

4.6 Visualization Tool

The visualization tool will enable the graphical representation of simulations and emulations, the effect of training actions on simulated and emulated systems as well as the status of the underlying components.

Using the visualization platform, the framework's operators will be able to select the desired training scenarios and tune their parameters. Moreover, this platform will be able to parse and visualize the CTTP model and the sub-models described in the previous sections and present the appropriate graphs to the users. The operators will utilize these graphs to select which parts of the cyber system should be simulated or emulated. The visualization platform is also responsible for the representation of the status of the simulated/emulated components and the effects of the training actions.

5 Conclusions

This paper presented the THREAT-ARREST solution – a platform for advanced cyber security training for medium to large organizations. At first, the organization's real system is analyzed, revealing the most severe threats and vulnerabilities. Then, a training programme is established which adheres to the organization's specific needs. The various concepts are formed as CTTP models and the overall learning procedures are monitored and adapted at runtime. Except from the ordinary on-line educational material (e.g. lectures, tutorials, videos, etc.), the advanced hybrid training involves serious games as well as emulated/simulated scenarios. The overall approach can cover the training against known and new attack cases and prepares the trainer to be able to detect, respond, and mitigate them under realistic circumstances.

Acknowledgements. This work has received funding from the European Unions Horizon 2020 research and innovation programme under grant agreements No. 769066 (RESIST) and No. 786890 (THREAT-ARREST).

References

1. Intel: A guide to the Internet of Things. Intel (2015). https://www-ssl.intel.com/content/www/us/en/internet-of-things/infographics/guide-to-iot.html
2. Storm, D.: Hackers allegedly attack polish LOT airline, 10 flights and over 1,400 people grounded. Computer World (2015). https://www.computerworld.com/article/2938485/hackers-allegedly-attack-polish-lot-airline-10-flights-and-over-1-400-people-grounded.html. article 2938485
3. Khandelwal, S.: United airlines hacked by sophisticated hacking group. The Hacker News (2015). https://thehackernews.com/2015/07/united-airlines-hacked.html
4. Hirschfeld, J.D.: Hacking of government computers exposed 21.5 million people. New York Times 9 (2015). https://www.nytimes.com/2015/07/10/us/office-of-personnel-management-hackers-got-data-of-millions.html
5. Newcomb, A.: Anthem hack may have impacted millions of non-customers as well. ABC News (2015). https://abcnews.go.com/Technology/anthem-hack-impacted-millions-customers/story?id=29212840
6. Al-Ghamdi, A.S.A.-M.: A survey on software security testing techniques. Int. J. Comput. Sci. Telecommun. **4**(4), 14–18 (2013)
7. Salas, M.I.P., Martins, E.: Security testing methodologies for vulnerabilities detection of XSS in web services and WS-security. Electron. Notes Theor. Comput. Sci. **302**, 133–154 (2014)
8. Hatzivasilis, G., et al.: AmbISPDM. Appl. Intell. **48**(6), 1623–1643 (2017)
9. Santa, I.: A users' guide: how to raise information security awareness. ENISA Rep. 1–140 (2010)
10. Manifavas, C., Fysarakis, K., Rantos, K., Hatzivasilis, G.: DSAPE – dynamic security awareness program evaluation. In: Tryfonas, T., Askoxylakis, I. (eds.) HAS 2014. LNCS, vol. 8533, pp. 258–269. Springer, Cham (2014). https://doi.org/10.1007/978-3-319-07620-1_23
11. Bird, J., Kim, F.: Survey on application security programs and practices. SANS Anal. Surv. 1–24 (2014)
12. Trustwave: Security testing practices and priorities. An Osterman Res. Surv. Rep. 1–15 (2016)
13. Hatzivasilis, G., et al.: WARDOG: Awareness detection watchdog for Botnet infection on the host device. IEEE Trans. Sustain. Comput. Spec. Issue Sustain. Inf. Forensic Comput. 1–18 (2019)
14. Hatzivasilis, G., Fysarakis, K., Askoxylakis, I., Bilanakos, A.: CloudNet anti-malware engine: GPU-accelerated network monitoring for cloud services. In: Fournaris, A.P., Lampropoulos, K., Marín Tordera, E. (eds.) IOSec 2018. LNCS, vol. 11398, pp. 122–133. Springer, Cham (2019). https://doi.org/10.1007/978-3-030-12085-6_11
15. Hatzivasilis, G.: Password-hashing status. Cryptography **1**(2), 1–31 (2017). MDPI Open Access Journal, number 10
16. Shillair, R., et al.: Online safety begins with you and me: convincing Internet users to protect themselves. Comput. Hum. Behav. **48**, 199–207 (2015)
17. Safa, N.S., Rossouw, V.S.: An information security knowledge sharing model in organizations. Comput. Hum. Behav. **57**, 442–451 (2016)
18. Beckers, K., Pape, S., Fries, V.: HATCH: hack and trick capricious humans – a serious game on social engineering. In: HCI Conference Fusion, Bournemouth, UK, pp. 1–3 (2016)
19. Boopathi, K., Sreejith, S., Bithin, A.: Learning cyber security through gamification. Indian J. Sci. Technol. **8**(7), 642–649 (2015)
20. Schreuders, Z.C., Butterfield, E.: Gamification for teaching and learning computer security in higher education. In: ASE, USENIX, Austin, TX, USA, pp. 1–8 (2016)
21. SANS: Online cyber security training. https://www.sans.org/online-security-training/

22. CYBERINTERNACADEMY: Complete cybersecurity course review on CYBERINER-NACADEMY. https://www.cyberinternacademy.com/complete-cybersecurity-course-guide-review/
23. StationX: Online cyber security & hacking courses. https://www.stationx.net/
24. Cybrary: Develop security skills. https://www.cybrary.it/
25. AwareGO: Security awareness training. https://www.awarego.com/
26. BeOne Development: Security awareness training. https://www.beonedevelopment.com/en/security-awareness/
27. ISACA: CyberSecurity Nexus (CSX) training platform. https://cybersecurity.isaca.org/csx-certifications/csx-training-platform
28. Kaspersky: Kaspersky security awareness. https://www.kaspersky.com/enterprise-security/security-awareness
29. CyberBit: Cyber security training platform. https://www.cyberbit.com/blog/security-training/cyber-security-training-platform/
30. Bundesamt für Sicherheit in der Informationstechnik (BSI)/Federal Office for Information Security, Germany. Protection Profile for the Security Module of a Smart Meter Gateway (Security Module PP) (2013)
31. Katopodis, S., Spanoudakis, G., Mahbub, K.: Towards hybrid cloud service certification models. In: International Conference on Services Computing, pp. 394–399 (June 2014)
32. Hatzivasilis, G., Papaefstathiou, I., Manifavas, C.: Software security, privacy and dependability: metrics and measurement. IEEE Softw. 33(4), 46–54 (2016)
33. Cichonski, P., et al.: Computer security incident handling guide. NIST Spec. Publ. 800(61), 1–79 (2012)

FINSEC Workshop

dAPTaset: A Comprehensive Mapping of APT-Related Data

Giuseppe Laurenza$^{(\boxtimes)}$ and Riccardo Lazzeretti

Research Center of Cyber Intelligence and Information Security (CIS),
Department of Computer, Control, and Management Engineering Antonio Ruberti,
Sapienza University of Rome, Rome, Italy
{laurenza,lazzeretti}@diag.uniroma1.it

Abstract. Advance Persistent Threats (APTs) are the most challenging adversaries for financial companies and critical infrastructures. Many open source platforms present various information about APTs but do not fully cover multiple edges of the diamond model, or may be easily used for research purpose. For this reason, we propose dAPTaset, a database that collects data related to APTs from existing public sources through a semi automatic methodology, and produces an exhaustive dataset.

1 Introduction

Cyber attacks arose since the first years of the Internet and they have continuously evolved in order to reach different goals and evade detection, making difficult to build effective defense strategies against them. Currently, cybercrime looks to be the greatest threat in the cyber world and it is estimated that it will cost 6 trillion dollars annually by 2021, according to a Cybersecurity Ventures report [6]. Among the possible adversaries, Advanced Persistent Threats (APTs) [8] are the most challenging ones. They possess sophisticated levels of expertise and significant resources which allow them to create opportunities to achieve their objectives by using multiple attack vectors. Differently from common threats, APTs usually attack a specific target and, as shown in several reports, financial services are in their top targets. For example, Anunak [2] and Carbanak [4] APTs targeted banks and other financial institutions. Typically, an APT carries on cyber campaigns with the goal of exfiltrating sensitive and secret information from the victims, or compromising the target infrastructure. To reach their goals, APTs follow a specific attack path [3] involving several steps, such as social intelligence to identify easy victims inside the target, malicious files delivering, data exfiltration, etc. Hence, several cybersecurity companies are carrying on several analysis on APT activities and releasing public reports that can be leveraged to improve the security of financial critical infrastructure. Stimulated by the importance of the topic, also academic research teams are performing several studies to provide innovative solutions that can be applied for cyber defense [5,7].

© Springer Nature Switzerland AG 2020
A. P. Fournaris et al. (Eds.): ESORICS 2019 Workshops, LNCS 11981, pp. 217–225, 2020.
https://doi.org/10.1007/978-3-030-42051-2_15

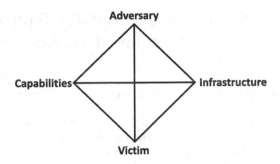

Fig. 1. Diamond model of intrusion

One interesting representation of APT attacks is through the *diamond model* [1], shown in Fig. 1, typically used to describe intrusions. In its simplest form, the diamond model describes that an *adversary* deploys a *capability* over some *infrastructure* against a *victim*. In this model, adversaries are APT groups, capabilities are malware, exploits, tools and techniques used, infrastructures are the physical and logical communication structures (IP addresses, domain names, etc.) and the victims are the targets (people, assets, financial organizations, critical infrastructures, etc.).

Many open source platforms present various information about APTs, but do not fully cover multiple edges of the model, or can be easily used for research purpose. **MITRE ATT&CK**[1] is a knowledge base created and maintained by MITRE containing information on APTs, tactics, techniques, and names of the adopted software. On the other side, it does not provide elements like malware, IP addresses, or domains. **APTNotes**[2] is a GitHub repository containing publicly-available reports and web articles related to APTs. Each report covers one or more of the diamond edges, but it lacks any standard data structure, so it is very difficult to take a comprehensive look among various documents. Moreover, one of the main problem when using these sources is the great inhomogeneities among the naming systems of different cybersecurity vendors. Hence, reports related to the same group can use different names. Unfortunately, despite the great number of released public reports and sources, there is not a comprehensive and updated public dataset that can be used to design, test and compare the different proposed methodologies. Thus, gathering information for fully understanding a particular APT is a long and complex process. It requires a huge manual effort to retrieve the information from different sources and merge them together.

In this short paper, we propose dAPTaset, a database that collects data related to APTs through a methodology that semi–automatically gathers information from different public sources, merges them and produces an exhaustive dataset. Our dAPTaset is a work in progress that aims to easily provide information to security researchers focused on APT analysis, classification, etc.

---

[1] https://attack.mitre.org/.
[2] https://github.com/aptnotes/.

2   Dataset Structure

In this section, we present the structure of the database we have created to store APT information. In designing the database we have taken into account the following arguments: (i) all the sources we use to build our dataset are considered as reports (also web pages) that can describe relationships among APTs and campaigns, APTs and different Indicators of Compromise (IOCs), such as samples or ip addresses, or even refer to other reports; (ii) information about reports can be useful to verify the source and check if it has been updated from last analysis and should be reprocessed; (iii) more names are attributed to the same APT, hence one of them (the one chosen by MITRE ATT&CK) is used to identify the APT while the others must be saved as aliases to ease the research; (iv) we are not interested in the campaigns, but their names can be useful to associate a report to an APT, when the APT name is not explicit, hence we consider campaign names as keywords.

Given those guidelines, dAPTaset is organized as in Fig. 2 and is composed by the following objects[3]:

APT is the fundamental concept and represents the attacker group. The table has only one field (apt_name) containing the common name of an APT, generally used for the group. To avoid the missing of string variants, APT names are stored with lower case letters and without any space or punctuations. We also store the original name as alias in KEYWORDS table.

KEYWORD contains all the words related to APTs, such as alias, campaigns, etc. These strings, together with the common name, are used to simplify APT recognition when analyzing a report. We also include a flag to distinguish between aliases and other keywords, where aliases are other names used to refer to the main APT group, while keywords can be any word (or also a small phrase) related to the APT. Such keywords can be used to associate a report to an APT, when the APT name is not provided in the report.

REPORT refers to all the collected and analyzed documents that contain information about APTs: pdf files or web pages. For each report, we store the hash of the document to easily verify whether two documents are the same but have different names, or to check whether a document has been updated and deserves to be analyzed again. We also include a simple description about the document and two fields to store the source, one representing the origin of the report and one the url from which the document can be downloaded, if the document comes from the web. Such information can be also useful for users interested to retrieve the original reports.

SAMPLE is related to the APT malware files. The table contains the various hashes of the malware used by APTs to perform their activities. Hashes are obtained by the *parsing* of the documents contained in the REPORT table.

---

[3] A detailed description of the database is provided in our github repository: https://github.com/dAPTaset/dAPTaset.

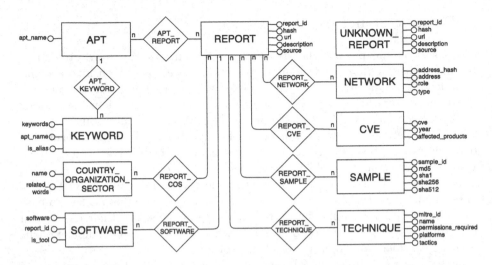

Fig. 2. ER Diagram (we have omitted two attributes in each entity that respectively contain the timestamp of the creation of the record and the one of its last modification).

From reports, we usually find only one of the possible hashes per file: MD5, SHA1, SHA256, etc. Other hashes are subsequently searched from other sources.

NETWORK table contains all the IOCs related to networking, such as ip addresses, urls or email addresses. Elements in this table are obtained by *parsing* the documents contained in the REPORTS table. Elements could be not necessarily malicious, hence we use a *role* field to describe their relationship with attacks, set through semi automatic validation.

CVE contains a list of *Common Vulnerabilities and Exposures* exploited by APTs during their activities. In addition to the identifier, this table also reports other information that can help analysts, such as the *affected_products* field that contains a list of software or devices affected by the vulnerability.

TECHNIQUE presents information about how APTs perform particular actions, such as obtaining high privileges, performing lateral movements or communicating with the command and control.

COS table contains all Countries, Organizations or Sectors that are related to APTs activities, such as the suspected victim sectors or state sponsors. For each entity we also include a list of possible alias or related keywords.

The database also contains two support tables (**UNKNOWN_REPORT** and **SOFTWARE**) to store data that need further investigation prior to become useful and be inserted into the real dataset. Many-to-many relationships between tables are implemented through new tables and sometimes contains some additional information. For example the **APT_COS** table has a field describing if the APT is targeting or is sponsored by a COS.

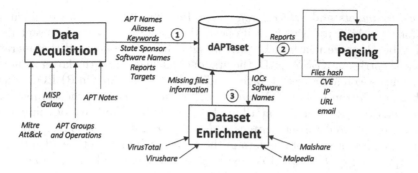

Fig. 3. Data collection

3   Data Collection

In this section, we provide an overview on how we collect data, detailing the origin and the processing. Figure 3 briefly describes the mechanisms.

3.1   Data Acquisition

The following are the main sources that we analyze to extract information and build the skeleton of our dataset. From them we principally acquire main names of APTs, their aliases, the suspected victims of their attacks, and the address of most of the public documents.

MITRE ATT&CK. The first source considered is *MITRE ATT&CK*, accessed through its GitHub repository. From there, we extract the following information: *name, aliases, description, malware names, tool names* (MITRE does not provide the hash of the capabilities), *techniques, tactics* and the list of *external references*. For each group we create an entry in the APT table, then we insert its *aliases* into keywords. We also store the MITRE group webpage in a record of the REPORT table, compute the hash of the group data, set url as the address of the corresponding webpage on the ATT&CK website, copy its description in the table, and set *"mitre"* as source. For each external reference, we download the report and create a new record in the REPORT table. Similarly, we extrapolate techniques to populate the relative table, and malware and tools names to create records into the SOFTWARE table.

APT Groups and Operations. Another useful resource is the *APT Groups and Operations* spreadsheet[4] created by Florian Roth. The spreadsheet is subdivided in tabs, each one related to a specific country/region to whom APTs have been attributed. In addition, there are two other tabs, one for other areas and one for groups with unknown location. Each row of the tabs represents a particular APT. These sheets have different columns, but they can be roughly grouped in: (common) *APT name, aliases, operations, malware, toolsets, targets,*

---

[4] https://apt.threattracking.com.

tactics, comments and *external references*. Periodically we fetch this document and for each APT row we check if one of the names or aliases is present in the APT table. If there is a match, then we add the other ones and the operation names as entries in KEYWORD, the first ones as aliases and the latter as normal ones. Then we create a record corresponding to the APT row in REPORT, using the hash of *Nation_CommonName* as hash (where *Nation* is the tab name and *CommonName* is the name attributed to the APT). We leave description and url fields empty and we set *"groups_and_operations_sheet"* as source. To have a common representation of the data in the *targets* column, we take advantages of the deep learning *Question Answering System* of DeepPavlov[5], an open source library for deep learning end-to-end dialog systems and chatbots. We used it to find which are the victim entities according to the text and then fill the COUNTRY_ORGANIZATION_SECTOR table. Names or abbreviations of nations are checked against data from RestCountries[6]. Last, we download the *external references* and we handle them as additional reports to be processed, in the same way described for MITRE ATT&CK.

APT Notes. Periodically, we download all the new documents from the repository, and we search inside them all the APT names and keywords we know, with the goal to link each report to a known APT. If we are able to attribute the report to an APT, we add it in the REPORT table, otherwise we insert a record in UNKNOWN_REPORT and we do not process the report.

MISP Galaxy Cluster. MISP[7] is a free and open source sharing platform for helping information sharing of threat intelligence. Usually, MISP users create different groups and share information only inside them. Even if it is possible to be part of different groups, the absence of a *general official* group does not allow a simple global sharing. The MISP project includes multiple sub-projects to support the operational requirements of analysts and to improve the overall quality of information shared. One of them is MISP Galaxy[8], that is a simple collection of clusters that can be parsed to add information to our dataset. Being the focus of our work on APTs, we analyze the *Threat Actor Cluster*. From it, we extract aliases of APTs to enrich KEYWORD table, suspected target and victims to be added to COUNTRY_ORGANIZATION_SECTOR table. Similarly to what we do for APT Groups and Operations, we check RestCountries to validate names and abbreviations of countries.

3.2 Report Parsing

As previously introduced, each recognized document is parsed to identify information that can enrich the database tables. We use IOCExtract from Microsoft Threat Intelligence Security Tools[9] to extract IOCs, file hashes, ip addresses and

---

[5] https://deeppavlov.ai.
[6] https://restcountries.eu.
[7] https://www.misp-project.org.
[8] https://www.misp-project.org/galaxy.html.
[9] https://github.com/microsoft/msticpy.

network urls. Moreover we use regular expressions to identify emails and CVEs. Finally we look for the presence of KEYWORD entries into the documents to find any possible relationship with APTs. For this purpose, we first check into title and metadata of the documents. If there is no match, we then look for keywords into the entire text. For any match, a relationships is created between the report and the related group.

3.3   Dataset Enrichment

dAPTaset is finally enriched through other cybersecurity websites: VirusTotal[10], VirusShare[11], Malshare[12] and Malpedia[13].

Hashes Unification. SAMPLES table contains various hashes collected from different documents, thus it is possible that more records refer to the same capability. This happens, for example, when we retrieve the md5 of a file from a report, and a different hash from another one. In addition to the undesired presence of more records, this can hide relationships between apt and report, because such samples can be linked to distinct reports. Using VirusTotal as a search engine, for each file we collect all the possible hashes in order to fill the empty fields. When there are hash repetitions, records are merged and existing relationships are linked to the new record.

Hashes Enrichment. dAPTaset also has a temporary SOFTWARE table. We search for malware names in all the previously listed websites in order to collect samples of these software. These new hashes must be verified before to link them to APT, so we take advantages of the Antivirus Vendor labels provided by VirusTotal to look for keywords and use them as a proof of correctness. Each time a new sample is correctly validated, we add it to the SAMPLE table.

Network Validation. NETWORK table contains network-related IOCs retrieved according to Sect. 3.2. To validate such elements, we check again Virus-Total. In the case of a match, we report a brief result of the response in the role column.

CVE Validation. Similarly to NETWORK table, also the CVE table needs validation and enrichment. For this purpose, we rely on the online repository CVEList[14]. For each *new* vulnerability extracted from a report, we check whether it is valid and then collect other information to enhance the data stored in the corresponding table.

3.4   Dataset Information

Using the methodology described, we have built dAPTaset. Currently, we found 88 different group names, described through 821 reports that allowed us to find

---

[10] http://virustotal.com.

[11] http://virusshare.com.

[12] https://malshare.com.

[13] https://malpedia.caad.fkie.fraunhofer.de.

[14] https://github.com/CVEProject/cvelist.

21841 binary hashes with 8927 unique files, 175 different techniques, 2620 network related IOCs and 169 CVEs related to APTs activities. dAPTaset can be downloaded from our github repository[15].

4   Conclusions and Future Improvements

In this short paper we have presented dAPTaset, a new database containing information about Advanced Persistent Threats. The main scope of this dataset is to collect information provided from several sources and present them in a simple, comprehensive and updated form, useful for investigation and test. dAPTaset covers all the edges of the diamond model and provides APT names, their aliases, and other information, such as all the available samples implemented or used by them, the CVEs exploited to perform their operations, etc.

As future works, we are interested to extend it with additional information related to Victims and Infrastructures with in-depth details that can help APT analysts. We would also enrich dAPTaset, by improving the report parsing step through more advanced text analysis. It will be interesting to perform advanced semantic analysis, or rely on artificial intelligence techniques in order to extract data related to behaviors, target, etc., and also improve the attribution to original attacking group directly from each report.

Moreover, dAPTaset is currently only a searchable dataset. In current version, verification and manual additions can be made only through direct queries. However a data visualization framework could allow analysts to easily inspect, update and fix the database.

Finally, we would like to enrich dAPTaset with other tables containing results of static and dynamic analysis made by various available tools such as PEframe[16], radare2[17], Cuckoo Sandbox[18], FakeNet[19], etc. Moreover it is our interest to also include results of scientific analysis performed by us or anyone else interested to contribute with the output of their analysis. This would provide different information that can be used to better understand, detect and analyze Advanced Persistent Threat activities.

References

1. Caltagirone, S., Pendergast, A., Betz, C.: The diamond model of intrusion analysis (2013)
2. Group-IB: Anunak: APT against financial institutions
3. Hutchins, E.M., Cloppert, M.J., Amin, R.M.: Intelligence-driven computer network defense informed by analysis of adversary campaigns and intrusion kill chains. Lead. Issues Inf. Warf. Secur. Res. 1(1), 80 (2011)

---

[15] https://github.com/dAPTaset/dAPTaset.
[16] https://github.com/guelfoweb/peframe.
[17] https://rada.re/.
[18] https://cuckoosandbox.org.
[19] https://github.com/fireeye/flare-fakenet-ng.

4. Lab, K.: Carbank APT: the great bank robbery
5. Laurenza, G., Aniello, L., Lazzeretti, R., Baldoni, R.: Malware triage based on static features and public APT reports. In: Dolev, S., Lodha, S. (eds.) CSCML 2017. LNCS, vol. 10332, pp. 288–305. Springer, Cham (2017). https://doi.org/10.1007/978-3-319-60080-2_21
6. Morgan, S.: Cybercrime report, 2017. Cybersecurity Ventures (2017)
7. Nath, H.V., Mehtre, B.M.: Static malware analysis using machine learning methods. In: Martínez Pérez, G., Thampi, S.M., Ko, R., Shu, L. (eds.) SNDS 2014. CCIS, vol. 420, pp. 440–450. Springer, Heidelberg (2014). https://doi.org/10.1007/978-3-642-54525-2_39
8. Ross, R.S.: Managing information security risk: organization, mission, and information system view. Tech. rep, NIST (March 2011)

Blockchain Based Sharing of Security Information for Critical Infrastructures of the Finance Sector

Ioannis Karagiannis[1], Konstantinos Mavrogiannis[2], John Soldatos[1],
Dimitris Drakoulis[1(✉)], Ernesto Troiano[3], and Ariana Polyviou[1,4]

[1] INNOV-ACTS LIMITED, 27, Michalakopooulou Street, Nicosia, Cyprus
{ddrakoulis,apolyviou}@innov-acts.com
[2] Singularlogic S.A, 3, Achaias & Trizinias Street, Nea Kifisia, Greece
[3] GFT Italia Srl, Via Alessandro Rimassa, 51/2s, Genoa, Italy
[4] University of Nicosia, Makedonitissis 46, Nicosia, Cyprus

Abstract. Recent security incidents in the finance sector have demonstrated the importance of sharing security information across financial institutions, as a means of mitigating risks and boosting the early preparedness against relevant attacks. However, financial institutions are in several cases reluctant to share security information beyond what is imposed by applicable regulations. In this paper, we introduce a blockchain-based solution for sharing security information in a decentralized way, which boosts security and trust in the information sharing process. We also illustrate how the information that is shared across financial institutions can serve as a basis for collaborative security services such as risk assessment.

Keywords: Security · Cyber security · Blockchain · Information sharing · Finance · Critical infrastructure protection

1 Introduction

1.1 Security Challenges in the Finance Sector

In recent years, we have witnessed a steady rise of cyber-security incidents against infrastructures of the financial sector, such as phishing, ransomware, and DDoS (Distributed Denial of Service) attacks. These incidents include notorious attacks, which have resulted in significant economic damage, while decreasing trust in financial institutions and questioning their social value. As a prominent example, the fraudulent SWIFT (Society for Worldwide Interbank Financial Telecommunication) transactions cyber-attack back in February 2016 resulted in $81 million being stolen from the Bangladesh Central Bank [1]. Likewise, the famous "Wannacry" ransomware attacked financial institutions and reaffirmed that the financial services industry is a primary target for cyber criminals. Hence, despite the increased investments of financial institutions in security, the critical infrastructures of financial organizations, remain vulnerable. This is highly due to

© Springer Nature Switzerland AG 2020
A. P. Fournaris et al. (Eds.): ESORICS 2019 Workshops, LNCS 11981, pp. 226–241, 2020.
https://doi.org/10.1007/978-3-030-42051-2_16

the growing sophistication of the IT technologies that are deployed by financial organizations, the rising complexity of the regulatory environment and the fact that several financial services (e.g., SWIFT and SEPA (Single Euro Payment Areas) involve multiple stakeholders and complex supply chain interactions. In order to address these challenges financial organizations can nowadays take advantage of leading-edge technologies for collecting and analyzing security data such as Big Data analytics and Artificial Intelligence (AI) techniques for security. These technologies enable the implementation of security workflows that comprise monitoring, analysis and automation activities. Indeed, Big Data systems are currently deployed in securing infrastructures and applications of the financial sector [2]. Nevertheless, these systems exhibit the following limitations:

- **Limited integration between physical and cyber security**. Data driven systems for the security of the finance sector are overly focused on cyber security and ignore physical security systems and assets such as CCTV (Closed Circuit Television) systems, intelligent visual surveillance, security lighting, alarms, access control systems and biometric authentication. This results in a fragmentation of vulnerability assessment, threat analysis, risk mitigation and response activities, which leads to increased costs and isolated (rather than integrated) security measures. Financial organizations can greatly benefit from holistic approaches in handling security incidents, which consider both cyber and physical assets of their critical infrastructures.
- **Poor stakeholders' collaboration for securing financial services**. In an era where financial infrastructures are more connected than ever before, their vulnerabilities are likely to impact other infrastructures and systems in the financial chain, dealing with cascading effects [3]. In this context, stakeholders' collaboration can be a key towards identifying and alleviating issues in a timely manner.

The exchange of security information across collaborating stakeholders of the financial services value chain can be a foundation for security collaboration in the relevant supply chain. In the scope of an integrated security approach, information for both cyber and physical security should be exchanged as outlined earlier. As a motivational example, one can consider an organization using a publicly exposed service of another organization as is common in financial supply chain services. This can be a physical security company contracted with a financial institution. In case a new vulnerability is detected, the security company needs to promptly share the risk level change along with information about the corresponding vulnerability. As part of the collaboration, the financial institution may apply relevant security measures (e.g., increasing physical security measures and increasing the data acquisition rates from CCTV cameras). As another example, a regulation violation in one financial institution can lead to increased risk level, which shall be immediately communicated to other participants of the supply chain. The latter participants could take advantage of this information in order to prevent a similar violation at their end.

1.2 Related Work

The value of security-related collaboration is already acknowledged by several security organizations and stakeholders. In Europe, collaboration is acknowledged as a key activity within every European national cyber security strategy. Specifically, collaboration is used to enhance cyber security at different levels, including threats sharing, risk assessment and awareness raising. This is the reason why formal structures like Information Sharing and Analysis Centers (ISAC) are established, along with relevant Public Private Partnerships (PPP) [4]. In the finance sector, the Financial Services Information Sharing and Analysis Center (FS-ISAC) [5] has been established, as an industry forum for sharing data about critical cybersecurity threats in the financial services industry.

The activities of the ISAC centers involve sharing information across stakeholders and supporting related collaborative workflows. Such workflows have also been implemented in other sectors of the economy (e.g., the maritime [6] and transport sectors [7]). Furthermore, collaborative security and information sharing options have been proposed in the literature (e.g., [8]), in order to support and complement conventional risk assessment techniques (e.g., [9, 10]). The rationale of information sharing is to trigger security processes like risk assessment and threat analysis, based on information received from other parties that join the collaborative security infrastructures.

One of the main issues in collaborative security is the trustworthiness and the security of the information sharing process at hand. Sharing data in a centralized database has some disadvantages. First, it requires a trusted third party (TTP) that will assume the ownership and will guarantee the integrity of the shared information. Second, it is susceptible to security attacks, which can comprise the shared data. These issues make financial organizations reluctant to share information (including security-related information), beyond what they are obliged to do as part of their compliance with regulations. To alleviate this reluctance, an approach that provides decentralized trust can be implemented. Such approach could be based on blockchain technology and the decentralized applications. In particular, based on the use of blockchain technology, financial organizations can share information in a shared distributed ledger in a secure and decentralized way, which provides distributed trust and alleviates the vulnerabilities of decentralized storage. Alternative technologies that could be employed include STIX (Structured Threat Information Expression) [11], a protocol developed by OASIS to model cyber threat intelligence. TAXII (Trusted Automated Exchange of Intelligence Information) [12] refers to the application-layer protocol developed by OASIS to exchange STIX data. TAXII runs on top of HTTP and can provide secure connections over SSL, if needed. But, TAXII is mainly a communication protocol and thus it does not provide storing capabilities. Thus, although it supports both publish-subscribe and client-server topologies, compared to blockchain, it lacks the guaranteed degree of confidentiality. Along the same lines, the alternative of pure P2P networks [13], could not provide a viable solution for sharing financial data. This is because the lack of solid authorization techniques could lead in information compromise, bad connections could possibly produce big network latency, while malicious files or messages can be easily implanted and consumed by other peers. For these reasons, information sharing is nowadays one of the most prominent blockchain use cases in the financial sector [14]. Existing literature provides a thorough analysis on the benefits arising by the use blockchain technology in the financial sector [15, 16].

1.3 Scope and Structure of the Paper

This paper contributes to existing literature by introducing a blockchain-based system for collaborative security in the finance sector. The system leverages the decentralization and distributed trust benefits of distributed ledger technologies in order to enable a secure and trustworthy exchange of security information across financial institutions. It is customized to the needs of financial organizations in terms of protecting their critical infrastructure in an integrated way. As such it acquires and processes information from the various physical and cyber security systems of financial organizations, while sharing such information with other participants of the financial services value chain. To this end, the blockchain based system is integrated within a Big Data system for security analytics, which provides the means for collecting security related information from physical and cyber security systems via a number of probes.

The information that is exchanged and processed through the blockchain-based system is modelled in a STIX (based format). STIX is extended to cover assets, services, attacks, threats and other forms of security information for the financial sector. This format is conveniently called FINSTIX and provides a standards-based way for representing the semantics of security information. The FINSTIX format is used by the Big Data security analytics platform, where the blockchain system for collaborative security is attached. From a functional viewpoint, the collaborative security system provides two main functionalities. First it enables organizations to receive information from other parties as a means of issuing alerts or activating security policies. Second it allows for collaborative assessment of risks.

The remaining of the paper is as follows: Sect. 2 introduces the Big Data security analytics system developed in the scope of the H2020 FINSEC project, which is conveniently called FINSEC platform. The collaborative security solution is therefore positioned within the architecture of the FINSEC platform. Moreover, as part of Sect. 2, the FINSTIX model is also introduced. Section 3 illustrates the design of the blockchain solution, while Sect. 4 provides insights on the practical implementation of the collaborative security system. Finally, Sect. 5 is the concluding section of the paper, which includes a short discussion of the pros and cons of the implemented solution.

2 Information Sharing Architecture

2.1 FINSEC Platform Overview

Aiming to elevate security collaboration in the financial services supply chain, this paper proposes an information sharing architecture, which is part of a wider platform for financial infrastructures security, namely the FINSEC platform. The implementation of the FINSEC platform is based on a state of the art microservices architecture. The platform encapsulates a Big Data system for security analytics, which provides the means for collecting security related information from physical and cyber security systems. The platform can be viewed as a n-tier architecture, with a lower layer (i.e., the edge layer) that interfaces with the actual physical and logical infrastructures. Moreover, it includes several cross-cutting services, which are not confined to providing support to a single tier, but rather support functionalities that may reside in any of the layers of the architecture. Overall, in-line with the previously outlined principles and building blocks, the n-tier architecture is just a projection of a modular architecture where every module, can in principle communicate with any other modules through proper interfaces. This is fully in-line with the concept of a modern microservices architecture, which is much more flexible than conventional monolithic architectures. Figure 1, illustrates the design and main building blocks of the platform's architecture, including both layered and cross-cutting building blocks.

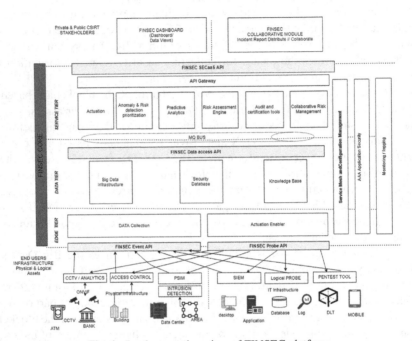

Fig. 1. Implementation view of FINSEC platform

The main tiers of the architecture enable the implementation of the previously presented building blocks and are as follows: (i) The Field Tier is the lower level and includes the probes and their APIs, whose role is extracting raw data from the physical and logical assets to be protected against threats. For example, CCTV analytics and SIEM (Security Information and Event Management) are involved in this layer to give useful information about potential attacks to the upper tiers; (ii) The Edge Tier contains the Actuation Enabler and a Data Collection module, which is needed to filter information as it flows towards the upper levels. The Actuation Enabler is authorizes actions to be applied by the upper layers onto the probes, such as the shutdown of a server in case of threat or the close of an automatic door of a protected room; (iii) The Data Tier is the logical layer where information is stored, and organized into three different storage infrastructures, providing consisting data access APIs to all other modules; (iv) The Service Tier is where the kernel applications and the security toolbox will be running (i.e. the security kernel of the platform), able to be used by external applications via proper APIs; (v) The Business Client Applications tier is the layer where end-users and business applications may actually get benefits from the platform capabilities. For example, the FINSEC dashboard enables the end-users to visually monitor in real-time the data and assets managed by the platform, while the (Supply Chain) collaboration module enables the sharing of information with other instances of the platform, including instances deployed in different business organizations.

The core platform, delimited by the blue bar in the picture, comprises three tiers, namely the Edge, Data and Service tiers which interact with the outside world with two main interfaces; northbound API and southbound API. (i) The northbound API towards higher level applications (e.g., end-user/business applications), called SECaaS (Security as a Service) API. It represents a consistent and unified view of the individual APIs exposed by the service tier high level services that represent the "major intelligence" of the platform. The SECaaS API is exposed and the API Gateway, which is the single-entry point to the system for external clients. Among other capabilities, the API Gateway provides and supports Authentication, Authorization, and accounting (AAA) services, which conceptually are part of the two cross-cutting vertical modules on the right of the figure (Application Security and Monitoring/logging). (ii) The southbound API interface, consisting of an "Event API" and a "Probe API", allows communication between the Edge Tier and physical and cybersecurity probes.

The SECaaS API is leveraged and invoked by external (north end) Business Client Applications (upper side of the figure). They are outside of the core platform and interact with it only through the SECaaS REST API. Typical examples of business client applications include: (i) The Dashboard application, a web-based GUI used by the profiled end-users of the platform; (ii) The Collaboration application, which enables the collaboration of multiple platform instances (data sharing etc.); (iii) Third parties' applications that exploit the capabilities of the platform, such as risk assessment and regulatory compliance applications. The Collaboration application is illustrated in following paragraphs, as it is based on the sharing of data in a blockchain infrastructure.

The Service Tier defines the high-level services that represent the "major intelligence" of the platform. The Service Tier services communicate with each other in three (3) possible ways: (i) Synchronous communications through their REST APIs. In this case, being the services internal to the platform, it is not necessary to use AAA functionalities; (ii) Asynchronous communications via an MQ bus; (iii) Asynchronous communications through the Database Infrastructure.

2.2 Security Information Modelling

Security Information Modelling is at the heart of the FINSEC platform and its blockchain-based Collaboration Services, as information across the various modules adheres to the same semantics and format. In particular, information exchanged and processed in the platform is modelled in a STIX-derived format, called FINSTIX, which serves as a standardized approach for representing the semantics of security information. Hence, the FINSEC platform incorporates a Collaborative Risk Assessment module that supports messages compliant with FINSTIX reference data model.

This data model provides constructs for representing risks, vulnerabilities, threats, as well as regulatory violations. Moreover, it includes parameters for configuring the collaborative security services. Also, the CVSS [17] (Common Vulnerability Scoring

System) library is employed for calculating risk levels. Vulnerability and impact levels are derived from CVSS metrics while threat levels result from historic events detected. Risk objects are defined using the "x-risk" FINSTIX object. "X-risk" is computed based on threat, impact and vulnerability levels and provides information about the risk level itself (individual, commutative or propagated), the service or asset related to it, as well as the threat this risk is calculated for. Services are supported using the "x-service" FINSTIX object. This object provides information about the criticality, the availability and other critical parameters such as the Organization or the domain/subdomain of the Service. Additionally, it provides a list of references of assets belonging to this specific service. Likewise, Vulnerabilities are modelled using the "x-vulnerability" object, whereas CVSS metrics as well as the domain of the vulnerability are defined by the security officer. Threats identified are related to a set of vulnerabilities. A Vulnerability can be exploited by a Threat. The risk level is dependent on the vulnerabilities that can be targeted by the threat. In the FINSTIX reference model, threats are represented as "x-threat".

Regulation violation objects are supported using the "x-regulation" object. The violation fields define a list of metrics such as the datasets affected, the financial damage or information regarding the vulnerability exploited, the adversary and of course, the dates the regulation violation took place. As part of the Collaboration Services of the FINSEC platform, Regulation violation messages will be sent to the corresponding regulation authority and sanitized information will be propagated to the blockchain infrastructure. Information about other stakeholders will be shared using the blockchain infrastructure while another channel will be utilized to send the regulation violation to the corresponding regulation authority. Finally, a configuration object called "x-risk-configuration" will be used to define the type of triggering (manual, automatic), risk level thresholds (e.g., trigger the computation when risk is Critical) and the input sources for a specific risk.

3   Collaborative Security System Design and Implementation

3.1   The Enabling Blockchain Infrastructure

The collaboration service operates in the context of the FINSEC platform and is based on the exchange of FINSTIX compliant objects and information. It is enabled by a blockchain infrastructure and fosters the exchange of messages related to events (FINSTIX x-events).

Specifically, each instance of the FINSEC platform controls and uses a blockchain Ethereum GETH node through which it interacts with the collaboration service. Additionally, the blockchain infrastructure is responsible for the exchange of FINSTIX compliant JSON (JavaScript Object Notation) messages between nodes (i.e., organizations deploying instances of the FINSEC platform). The blockchain nodes are responsible for the verification of transactions which encapsulates messages and synchronization (delivery) of those messages to all other nodes. An organization publishes a message by invoking an Ethereum smart contract. However, before the message is published in the form of a blockchain transaction on the blockchain, the transaction undergoes a validation/verification process. After the transaction is verified, the message is made available on all nodes.

The functionality of the collaboration service is supported by an (Open) API. Other services are therefore able to use the API in order to interact with the collaboration service. Hence, the API abstracts the complexity of the blockchain infrastructure and provides a generic collaboration interface to other services. In this context, it also enables publish-subscribe message interactions from the blockchain infrastructure to a message bus infrastructure (like Apache Kafka) and vice versa.

As already outlined, an Ethereum blockchain is used to implement the inter organizational message exchange service. Smart Contracts Code developed in the Solidity Domain Specific language enables the participating FINSEC nodes to interact through the Ethereum network. The implemented Ethereum network is based on the open source implementation of Ethereum, but is setup as a permissioned blockchain infrastructure. The latter provides control over the blockchain members and is operated by the FINSEC consortium, while being fully decoupled from the public Ethereum blockchain.

3.2 Blockchain Infrastructure: Benefits, Drawbacks and Design Options

The main driving force behind using a blockchain as the base of the collaboration module is that it provides data immutability and consequently integrity. This is important for financial institutions that exchange security-related data since they use them to make informed decisions related to physical and cyber security. An additional benefit is that blockchain provides constant data availability since they are stored on every node of the blockchain network. Furthermore, a blockchain is one easy and robust way to achieve the Confidentiality Integrity and Availability (CIA) properties that are required for trustworthy interactions between the financial institutions. In particular, this can be optimally achieved by means of a permissioned blockchain, as the latter controls nodes' permissions in a way ensuring that only nodes that are members of the permissioned network can write and read data on it. This property ensures the confidentiality of data, which is particularly important for the case of the financial sector as very sensitive data are handled. Another benefit stems from the use of the Ethereum blockchain, which is a tested solution that has been used in a variety of applications and is backed up by a huge community of developers and integrators worldwide.

Nevertheless, a blockchain based solution incorporates some drawbacks. One of the main drawbacks of a blockchain network is its poor performance in terms of transaction delay, which makes it inappropriate for real time applications. This poor performance stems from the need to verify and validate a transaction by means of Proof-of-Work (PoW). In conventional Ethereum blockchain networks the transaction verification processes can take several seconds, which is intolerable for real-time transactions. In the scope of the FINSEC collaboration service, this can be a set-back for security scenarios that require fast information exchange and collaborative interactions. Note however, that permissioned blockchains could partly alleviate the transaction latency issues, as they can bypass the requirement for PoW and related distributed consensus. This enables permissioned blockchain infrastructures (such as Hyperledger Fabric and Corda/R3) capable of concluding tens or even hundreds of transactions per second. Compared to public blockchains, such approach offers an improved performance.

Additionally, trust associated to information sharing on the blockchain may be regarded as a drawback. This is because, while some blockchain solutions, provide hierarchy capabilities, others consider all nodes equal. For example, Ethereum supports a naive approach, providing all participating partners the same privileges. A potential solution to such issues is Hyperledger Fabric, as it is capable to support a more complex trust schema. A distributed trust authority can be easily applied on top of Hyperledger Fabric and thus, control the privileges of each node based on predefined criteria or algorithms. Additionally, solid authentication and authorization of peers in a permissioned blockchain could amplify trust levels in a blockchain environment.

Another drawback of a blockchain network is that it consumes much electrical power whereas the possibility of attacks against it (e.g., compromising the 51% consensus mechanism) cannot be ruled out. Nevertheless, this risk is also lowered in the scope of collaboration by means of a permissioned blockchain, as each node is fully controlled and operated by a financial institution. Hence, the time required for transactions to be validated as well as the transaction validation and verification difficulty, can be regulated by the participating entities. Thus, both transaction delays and electricity consumption can be reduced. Overall, in the context of collaborative security, the use of a permissioned blockchain infrastructures provides several benefits over conventional public blockchain networks.

3.3 Collaborative Module Implementation Overview

The collaboration module implements collaborative security functionalities leveraging on information from other blockchain participants. It uses the blockchain network both for the underlying infrastructure and for storing exchanged messages. As outlined, a smart contract, written in Solidity and deployed on the blockchain, enables organizations to post and retrieve messages, as well as to receive notifications every time a new message is posted to the collaboration module. Such functionalities are performed via REST endpoints. The documentation of the available endpoints is provided in YAML language. Any organization (i.e., blockchain participant) can add a new message to the collaboration tool through an HTTP POST request. As soon as the message is posted, it is inserted in a blockchain transaction and a hash is attached to the transaction so as to functions as a checksum for integrity check purposes. In addition to the POST request/endpoint that enables an organization to publish a message to the Collaborative Module, there are other four types of GET requests/endpoints:

- The GET '/messages/index/{index}' request allows an organization to retrieve a specific message, which was transferred via the collaboration module, by providing the collaboration index number. The number is automatically incremented in every newly created transaction. This process is performed when a message is published.
- The GET '/messages/uuid{uuid}' request concerns the ability to retrieve a message, which was transferred through the collaboration module by inputting the message's unique id.
- The GET '/messages' request provides the ability to retrieve metadata about each message that has been submitted to the collaboration tool by the time of that GET request.
- The GET '/transactions/{hash}' request via which information regarding a transaction can be retrieved by using as search criterion the hash of the particular transaction.

The FINSEC collaborative module also uses HEAD YAML requests. In this case, the HEAD request enables simplified retrieval of data related to the original messages such as the total amount of messages that have been submitted so far to the collaboration tool.

Typically, the flow of data in the collaborative module starts by creating a collaboration message and appending a unique identifier to it. As soon as the message is reviewed, it is approved for submission to the other collaboration tool participants. Afterwards, the message is transferred to the collaboration API endpoint, which in turn submits it to the blockchain smart contract. The information regarding the smart contract address, the account of the sender and user authentication are enclosed in the collaboration API. Then, the blockchain nodes verify the transaction. Following the verification stage, the transaction that contains the message is stored on the blockchain and is accessible by every node. Once the transaction is included on the blockchain, a notification is sent to all nodes describing the message exchange. Security Monitoring and Alerts in the Blockchain Network.

A validation process ensures the security of the blockchain transaction, whereas the use of Ethereum smart contract enables an organization to interact (read, append) with the Ethereum blockchain. Additionally, the methods (or functions) of the smart contract append to the message the timestamp, which indicates the time of the share.

For example, in the case that messages are exchanged between two organizations (Organization 1 (O1) and Organization 2 (O2)), each one of the two organizations, controls and operates a blockchain node. Once O1 publishes on the Blockchain ledger a STIX compatible JSON message via an Ethereum smart contract call, the blockchain transaction undergoes a validation/verification process before being published. As soon as the transaction is verified the message is made available on all nodes. Then, O2 can send a request to retrieve the new message. In the case that there is a message feed that has subscribers, every time an organization submits an event message, every organization and members of it, subscribed to this specific message feed, gets a notification. If O1, publishes a STIX compatible JSON message by invoking an Ethereum smart contract, then organization 2 which is already subscribed to receive notifications gets a POST request with the metadata (ID, Timestamp, Sender Address, Message Type) of the message that was just posted. If necessary, the entire message can be retrieved by querying it through its identifier (ID).

3.4 Collaborative Risk Scoring and Assessment

The collaboration service also incorporates a risk assessment approach, which leverages risk assessment input from various sources, notably:

- A Risk Assessment Engine (RAE), used inside the FINSEC BigData platform for security analytics. The RAE module is a tool developed by ATOS, one of the partners of the FINSEC consortium and is an integral element of the FINSEC platform.
- A Collaborative Risk Assessment Engine (CRAE), developed in the scope of the H2020 MITIGATE project and used to perform risk calculations based on multiple inputs.

Data from risk calculations performed by RAE and CRAE are combined, in order to generate collaboration data and distribute them to the Collaboration Service. Figure 2, provides a high-level description of the interactions between these components as part of a risk scoring scenario.

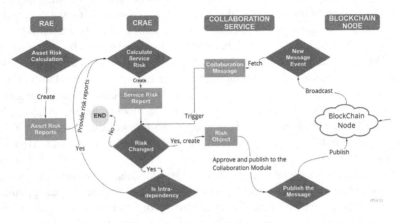

Fig. 2. Components interaction

As shown in Fig. 2, a Risk level change of an Asset is triggered by the RAE, whereas the CRAE fetches the report from the RAE and calculates all service risks related to this asset. In the case that a Service risk level changes, CRAE will recursively calculate risks for all internal dependent services. For every Service risk level change, a FINSTIX risk object will be created and after the security officer's approval will be sent to the Collaboration Module. The module is responsible for Publishing the risk object message to the blockchain infrastructure. In case of external Risk level changes, CRAE will fetch the information needed since it will be subscribed in the Collaboration Service and "listens" to risk updates.

The CRAE has been integrated with the blockchain infrastructure described in earlier paragraphs. Hence, it works based on input either from the RAE or the blockchain infrastructure for collaborative information sharing. The RAE provides information on assets' risks, while the blockchain infrastructure holds risk information for both services and assets calculated inside other Organizations. The CRAE may also integrate input from additional sources, including other modules of the FINSEC platform such as the Analytic Tools and sources of the Data Tier presented in Sect. 2. In FINSTIX notation, the inputs to the CRAE include: (a) x-risk and x-vulnerability objects (from the RAE), (b) x-vulnerability, x-threat, attack-pattern, malware, intrusion-set, campaign from the analytic tools and (c) x-asset, x-vulnerability from Data Tier.

Note also that the Data Tier provides critical information about the infrastructure of the Organization. A small change associated with the risk of an asset (example e.g., a version update of a web server) may change completely the Risk levels of all the Services dependent on that asset. Analytic tools on the other hand, may identify a new adversary. This identification will also affect the overall Service risk. For example, if a Service's asset has one known vulnerability and the analytic tools detect a malware that can exploit this specific vulnerability, the risk level of both the Asset and the Service must be updated.

The CRAE produces the following outputs: (a) Risk objects, (b) Regulation violation objects, (c) Threat objects, (d) Vulnerability Objects. In particular, Risk objects will refer to either a Service or an Asset of the Organization and will depict the risk calculated based on the current impact, threat and vulnerability levels. The exact calculation formula is derived from H2020 MITIGATE project. Regulation violation objects will be produced by a security officer who will fill a questionnaire as soon as possible to deal with a regulation violation (e.g. GDPR violation). Threats and vulnerabilities will be provided by one or more security officers. A successful risk assessment process implies the identification of Threats as well as known vulnerabilities inside an Organization. As a first step threats and vulnerabilities can also be provided manually by a security officer. However, dealing with all the vulnerabilities and threats manually is not possible. This is the reason why we are planning to implement tools like OpenVas to automatically detect vulnerabilities inside a network, or integration with vulnerability databases like the NVD (National Vulnerability Database).

In terms of communication between the various components of Collaborate Security Solutions, a Message Bus architecture is used, powered by an Apache Kafka infrastructure. In line with the FINSEC platform architecture, the RAE and the CRAE communicate with each other through the Bus, which allows all FINSEC components living in the Service tier to publish and subscribe to it. Furthermore, the RAE and the CRAE will also communicate directly with each other by consuming exposed REST endpoints. Figure 3, illustrates the communication methods between all involved components.

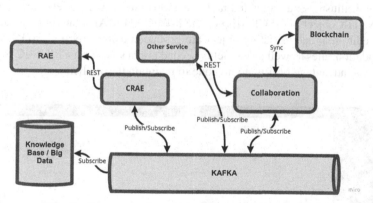

Fig. 3. Communication mechanism between components

As illustrated in Fig. 2, the Collaboration Module will also publish/subscribe to the Kafka Message Bus. In practice, information stemming from the blockchain is pulled in a Kafka channel, while new messages that are to be shared are published to another channel. The Collaboration module receives messages from the message bus and dispatches them to the blockchain infrastructure.

4 Demonstration and Validation

4.1 Managing FINSTIX Objects

The prototype implementation of the blockchain-based Collaborative Risk Assessment infrastructures supports different users and roles, with various privileges associated with management of assets, vulnerabilities and risks. In practice, the latter operations enable the management of all relevant FINSTIX objects, including:

- Creating, updating, listing, and deleting assets.
- Create, updating, listing and deleting vulnerabilities.
- Creating, updating, listing and deleting regulations.
- Sharing information through posting to the Collaboration Module.
- Fetching information stemming from the Collaboration Module.

Relevant management operations are supported through an administration panel.

4.2 Collaborative Risk Calculations

Risk calculations are supported at an individual/asset level and a median formula is applied in case of a Service Risk calculation. The risk calculation is triggered whenever a user creates, updates, edits or deletes a vulnerability. The corresponding CVSS vector is generated and the CRAE runs its computations as a background job. Security officers receive a notification every time a new FINSTIX object is fetched by other components.

Figure 4, illustrates a paginated table developed to provide asset information. For every FINSTIX object in the CRAE (i.e., the MITIGATE RAE), the forms to add a new object or edit an already existing object are produced using FINSEC JSON schemas. Thus, validation rules as well as the fields needed are in sync with a FINSEC repository providing the advantage of little to no code to maintain the application.

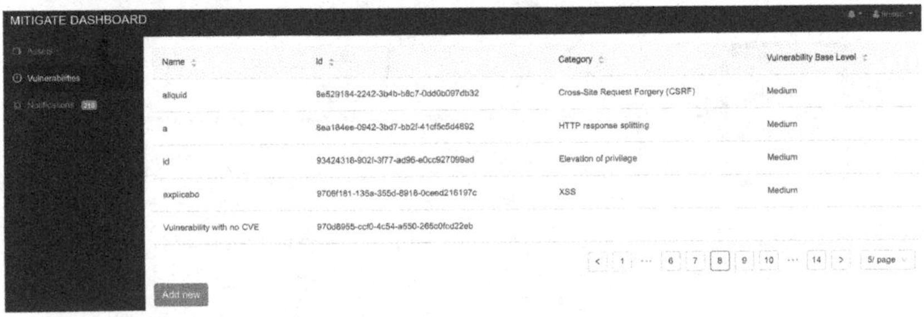

Fig. 4. Paginated table developed to visualize asset information

After generating a new FINSTIX object, the security officer is prompted to apply the relations to other objects. In the case a user will need to provide Vulnerabilities and Services while, when adding a new Vulnerability, the security officer needs to associate it with one or more Threats as illustrated in Fig. 5.

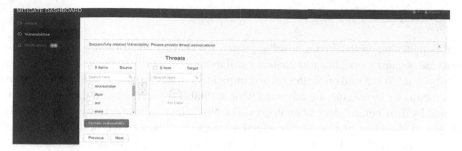

Fig. 5. Object relations – UI

Notifications (other FINSTIX objects) created by other users of the (MITIGATE) CRAE and/or the blockchain infrastructure can be accessed by the left sidebar (Notifications/bell icon). After the review, the security officer can mark the notification as read, or apply further actions. Figure 6 illustrates the notifications user interface.

Finally, a security officer, can check the object created and send it to the collaboration module, as illustrated in Fig. 7.

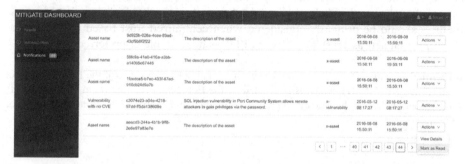

Fig. 6. Notifications - UI

Fig. 7. Collaboration Module, Sharing Object Prompt

5 Conclusions

In this paper we introduced a novel approach for sharing security information across financial organizations, towards enabling collaborative security in the financial services supply chain. It is based on the design and implementation of a blockchain infrastructure, as a means of leveraging the advantages of auditability, security and distributed trust offered by distributed ledger technologies. The blockchain infrastructure is appropriately integrated to a wider platform for financial services security, which is destined to protect both cyber and physical assets. Based on information exchanged in the blockchain, a set of collaborative risk assessment functionalities have been developed and validated.

Along with the presentation of the benefits of a blockchain based approach to security information sharing and security collaboration, we have also discussed the drawbacks of the approach when compared to the conventional solution of sharing data in a high-end shared database. In particular, blockchains present some proclaimed performance and privacy control limitations, while being associated with high energy consumption. These limitations can be alleviated based on the development, use and operation of a permissioned blockchain, rather than relying on public blockchain infrastructure. Nevertheless, even permissioned blockchains have their limits. For example, while they can handle some hundreds of transactions per second, their performance still lags behind the state-of-the-art centralized cloud-based databases. As a result, blockchain based infrastructures should be primarily considered when centralized trust based on a financial institution that acts as Trust Third Party (TTP) is not a viable or preferred option.

Acknowledgements. Part of this work has been carried out in the scope of the FINSEC project (contract number 786727), which is co-funded by the European Commission in the scope of its H2020 program. The authors acknowledge valuable help and contributions from all partners of the project.

References

1. Maurer, T., Levite, A., Perkovich, G.: Toward a global norm against manipulating the integrity of financial data. Economics Discussion Papers, 38, Kiel Institute for the World Economy, Kiel (2017)
2. Hussain, K., Prieto, E.: Big data in the finance and insurance sectors. In: Cavanillas, J.M., Curry, E., Wahlster, W. (eds.) New Horizons for a Data-Driven Economy, pp. 209–223. Springer, Cham (2016). https://doi.org/10.1007/978-3-319-21569-3_12
3. Rinaldi, S.M., Peerenboom, J.P., Kelly, T.K.: Identifying, understanding and analyzing critical infrastructure interdependencies. IEEE Control Syst. Mag. **21**(6), 11–25 (2001)
4. European Union Agency for Network and Information Security: Safeguarding the global financial system by reducing cyber-risk, Heraklion (2016)
5. Financial Services Information Sharing and Analysis Center. https://www.fsisac.com/. Accessed 09 July 2019
6. Ntouskas, T., Polemi, N.: A secure, collaborative environment for the security management of port information systems. In: 5th International Conference on the Internet and Web Applications and Services, pp. 374–379, IEEE Press, Barcelona (2010)

7. Theoharidou, M., Kandias, M., Gritzalis, D.: Securing transportation-critical infrastructures: trends and perspectives. In: Georgiadis, Christos K., Jahankhani, H., Pimenidis, E., Bashroush, R., Al-Nemrat, A. (eds.) e-Democracy/ICGS3 -2011. LNICST, vol. 99, pp. 171–178. Springer, Heidelberg (2012). https://doi.org/10.1007/978-3-642-33448-1_24
8. Kampanakis, P.: Security automation and threat information-sharing options. IEEE Secur. Priv. **12**(5), 42–51 (2014)
9. European Network and Information Security Agency: Inventory of Risk Management/Risk Assessment Methods. http://rm-inv.enisa.europa.eu/rm_ra_methods.html. Accessed 09 July 2019
10. Ekelhart, A., Fenz und, S., Neubauer, T.: Automated risk and utility management. In: 6th International Conference on Information Technology: New Generations, pp. 393–398. IEEE Computer Society, Las Vegas (2009)
11. Jordan, B., Piazza, R., Wunder, B.: Stix Core Concepts. https://docs.oasis-open.org/cti/stix/v2.0/stix-v2.0-part1-stix-core.html. Accessed 09 July 2019
12. Wunder, J., Davidson, M., Jordan, B. TAXII™ Version 2.0. https://docs.google.com/document/d/1Jv9ICjUNZrOnwUXtenB1QcnBLO35RnjQcJLsa1mGSkI/edit. Accessed 09 July 2019
13. Parameswaran, M., Susarla, A., Whinston, A.B.: P2P networking: an information-sharing alternative. Computer **34**(7), 31–38 (2001)
14. Bosco, F., Croce, V., Raveduto, G.: Blockchain technology for financial services facilitation in RES investments. In: 4th International Forum on Research and Technology for Society and Industry (RTSI), pp. 1–5. IEEE Italy Section, Palermo (2018)
15. Guo, Y., Liang, C.: Blockchain application and outlook in the banking industry. Financ. Innov. **2**(1), 24 (2016)
16. Rosati, P., Čuk, T.: Blockchain beyond cryptocurrencies. In: Lynn, T., Mooney, J.G., Rosati, P., Cummins, M. (eds.) Disrupting Finance. PSDBET, pp. 149–170. Springer, Cham (2019). https://doi.org/10.1007/978-3-030-02330-0_10
17. Common Vulnerability Scoring System. https://www.first.org/cvss/v3.0/cvss-v30-specification_v1.9.pdf. Accessed 09 July 2019

Bunkers: Jail Application Level Firewall for the Mitigation and Identification of Service Takeover Attacks on HardenedBSD

Alin Anton[✉] and Răzvan Cioargă

Department of Computer and Information Technology,
Faculty of Automation and Computers, Politehnica University Timisoara,
2nd Vasile Parvan Avenue, 300223 Timis, Timisoara, Romania
{alin.anton,razvan.cioarga}@cs.upt.ro

Abstract. Jails are a lightweight operating-system based virtualization framework that allow safe delegation of subsets of a FreeBSD operating system to guest root users. HardenedBSD is a security-enhanced fork of FreeBSD, with Jail capabilities. In this paper we introduce Bunkers for Bank IT infrastructure security. Bunkers are security-enhanced HardenedBSD jails having only UNIX domain sockets enabled, and refusing all other types of socket creation including networking sockets. Bunkers also disable the execve() system call inside and only allow bit exact validated binaries from a global whitelist to be loaded and executed. The main objectives are to prevent elevation of privilege attacks and to isolate remote payloads and exploits from their source of origin. Bunkers detect, log, monitor and prevent all attempts to use network communications or unwanted binaries by isolating all the internal processes to UNIX domain sockets and filtering the execve() system call. Two use-cases are presented for isolating the ClamAV antivirus engine and all the necessary compressed file unpackers into HardenedBSD Bunkers: for e-mail security in a store and forward system and a real mail server and for web browsing security through the Squid proxy. Extensive benchmarks show that in both cases, for store and forward systems and for timely content delivery web systems the impact of the Bunker kernel module is comparable to rival approach Integriforce or with Regular Jails. More importantly, enforcing UNIX domain sockets for internal communication provides faster and safer inter-process communication mechanisms, between service processes and between Jails. The bit-exact execve() firewall has a consistent 13%–19% additional computation regardless of the type of service protected (web application firewall, SQL database). For the utmost security of mission-critical services we consider the results to be adequate.

Keywords: System call · Firewall · Bank Antivirus · Bank database · Microfinance

© Springer Nature Switzerland AG 2020
A. P. Fournaris et al. (Eds.): ESORICS 2019 Workshops, LNCS 11981, pp. 242–257, 2020.
https://doi.org/10.1007/978-3-030-42051-2_17

1   Introduction

Jails are a lightweight operating-system based virtualization framework that allow safe delegation of subsets of a FreeBSD[1] operating system to guest root users [6]. The origins lie in the chroot() system call which transforms a process's filesystem namespace by modifying the process-local root vnode (fn_rdir) to differ from the boot-time global root vnode [11].

HardenedBSD[2] is a security-enhanced fork of FreeBSD having Jail capabilities. Table 1 shows proeminent features comparison between mainstream FreeBSD (F), NetBSD[3] (N), OpenBSD[4] (O) and the HardenedBSD (H) operating system. According to Furnell delayed application updates and ignored security patches are frequent denominators for network breaches of software with known vulnerabilities [4]. Externalization of services on remote networked operating systems has become a very convenient paradigm for both users and private companies alike. Cloud computing for instance provides significant benefits of scalability and elasticity at reduced costs [14]. The reduced costs however come with the price of increased security and privacy risks [15].

The HardenedBSD team has done extensive efforts in order to mitigate for unpublished software vulnerabilities and late application updates [21]. For this reason HardenedBSD was selected as the operating system of choice for developing our bunker services such as Bank E-mail Antivirus Bunker and Bank Web Proxy Antivirus Bunker.

The chroot() system call is by design a namespace transformation tool, having been used at origins for isolating package building and testing scripts and compilation processes for various versions and distributions of a software. The jail on the other hand is by design a high-level security prison where a number of services can be run inside a virtual operating system running the same kernel as the host. This makes the jail a high performance container with solid security constraints, having a separate IP and the possibility to enforce a non-priviliged username and its own securelevel. The software installed inside a jail does not have to be recompiled or made aware of the prison in any way. At the opposite pole, whenever the source code of the service is available Capsicum can replace the chroot() method by providing application-centered sandboxing security [20]. However, modifying the source code is just the first step and a thorough application-based strategy is necessary for each recompiled service. Capsicum by itself does not automatically provide the stability and protections against abuse and resource consumption available within a jailed kernel but the two security mechanisms can be combined for better security resilience. Oracle Solaris has zones [5], which can be used for the virtualization of different operating systems but these are not security-oriented by design. Zones, for instance, can be used to run foreign operating systems like GNU/Linux. The Linux kernel can be contained with Linux Containers (LXC) [8], providing virtual private

---

[1] https://www.freebsd.org.
[2] https://www.hardenedbsd.org.
[3] https://www.netbsd.org.
[4] https://www.openbsd.org.

Table 1. HardenedBSD (H) exploit mitigation features compared to FreeBSD (F), OpenBSD (O) and NetBSD (N) operating systems [21]

Feature	H	F	O	N
ASLR	x	x	x	x
PIEs	x		x	x
RELRO + BINDNOW	x		x	
Ports PIE, RELRO, BINDNOW			x	
StaticPIE			x	
SEGVGUARD	x			
WX Part One	x		x	x
WX Part Two	x			x
Sysctl Hardening	x			
Net stack hardening	x		x	
Exec FIE	x			x
Boot Hardening	x			
Procfs/linprocfsHardening	x		x	
LibreSSL			x	
SROP Mitigation			x	
Most Of Base Sandboxed			x	
Trusted Path Execution	x			
Safe Stack In Base	x			
Safe Stack In Ports	x			
(CFI) InBase	x			
(CFI) InPorts	x			
Base Retpoline	x			
Ports Retpoline	x			
IntelSMAP+SMEPSupport	x	x	x	x

systems-like isolation. The weaker isolation guarantees of LXC have been known [1] since "linux containers were not designed for security" [9]. Unlike jails, these compartmentalization approaches are not security-oriented by design.

Trusted path execution initially presented in the Phrack magazine [12] provides kernel-level mechanisms for verifying a program's path before allowing the contents to run [13]. NSA's seLinux [2] and Grsecurity [17] include the idea however the contents of the binary files have to be protected also otherwise the trusted path in reality only protects the name of the file and its location. This has been addressed in NetBSD using Veriexec cryptographic checksums to validate the contents of a file before allowing execution [18]. A similar technology is called Integriforce in HardenedBSD (ExecFIE in Table 1) and is used in our measurements for reference [22]. Advances in computational power and

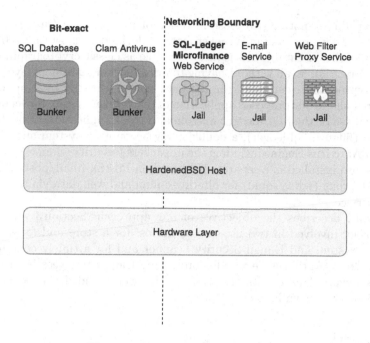

Fig. 1. HardenedBSD bunker model

cryptography research show that important cryptographic hash functions can be exploited to produce collisions, meaning the ability for an attacker to counterfeit file contents so that it produces the same checksum and appears to be valid and trustworthy. This may be unfeasible for a regular attacker targeting financial data, but it certanly is not impossible [16,19]. The SHA2 family of ciphers is considered unbreakable, but the implementations still require all the bits in the target file to be used as input for the hash function in order to produce the hash. That is, in order to compute the SHA2 checksum for a binary file all the bytes in the file need to be read just as when comparing two binary files byte by byte. Regardless of how secure a hash function or a block cipher is considered to be for the time being, there is no known way to mathematically prove it to be unbreakable. Consequently, in order to completely mitigate for this theoretical limitation, we decided to sacrifice some kernel memory storage in the order of a few megabytes in kernel space in order to implement bit-exact comparisons for executable files in the Bunker.

On a different plate, Microsoft's Authenticode has been abused by Stuxnet and Flame, and various other code-signing ecosystems for multiple platforms all share the same threat model [7]. Solutions like [3,10] may expose the entire operating system to total foreign control if the private system key is stolen or compromised. We address this risk by not trusting executable files based on their digital signature, and instead, we only trust bit-exact verified content for the Bunker.

Having almost nothing to loose in terms of performance (just a few more megabytes of data residing in kernel space), we decided to show that a bit-exact validation of the executable files is just as feasible as classic cryptographic validations like Integriforce, all without having to introduce an additional layer of trust having cryptographic complexity in the trust model (security by simplicity).

Figure 1 shows our proposed application of the Bunker system for securing the SQL Database of the SQL-Ledger microfinance web application from the ports collection (finance/sql-ledger), a double entry accounting system and ClamAV, the Clam Antivirus Engine including the unpackers (security/clamav). An e-mail service is also installed in a separate jail based on Postfix (mail/postfix) and the Squid web proxy (www/squid) for filtering e-mail and web data via the ClamAV bunker service.

Section 2 describes the objectives of our approach. Section 3 presents the methodology involved in two use-case scenarios, for a store and forward Bank Antivirus System and E-mail Security Scanner and for a timely content delivery Web Proxy Antivirus Service for protecting Bank employees from malware and ransomware. The results are presented in Sect. 4 and discussed in Sect. 5. Conclusions are drawn in Sect. 6.

2   Objectives

1. Our first objective is to render remote exploits and payloads unresponsive within the Bunker by isolating the remote attacker from the vulnerable system.
2. Our secondary objective is to provide intrusion detection for the HardenedBSD jail system by using the global system log in order to record any attempt to execute socket() with AF_INET networking capability.

3   Methodology

The kernel module has been compiled for HardenedBSD 11.2 on a 4 core machine with Intel i5 4460 @ 3.2 GHz, 16 GB RAM and 20 GB HDD.

For our measurements the global system /etc/bunkerjail.conf file contains:

```
ClamAV
```

the names of the jails converted into bunkers, one word each line.

In order to test the solution two use-case scenarios are designed and implemented as follows.

3.1   Bank E-Mail Antivirus Bunker

The Bank e-mail service is a store and forward system where file attachments are stored and scanned before being inserted into the Bank employee's Inbox. The scenario is shown in Fig. 2. For this we used a real mail server, with Postfix compiled statically inside a jail. ClamAV from ports (security/clamav) has been compiled statically inside another jail (which makes the object of this performance review), with and without the bunker mode enabled.

ClamAV is set to scan all incoming mails. Five test e-mail addresses were created on the mail server for this performance review:

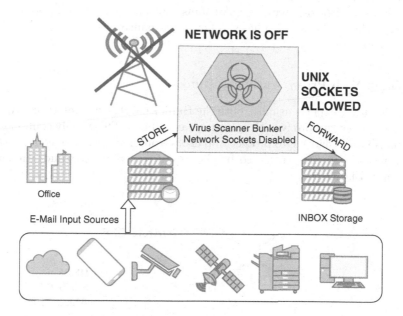

Fig. 2. Bank E-mail Virus Scanning Bunker with Isolated UNIX sockets inside a Jail

1. postal.test1@example.org,
2. postal.test2@example.org,
3. postal.test3@example.org,
4. postal.test4@example.org,
5. postal.test5@example.org.

Postal from the ports collection (benchmarks/postal) is used to test the performance of the Postfix (mail/postfix) mail server.

For this scenario two test cases have been used, each with and without the bunker mode:

1. 10 threads, 500 emails per thread;
2. 20 threads, 100 emails per thread;

Each thread opens a connection to the mail server and sends any random number of emails (between 1 and the number stated above, 500 or 100) and closes the connection afterwards; postal repeats this indefinitely. There are a number of threads/connections which are executed simultaneously (10 or 20). There is

50% chance of using a SSL connection (5/5 or 10/10 normal/SSL connections for the number of threads above). Each message has between 25 and 35 KB in size (randomly generated text). Every minute postal reports the number of emails successfully sent over the passing minute, the size of all data sent, the number of errors, the number of connections and the number of SSL connections. The tests were allowed to run over 120 min.

We compare Bunkers with Regular Jails and also with rival approach Integriforce, to show that our idea has similar performance results in terms of e-mail datarate capacity.

3.2 Bank Web Proxy Antivirus Bunker

Bank IT security experts usually route the Bank's employees' web traffic through an outbound security proxy with antivirus capabilities. This timely content delivery scenario uses ClamAV to protect web users from malicious web content traffic by scanning all the files presented by the Squid proxy (www/squid) on the fly, as shown in Fig. 3.

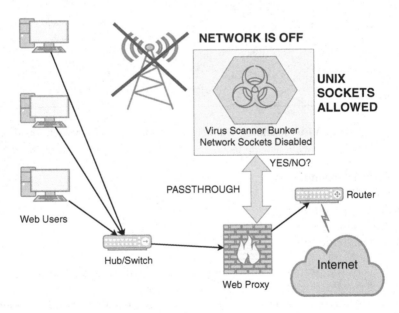

Fig. 3. Bank Web Proxy Virus Scanning Bunker with Isolated UNIX sockets inside a Jail

Squid from the ports collection is configured to run as a proxy server on port 3128. Squidclamav (www/squidclamav) is used to scan all proxy server traffic through c-icap (www/c-icap) server. Polygraph (benchmarks/polygraph) is used for benchmarking the configuration. Polygraph uses a client server architecture to simulate heavy traffic in a web proxy. The Squid proxy has been inserted between polygraph server and client and performance has been measured.

There are two cases whose performance have been evaluated with and without squidclamav (both with and without bunker mode on), measuring data throughput.

We compare Bunkers with Regular Jails and also with rival approach Integrifoce in order to show that our solution has similar performance under real web browser heavy load conditions in terms of data rate.

3.3 Bit-Exact Execve() Web Service Firewall for Bank's Web Applications

Web applications are a common way for providing thin clients to Bank employees in a local area network. The bit-exact execve() feature of our Bunkers can be used to monitor and protect whitelisted web applications provided that their binary form is statically compiled. Language interpreters like PHP or Perl can also be whitelisted in order to allow the scripts inside to work. The SQL-Ledger microfinance web application from the ports collection (finance/sql-ledger) has been used in the bit-exact execve() configuration only, connected to a separate Bunker for the PostgreSQL database via local UNIX sockets.

The bunker module has been compiled for HardenedBSD 11.2 on a 4 core machine with Intel i5 4460 @ 3.2 GHz, 16 GB RAM and 20 GB HDD. In order to evaluate the performance impact of the module 3 jails are configured each using a statically compiled version of the following ports based on FAMP: a web server (www/apache24), (lang/php73) and (databases/mysql80-server), and the other 2 jails are configured with (www/nginx) and (www/lighttpd) for web service respectively. A MySQL table with 1000000 records is populated with random data. Each row has 5 columns: id, random_int, random_int, random_varchar(20), random_varchar(20). The (benchmarks/siege) tool is used from the ports collection with 20 concurrent accesses and 50 repetitions each. Thus, 1000 measurements are performed for each configuration. For each test, its execution time has been recorded in the PHP file containing the test. The total execution times given by the siege tool were ignored as they contain network time and delays. After a single execution the PHP file records a single line in a comma separated values results file (.csv); the line contains 5 values (one for each test and a total).

The scenario described above has been repeated with jails containing only the necessary binary files and scripts. All the executable files are statically linked and have no outside library dependencies.

Our PHP test is used to evaluate performance for "SELECT" queries which are evaluated by a MySQL and a PostgreSQL server. The test is executed on a database containing a single table with 1,000,000 records with random generated values. There are 5 columns: id, int1, int2, string1, string2. Column id is the primary index, autoincrement, contains values from 1 to 1,000,000. The second and third columns are integers containing random generated values in the interval of 1 to 1,000,000. The fourth and fifth columns' type is varchar(20) and contains random generated 20 characters strings.

The test has been inserted into the same PHP file which has been provisioned to calculate the execution times.

The PHP file has been executed using the (benchmarks/siege) tool using the following scenario: 20 concurrent accesses, 50 repetitions for each of the 20 accesses. Thus, 1000 data sets have been collected for each measurement with the siege tool.

For each test, its execution time has been recorded in the PHP file containing the test. The total execution times given by the siege tool were ignored as they contain network time and delays.

After each execution, the PHP file records a single line in a comma separated values results file. The line contains 5 values (one for each test and a total). The scenario described above has been repeated with jails containing only the necessary binary files and scripts. All the executable files are statically linked and have no outside library dependencies.

The scenario has been repeated with 3 types of jails using the following configurations for a PHP and MySQL/PostgreSQL web server: Apache, Nginx, and Lighttpd as popular solutions. We also use the default PostgreSQL benchmarking tool provided by the database, pgbench, which shows performance results in the same margin.

4   Results

Results are provided by measuring the performance impact of our kernel module in two ClamAV installations: a store and forward e-mail system with and without the bunker mode enabled, and a timely content delivery web proxy antivirus as follows.

4.1   Bank E-Mail Antivirus Bunker

Figure 4 shows 240 measurement points, 120 for a regular Jail configuration and 120 for a Bunker. The amount of e-mail data sent in a minute spans between 12–20 Mb using small random messages of 25–35 Kb each.

Bunker mode shows similar performance and data rate as compared to Regular Jails and with the rival approach Integriforce, which uses cryptographic checksums to validate executable file contents. The reason for this is Postfix[5], which does not spawn new processes when receiving heavy loads of e-mail data, using threads instead.

Figure 6 shows 240 measurement points, 120 for a regular Jail configuration and 120 for a Bunker. The amount of e-mail data sent in a minute spans between 25–40 Mb using small random messages of 25–35 Kb each.

Bunker mode shows the same performance and data rate when compared to rival approach Integriforce, based on cryptographic checksums, and also with Regular Jails. This again has to do with how Postfix handles parallel connections, using threads instead of forking new processes.

---

[5] https://www.postfix.org.

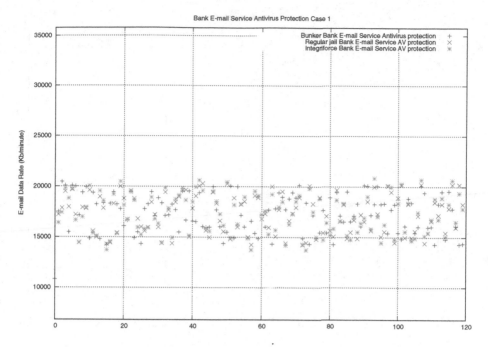

Fig. 4. Postfix 10 Threads 500 E-Mails per Thread 25–35 Kb each

4.2   Bank Web Proxy Antivirus Bunker

Figure 5 shows the data rate measurement results obtained using the Polygraph benchmark from the ports tree (benchmarks/polygraph).

Both regular HardenedBSD Jails and Bunkers show similar performance, with a constant data rate oscillating less than $+/-$ 100 Kb/s around the value of 1500 KB/s. Integriforce and regular jails have very similar performance, only distinguishable in the raw data set, both performing slightly better than Bunkers. This is explained by the additional kernel memory required by the Bunker in order to operate. SquidClamAV seems not to fork or spawn new processes therefore having not impact when comparing Integriforce with regular jails.

The test took 8 min and 20 seconds to perform and transferred a total of 738.5 Mb with 1400–1600 Kb/s.

The mean value of 1500 KB/s is shown using a horizontal line for convenience.

The two negative spikes in Fig. 5 for the regular Jail at measurements 45 and 79 and the positive spike at measurement 58 compared to the Bunker data rate are independent to the bunker kernel module. Unix domain sockets are used in both cases, using the same ClamAV configuration. These events may be related to sockets and file system buffers and are completely unrelated to our implementation.

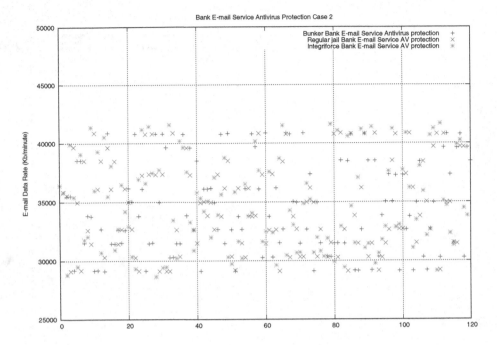

Fig. 5. SquidClamav Polygraph Benchmark Datarate for 100 Measurements

Congestion control is used also for UNIX domain sockets communication resulting in the 200 Kb/s oscillatory effect.

It is important to notice that rival approach Integriforce, and also Regular Jails, have similar performance and data rate when compared to our Bunker idea which also provides network isolation.

4.3 Bit-Exact Execve() Web Service Firewall for Bank's Web Applications

In all our tests the time is measured in seconds and it is used to compute the mean value based on 1000 samples with confidence intervals of 95%. In total 12000 measurements are performed using the siege tool.

The observable 13%–19% performance penalty in the case of web services in Fig. 7 is due to multiple child processes being spawned by the web daemons in order to handle the load. The execve() system call and the binary file validations are used only when the Bunker requires new processes. Also, AF_INET sockets had to be re-enabled in the web service Bunker in order to avoid using a reverse proxy, leaving only the bit-exact validation active.

The bit-exact filter of execve() has also been tested by populating the same postgresql (databases/postgresql) database used by the SQL-Ledger Micro-finance Web Application using the standard postgresql benchmarking tool pgbench.

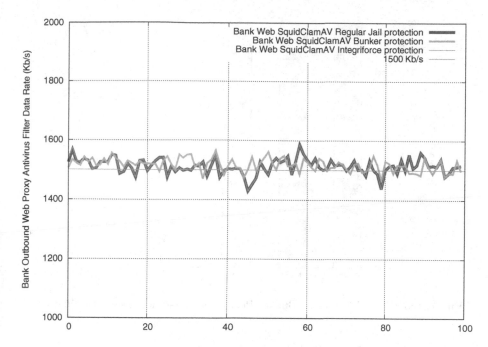

Fig. 6. Postfix 20 Threads 100 E-Mails per Thread 25-35 Kb each

The tool is called to populate a 10 million entry table:

```
# pgbench -i -s 100 benchmark -U postgres
```

and later to benchmark the database system with the bunker mode enabled:

```
pgbench -c 1000 -j 100 benchmark -U postgres
starting vacuum...end.
transaction type: TPC-B (sort of)
scaling factor: 100
query mode: simple
number of clients: 1000
number of threads: 100
number of transactions per client: 10
number of transactions actually processed: 10000/10000
latency average: 1803.432 ms
tps = 554.498281 (including connections establishing)
tps = 568.914833 (excluding connections establishing)
```

and also without the module:

```
...
latency average: 2341.324 ms
tps = 645.531954 (including connections establishing)
tps = 672.051051 (excluding connections establishing)
```

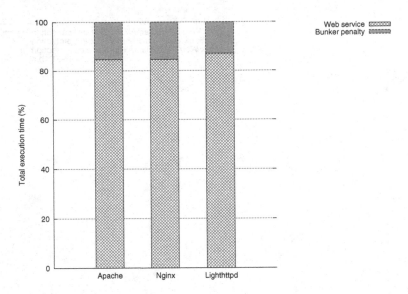

Fig. 7. Bank Web Application Bunker Penalty for bit-exact execve() validation

It can be seen that the filtering of the execve() using bit-exact comparisons against the image of the statically compiled postgresql binary and also the AF_UNIX socket test together bring a 554/645 15% impact on the transactions per second (tps) metric shown above by the tool, since PostgreSQL uses child processes in order to handle the heavy load.

5   Discussion

The Bunker idea originates in the desire to securely isolate critical financial services running on UNIX platforms like financial databases of a Bank and antivirus engines protecting a Bank's employees and IT systems. This has been obtained by virtualizing a HardenedBSD kernel using the Jail security mechanism, and by selectively blocking it from all outside world communications.

In the event that any of the mitigation techniques in HardenedBSD should fail, the Bunker securely isolates any remote attacker from the processes running inside the Bank system. Also, the Bunker requires a bit-exact execve() whitelist of binary files to be loaded in global kernel space (outside the bunker itself). Only this select list of files can have an identical copy inside the bunker and is allowed to run inside.

Such a configuration is possible given that the Bunker exchanges data with other Bunkers and also with regular Jails using UNIX domain sockets, visible as files.

Jails and Bunkers alike can optionally have a number of Matryoshka prisons recursively contained while also sharing parts of the file system with each other.

The ClamAV antivirus has been chosen based on the fact that it is free software and that antiviruses require external unpackers and libraries in order to decompress e-mail attachments. Such packers are frequently closed-source and notoriously buggy leaving room for zero-day exploits and unknown vulnerabilities.

Consequently, the ClamAV antivirus is perfect for the bunker since no communication with the outside world is necessary for files to be scanned. Antivirus signatures can be installed from outside the bunker using automated crontab scripts.

HardenedBSD Gateways have to route packets between network interfaces, leaving regular Jails vulnerable to misconfigurations and data leaks. All regular Jails, by default, have an IP address and can use internet sockets as well as optionally raw sockets, disabled by default.

Bunkers completely remove the idea of non-UNIX socket communication for a select list of regular Jails given in the global /etc/bunkerjail.conf.

Store and forward systems do not require timely responses like the web does, and antivirus scanning time may quietly take place inside a Bunker without exposing the file unpackers to the outside world.

On the other hand, timeliness and fluency is of critical importance for web proxies, thus online antivirus scanners for the proxied data require more powerful hardware resources and communication bandwidth.

Regardless of the type of system in use, our goal was to stress test the socket system call to see if there are any negative consequences due to the additional Bunker code.

The benchmarks show that the method used has negligible impact on the system while providing higher security standards and peace of mind for the system administrator. Our bit-exact execve() whitelisting solution has similar performance and data rate as the rival approach Integriforce, which is based on cryptographic checksums.

When compared to Integriforce and Regular Jails, Bunkers also provide complete network isolation and security by simplicity. The more complex the code and a cryptograhic implementation is, the higher the chance for mistakes to remain hidden. We also avoid using file paths as validation, which is known to produce race conditions due to the way the kernel buffers receive filesystem data in both BSD-like and GNU/Linux based operating systems.

One limitation of the Bunker use case is that network isolation has to be disabled when protecting services which require direct access to the internet, like a web service having the SQL-Ledger microfinance application on top of it. Future versions should consider protocol enforcers in order to limit the network traffic and enforce a valid HTTP or SMTP protocol over the socket.

6   Conclusions

Bunkers are security-enhanced HardenedBSD Jails which disable the socket() system call except for UNIX domain sockets. The module has been tested against popular e-mail and web antivirus configurations using ClamAV, the free software antivirus.

The idea is novel for HardenedBSD jails. HardenedBSD was selected as the operating system of choice for developing our bunker services such as Bank E-mail Antivirus Bunker, Bank Web Proxy Antivirus Bunker, and Bank databases because it provides enhanced exploit mitigation techniques for unknown vulnerabilities and zero-day exploits which affect critical financial services.

Bunkers can be used for any possible UNIX service that is part of the critical infrastructure of any Bank, provided that the binary executable file for the service is statically compiled and that the service can communicate using local UNIX sockets.

The kernel module is designed from scratch to only affect jails having no impact outside on the global system which may also run other, non-jailed services. These are going to remain unaffected. The module intercepts and replaces the native socket() system call with a wrapper. All security checks are only active when the module code runs inside a jail prison. Bunkers can be selectively nominated in the /etc/bunkerjail.conf global system file.

The module also logs any attempt to execute the socket() system call inside a Bunker. This provides a mechanism for intrusion detection since logs inside the jail can be monitored in real-time or mirrored on the global system with append-only permissions.

The source code for our kernel module and the measurement data can be provided on request.

1. Our first objective was to render remote exploits and payloads unresponsive within the Bunker by isolating the remote attacker from the vulnerable system. This has been achieved by intercepting the socket() system call with the Bunker kernel module and filtering out all non-UNIX (domain) sockets, including networking AF_INET and PF_INET6 code. The bunker is isolated from the outer world.
2. Our secondary objective was to provide intrusion detection for the HardenedBSD Jail system by using the global system log in order to record any attempt to execute socket() with AF_INET networking capability. All socket() calls having anything but UNIX domain sockets return permission denied for any process active inside the bunker.

Acknowledgement. We acknowledge Dr. Luca Verderame, our shepherd, and the anonymous reviewers for help improving this paper.

References

1. Arnautov, S., et al.: SCONE: secure linux containers with intel SGX. In: 12th USENIX Symposium on Operating Systems Design and Implementation (OSDI 2016), pp. 689–703, USENIX Association, Savannah (2016)
2. Bauer, M.: Paranoid penguin: introduction to seLinux. Linux J. **2007**(154), 15 (2007)

3. Crooks, A.: NetPGP and Signed Execution. https://www.netbsd.org/agc/netpgp-signedexec-2012.pdf. September 2012
4. Furnell, S.: Vulnerability management: not a patch on where we should be? Netw. Secur. **2016**(4), 5–9 (2016)
5. Oracle Inc.: Enterprise Manager Ops Center User's Guide 11g Release 1 Update 3 (11.1.3.0.0) Chapter 12 Oracle Solaris Zones. Oracle Inc., November 2011
6. Kamp, P.-H., Watson, R.N.M.: Jails: confining the omnipotent root. In: Proceedings of the 2nd International SANE Conference (2000)
7. Kim, D., Kwon, B.J., Dumitraş, T.: Certified malware: measuring breaches of trust in the windows code-signing PKI. In: Proceedings of the Conference on Computer and Communications Security, CCS 2017, pp. 1435–1448. ACM, New York (2017)
8. Canonical Ltd.: Linux containers LXC (2019). https://linuxcontainers.org/. Accessed 2019
9. Mattetti, M., Shulman-Peleg, A., Allouche, Y., Corradi, A., Dolev, S., Foschini, L.: Automatic security hardening and protection of linux containers. In: Workshop on Security and Privacy in the Cloud, September 2015
10. McCorkle, E.: A trust infrastructure for FreeBSD. In: BSDCan - The BSD Conference, Ottawa, June 2018
11. McKusick, M.K., Neville-Neil, G.V., Watson, R.N.M.: The design and implementation of the FreeBSD operating system, 2nd edn. Addison Wesley, Boston (2015)
12. Phrack: Hardening the Linux Kernel: Trusted Path Execution. Phrack Mag. **8**(52), 6–20 (1998)
13. Rahimi, N.A.: Trusted Path Execution for the Linux 2.6 kernel as a Linux Security Module (2004)
14. Samarati, P.: Data security and privacy in the cloud. In: Proceedings of 10th International Conference on Information Security Practice and Experience (ISPEC 2014), Fuzhou, China, May 2014
15. Samarati, P., De Capitani di Vimercati, S.: Data protection in outsourcing scenarios: issues and directions. In: Proceedings of the 5th ACM Symposium on Information, Computer and Communications Security (ASIACCS 2010), Beijing, China, April 2010. invited paper
16. Stevens, M., Bursztein, E., Karpman, P., Albertini, A., Markov, Y.: The first collision for full SHA-1. In: Katz, J., Shacham, H. (eds.) CRYPTO 2017. LNCS, vol. 10401, pp. 570–596. Springer, Cham (2017). https://doi.org/10.1007/978-3-319-63688-7_19
17. The Grsecurity project: Filesystem hardening: Trusted Path Execution 2019. https://www.grsecurity.net. Accessed 2019
18. The NetBSD Project: The NetBSD Guide Part III chapter 20: NetBSD Veriexec subsystem (2019). https://www.netbsd.org/docs/guide/en/index.html
19. Wang, X., Yu, H.: How to break MD5 and other hash functions. In: Cramer, R. (ed.) EUROCRYPT 2005. LNCS, vol. 3494, pp. 19–35. Springer, Heidelberg (2005). https://doi.org/10.1007/11426639_2
20. Watson, R.N.M., Anderson, J., Laurie, B., Kennaway, K.: A taste of Capsicum: practical capabilities for UNIX. Commun. ACM **55**(3), 97–104 (2012)
21. Webb, S., Salcedo, B.: HardenedBSD Easy Feature Comparison (2019). https://hardenedbsd.org/content/easy-feature-comparison. Accessed 2019
22. Webb, S., Salcedo, B.: HardenedBSD Integriforce (2019). https://github.com/HardenedBSD/secadm. Accessed 2019. secadm 0.2

A Language-Based Approach to Prevent DDoS Attacks in Distributed Financial Agent Systems

Elahe Fazeldehkordi[1,2], Olaf Owe[2(✉)], and Toktam Ramezanifarkhani[2]

[1] Department of Technology Systems, University of Oslo, Oslo, Norway
[2] Department of Informatics, University of Oslo, Oslo, Norway
{elahefa,olaf,toktamr}@ifi.uio.no

Abstract. Denial of Service (DoS) and Distributed DoS (DDoS) attacks, with even higher severity, are among the major security threats for distributed systems, and in particular in the financial sector where trust is essential.

In this paper, our aim is to develop an additional layer of defense in distributed agent systems to combat such threats. We consider a high-level object-oriented modeling framework for distributed systems, based on the actor model with support of asynchronous and synchronous method interaction and futures, which are sophisticated and popular communication mechanisms applied in many systems today. Our approach uses static detection to identify and prevent potential vulnerabilities caused by asynchronous communication including call-based DoS or DDoS attacks, possibly involving a large number of distributed actors.

Keywords: DoS attacks · DDoS attacks · Active objects · Agent communication · Asynchronous methods · Static analysis · Static detection · Call-based flooding

1 Introduction

Today distributed and service-oriented systems form critical parts of infrastructures of the modern society, including financial services. In the financial sector security and trust are essential for users of financial services [19]. Security breaches may lead to significant loss of assets, such as physical or virtual money, including cryptocurrencies and bitcoins. In addition, successful attacks on services of a financial institution may damage the trust of customers, which indirectly may hurt the institution [18]. According to [1,12,17], a main threat on financial institutions is Distributed Denial of Service (DDoS) attacks. Protection against DoS/DDoS attacks is therefore crucial for financial institutions. Slow website responses caused by targeted attacks, can imply that customers cannot access their online banking and trading websites during such attacks. Both network layer and application layer DDoS attacks continue to be more and

© Springer Nature Switzerland AG 2020
A. P. Fournaris et al. (Eds.): ESORICS 2019 Workshops, LNCS 11981, pp. 258–277, 2020.
https://doi.org/10.1007/978-3-030-42051-2_18

more persistent according to a report from the Global DDoS Threat Landscape Q4 2017. Based on this report, it becomes easier and easier to launch DDoS attacks, and one may even purchase botnet-for-hire services that provide the basis for starting a hazardous DDoS attack. Financial institutions are recommended to monitor the internet traffic to their websites in order to detect and react to possible threats. However, this kind of run-time protection may slow down or temporarily shut down the websites.

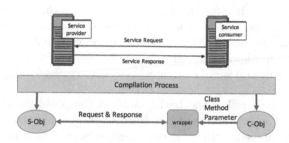

Fig. 1. Distributed communication. S-Obj stands for server object and C-Obj for consumer object.

Unintended attacks on customers from a financial institution may easily destroy the customer's trust and confidence and result in reputation damage. If customers cannot trust an institution, they may quickly shift to a different institution, due to competition between the many different financial institutions and service providers. Even a single unfortunate incident of a financial service provider could be enough to influence customers. One should make sure that the software is not harmful for the customers before running it, and this makes static (compile-time) detection more important than in other areas. Thus, in the financial sector static detection is a valuable complement to run-time detection methods, and seems underrepresented.

Call-based *flooding* is commonly seen in the form of application-based DDoS attacks [6]. To prevent DoS/DDoS flooding attacks in a manner complementary to existing approaches, we propose an additional layer of defense, based on language-based security analysis. We focus on DDoS attacks that try to force a (sub)system out of order by flooding applications running on the target system, or by using such applications to drain the resources of their victim.

In this paper, we consider a high-level imperative and object-oriented language for distributed systems, based on the actor model with support of asynchronous and synchronous method interaction. This setting is appealing in that it naturally supports the distribution of autonomous concurrent units, and efficient interaction, avoiding active waiting and low-level synchronization primitives such as explicit signaling and lock operations. It is therefore useful as a framework for modeling and analysis of distributed service-oriented systems. Our language supports efficient interaction by features such as asynchronous and non-blocking method calls and first-class futures, which are popular features applied in many distributed systems today. However, these mechanisms make it even easier for an attacker to launch a DDoS attack, because undesirable waiting by the attacker can be avoided with these mechanisms.

We propose an approach consisting of static analysis. We identify and prevent potential vulnerabilities in asynchronous communication that directly or indirectly can cause call-based flooding of agents. More precisely, we adapt a general algorithm for detecting call flooding [14] to the setting of security analysis and for detection of distributed denial of service attacks adding support for many-to-one attacks. The algorithm detects call cycles that might overflow the incoming queues of one or more communicating agents. Each cycle may involve any number of agents, possibly involving the attacked agent(s).

The high-level framework considered here is relevant for a large class of programming languages and service-oriented systems.

Outline. Section 2 describes the background of the problem. Related work is discussed in Sect. 3. The active object framework is explained in Sect. 4. Our static analysis to prevent attacks is described in Sect. 5. Examples of possible DoS/DDoS attacks are given in Sect. 6. The final section concludes and suggests future work.

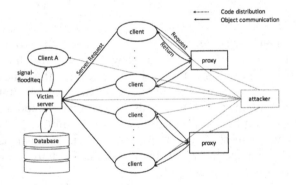

Fig. 2. Distributed object communication in DDoS.

2   Overview

In distributed system communication there is an underlying distributed object system as shown in Fig. 1. In such a distributed system, classes such as server or client classes would be instantiated by objects, and communication is established in the form of method calls, usually wrapped in XML or other forms. Therefore, communication in a distributed system is implemented by method calls between objects. If there is a possibility of flood of requests to the service provider (S-Obj) from the consumer object(s) (C-Obj) in this figure, a DoS attack is probable.

Call-Based Flooding Attacks. To launch a DoS attack, the attacker may try to submerge the target server under many requests to saturate its computing resources. To do so, flooding attacks [6,20] by method calls are effective, espe-cially when the server allocates a lot of resources in response to a single request. Therefore, we detect:

- call-flooding: flooding from one object to another.
- parametric-call-flooding: flooding from one object to another when the target object allocates resources or consumes resources for each call.

In the case of call-flooding, communications are just simple requests like a simple call without parameters or parameters that do not lead to resource consumption. Parametric-call-flooding is when requests usually include parameters in a non-trivial manner. Such requests usually trigger relatively complex processing on the server such as access to a database. Parametric-call-flooding is more effective than call-flooding because it takes fewer requests to drown the target system. However, call-flooding are more common and easier for attackers to exploit.

Categories of Call-Based Flooding Attacks: DoS or DDoS Possibilities

one-to-one (OTO): If thousands of requests every single second come from one source object to a target object, then it is a *one-to-one (OTO) DoS attack*. The intent of the flooding might be malicious, or even undeliberate call cycles. Communication between Client A and the victim server in Fig. 2 is an example of this attack.

many-to-one (MTO): If the incoming flooding traffic originates from many distinguishable different sources, then it is a *many-to-one (MTO) DDoS attack*. Figure 2 shows a distribution of code between clients and a server, and proxies.

one-to-many (OTM): A *one-to-many attack* appears if a system makes an unlimited number of requests to many objects simultaneously. Such an attack can be serious since many target objects are attacked at the same time.

Static Attack Detection and Prevention. For any set of methods that call the same target method, a call cycle could be harmful. The methods might belong to the same or different objects with the same or different interfaces. In the case of normal blocking calls, where the caller is blocking while waiting for the response, making a flood of requests also means receiving a flood of responses. And thus in the case of OTO, it may cause a self DoS for the attacker. With the possibility of non-blocking calls in a distributed setting, it is more cost-beneficial for an OTO attacker to launch a DoS, because then undesirable blocking by the attacker is avoided. By means of futures and asynchronous calls, a caller process can make non-blocking method calls.

The possibility of unbounded object creation, referred to as *instantiation flooding* [8], could cause resource consumption and DoS that could be detected statically, especially if those objects and their communication can cause flooding requests from the bots, such as the customers in our example. It is even worse if there is instantiation flooding on the target side of the distributed code. This can be detected by static analysis of the target. (See the example in Fig. 10.)

Our static analysis detects explicit or implicit call-flooding. Static detection is accomplished by static analysis at compile time and informs the programmer about the possibility of program exploitation at runtime.

3   Related Work

A DoS attack, or its distributed version, happens when access to a computer or network resource is intentionally blocked. Considering the exploited vulnerabilities, these attacks might be classified by resource consumption attacks or flooding attacks, of which the latter category is the most common [6]. In this paper, we aim to prevent distributed code to be exploited by attackers to launch a DoS attack by detection of possible call-based flooding in both of the target and zombie sides. To do so, we analyze the distributed code to make an additional layer of defense against DoS or DDoS attacks.

In the following, we discuss related works for preventing application-based DDoS attacks using static detection. In the paper presented by Chang et al. [3], a novel static analysis approach was introduced in order to detect semantic vulnerabilities in networked software that might cause denial of service attacks because of resource exhaustion. Their approach is implemented in a tool named SAFER: Static Analysis Framework for Exhaustion of Resources. SAFER integrates taint analysis (in order to compute the group of program values that are data-dependent on network inputs) and control dependency analysis (for computing the group of program statements whose execution can affect the execution of a given statement) toward detecting high complexity control structures that can be caused by untrusted network inputs. The tool applies the CIL static analysis framework and combines different heuristics for recognizing loops and recursive calls. Compared to our work the SAFER approach is oriented toward detecting server attacks from within the server code, whereas our approach is mainly targeting server attacks from an external attacker, or a combination of external agents. An attacker needs to understand the code of the server in order to find weaknesses that can be triggered by specific inputs. In contrast, our approach is detecting attacks caused by coordination of several agents and/or servers in a distributed setting.

Another work that detects resource attacks from within the server code is presented by Qie et al. [15]. In their toolkit, they check for possible "rule" violations at runtime. This work is complementary to ours, since our work is oriented toward static detection. Gulavani and Gulwani [7] describe a precise numerical abstract domain. This domain can be used to prove the termination of a large class of programs and also to estimate valuable information such as timing bounds. In order to make linear numerical abstract domains more precise, they make use of two domain lifting operations: One operation depends on the principle of *expression abstraction*. This describes a set of expressions and determines their semantics by use of a selection of directed inference rules. It works by picking up an abstract domain and a group of expressions, such that their semantics are described by a group of rewrite rules, in order to construct a more precise abstract domain. The second domain constructor operation picks up a linear arithmetic abstract domain and constructs a new arithmetic domain that is able to represent linear relations through introduction of max expressions. Another approach to estimate worst-case complexity is presented by Colon and Sipma [4]. These approaches [4,7], in which the complexity of loops and recursive calls has been estimated using structural analysis, are widely complementary to our work.

Zheng and Myers [21] propose a framework for using static information flow analysis in order to specify and enforce end-to-end availability policies in programs. They extend the decentralized label model to include security policies for availability. This work presents a simple language with fine-grained information security policies described by type annotations. In addition, this language has a security type system to reason about end-to-end availability policies. Various examples have been discussed, in which abuse of an availability policy can represent denial of service attacks.

In a work by Meadows [13], a formal analysis has been developed in order to apply the maximum benefit of tools and approaches that have already been used to strengthen protocols against denial of service attack. This analysis has been done at the protocol specification level. Also, different ways in which existing cryptographic protocol analysis tools can be modified for the purpose of operating in this formal framework, have been demonstrated. In contrast, we do a detailed static analysis of source code both inside and outside a server. The class of software vulnerabilities that we can detect is more complicated than what appears just at the network-protocol specifications level. Moreover, vulnerable sections of the source code have been identified in our work.

The current work shows how the static analysis method for detection of flooding can be used for detection of DoS and DDoS attacks. This general idea was also outlined by the same authors in an extended workshop abstract [16]. Moreover we here discuss why this is particularly harmful in the financial sector, where both economic assets and customer trust are at risk. Furthermore we simplify and adapt the static analysis method of [14] to the setting of financial service systems, extending it to detect many-to-one attacks involving unbounded creation of objects (as demonstrated in the example in Fig. 10), as well as hidden attacks, neither of which were detected by the original method of [14].

4   Our Framework for Active Object Systems

The setting of concurrent objects communicating by asynchronous method calls combines the Actor model and object-orientation, and is referred to as *active objects*. Active object languages are suitable for modeling and implementing distributed applications, letting a distributed system be modeled by a number of active objects that interact via asynchronous method calls. The active object model provides natural description of autonomous agents in a distributed system, and the *future mechanism* provides an efficient communication primitives [2,11], allowing results computed in a distributed setting to be referred to and shared.

A future is a read-only placeholder for a method result value and may be referenced by several objects. Moreover, the addition of *cooperative scheduling*, as suggested in the Creol language [10], allows further communication efficiency, by adding process scheduling control in the programming language, and passive waiting. This is achieved by including statements for suspension control, and letting each object have a process queue for holding suspended processes. We consider a core language for active objects with future-based communication primitives, inspired by Creol and ABS [9]. The objects are concurrent units distributed over a network, and their identity is globally unique. An object has a process queue, as well as a queue for incoming method call requests, and can perform at most one process (i.e., remaining part of method call) at a time. A process can be suspended by an **await** statement, allowing other (enabled) processes to continue. When a process is ended or suspended, the object may continue with an incoming call request or other enabled process from the process queue (if any). The **await** statement allows a process to wait for a Boolean condition to be satisfied, or for a future value to be available. The statement is enabled when the waiting condition/future is satisfied/available. The **await** statement enables high-level process control, instead of low-level process synchronization statements such as signaling and lock operations.

Our core language is a typed, imperative language. An assignment has the form $x := e$ where the expression e is without side-effects. All object variables (i.e., object references) are typed by an interface, and an interface specifies the set of methods that are visible through that interface. The interfaces of a class protect and limit the object communication, and in particular shared variable interaction is forbidden. Local data structure is made by data type declarations, indicated by **data**, and a functional data type sublanguage is used to create and manipulate data values. Data values are passed by value, while object variables are passed by reference. The language supports first-class futures. The basic interaction mechanisms (by method calls/futures) are as follows:

- $f := o!m(\bar{e})$ – the current object calls method m on object o with actual parameters $\bar{e}$. A globally unique identity u identifying the call is assigned to the future variable f. A message is then sent over the network from the current object to object o. When object o eventually performs the method and the method gives a result defined by a **return** statement, that result is placed in a (globally accessible) future with identity u, and the future u is then said to be *resolved*. Any process of any object that knows u may access the future value or wait for it to be available.
- $x := \textbf{get}\ f$ – this statement blocks until the value of the future f is available, and then that value is assigned to the variable x. (Here f may be an expression resulting in a future identity.)
- **await** c – this statement suspends if the Boolean condition c is not satisfied, and is enabled when c is satisfied,
- **await** $x := \textbf{get}\ f$ – this statement suspends if the value of f is not yet available, and is enabled when the future is available. Then the future value is assigned to x. The statement **await** f suspends when f is not resolved.

The statement sequence $f := o!m(\bar{e}); x := \textbf{get } f$ corresponds to a traditional blocking call, and is abbreviated $x := o.m(\bar{e})$ using the conventional dot-notation. The statement sequence $f := o!m(\bar{e}); \textbf{await } f; x := \textbf{get } f$ is abbreviated $\textbf{await } x := o.m(\bar{e})$ and corresponds to a non-blocking call, since the **await**-statement ensures that the future is available before the **get**-statement is performed. If the result value is not needed, we may simplify the syntax to $o.m(\bar{e})$ for blocking calls and $\textbf{await } o.m(\bar{e})$ for non-blocking calls. And if the future is not needed, $f := o!m(\bar{e})$ may be abbreviated to $o!m(\bar{e})$, in which case the future cannot be accessed (since it is not stored in a future variable).

Object creation has the syntax $x := \textbf{new } C(\bar{e}) \textbf{ at } o$, where the class parameters behave like fields (initialized to the values of $\bar{e}$) except that they are read-only, and the new object is created locally at the site of object o. With the syntax $x := \textbf{new } C(\bar{e})$ the new object is located anywhere in the distributed system.

One may refer to the current object by this and to the caller object by (the implicit method parameter) caller. Self calls are possible by making calls to this, and recursion is allowed. *Active behavior* is possible by making a recursive self call in the constructor method (given as a nameless method). By means of suspension, the active self behavior may be interleaved with execution of incoming calls from other objects, thereby combining active behavior and passive behavior. If- and while-statements are as usual.

We assume all class parameters and method parameters (including this and caller) are read-only. This helps the static analysis by reducing the set of false positives. For methods that return no information we use a predefined type *Void* with only one value, *void*. For simplicity we omit **return** *void* at the end of *Void* methods in the examples.

5   Static Analysis to Prevent Attacks

We base our approach on the static analysis of flooding presented in [14] for detection of flooding of requests, formalized for the Creol/ABS setting with futures. We adapt this notion of flooding to deal with detection of DDoS attacks, which have a similar nature. The static analysis will search for flooding cycles in the code, possibly involving several classes. According to [14] (unbounded) flooding is defined as follows:

Definition 1 (Flooding). *An execution is* flooding with respect to a method m *if there is an execution cycle C containing a* call *statement to a method m at a given program location, such that this statement may produce an unbounded number of uncompleted calls to method m, in which case we say that the call is* flooding with respect to C *in the given execution.*

Like in [14], we distinguish between weak flooding and strong flooding. Strong flooding is flooding under the assumption of so-called *favorable* process scheduling, i.e., enabled processes are executed in a fair manner.

Definition 2 (Strong and weak flooding). *A call is* weakly flooding *with respect to a cycle C if there is an execution where the call is flooding with respect to C. And a call is* strongly flooding *with respect to a cycle C if there is an execution with fair scheduling of enabled processes where the call is flooding with respect to C.*

Strong flooding reflects the more serious flooding situations that persist regardless of the underlying scheduling policy. In the detection of strong flooding, a *statically enabled* node is considered strongly reachable if each of its predecessor flow nodes are strongly reachable. All statements are statically enabled, apart from **get**/**await** statements. A **get** statement or an **await** on a future/call is statically enabled if the corresponding future/result is available, detected statically if the corresponding return statement is strongly reachable or another **get**/**await** statement on the same future is strongly reachable. We rely on a static under-detection of the correspondence between return statements and futures. In the examples this detection is straight forward. With respect to DDoS, weak flooding of a server is in general harmless unless the flooding is caused by a large enough number of objects. Strong flooding is dangerous even from a single attacker.

---

1. Make separate *control flow graphs* (CFGs) for each method. Include a node for each *call*, *get*, *await*, *new* (for object creation), *if* and *while* statement, as well as an initial *starting* and a final *return* node.
2. Add call edges from call nodes to the start node of a *copy* of the called method. In case the call is recursive, simply add a call edge to the existing start node.
3. Identify any cycles in the resulting graph (including all copies of the CFGs).
4. Assign a unique label to each call node, and assign this label to the *start* and *return* node of the corresponding copy of the method CFG.
5. Make *put* edges from the *return* nodes to the corresponding *get*/*await* nodes. This requires static flow analysis, possibly with over-approximation of *put* edges.

Fig. 3. Control flow graph.

Consider a cycle C in the control flow graph G resulting from Fig. 3:

1. Mark all nodes in C as *strongly-reachable (SR)*, and the rest as (initially) *not reachable*.
2. From the entry point to the cycle, follow all flow and call edges in a depth-first traversal of G and mark the nodes as *weakly-reachable (WR)*, *strongly-reachable (SR)*, or neither, as defined in Def. 3.
3. If the previous step results in any changes to the *SR* or *WR* node sets, go to step 2.
4. Report flooding of call n if $n \in (calls - comps)$ where $calls = \{n \mid call_n \in WR\}$ and $comps = \{n \mid return_n \in SR \vee get_n \in SR\}$.

Fig. 4. Algorithm for detecting flooding by means of *calls* and *comps* sets in a given cycle.

Following [14], flooding is detected by building the control flow graph (CFG) of the program, locating control flow cycles as outlined in Fig. 3, and then analyzing the sets of weakly reachable calls, denoted *calls*, and the set of strongly reachable call completions, denoted *comps*, in each cycle. Flooding is reported for each cycle with a nonempty difference between *calls* and *comps*, as explained in Fig. 4. Note that the abbreviated notations for synchronous calls and suspending calls are expanded to the more basic call primitives, as explained above. We assume that assignments (other than calls) will terminate efficiently and therefore ignore them in the CFG. For each method the CFG begins with a start node and ends with a return node (even for void methods) – the latter helps in the analysis of method completion. We next define *weakly and strongly reachable nodes*. The detection of strongly reachable nodes uses a combination of forward and backward analysis, and is simplified compared to [14]:

Definition 3 (Weakly and strongly reachable nodes). *Consider a given cycle C. Weakly reachable (WR) nodes are those that are on the cycle or reachable from the cycle by following a flow edge or a call edge.*

A node is strongly reachable (SR) if it is in the given cycle or is reachable from an SR node without entering an if/while node nor passing a wait node (get/await) outside the cycle, unless the return node of the corresponding call is strongly reachable. A return node is SR if there is a SR get/await node on the same future. And a node is SR if all its predecessor nodes are SR.

We consider two versions of SR, the optimistic, *where we follow call edges (as indicated above), and the* pessimistic, *where we follow a call edge n only when the call is known to complete, i.e., when $n \in SR$ before following the call edge. (As above we follow flow and put edges without restrictions.)*

The optimistic version is used to find unbounded flooding under the assumption of favorable scheduling, i.e., *strong flooding*. The pessimistic version is used to detect unbounded flooding without this assumption, i.e., *weak flooding*. Detection of strong flooding implies detection of weak flooding, but with less precise details about which calls that possibly may cause flooding. If there is a call causing weak flooding wrt. a given cycle, pessimistic detection will report this call or a call leading to this call. If there is a call causing strong flooding for a given cycle C, optimistic detection will report this call. Our notions of optimistic and pessimistic reachability cover a wider class of nodes than in [14]. The soundness of [14] can be generalized to our setting.

6   Examples of Possible DoS/DDoS Attacks

An Example of Flooding Cycles. We consider here an example of a possible DoS attack on customers caused by a financial institution. The attack may be unintended by the institution, but may result from an update supposed to give better efficiency, by use of the future mechanism to reduce the amount of data communicated over the network.

We imagine that the financial institution has a subscription *service* for customers, such that customers can register and receive the latest information about shares and funds, through data of type "newsletter", here simply defined as a product type consisting of a *content* and a *date*. The financial institution uses a method signal to notify the customers about new information about shares. In the first version, each call to signal has the newsletter as a parameter. This may result in heavy network traffic and many of the newsletters may not be read by the customers. In the "improved" solution, each call to signal contains a reference (by means of a future) to the newsletter rather than the newsletter itself. However, this allows the subscription service system to send signal calls even before the newsletter is available, and as we will see, this can cause a DoS attack on the subscribing customers.

In order to handle many customers, a (dynamic) number of proxies are used by the service object, and an underlying newsletter producer is used for the sake of getting newsletters, using suspension when waiting for news. The proxies are organized in a list (*myCustomers*), growing upon need. In both solutions, futures are used by the service object to avoid delays while waiting for a newsletter to be available. In this way the service object can continuously respond to customers. The interfaces are shown in Fig. 5. We abbreviate "Newsletter" to "News". Figure 6 represents a high-level implementation of the publish/subscribe model, adapted from [5]. A multi-cast to each object in the *myCustomers* list is made by the statement *myCustomers!signal(ns)* in line 16. If we shift requiring the actual newsletter to have arrived, from the Proxy (as shown by the statements *ns:=get fut; myCustomers!signal(ns)* in the original *publish* method) to the Customer (i.e., *news:=**get** fut* in the modified *Customer.signal* method). This change in the program causes flooding of customers.

```
1      data News == (String content, Int date) // a product data type
2      interface ServiceI{
3            Void subscribe(CustomerI cl)  // called by Clients
4            Void produce()}  // called by Proxies
5      interface ProxyI{
6            ProxyI add(CustomerI cl) // called by Service
7            Void publish(Fut[News]fut)} // called by Service
8      interface ProducerI{
9            News detectNews()} // called by Service
10     interface NewsProducerI{
11           Void add(News ns) // called when news arrives
12           News getNews()} // called by Producers
13     interface CustomerI{
14           Void signal(News ns)} // called by Proxies
```

Fig. 5. The interfaces of the units in the subscription example.

```
1    class Service(Int limit, NewsProducerI np) implements ServiceI{
2      ProducerI prod; ProxyI proxy; ProxyI lastProxy; //declaration of fields
3      { prod := new Producer(np); proxy:= new Proxy(limit,this);
4        lastProxy:=proxy; this!produce()}
5      Void subscribe(CustomerI cl) {lastProxy:=lastProxy.add(cl)}
6      Void produce(){ Fut[News]fut :=prod!detectNews();
7        proxy!publish(fut)}} // sends future
8
9    class Proxy(Int limit,ServiceI s) implements ProxyI{
10     ProxyI nextProxy; List[CustomerI] myCustomers:=empty; //fields
11     ProxyI add(CustomerI cl){ ProxyI lastProxy:=this;
12       if length(myCustomers)<limit then myCustomers:=append(myCustomers,cl)
13       else if nextProxy=null then nextProxy:= new Proxy(limit,s) fi;
14       lastProxy:=nextProxy.add(cl) fi; return lastProxy}
15     Void publish(Fut[News]fut){ News ns :=get fut; // wait for the future
16       myCustomers!signal(ns); // multi-cast the result
17       if nextProxy=null then s!produce() else nextProxy!publish(fut) fi}}
18
19   class Producer(NewsProducerI np) implements ProducerI{
20     News detectNews(){ News news; news:=np.getNews(); return news}}
21
22   class NewsProducer() implements NewsProducerI{ List[News] nl;
23     Void add(News ns){nl:=append(nl,ns)}
24     News getNews(){News n; await nl /= empty; n:=first(nl); nl:=rest(nl); return n} }
25
26   class Customer implements CustomerI{ // Consumer of news items:
27     News news; // the latest news
28     Void signal(News ns){news:=ns}}
```

Fig. 6. Classes providing an implementation of the subscription example.

```
1    class Proxy(Int limit,ServiceI s) implements ProxyI{
2      ProxyI nextProxy; List[CustomerI] myCustomers:=empty;
3      ProxyI add(CustomerI cl){ ... }
4      Void publish(Fut[News]fut){
5        myCustomers!signal(fut); // sends future, no waiting
6        if nextProxy=null then s!produce() else nextProxy!publish(fut) fi}}
7
8    class Customer implements CustomerI{ News news; ...
9      Void signal(Fut[News] fut) { news:=get fut}} // blocking wait
```

Fig. 7. DoS attack by a variation of the subscription example.

Service.produce asynchronously calls Producer.detectNews (Pd), line 6 of Fig. 6
Service.produce asynchronously calls Proxy.publish (Xp), line 7 of Fig. 6
Proxy.publish asynchronously calls Customer.signal (Cs), line 5 of Fig. 7
Proxy.publish asynchronously calls Service.produce (Sp), line 6 of Fig. 7

Each iteration of this cycle generates an asynchronous call to *Proxy.publish*, which again produces an asynchronous call to *Producer.detectNews*, which is not processed as part of this cycle, nor is its processing synchronized call with the cycle. An unbounded number of suspended calls to *Producer.detectNews* can be produced by this cycle. We then say that the cycle is flooding. The flooding cycle identified above is harmless provided the customers are able to process their signal calls as fast as the cycle iterations. The programmer will be warned by our algorithm about each possible flooding, and should determine whether it is a real problem.

In contrast, the modified program version (Fig. 7) does not wait in *Proxy.publish* (doing *ns:=**get** fut*) until the newsletter is produced. Instead the future is directly passed to another asynchronous call (*myCustomers!signal(fut)*) in line 5 of Fig. 7 through the method *Proxy. publish*, this removes any progress dependency between the cycle producing the *Producer.detectNews* and *Customer.signal* calls and the processing of those calls. The completion of the *Producer.detectNews* and *Customer.signal* calls does not

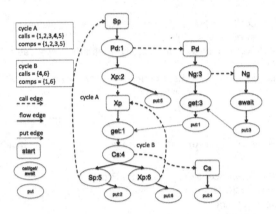

Fig. 8. The graph and call/comp sets for the original version of the program (Fig. 6).

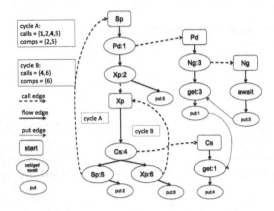

Fig. 9. The graph and call/comp sets for the modified version of the program (Fig. 7).

only depend on the speed of code execution, but depend on the rate of newsletter items arrivals. Practically, this flooding cycle generates a number of unprocessed calls that quickly grows to system limits.

Applying the Algorithm to the Example. Following [14], the *call* and *comps* sets for the two publish/subscribe versions are shown in Figs. 8 and 9. Method names are abbreviated with two letters as indicated above, letting Ng abbreviate method *getNews* of interface *NewsProducerI*. There are two cycles in Fig. 8, i.e., cycle A and B. We have a flooding on the call to *Customer.signal* (Cs) in both cycles. However, this flooding does not reflect an actual flooding since the Customer objects easily keep up with the calls since the amount of work required by the Customer to complete a signal call is trivial. The execution rate is restricted with respect to the actual arrival of new items from the *NewsProducer* (by the blocking call in the proxies), and therefore, the rate of produced asynchronous calls to *Customer.signal* by this cycle is limited. Thus this is an example of *weak flooding* that is harmless. Furthermore, cycle B is not infinite since it goes through the chain of Proxies. The modified version of the program is shown in Fig. 9. This version is displaying *strong flooding*. The flooding-cycle of Pd (Producer.detectNews) through both cycles is dangerous and will cause flooding of the system instantly. In version 1, there is a *get* in cycle A that regulates the speed of this cycle, whereas in the modified version there is no *get* in cycle A.

An Example of Instantiation Flooding. The example in Fig. 10 shows how a *ClientDistribution* object can cause an attack by using an unbounded number of clients to flood the same server s, due to an unbounded recursion of the *run* method. The initialization of the attacker object of class ClientDistribution connects to a client, and the client does the registration of the server object. The attacker may start such a communication with lots of clients to register at the same server. (For simplicity, interfaces are omitted here.) Each client

```
1   class Attacker(ServerI s) {
2     {this!run(); } // initialization
3     Void run() { ClientI c := new Client();
4       c!connect(s); this!run() } // terminate & make recursive call
5   }
6   class Client() implements ClientI{
7     Nat connect(ServerI s){
8       Nat n := s.register();// blocking call, not causing flooding
9       return n }
10  }
11  class Server(DataBase db) implements ServerI{ {...} // Initialization
12    Nat register(){Nat n :=0; if okcheck(caller) then Bool ok := db.open();
13      if ok then n:=db.add(caller); db.query(...); db.close() fi fi; return n }
14    //register requires time and resources
15    ... }
```

Fig. 10. Flooding by unbounded creation of innocent clients targeting the same server.

is innocent in the sense that it does not cause any attack by itself. By finding such a vulnerability in the ClientDistribution, an attacker can cause the flooding attack by calling run(). In addition, the non-blocking call in this method helps the attacker because the method does not wait for the connect calls to complete, therefore it is able to create more and more workload for the server s in almost no time. The execution of f:=c!connect(s) causes an asynchronous call and assigns a future to the call. Thus no waiting is involved. The run method recursively creates more and more objects, located somewhere in the distributed network. Therefore, the attacker creates flooding by rapidly creating clients that each performs a resource-demanding operation on the same server. Static analysis detects such attacks by finding a call loop (in this case inside run) which is also targeting the same server.

In this example, if the object creation in run had happened locally, an explicit instantiation flooding that consumes all the resources in an object will happen, which is a self DoS attack. However, since the object creation is distributed, the example in Fig. 10 shows an implicit attack because of targeting the same server by different clients.

Static Analysis of the Instantiation Example. Consider the example in Fig. 10. For the run method of class ClientDistribution, the following cycle is detected:

the initialization of the attacker calls *run*
run creates a client object *c*
run calls c!connect(s)
run terminates and calls itself recursively in an asynchronous call.

The *run* call has a call edge to the flow graph of *connect* (call 1), and *connect* has a call edge to the flow graph of *register* (call 2). The call to *register* waits for completion of *register* since it is a blocking call, and the database calls (call 3) made by *register* wait for the completion of these database calls. The code for the

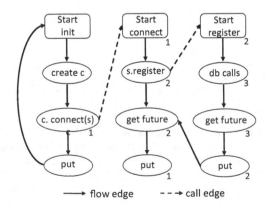

Fig. 11. Static detection of flooding using unbounded creation.

database is not given, and therefore the analysis will be worst-case by considering the termination of such calls non-reachable (unless indirectly found strongly reachable). The control flow graph is given in Fig. 11. The set of weakly reachable call nodes of the cycle, i.e., *calls*, are $\{1, 2, 3\}$ with optimistic detection, and $\{1\}$ with pessimistic detection. And the set of strongly reachable calls, i.e., *comps*, is empty in both cases. This gives that the set of potentially flooding calls, given by *calls* − *comps*, is $\{1\}$ (c.connect) with pessimistic detection and $\{1, 2, 3\}$ with optimistic detection. However, in this case, call 1 does not reflect a real flooding since each call is on a separate object, but call 2 (s.register) and call 3 (the db calls) do. We detect strong flooding. The example may be improved by using suspending calls (using **await**) on the database operations.

6.1   Modification of the Static Detection to DDoS

As seen in Fig. 2, a DDoS attack on a server is often made through many innocent clients. This is hard to detect from the server side at runtime since each client may behave in an acceptable manner, and since the real attacker is hidden behind the clients. The original detection method [14] is not oriented towards such attacks, since it is not aware of the number of generated objects of a class. Moreover, the approach is using as an assumption that *an execution has a bounded number of objects*. Nevertheless, if applied to the example in Fig. 10, it will report a possible attack on the clients (treating all customers as one object), but not an attack on the Service server, which is the real attack. A draw-back is that there could be reported more false positives due to overapproximation.

A weakness with pessimistic detection is that the *connect* call, but not the *register* call, would be reported. Although the former call leads to the second, the detection result is not appropriate since a harmless call is reported and not the harmful one. Another weakness is that the attack would not be discovered when removing the connect call from the attacker class and instead letting the register call be caused by the init method of class Client. (In this case the method parameter *s* should be transferred as a class parameter.) The reason for this is that indirect calls due to object generation are ignored (since by assumption there cannot be unboundedly many such calls). To compensate these weaknesses, we make two modifications wrt. [14], described below:

First, we modify the static analysis by viewing a **new** C statement as a special kind of a call statement with its own associated call number and a call edge to a copy of the *init* code of class C, which again may have further calls, treated as usual. More precisely, we treat **new** C as a *simple* call statement (like $new!C(classparameters)$) except that the *new* object is not known before the call) since the **new** statement does not wait for the *init* to complete. This allows us to see the generation of objects and to follow all implicit calls from the initialization code. Thus we can detect instantiation flooding attacks depending on call indirectly caused by object initialization. We may assume that an initialization cannot generate flooding in itself since each initialization is on a new object. Thus the call numbers associated with object creation can be included in *comps*. Furthermore, one more call on a new object cannot generate flooding on this object (unless in a cycle after the object creation). The same goes for a finite number of calls on a new object, if it can be detected statically that all these calls have the same new object as callee. These calls can also be included in *comps*. In the example of Fig. 10, we detect that the call c!connect is to the new Client object, and this call will then not be reported with the improved static detection.

Secondly, since implicit calls are important in DDoS attacks, we follow all call edges in the calculation of WR nodes, even in the pessimistic version. The resulting improved static detection method can then also detect the hidden attacker in all versions of the instantiation example, as shown below. Since the improved static detection method depends on static detection of same callee, we briefly discuss how to incorporate this: Two calls in the same method activation have the same callee if the callee is the same variable, and it is either

- a read-only variable (such as a parameter),
- a local variable and there are no updates on this variable between the calls, or
- a field variable and there are no updates on it nor suspension between the calls.

The first of these calls may be an object creation $x := \mathbf{new}\ C(\ldots)$, and the second a call with x as callee (provided one of the conditions above are satisfied for x). This suffices for the example with the two calls $c := \mathbf{new}\ Client()$ and $f := c.connect(s)$. This detection could be improved in several ways. In particular, we may detect that the actual parameter s in the latter call refers to the same object for all activations of *run* since s is a read-only class parameter and the recursive *run* call is on the same object (since this is read-only). This could be used in the detection algorithm to see that all $s.register$ calls refer to the same server s, which gives a clear indication of a DDoS attack.

Instantiation Example Revisited. We reconsider the example in Fig. 10, using the improved static detection algorithm. Now the *create c* node of Fig. 11 is represented as a call, say call 0. For the original version of the example, the initialization is empty so call 0 is considered terminating ($0 \in comps$). We get $calls = \{0, 1, 2, 3\}$ where 0 corresponds to the creation of the new C object. But call 0 (c:= new Client) and call 1 (c!connect) do not generate flooding since they are on a new object. Thus $comps = \{0, 1\}$. This shows that there is a possibility of call flooding through call 2 (s.register) and call 3 (the db calls); and these correspond to actual attacks. For the modified version of Fig. 10, where the register call is caused by the Client initialization, we get a similar analysis except that there is no call 1 (c!connect) since this is incorporated in the Client initialization. Thus we get that $calls = \{0, 2, 3\}$ and $comps = \{0\}$. Here the presence of call 0 enables us to detect call 2 in the (modified) initialization code and thereby also call 3 (and both correspond to possible flooding).

7   Conclusion

In this paper we have considered denial of service attacks, formulated in a high-level imperative language based on concurrent objects communicating by asynchronous calls and futures, thereby supporting asynchronous as well as synchronous communication. The language includes mechanisms for process control allowing non-trivial process synchronization by means of cooperative scheduling. We adapt a static detection algorithm developed for analysis of flooding to this setting, in order to detect possible denial of service attacks. This kind of static analysis is useful in the financial sector, because the aspect of trust between customers and service providers is essential, perhaps more so than in other application areas, and therefore static detection is valuable.

We have illustrated the approach on examples of distributed systems in the financial sector, including versions of a one-to-many attack and a many-to-one attack. In the first example a financial institution notifies a number of subscribing customers. We have seen that a revision of the basic notification software used by the financial institution, intended to be more efficient, actually implies a one-to-many attack on the subscribing customers. In this example, the financial institution was responsible for the attack, which could lead to loss of reputation and of customers. Static detection solved the situation here since the detection is made before the program is run. The underlying detection algorithm is sound for call-based coordinated attacks, provided the source code of the objects involved in the coordinated attack is available. In the many-to-one example, an attacker object causes an attack by using an unbounded number of clients, each innocent, to flood the same server s, letting a new client be created in each cycle.

In this paper we have adapted a general algorithm for detecting flooding [14] to the setting of DDoS and improved it to deal with unbounded object generation and to better reveal hidden attacks. Our framework can deal with advanced programming mechanisms including suspension and first-class futures considering distributed systems at a high-level of abstraction. It is therefore relevant for high-level modeling and prototyping of distributed software solutions. In future work, we suggest to complement the static checking with dynamic runtime checking since static detection methods give a degree of over-estimation. This could give a more precise combined detection strategy.

Acknowledgments. We thank the reviewers for significant feedback. This work is supported by the *IoTSec* project, the Norwegian Research Council (No. 248113/O70), and by the *SCOTT* project, the European Leadership Joint Undertaking under EU H2020 (No. 737422).

References

1. Ashford, W.: DDoS is most common cyber attack on financial institutions (blog post, 2016). https://www.computerweekly.com/news/4500272230/DDoS-is-most-common-cyber-attack-on-financial-institutions/

2. Boer, F.D., et al.: A survey of active object languages. ACM Comput. Surv. (CSUR) **50**(5), 76 (2017)

3. Chang, R., Jiang, G., Ivancic, F., Sankaranarayanany, S., Shmatikov, V.: Inputs of Coma: static detection of denial-of-service vulnerabilities. In: 22nd IEEE Computer Security Foundations Symposium (CSF 2009), pp. 186–199. IEEE Computer Society (2009)

4. Colóon, M.A., Sipma, H.B.: Synthesis of linear ranking functions. In: Margaria, T., Yi, W. (eds.) TACAS 2001. LNCS, vol. 2031, pp. 67–81. Springer, Heidelberg (2001). https://doi.org/10.1007/3-540-45319-9_6

5. Din, C.C., Owe, O.: A sound and complete reasoning system for asynchronous communication with shared futures. J. Log. Algebraic Methods Program. **83**(5), 360–383 (2014)

6. Douligeris, C., Mitrokotsa, A.: DDoS attacks and defense mechanisms: classification and state-of-the-art. Comput. Netw. **44**(5), 643–666 (2004)

7. Gulavani, B.S., Gulwani, S.: A numerical abstract domain based on *expression abstraction* and *max operator* with application in timing analysis. In: Gupta, A., Malik, S. (eds.) CAV 2008. LNCS, vol. 5123, pp. 370–384. Springer, Heidelberg (2008). https://doi.org/10.1007/978-3-540-70545-1_35

8. Jensen, M., Gruschka, N., Herkenhöner, R.: A survey of attacks on web services. Comput. Sci. Res. Dev. **24**(4), 185 (2009)

9. Johnsen, E.B., Hähnle, R., Schäfer, J., Schlatte, R., Steffen, M.: ABS: a core language for abstract behavioral specification. In: Aichernig, B.K., de Boer, F.S., Bonsangue, M.M. (eds.) FMCO 2010. LNCS, vol. 6957, pp. 142–164. Springer, Heidelberg (2011). https://doi.org/10.1007/978-3-642-25271-6_8

10. Johnsen, E.B., Owe, O.: An asynchronous communication model for distributed concurrent objects. Softw. Syst. Model. **6**(1), 35–58 (2007)

11. Karami, F., Owe, O., Ramezanifarkhani, T.: An evaluation of interaction paradigms for active objects. J. Log. Algebraic Methods Program. **103**, 154–183 (2019)

12. Lambert, K.: Protecting financial institutions from DDoS attacks (blog post, 2018). https://www.imperva.com/blog/protecting-financial-institutions-from-ddos-attacks/

13. Meadows, C.: A formal framework and evaluation method for network denial of service. In: Proceedings of the 12th IEEE Computer Security Foundations Workshop, pp. 4–13 (1999)

14. Owe, O., McDowell, C.: On detecting over-eager concurrency in asynchronously communicating concurrent object systems. J. Log. Algebraic Methods Program. **90**, 158–175 (2017)

15. Qie, X., Pang, R., Peterson, L.: Defensive programming: using an annotation toolkit to build DoS-resistant software. CM SIGOPS Oper. Syst. Rev. **36**(SI), 45–60 (2002)

16. Ramezanifarkhani, T., Fazeldehkordi, E., Owe, O.: A language-based approach to prevent DDoS attacks in distributed object systems. In: 29th Nordic Workshop on Programming Theory. Turku Centre for Computer Science, November 2017 (extended abstract, 3 p.)

17. Urrico, R.: Denial of service attacks overwhelmingly target financial services: Verisign. Credit Union Times (2018). https://www.cutimes.com/2018/07/03/denial-of-service-attacks-overwhelmingly-target-fi/?slreturn=20190713065814/

18. Wilczek, M.: Why banks shouldn't be in denial about DDoS attacks (blog post, 2018). https://www.globalbankingandfinance.com/why-banks-shouldnt-be-in-denial-about-ddos-attacks/

19. Zahoor, Z., Ud-din, M., Sunami, K.: Challenges in privacy and security in banking sector and related countermeasures. Int. J. Comput. Appl. **144**(3), 24–35 (2016)
20. Zargar, S.T., Joshi, J., Tipper, D.: A survey of defense mechanisms against distributed denial of service (DDoS) flooding attacks. IEEE Commun. Surv. Tutor. **15**(4), 2046–2069 (2013)
21. Zheng, L., Myers, A.C.: End-to-end availability policies and noninterference. In: 18th IEEE Workshop Computer Security Foundations, CSFW-18 2005, pp. 272–286 (2005)

Author Index

Printed in the United States
By Bookmasters